FREEDOM WITHOUT VIOLENCE

Freedom Without Violence

RESISTING THE WESTERN POLITICAL TRADITION

Dustin Ells Howes

OXFORD
UNIVERSITY PRESS

OXFORD
UNIVERSITY PRESS

Oxford University Press is a department of the University of Oxford. It furthers
the University's objective of excellence in research, scholarship, and education
by publishing worldwide.Oxford is a registered trade mark of Oxford University
Press in the UK and certain other countries.

Published in the United States of America by Oxford University Press
198 Madison Avenue, New York, NY 10016, United States of America.

© Oxford University Press 2016

First Edition published in 2016

Cataloging-in-Publication data is on file at the Library of Congress
ISBN 978-0-19-933699-9

9 8 7 6 5 4 3 2 1
Printed by Sheridan, USA

For Madeline and Henry

There is no word that admits of more various significations, and has made more varied impressions on the human mind, than that of liberty.

—MONTESQUIEU

To raise the question, what is freedom? seems to be a hopeless enterprise. It is as though age-old contradictions and antinomies were lying in wait to force the mind into dilemmas of logical impossibility so that, depending which horn of the dilemma you are holding on to, it becomes as impossible to conceive of freedom or its opposite as it is to realize the notion of a square circle.

—HANNAH ARENDT

Contents

Acknowledgments

THE IDEA FOR this project sprang from a conversation with David Andrews in a car ride coming back from my first academic position at SUNY-Oswego in 2006. Both of us opposed the war in Iraq, but we disagreed about how the Bush administration had been able to convince the American people to invade. Toward the end of the conversation, as we were pulling up to his house I remember saying something like: "Isn't there something wrong with how we use the word freedom, if it can be used to justify this war?" Many people have provided support for me in many different ways over the last decade as I have tried to answer this question.

Liz Markovits, Rick Moreland, and Wayne Parent read significant portions of the book and offered challenging and useful comments. A number of people read the entire manuscript and offered extensive comments. Libby Anker, Brien Hallett, Farah Godrej, and Jonathan Weiler each contributed important insights that helped shape the character and tone of the book. Michael Lienesch made this a much more readable and elegant book with his meticulous and incisive suggestions. Amy Shuster influenced the manuscript significantly through our conversations about Plato and various things she has called to my attention over the years. I fear I have not been able to live up to the high caliber of commentary in my revisions, but I hope my most engaged interlocutors will take solace in the fact that they improved the manuscript significantly even as it may fall short of their highest expectations. Colin Ward, Trevor Shelley, and Gargi Aleaz provided able research assistance. Rudy Hernandez helped with the Aquinas citations. Cecil Eubanks has provided exceptional professional support. LSU students in my class "Theories of Freedom" in the Fall of 2009 and Spring of 2014 helped me to think through and develop many of the ideas that appear in the book.

The Louisiana Board of Regents provided an ATLAS grant for Fall 2011 through the Summer 2012, without which the book would not have been possible. Louisiana State University provided much-appreciated Manship Summer Research Awards in 2011 and 2014.

Portions of chapters 1 and 2 were published in "The Nonviolent 99" for #OccupyThought on the New Everyday, a Media Commons project on March 15, 2012. A shorter version of chapter 3 was published as "Defending Freedom with Civil Resistance in the Early Roman Republic" in *Civil Resistance: Comparative Perspectives on Nonviolent Struggle* edited by Kurt Schock with University of Minnesota Press in 2015. A shorter version of chapter 2 was published as "Nonviolent Liberation" in *Non-violence: Challenges and Prospects* edited by Bidyut Chakrabarty with Oxford University Press India in 2014.

A vibrant and diverse group of colleagues and friends provided emotional, physical, and intellectual sustenance. They include Seth Baldwin, Maureen Baldwin, Chris Hardy, James Niels Rosenquist, Ian Finseth, Stephanie Hawkins, Jonathan Weiler, Adam Schiffer, Becky Schiffer, Aaron Espinosa, Greg Petrow, Alec Ewald, Carisa Showden, Erin Carlston, Bennett Hazlip, Erin Taylor, Heather Raffo, Jan Krummrey, Ruth Bowman, Michael Bowman, James Stoner, Tim Slack, Tracy Rizzuto, Derek Barker, Karuna Mantena, Stephen Zunes, Ronald Terchek, Jennifer Rubenstein, Alexander Livingston, Eric McGillivray, Karl Widerquist, Anthony Parel, Bidyut Chakrabarty, Alexander Gourevitch, Joan Cocks, Catia Confortini, Jane Gordon, Mark Lance, Olivia Guaraldo, Susan Bickford, Patricia Owens, Hollie Mann, Brian Duff, Joel Winkelman, Gaurav Desai, Delia Popescu, Keally McBride, Peggy Kohn (but you still owe me some comments), Adriana Cavarero, Dana Villa, Jas Sullivan, Jacqueline Stevens, David Clark, Rachael Harrell, Irene Goldzer, Amy Chrisman, Diane Stone, Laura Moyer, Greg Van Steeg, Dana Berkowitz, Bill Clark, Katherine Surek, Judy Roberts, and David Glickman. My dear friends Wayne Parent, Wonik Kim, and Rick and Susan Moreland provided seemingly endless wonderful meals, intellectual stimulation, and emotional support.

I am fortunate to have a large and loving family that has supported me throughout this process and throughout my life. They include Janet Howes, Ed Gwisdalla, Robert Howes, Randy Stoddart, Joann Stoddart, Marilyn Kelly, Colleen Howes, Randy Howes, Jason Howes, Shannon Fisher, Cory Howes, Anna Howes, Russell Howes, Sue Vincent, Betty Howes, Russell N. Howes, Freda Ells, Garland Ells, Lloyd Hall, Charles Hall, Kim Hall, Sharon Hall, William "Deed" Houpt, Dan Hall, Sarah Hall, and Chris Harpst.

Angela Chnapko has been everything one could ask for in an editor. The anonymous reviewers provided much-needed support and made perceptive and helpful suggestions for improving the manuscript.

Our children Madeline Rose Hall Howes and Henry Lloyd Hall Howes were born while I was writing this book. We relied upon many people to help us with their care, but Ashley Williams, Lula Cain, and the good folks at University Presbyterian Daycare deserve special mention.

In the process of finishing this book, I became disabled and dependent upon the physical and emotional support of many professionals. They include Bob Pascuzzi, Stanley Masinter, Kathryn Leskis, Rashmi Gangamma, Tracie Jackson, Christopher Bester, Rose Karuzis, Amie Robbins, Tracy White, Tammy Stewart, Connie Johnson, Jessica Jackson, Jodi Pearce, Desma Reaves, Lanesha Johnson, Monique Orr, Curt Shults, and Jadi Mitchell. We could not have afforded to pay for this help without the donations of many, many people to our Crowd Rise site. This outpouring of support was truly humbling and we keep each and every one of you in our hearts.

My brother Brandon Howes and his wife Erin McCrea swooped in and came to my rescue in my hour of greatest need. Their boundless love and energy continue to amaze me.

My greatest love and favorite person in the world is Rachel Hall. To say anything more would be too complicated. To say anything less would diminish the fact that my intellectual and emotional life is unimaginable without her.

FREEDOM WITHOUT VIOLENCE

[Slave] camps under the flag of freedom, massacres justified by philanthropy or by a taste for the superhuman, in one sense cripple judgment. On the day when crime dons the apparel of innocence—through a curious transposition peculiar to our times—it is innocence that is called upon to justify itself. . . . Our purpose is to find out whether innocence, the moment it becomes involved in action, can avoid committing murder.

ALBERT CAMUS

Introduction

THE MOTTO OF the Joint Task Force Guantánamo is prominently displayed on gates outside the detainment camp: "Honor Bound to Defend Freedom" (figure 0.1). It might strike us as brazen, offensive, or ironic to emblazon the word freedom on a prison. In a place where the United States government has taken such extraordinary efforts to delimit, control, and degrade the human body and mold, humiliate, and destroy the human personality, the use of the word seems particularly strange and cynical. Stress positions, sensory deprivation, sensory bombardment, sleep deprivation, sexual humiliation, extreme isolation, and indefinite detention without charges far surpass our common-sense notions of violating freedom. In response to a hunger strike, prisoners in Guantánamo were force-fed by way of restraint and feeding tubes, and a federal judge upheld the government's right to do so in order to prevent them from committing suicide.[1] Such extreme domination not only seems to give up the lie that this place has something to do with freedom but also establishes the truth that it institutionalizes precisely the opposite: torture, oppression, and slavery.

Yet one of the premises of this book is that the words on the sign outside Guantánamo should be taken seriously and are worthy of investigation. Most citizens in the United States take for granted the idea that their government and military in particular are charged with "defending our freedom." A core element of how soldiers are honored in the United States is captured in the idea that their sacrifices and deaths, as well as the violence they do to others, are for the purpose of defending freedom. How is it that the world's oldest liberal democracy has come to understand violence as a critical element of preserving liberty? Part II of this book

FIGURE 0.1 The entrance to Camp 1 in Guantanamo Bay's Camp Delta. Photo by Kathleen T. Rhem. US Department of Defense

explores the history of the idea of defending freedom. Perhaps surprisingly, it is a relatively recent one. Although the idea of defense as a legitimate justification for violence is an ancient one and the idea of freedom as a primary political value dates back to at least the fourth century BC, it is only in the last few centuries that the two have been combined. More surprising still is that the idea that one could and should defend freedom *without* violence—indeed, by refusing to participate in wars—long predates the idea of defending freedom with violence.

The sign on the gates at Guantánamo recalls other prison camps that invoke freedom at their entrances. Those arriving at the Nazi concentration camps of Dachau and Auschwitz, for instance, were greeted by the words *Arbeit Macht Frei*, or "Work Makes Freedom" (figure 0.2). We might consider such signs to be simply absurd or offensive given the realities of the concentration camps. But the words should be taken seriously. Although sometimes deeply critical of the thought and practices of liberal democracies, nationalist and socialist thinkers typically share the tendency to hold up freedom as a primary value. However, instead of claiming that violence is necessary to defend freedom, many of the practitioners and theorists of nationalism and socialism have asserted that free-dom can and should be exercised and expressed through violence. That is, not only can violence be a means to freedom, or a way to preserve it in the face of

FIGURE 0.2 View of the entrance to the main camp of Auschwitz (Auschwitz I). US Holocaust Memorial Museum

challenges, but its very practice is seen as commensurate with freedom. Thus while there are serious disagreements between and among liberals, nationalists, and socialists as to the proper role of violence in politics, the connection between some form of collective freedom and violence runs deep in the thought and practices of each of them. Indeed, the idea that freedom can be exercised through violence and warfare is part of the very fabric of what we have come to call the Western political tradition.

The origins and founding of freedom in the Western tradition are conflicted concerning the issue of violence. Today a wide range of political ideologies generally assume that violent revolutions are necessary to establish freedom from tyranny and liberate people from slavery. But the near unanimity among modern ideologies regarding the necessity of violence for attaining freedom is somewhat surprising given that one of the oldest stories of liberation in the Western tradition is that of the Israelites escaping from Egypt. The story contains numerous elements of violence, including Moses's killing of an Egyptian prior to his escape into the desert and the destruction of the original inhabitants of Canaan prior to taking possession of the Promised Land. However, the Exodus itself—the moment of liberation— has many of the critical features that we have come to associate with nonviolence. Moses inspires the Jewish people to resist their oppressors by withdrawing from participation in tyranny. Their oppressors are destroyed by acts of God and as a result of their own arrogance, as opposed to violent resistance on the part of Jews. Similarly, the scant evidence we have of the founding of democratic Athens suggests that a collective act of refusing cooperation combined with an attitude of restraint toward the Spartan occupiers may have played a crucial role in ushering in Cleisthenes' reforms. Although the threat of violence was present, there is no evidence that the democratic founding came about through a war (I discuss this in chapter 5). Likewise, the founding of the Roman Republic involved acts of self-sacrifice, the avoidance of military conflict, and the use of moral suasion to gain the support of the Roman people in ousting the Tarquin tyrants (I discuss this in chapter 3).

So how then did we get here? How and why has freedom become entangled with violence, warfare, prisons, torture, and slavery? The first six chapters of this book explore the long history of the relationship between freedom and violence in the Western political tradition. Although I touch upon many of the major events and thinkers related to freedom in the Western tradition, I do so thematically instead of chronologically. The book is organized in this unconventional way for two reasons. First, violence and freedom are connected to each other in the tradition in three distinctive ways, which appear and recede over time. A chronological rendering would be an obstacle to drawing out these themes and tracing their genealogies. Second, it turns out that the relative ease or difficulty of breaking the connection between violence and freedom, both historically and philosophically, depends upon which theme is being considered. I have organized the three themes in order to slowly ratchet up the level of difficulty for would-be advocates of freedom without violence. Parts I, II, and III explore the themes of liberation, defending freedom, and collective freedom, respectively. Along the way, I highlight the contested connection between freedom and violence by pointing to nonviolent efforts within and without the tradition. However, by the time I reach chapter 6, the challenges for nonviolence have become sufficiently great to require a thoroughgoing theory of nonviolent freedom, which I present in Part IV.

The dominant ideologies of the last two hundred years not only assert that violence is necessary to attain freedom but insist that the historical record tells us that freedom can only be attained through violence. A major purpose of this project is to contest that received wisdom. Resistance to the heritage of freedom through violence can be found in the thought and movements of non-Western peoples and thinkers who have mustered powerful political responses to and theoretical critiques of Western violence in the name of freedom. I draw upon some of those thinkers and movements here, especially in Part I and later in my discussion of Gandhi in Part IV. But for the most part, I highlight overlooked movements and underappreciated thinkers within the purview of Western histories and texts.[2] Some of the events and ideas I draw attention to are de-emphasized or understood as only complimentary parts of what are typically considered to be the main events of Western history. However, some of the events I explore are so unimaginable given our predisposition to privilege violence, that they are disputed by skeptical historians. Similarly, some of the ideas I recover are so counter to our basic assumptions about politics that professional political theorists are unlikely to be familiar with them.

So the first six chapters of this book explore the long history of the familiar theme of freedom in an unusual way. Part I seeks to demonstrate that examples from the last three centuries have shown that violent revolutions often undermine the very brand of freedom that they hope to attain. Nonviolent revolutions, by contrast, have shown much more consistency and effectiveness if we account for their major achievements and consider them in light of the long-term prospects for achieving political freedom. Chapter 1 explores attitudes toward violence in the American, French, Haitian, Bolshevik, and other revolutions. In chapter 2, I contrast those violent efforts with the nonviolent struggle for freedom initiated by the abolitionists who took on the worldwide slave trade, the women's rights movement of the nineteenth and twentieth centuries, and nonviolent resistance to colonialism and tyranny in every part of the world in the twentieth and twenty-first centuries. When it comes to freedom as a process of liberation, nonviolence has quite clearly demonstrated its effectiveness.

Part II begins by excavating frequently overlooked ways of defending freedom in the Roman Republic. Chapter 3 examines the founding of the Roman Republic, the secessions of the plebs, and the subversion of the Republic to show that defending freedom is possible without violence. But my primary purpose in this section is to trace the origins of the modern concept of defending freedom with violence. In chapter 4, I show how conceptions of liberty formed in the Middle Ages were welded to just war arguments for self-defense that emerged in the early modern period. The liberal and republican thinkers of the seventeenth and eighteenth centuries made the idea of defending freedom the primary justification for the sovereignty and violence of the state. At the same time, these ideas ensconced the parallel if somewhat competing idea of the citizen militia, which called for the democratization of firearms as a critical means for securing freedom. These arguments laid the foundations for the present international state system, and continue to dominate the politics of liberal democracies. Although the history of the Roman Republic provides us with some clues, the nonviolent alternatives are not immediately obvious.

Part III traces the history of the idea that freedom as a collective capacity to rule ourselves requires violence and resistance to that idea within the tradition. Chapter 5 takes us to the origin of democracy in the West by examining the Golden Age of Athenian politics, when Pericles introduces the idea that freedom can be expressed and exercised through warfare. I show how the defeat of Athens in the Peloponnesian Wars and the subsequent response of women, playwrights, and philosophers raised questions about the connection between freedom and violence. But I also demonstrate how Aristotle's revised version of patriarchal freedom helped Pericles' ideal survive and retain legitimacy. I then go on to explore nationalism and socialism over the last two centuries, where the idea that collective freedom can be exercised and expressed through violence was resuscitated and came to full fruition. Chapter 6 describes the close relationship between the state, popular sovereignty, violence, and conceptions of freedom. With the defeat of the Axis powers in World War II, liberal democracies embraced the language of *defending* freedom (for instance, the War Department in the United States became the Department of Defense in 1949). In addition, the labor movement and the role of the general strike in particular have had a complex and contested relationship to violence, sometimes modeling a way to exercise collective freedom nonviolently. Yet the question remains, as perhaps the most enduring political challenge in considering the relationship between violence and freedom: Is it possible for us to rule ourselves without violence?

Part IV takes up this challenge by developing a concept of nonviolent freedom and playing out its political implications. I begin by wading into long-standing debates surrounding the existence and nature of the free will. In chapter 7, I argue that there are certain irrevocable facts of freedom. Irrespective of our social, economic, or political situation, every individual retains a capacity for freedom in a very particular sense. Through a critical reconstruction of Hannah Arendt's exploration of free thought, free willing, and free action, I argue that each individual has the capacity for spontaneous and creative action, and that we are each separated from one another to a certain degree. Although these facts of freedom make physical violence possible, they also cannot be secured or defended by violence. Most crucially, the facts of freedom decisively refute the idea that violence is necessary. No individual is constrained by circumstances in such a way where they must do violence. Acknowledging the dangers of this individualistic view and attempting to avoid its pitfalls, I show that this minimalist understanding of freedom requires that we become aware of the facts of freedom in order for them to be fully realized. This awareness introduces a social and political element to nonviolent freedom, which sets up my attempt to demonstrate the significance of these philosophical claims in practice.

Chapter 8 begins by squarely addressing the problem of defending free societies from internal subversion and external invasion. Recovering the frequently overlooked arguments of the sixteenth-century thinker Étienne De La Boétie, I show how the existence of the facts of freedom makes tyranny impossible without the consent and active participation of the oppressed. The contemporary work of Gene Sharp (and others) on civilian-based defense provides significant historical evidence that widespread awareness of the facts of freedom allows people to exercise power in a way that can check even the most brutal invaders and dictators. I also examine how techniques of restorative justice might replace prisons and substitute nonviolent means for the traditional, police-based justice system in dealing with crime.

I then turn to the issue of collective self-rule. To construct a robust concept of nonviolent freedom, I turn to three prominent attempts to distance freedom from violence. Isaiah Berlin, in the liberal tradition, Hannah Arendt, in the republican tradition, and Immanuel Kant, in the tradition of moral philosophy, each attempt to develop a brand of political freedom that is contrary to, mitigates against, or cannot be reduced to violence. Although each has important strengths, I argue that they all come up short. Gandhi's concept of swaraj (often translated as "freedom" but literally meaning "self-rule") corrects and compliments each of these thinkers. While strongly emphasizing individual liberty, Gandhi argues that rights can only emanate in practice from the fulfillment of duties. While not shying away from endorsing dramatic, collective action in politics, Gandhi shows how such rule does not have to rely upon slavery or a laboring underclass but instead can take as one of its very purposes collectively addressing the physical well-being of those most in need. And while endorsing the view that morality and truth-seeking are central to politics, Gandhi develops the method of satyagraha as a way of allowing others to correct and contest their own necessarily partial views of the truth.

In his experiments with methods of nonviolence, Gandhi discovers a way for the free will and one's conscience to intervene in politics while minimizing the risk of being imperious or tyrannical. In his constructive program of village cottage industries, he envisions a decentralized form of self-rule, which attends to, relies upon, and integrates our moral, emotional, rational, and physical capacities. His view of freedom neither reduces it to physical security nor devalues human life and physical suffering. His concept of swaraj counts upon individuals to rule themselves responsibly, and yet describes in detail how to exercise power collectively.

I have tried to write a book in the spirit of nonviolent action, which addresses itself to the amorphous and daunting "Western political tradition." This involves being fastidious and unrelenting in identifying and tracing the ways in which that tradition is implicated in violence. Resisting the Western political tradition means refusing to abide by the idea that violence is necessary for freedom. In the words of two puzzling and disturbing signs, erected on prison camps by regimes claiming to be on opposite sides of the contemporary ideological spectrum, we find clues that I pursue over twenty-five hundred years of political thought and history. I try to understand how it is that the activities and experiences of the people in these two camps can be understood as consistent with freedom. Moreover, in pursuing the meaning of these two signs, I find a whole range of related ironies and contradictions. From the "freedom" to bear arms to the "freedom" to sell one's labor for wages, freedom is closely tied to various manifestations of everyday violence. The physical imposition, use, and destruction of persons by other persons might seem at first to be the opposite of freedom, but it is not so in our tradition.[3]

In writing, I have also tried to avoid unfair characterizations of the tradition even as I resist it. The arguments for the necessity of violence in defending freedom and the centrality of violence and warfare for expressing and exercising freedom are powerful and persuasive, and have not been adequately, or at least not systematically, addressed by the advocates of nonviolence. The Western political tradition, far from being monolithic or uncomplicated, involves and incorporates a great deal of resistance already. But taking the dominant narratives of the tradition seriously is the best way to squarely address the problems they raise.

Yet we might well ask whether political theory can still be an act of resistance. I say "still" because clearly political theory has altered the course of human events. However, it would seem that the written word may be among the least effective forms of resistance when unaccompanied by corresponding political action. "Professional" political theorists such as myself get tenure and promotions for writing books, and we typically risk very little in publishing, at least those of us in free societies. For these reasons, there is good reason to be skeptical that a book such as this one can be an act of resistance.

However, I am hopeful that this work can serve as an act of resistance in at least one respect. The idea that violence can help us attain, defend, express, or exercise freedom has proven to be extraordinarily resilient and seductive in both free and unfree societies. The idea that one last revolution will usher in a new era of freedom, or that one more prison, one more cop on the beat, or one more advanced weapons system will keep us safe and preserve our way of life, is based upon a reading of events past. I have tried to show that freedom can be attained, defended, and exercised without violence. As it turns out, this challenges our most sacred assumptions about the meaning of freedom and what it means to be a free society. The romance of heroes fallen and ancestors having died for freedom may withstand scrutiny if we refocus our attention upon different heroes and ancestors. The possibility of ruling ourselves freely depends upon becoming aware of our capacity to resist the violence of others without violence and resisting the belief that exercising superior violence makes us free.

PART I

Liberation

[It] is the intuition of the colonized masses that their liberation must, and can only, be achieved by force.

FRANTZ FANON

1

Revolting Revolutionaries

IT MAY BE that nearly every oppressed person at some point imagines using violence to strike back at her or his oppressors. With the swing of a fist, the pull of a trigger, or the explosion of a bomb, one can destroy or humble the purveyors of economic, physical, and psychological violence. This chapter tells the story of how liberation came to be associated with violence in the modern West and eventually the world. It suggests that the Age of Revolutions was characterized by contradictions and hypocrisies that raise difficult questions about how to achieve freedom, and that those difficulties carry over into later socialist and postcolonial revolutions. We typically look to the American and French Revolutions as founding moments for freedom. In the American case, the founding was significant because it completely severed ties with the authority of a monarch, creating a government grounded solely upon a mutually agreed-upon Constitution. The French case sent shock waves through Europe by executing the king and queen, establishing a new secular religion and instituting suffrage without property qualifications for all male citizens. In figuring these two revolutions as the primary and original spurs to political freedom, we tend to obscure how violence in them persistently undermined the lofty ideals and practical aims of the revolutionaries.

Both inspired other liberation movements around the world. While I deal with a number of different examples, the Haitian and Bolshevik Revolutions take pride of place. The former is the only slave rebellion in the history of the world to result in a new government run by those formerly enslaved. The latter sought to redefine revolution and freedom in terms of the economic well-being of the masses. Both were plagued by the problems of internecine violence that afflicted the American and French experiences. The hallmarks of liberation sought through violence are

temporary triumph followed by eventual failure, leading to freedom that in practice looks more like slavery, and solidarity that is imperiled by recrimination and
assassination.

To a remarkable extent, certain themes, issues, and problems appear across the
various literatures advocating liberation. First, every political liberation movement
begins with the identification and critique of oppression as practiced *by others*.
Liberals set out to undermine the authority of tyrannical monarchs and landed aristocrats who arbitrarily control the lives of merchants and serfs. Communists take
to task the capitalist class for extracting surplus value from the labor of workers and
violently transforming it into a system of private property that alienates humanity. Anti-colonialists highlight the fact that Europeans have systematically enslaved
and exploited the people of the world on the basis of theories of cultural and racial
superiority. Feminists show how men work to keep women as unequal partners,
second-class citizens, and outright concubines. Gay liberation involves exposing the
legal and normative privileges of straight people. The liberation of a nation depends
upon identifying a dominant occupier, class, religion, or ethnic group that claims
superiority and monopolizes power.

Second, liberation movements identify overt physical violence as emblem-
atic of and a critical means for sustaining the psychological, emotional, and economic dimensions of oppression. Tyrants extract taxes, military service, and fealty
under threat of death and hold arbitrary power over the life and death of subjects.
Capitalists use the police state and the army to crush unions, defend property,
and fight other capitalists. Europeans use armies and slavery to colonize the world
and lynching, rape, and the police state to enforce the second-class status of people of color. Men confine, beat, and rape their wives, girlfriends, and mistresses to
uphold masculine superiority. One ethnic or religious group sometimes attempts to
"cleanse" the community of another. Heterosexuals enforce their privileges through
bullying and murder. Every liberation movement demands putting an end to these
instances of physical violence by certain identifiable others, and sets out to disman-
tle the institutions and norms that sustain such violence. Since the belief systems
and practices of oppressors dominate the psychology and bodies of the oppressed,
liberators offer arguments against the idea that such violence is justified and necessary. One of the first tasks of every liberation movement is to make the claim that
there is nothing inevitable or natural in the physical violence of the oppressors.[1]

Among these common concerns, the issue of whether and how to use violence
in response to the violence of oppressors stands out because it has so often been
the cause of division and disagreement. Nearly every movement carries on an internal discussion regarding the use of violence as a means to liberation. The physical
violence of oppressors is always a focus of critique, but debates about whether or

not to use violence in return—and, if so, when and how much—plague liberation traditions. In what follows, I trace some exemplary disputes about the use of violence, exploring the contradictions that arise in some of the signature violent revolutions of the last three centuries. The American, French, Haitian, and Bolshevik Revolutions all embraced some degree of violence, but the movements were deeply divided and frequently self-destructive in their disputes regarding its use. In the following chapter, I will explore liberation traditions that claim nonviolence is sufficient even in the face of the most egregious and oppressive violence.

"CRUEL MODERATION" AND ENLIGHTENED VIOLENCE: THE AMERICAN AND FRENCH REVOLUTIONS

Most eighteenth- and nineteenth-century republicans and liberals thought that advancing the rights of man required collective action that would involve bloodshed. However, their estimations of exactly how much violence was necessary or justified varied widely. They looked to precedents such as England's Glorious Revolution (1688) and ancient precedents from Greek democracy and the Roman Republic. However, their views were also deeply informed by their own attempts to dominate native peoples in the Americas. European dreams of freedom arose in part from the resistance they met in trying to colonize land where others already lived. The encounters strongly influenced both their conceptions of liberty and their understandings of violence. On the one hand, indigenous people were figured as providing models of individual freedom and communal equality in the "state of nature"—noble savages. On the other hand, as European colonists met with resistance to their efforts to dominate North and South America, the same people were figured as lawless, amoral animals—heathen savages.

In their revolution against King George, the British colonists of North America set out to imitate American Indians in both respects. Many of the practices and ideas that led the colonists to call for the liberation of "Americans" were paradoxically inspired either directly or indirectly by the continent's original inhabitants. In perhaps the most important protest leading up to the War, the Sons of Liberty dressed as Mohawk Indians threw taxed tea into Boston Harbor, performatively identifying themselves with the inhabitants of "their" new continent against the Old World. Although George Washington (1732–1799) shunned the tactics, Francis Marion (1732–1795), Thomas Sumter (1734–1832), and others deployed "the Indian way of fighting" against British and loyalist regulars during the war, delivering decisive blows in the Southern colonies.[2] Some argue that the Virginia elite were pressed to seek independence as a way of channeling and deflecting the violent turmoil and rebellion wrought by debtors, slaves, and native peoples in the colony.[3] And when drawing up the new Constitution, some of the founders may have looked to the Great Law of Peace of the Iroquois or Haudenosaunee Confederacy. The French baron and political theorist Montesquieu (1689–1755) and others had described the tripartite branches of government, but the six Iroquois Nations provided a model of how to rhetorically, theoretically, and practically bring a collection of diverse political entities together under one common governing body.[4]

Before and during the Revolution, how to respond to the British government's transgressions was the cause of much debate. The range of opinions ran from American Quakers, most of whom agreed that British policies were wrong but were categorically opposed to the use of violence and war,[5] to Sons of Liberty and Committees of Safety, who destroyed property and killed or routed colonial loyalists and British officials. Philadelphian and Quaker John Dickinson (1732–1808) wrote most of the Olive Branch Petition and played a major role in convincing the First Continental Congress to offer it to Great Britain in July of 1775 in an attempt to resolve the conflict without complete independence or a full-scale war. Others averred, and when King George III rejected the petition and declared the colonies in rebellion, the Second Continental Congress tasked the Virginian polymath Thomas Jefferson (1743–1826) with writing the Declaration of Independence (1776).

The debate about violence among the new Americans led to a distinctive stance on the relationship between war and liberty. The Declaration of Independence articulated a case for complete independence and separation, undermined the legitimacy of British rule, and generally advanced the case for revolution. Yet, it was a declaration of war notable for its lack of inflammatory language.[6] Instead of demonizing the crown, calling for the death of aristocrats, or invoking bloodshed and terror, Jefferson and the other signatories levied specific legal grievances and forwarded lofty philosophical principles. Likewise, Thomas Paine's (1736/7–1809) *Common Sense* (1776) was a forceful case for coming together to fight the war that nonetheless refrained from rhetorically invoking and endorsing violence as central to the American cause. Instead, the English-born Paine associates violence and war with the tyrants of Old Europe,[7] in contrast to the American revolutionaries who use arms as a "last resource" and only at "the choice of the king."[8]

Subsequent events on the world stage tested the intellectual coherence and political practicality of the American approach. In the events leading up to the French Revolution, disputes about violence among the liberators became the cause of internecine violence. The French general Lafayette (1757–1834) had pushed France to support the American Revolutionary War, and had served as a major-general under George Washington in fighting the war against the British. Yet upon his return to France, acting in his role as a commander of the National Guard, he had ordered troops to fire on republican demonstrators on the Champs de Mars in July of 1791.

Although the demonstrators had hung two suspected royalist saboteurs, French troops killed scores of the unarmed protestors, suggesting that Lafayette saw an organized war against a monarch as legitimate but also thought the violence of monarchs should be deployed against an unruly mob.[9]

Others took the case for violence against the monarchy further. The Jacobin Club leader Maximilien Robespierre (1758–1794), Saint-Just (1767–1794), and the Committee for Public Safety guillotined those who decried the violence of the people, including leaders of the revolution such as Georges Danton (1759–1794) and Camille Desmoulins (1760–1794). "Cruel moderation," observed Robespierre, was the work of "false patriots."[10] The Jacobins also executed those who thought Robespierre was too moderate, namely, members of Jacques Hébert's (1757–1794) faction. Far from denying Edmund Burke's (1729–1797) charge in *Reflections on the Revolution in France* (1790) that the novice rulers would embrace terror,[11] Robespierre argued that the king (and eventually all others the Committee of Public Safety suspected) should be made to feel the "salutary terror of the people's justice."[12]

Burke's tract became a foundational text for conservatives, but in one respect he and the Jacobins were in agreement: the women of the French Revolution were a menace. Even as he supported the American Revolution, Burke worried that the actions of the radical mob of women who forced the King to come to Paris to attend to the basic material needs of the people went too far.[13] The women that Burke thought portended the coming terror were the lifeblood of the revolution, but they were excluded from taking part in the official business of the new Republic.[14] In response to the Declaration of the Rights of Man and of the Citizen (1789), Olympe de Gouges (1748–1793) penned the Declaration of the Rights of Woman and the Female Citizen (1791) and her own version of Rousseau's *Social Contract*, arguing for marriage grounded in gender equality. Along with advocating for slaves in the colonies, she opposed the execution of the king and wrote critically about Robespierre and the Jacobins, even after they imprisoned her. She was guillotined early on in the Terror.

The French Revolution was hotly debated by the newly liberated Americans. Thomas Paine, like Lafayette from the French side, directly participated in the Revolution, writing *Rights of Man* (1791) in reply to Burke's *Reflections* and eventually joining the National Convention as an honorary French citizen. Yet when it came to the issue of whether or not to kill the king, Paine balked, arguing that the king should be tried and exiled to the United States. Arrested by Robespierre and the Jacobins, Paine narrowly escaped the guillotine,[15] his tenuous moderation nearly costing him his life.

Jefferson initially embraced the methods of the Terror, writing in a 1793 letter that although his "affections have been deeply wounded by some of the martyrs to the cause" he would rather see "half the earth desolated" if those who remained were "left free."[16] He had a similar response to Daniel Shays' Rebellion (1786–1787), the uprising of Revolutionary War veterans who were burdened with heavy taxes and could not pay their debts to Massachusetts. Though he distanced himself from their motives, Jefferson said the rebels were ignorant but not malicious. Where others thought the rebellion showed the need for a new Constitution with a strong executive,[17] Jefferson thought there was not much to fear:

> What country before ever existed a century & half without a rebellion? & what country can preserve its liberties if their rulers are not warned from time to time that their people preserve the spirit of resistance? Let them take arms. The remedy is to set them right as to the facts, pardon & pacify them. . . . The tree of liberty must be refreshed from time to time with the blood of patriots & tyrants. It is its natural manure.[18]

In this 1787 letter, Jefferson demonstrates a distinctive position on violence, describing it as a necessary and natural means to ensuring liberation. Moreover, echoing Niccolò Machiavelli, he argues that republican liberty must regularly be renewed and refreshed with revolutionary violence.[19] However, it is also likened to manure. In both his response to the French Revolution and Shays' Rebellion, Jefferson suggested that violence is a (perhaps unfortunate) necessity for establishing and maintaining freedom. It would be a view consistent with his understanding of slavery.

FROM FIELD HANDS TO "CULTIVATORS": REVOLUTIONIZING SLAVERY IN THE AMERICAS

Jefferson later wrote to Lafayette that the French Revolution had been excessive. Lafayette returned the favor by calling Jefferson to task for failing to rectify the hypocrisy of American slavery, calling it a "wide blot on American philanthropy."[20] Jefferson soured on the French Revolution for a number of reasons, but among them was what he must have taken to be a surprising turn: the Republic's decision to abolish slavery in 1794.[21] Failing to realize the reverberations the American Revolution would have in France,[22] he certainly did not imagine that the French revolutionaries, Robespierre among them, might apply their lofty ideals to their own colonies.[23]

There was good reason to believe that even a republican France would support slavery. France's prized colonial possession San Domingo was the most profitable European colony in the Americas and held half a million slaves. Yet an indigenous slave rebellion, divisions among royalist and republican French officials, and the political circumstance of three European powers vying for control of the colony changed the political dynamics in favor of abolition. The leaders of the American and French Revolutions were primarily preoccupied with debating the proper means for obtaining their own liberty from monarchs, but their actions unleashed a transatlantic debate as to whether or not slavery—and all of its concomitant murder, torture, and rape—could be made consistent with freedom.

The people of what would become Haiti had an answer. During the summer of 1791, a *papaloi*, or voodoo priest, named Boukman (d. 1791) organized and led a rebellion of slaves in the northern part of San Domingo. In a matter of weeks, they implemented a rampage of vengeance for years of oppression that threatened the very existence of slave owners on the French side of the island.[24] The Spanish controlled the other half of the territory and joined forces with the leaders of the rebellion. Royalist Spaniards and the slaves of French planters aligned themselves against republican France, an ironic alliance recurrent in the history of slave rebellions.

There was no disagreement among the rebel leaders as to the necessity of violence against those who had oppressed them so brutally. However, as with the bourgeois Europeans, the amount and timing of it was a subject of serious dispute. In the initial rebellion, three leaders came to the fore—Georges Biassou (1741–1801), Jean François (d. 1805), and Jeannot—all three of whom sanctioned the killing of their former masters, the rape of their wives and daughters, and the burning of plantations.[25] Indeed, Jeannot believed the discipline and obedience of the slaves themselves required a measure of brutality to complement cruelty toward the enemy. Judging that he had gone too far, Jean François arrested, tried, and killed him.[26]

A fourth leader, Toussaint Louverture (circa 1743–1803), had a very different attitude. Before he joined the rebellion, he worked to ensure the safety of his former master Bayon de Libertat and his family.[27] Toussaint's remarkable career, which culminated in an independent Haiti and the abolition of slavery on the island, was marked by disputes with rivals and one-time allies regarding when and how to use force, disputes that raised questions about the very nature of freedom itself. When the French Assembly abolished slavery, Toussaint and his supporters went over to the French side while Biassou and Jean-François continued to fight them in alliance with the Spanish. Over a ten-year period, black, mulatto, and white revolutionaries questioned Toussaint's use of force to return former "field hands" to the plantations, now as "cultivators," a policy that blurred the line between freedom and slavery. Those who lined up against Toussaint tried to topple him with force.[28] Toussaint bested them all and restored some of the white planters, including his former master de Libertat.[29] All the while, he vigorously defended the island from the attacks of the Spanish, the British, and Napoleon's France.

Once again, a violent revolution resulted in stark contradictions. Each European power tried to reestablish European control of the island with the prospect of restoring slavery. Toussaint's National Assembly instead drafted a Constitution (1801) that abolished it. However, the Constitution also made Catholicism the official religion of Haiti (effectively outlawing voodoo) and tied freed slaves to their plantations.[30] The only successful slave rebellion in the history of the world inspired people around the globe and pointed to the hypocrisies of the so-called republics that codified and perpetuated slavery. Yet, Haiti too was haunted by the hypocrisies that persistently crop up in liberation movements that use violence to obtain and secure freedom.

These three interrelated revolutions were all influential in the struggle of *criollos* in South America to gain independence from Spain and Portugal. As was the case in the United States, slaveholders were divided between royalists and republicans. More directly, the invasion of Spain by Napoleon (1808) for nominally republican purposes left the colonies effectively independent.[31] On the issue of slavery, Simón Bolívar (1783–1830), the great liberator of South America's colonies, was directly influenced by Haiti. After the first Venezuelan Republic fell, the British refused to give him safe harbor in Jamaica. He went to Haiti, where El Liberator received the material support necessary to launch a successful effort against the Spanish— on the condition that he would abolish slavery in the newly independent states of South America. (The question of uniting the new states or keeping them separate was also a subject of violent dispute.[32]) The Haitian Revolution also played a role in the United States, where it intensified the urgency of both the abolitionist and pro-slavery causes.[33]

LIBERATING WORKERS WITH BOURGEOIS METHODS: THE COMMUNIST REVOLUTIONS

The issue that was the cause of so much dispute in Haiti—the meaning of liberty in relation to labor—would come to define violent struggles for freedom in the nineteenth and twentieth centuries. In addition, the North and South American colonists who looked to the freedom and military tactics of indigenous Americans for inspiration in their rebellions[34] outlined principles that would influence the indigenous peoples of Asia and Africa. Those revolutions would expel or recapture political control from the European colonists themselves. However, far from resolving the contradictions of the earlier revolutions, the socialist, communist, and anti-colonial movements further intensified them.

The ideas that would percolate into communist revolutions were centrally concerned with how to free human beings from violence. The needs of the body were used to enslave people to the productive forces of capitalism. The serfdom of feudalism and the tyranny of kings had been replaced with the alienated labor of industry and the bureaucracy of republican government. For many nineteenth-century thinkers, the problem of industrialization was one of both mode of production and scale of production, and many of the solutions—from the likes of Charles Fourier (1772–1837), John Ruskin (1819–1900), and Leo Tolstoy (1828–1910)—were as radical as they were pacifist. These thinkers imagined small, self-sufficient, highly democratic communes where people could labor with dignity. Tolstoy in particular understood war and forced conscription as part and parcel of the destructive effects of industrial economies. Labor was dehumanized and impoverished. Militaries were brutal and destructive, sacrificing the lives of ordinary people for the aims of elites, capitalists, and bureaucrats.[35]

Yet in the mid-nineteenth century, a generation of communists rejected the experiments of the socialist radicals as insufficient. Accusing other socialists of being conservative, reactionary, and bourgeois,[36] these communists, led by Karl Marx (1818–1883), mustered a critique of their fellow socialists that embraced a theory of change first outlined by bourgeois revolutionaries. Liberals and republicans had argued that individual liberties and the protection of property rights required violence in response to the violence of tyrants and the arbitrary will of purportedly divine rulers. Indeed as we will see in Part II of this book, tyrants and slave masters were understood to operate outside of the rule of law, physical force used for the purpose of liberation was not really "violence" at all—it comported with natural law and the strictures of reason.[37] In turn, communists argued that violence was necessary for freedom because it was the only way to precipitate the end of the capitalist mode of production and assure the well-being of all the people. Proletarian revolution required doing violence to the property rights and individual liberties of capitalists, just as the earlier liberation movements did violence to the title-holders and aristocrats.[38]

Both bourgeois and communist revolutionaries faced similar problems in grappling with how to translate their justifications for violence into a system of governance. On principle, the revolutionaries in each school were skeptical of the state. For instance, John Locke (1632–1704) opined that tyrants ought to be overthrown even if the alternative was little or no government. Strongly tempering Thomas Hobbes's (1588–1679) concern with preserving stability and order, he argued that the social contract was more convenient than the state of nature—but that bad governments were worse than no government at all.[39] Likewise, Marx argued that parliamentary democracies were committees for the bourgeoisie and would eventually wither away. States would no longer be necessary when workers owned the means of production.[40] Yet in practice, communists were deeply divided regarding the proper role of the state, reflecting in part the ambivalence and contradictions in Marx's own thought.

A primary issue for communists of the late nineteenth and early twentieth centuries was whether the purpose of the revolution was to destroy the bourgeois state or transform it, using it for communist purposes. The issue involved violence in two respects: First, how would the revolution be conducted? Second, what kind of rule did communism imply once the revolution was over? For anarchist communists such as Mikhail Bakunin (1814–1876) and Peter Kropotkin (1842–1921), the republican dream of a liberated humanity had turned into the nightmare of nationalism. The armies of states mobilized one people against another, and the police forces of states enforced property rights and kept the peasants and workers poor. Because the bureaucratic state and capitalism could not be separated, the solution was a radically different alternative.[41] The main work of the revolution certainly involved violence, but for anarchists it would involve smashing the state, not co-opting it. Even so, this act might not require that much physical force, simply because the people had such overwhelming numbers on their side.[42] When the capitalists had been forced to give up their property, the remaining tasks would involve educating the populace and nourishing radically participatory and local forms of governance.[43]

For Vladimir Lenin (1870–1924) and Leon Trotsky (1879–1940) no revolution could succeed, at least not in any satisfactory time frame, without using the bureaucracy, mechanized army, and police force of the state. Counterrevolutionary forces would overrun the revolution if its supporters did not have the institutional and material resources to match them. All of the capitalist states would line up against communism. Further, dissent from within had to be suppressed because discipline and unity were essential to the success of the revolution.[44] As with the earlier bourgeois revolutions, these disputes about violence themselves led to violence among the revolutionaries. The most infamous incident, which is still a matter of contention among contemporary communists, was the suppression of anarchists in Petrograd (1921) by Lenin. Workers and sailors from the naval fortress Kronstadt went on strike amidst worsening economic conditions and demanded, among other things, the right of unions and peasant associations to speak and organize freely. Thousands died in the assault commanded by Trotsky.

The towering figure of Karl Marx played an ambiguous role in the dispute between statists and non-statist communists, in that Marx's position on the issue of state violence is somewhat obscure. In a speech at Amsterdam in 1872 after the Congress of the First International, Marx raised the possibility that in countries such as the United States, England, and Holland, the workers "can attain their goals by peaceful means."[45] Yet, understood in its historical context, one wonders if the remark was not a kind of tributary paean to an enemy recently defeated. The just-concluded Congress had expelled the anarchists.

Ostensibly, Bakunin was expelled because of corruption, but there is strong evidence that his relationship with a young revolutionary named Sergey Nechaev (1847–1882) and the general sense that there were "'proportionally more homosexuals and effeminates'" among the anarchists was used by Marx to discredit them.[46]

Anarchists were more apt to understand sexual freedom as part and parcel of liberation. By connecting this with their skepticism of the state, Marx could deride them as weak, effeminate, and bourgeois. Anarchists like Bakunin subsequently amplified their criticisms of Marx's willingness to use violence as "authoritarian communism"[47]; Marx and Friedrich Engels (1820–1895) continued to dispute the charge that their endorsement of violence was tyrannical.[48] Among the next generation of communists, the conflict came to center around the meaning of Marx's phrase "the dictatorship of the proletariat." The Czech-Austrian political theorist and influential Marx interpreter Karl Kautsky (1854–1938) claimed the phrase was neither antidemocratic nor pro-violence if taken in proper context. Lenin and Trotsky claimed that Marx meant to fully endorse both the dictatorial power of one person and the use of terror as a means to political ends. Kautsky argued that it was one thing for the nationalists to use terror, but it was hypocritical for the communists to do so because Marx held life to be sacred. To this Trotsky responds:

> As for us we were never concerned with the Kantian-priestly and vegetarian-Quaker prattle about the "sacredness of human life." We were revolutionaries in opposition, and have remained revolutionaries in power. To make the individual sacred we must destroy the social order which crucifies him. And this problem can only be solved by blood and iron.[49]

Joseph Stalin (1878–1953) was even more enamored with the means of state violence, eventually leading to the imprisonment and death of millions in forced labor camps and purges. This, in part, led to a split with Trotsky that ended with Trotsky's exile and assassination. Trotsky had been Lenin's point man in crushing the anarchists but was eventually destroyed himself.

DESTROYING AND BECOMING THE OTHER? THE WORLD PUSHES BACK AGAINST EUROPE

In Asia, Africa, and the Middle East, the anti-colonial movements of the twentieth century were characterized by a wide range of ideas about the meaning of freedom and the tactics required to obtain it. In China, Mao Zedong (1893–1976) adapted the Leninist model to a rural population and mobilized the peasantry against the nationalists by way of the Long March, a strategic military retreat that won the communists the popular support of millions.[50] In Africa, leaders like Patrice Lumumba (1925–1961) in Congo and Kwame Nkrumah (1909–1972) in Ghana took a relatively moderate pan-African view of socialism. In the Middle East, secularists like Saddam Hussein (1937–2006) in Iraq rose to power along with Islamic revolutionaries like Ayatollah Khomeini (1902–1989) in Iran. These leaders all thought some degree of violence was necessary for liberation from Western imperialism, but their estimations varied widely and changed over time. For instance, Khomeini and the Islamic Revolution in Iran was at first almost entirely nonviolent, but Khomeini's anxieties about Western influence led him to implement a repressive post-revolutionary government.

Of particular note is that the latter half of the twentieth century was characterized by liberation movements that specifically sought to expel the militaries of the United States and the Soviet Union, two countries that held up their own revolutions as the inspiration for liberation movements around the world. In Vietnam, Ho Chi Minh (1890–1969) and the North Vietnamese fought a campaign against overwhelming force and successfully repelled the Americans after suffering upwards of one million deaths.[51] In Afghanistan, a ragtag group of tribal fighters expelled the Soviets after a brutal occupation (1979–1989). In both cases, the United States and the Soviet Union had far superior military forces and inflicted more casualties than they suffered by some orders of magnitude. Yet overwhelming violence failed to persuade the populations of both countries to accept foreign rule or adopt their preferred systems of government or brand of freedom. Perhaps the most perverse manifestation of the close connection between liberation and violence came in Cambodia. In response to saturation bombing by the United States (in the name of keeping Southeast Asia free), Pol Pot's (1925–1998) regime implemented a Maoist model of agrarian socialism that promised freedom from Western imperialism but ended in vicious repression and the deaths of a significant portion of the population of the country.

Ideologically, the poles of opinion on the issue of violence among postcolonial thinkers are perhaps best represented by Franz Fanon (1925–1961) and Mahatma Gandhi (1869–1948). Fanon argued that in Algeria:

[The nationalist militant] discovers in real action a new form of political activity . . . These politics are the politics of leaders and organizers living inside history who take the lead with their brains and their muscles in the fight for freedom. . . . Violence alone, violence committed by the people, violence organized and educated by its leaders, makes it possible for the masses to understand social truths and gives the key to them.[52]

By contrast, Gandhi averred that freedom, or swaraj (self-rule), could not be won through violence. Adopting the tactics of violence and embracing the bureaucratic state might appear to achieve independence from the West, but it would in fact turn colonized peoples into a replica of so called Western "civilization."[53] True liberation involved something different.

In positing that some are oppressors and others are the oppressed, liberation movements respond to the dehumanizing ideologies and practices of oppressors by creating overly simplistic identities that exacerbate the oppression of certain members who are nominally within the group. For instance, in identifying themselves as victims of the tyrannical policies of the British government, American Revolutionaries simultaneously reinforced their freedom to enslave African Americans and kill or expel American Indians. In upholding the good character and capabilities of the Russian working class, Lenin railed against the homeless and the criminal element, whom he felt hindered the progress of the Bolshevik Revolution.[54] In their attempt to create a utopian agricultural community for all Cambodians, the Khmer Rouge demonized and murdered hundreds of thousands of urban dwellers.

Nowhere are the disputes and contradictions within and among liberation movements more apparent than with respect to the issue of violence. In this chapter, I have traced a circuitous and harrowing conversation about the proper use of violence in the struggle for political and economic freedom over the last three centuries. Another way to tell this story would be to attempt to account for the sheer number of those killed in the revolutions I explore in this chapter. However, disputes among historians as to the number of casualties in these wars as well as how to account for the loss of life due to related factors such as disease prevent a precise accounting. Moreover, the freedom of one group often seemed to come at the expense of another. So we might, for instance, include in the tally of those killed or violated as a result of the American Revolution the genocide of indigenous Americans and the codification of slavery in the resulting Constitution. Each call for liberation seems to belie the freedom of others who are subjected to violence and deprivation, and at the same time sets in motion new aspirations from new groups of people. Each call for moderation and nonviolence is vulnerable to the charge of accommodation and conservatism, and yet when revolutions combine the zeal for liberty with an equal zeal for violence it threatens to destroy the aims of the revolution by raising up a tyrant, creating a new form of slavery, or devolving into a bloodbath.

If fire-fighters fight fires and crime-fighters fight crime, what do freedom-fighters fight?
GEORGE CARLIN

2

Nonviolent Liberation(s)

THE RECORD OF the signature violent revolutions of the last three centuries is checkered. In the last chapter, we found internecine violence within liberation movements and freedom fighters who themselves became oppressors. By only considering successful violent revolutions I limited the analysis, but an even more discouraging story might emerge if we considered all of the failed violent revolutions fought in the name of freedom. Even so, the human toll of the successful revolutions alone raises hard questions about the measure of success and the meaning of liberation and freedom. In what follows, I partially resolve some of those questions by putting the violent revolutions explored in the last chapter in historical perspective. Through an examination of exemplary nonviolent liberation movements over roughly the same time period, the idea of nonviolent freedom begins to come into focus.

Liberation implies a process that changes the condition of those liberated and the state of the world more generally. What that process looks like and what it means to be liberated have extraordinarily diverse meanings in political thought. Liberation from slavery and colonization, women's liberation, liberation from tyrants, black liberation, gay liberation: these movements differ from one another in important respects and at times may have even seemed to be mutually exclusive. It is no surprise then that not only violent revolutions but also nonviolent ones have been hampered by contradictions and infighting. The abolitionist and civil rights movements often dismissed or opposed the liberation of black women in an effort to invigorate a brand of black masculinity.[1] Some Second Wave feminists went out of their way to distinguish themselves from and defend themselves against "charges" of lesbianism. As mainstream lesbian, gay, bisexual, and transgender (LGBT) rights groups make marriage equality and property rights the centerpiece of the struggle, it reinforces the idea that queer identities that reject monogamy and marriage are abnormal and illegitimate.[2]

In this chapter I will show that nonviolent liberation movements are generally much less prone to self-destruction, hypocrisy, and contradiction than their violent counterparts. Instead, they are characterized by remarkable consistency and coherence, both within and among themselves. When nonviolent movements have been derailed and turned to violence, the character of the progress they seek is frequently compromised, as using violence as a means to freedom erodes the very character of freedom. The through-line of liberation thought that runs from mid-century abolitionists in the United States to Gandhi's development of satyagraha in South Africa and India to the present-day use of nonviolence in revolutions around the globe contains the idea that liberation involves rejecting not only the violence of others, but the use of violence to liberate oneself.

THE INTRACTABILITY OF SLAVERY AND FREEDOM

As I mentioned above, the Haitian Revolution is the only successful slave rebellion in the history of the world. When considered as an indication of the effectiveness of violence in achieving human ends, this remarkable fact cuts two ways. On the one hand, it can be understood as a profound affirmation of the political power of human violence, in that slavery itself is a form of physical subjection that is sustained by violence. Once established, the institution of slavery is extremely difficult to remove.[3] Indeed, while slaves have always found ways to resist their masters, historians of slavery tell us that millions toiled for the benefit of others in dire conditions from the beginning to the end of their lives, for generation upon generation.[4] Liberation requires something more, and that something more is not guaranteed by the condition of slavery.

On the other hand, the fact that only one violent rebellion against slavery in the history of the world has succeeded seems to undermine the assumption that violence, at least for the purposes of liberation, is effective—let alone the critical factor—in overturning slave systems. This is particularly true if we consider the fact that while not all enslaved people have rebelled, those who have done so have sometimes mustered extraordinary organization, courage, and persistence. Where the Haitian Revolution succeeded, the near-constant plots, rebellions, and organized violent resistance in Jamaica did not. The slave rebellions in the later years of the Roman Republic, including the one famously led by Spartacus (111–71 BC), involved tens of thousands of people. In one instance, the republic slaughtered upwards of 100,000 slaves to put down a rebellion.[5] Such uprisings sometimes succeeded temporarily and sometimes inspired reforms, but in the history of the world, only the single instance of the Haitian Revolution has won freedom for slaves by the violent rebellion of slaves themselves.

Is there something about using violence for subjugation that makes it more effective than violence used for the purpose of liberation? Not if we consider a second, equally remarkable historical fact. No one has ever managed to enslave another people in situ.[6] That is, enslaving people always requires taking them away from their native culture and homeland. Techniques such as dispersing family members, mixing slaves who speak different languages, and generally removing as many common points of identity as possible are all tried-and-true tactics of slave masters. Europeans attempted to enslave the indigenous people of the Americas but failed, sometimes taking their resistance as a model of freedom for themselves, while eventually resorting to genocide and geographic containment as a response to it.[7] People will simply refuse to be completely humiliated and subjugated, to the point of sacrificing everything, if they are living in their homeland and in the company of other members of their community.

THREE LIBERATION MOVEMENTS IN ONE

It would seem then that both freedom and slavery are somewhat intractable, and that violence, both as a means for overcoming slavery and as a means for imposing it, has definite limits. But this finding raises the question, how do we explain the worldwide abolition of slavery? Although slavery had been banned by individual political entities even in ancient times, for almost all of human history some or most governments allowed or directly participated in the practice. Yet concurrent with the violent revolutions of the late eighteenth and early nineteenth centuries, the largely nonviolent abolitionist movement achieved extraordinary success in putting an end to legally sanctioned slavery.[8] In a worldwide campaign that operated in fits and starts, abolitionism made slavery into a signature moral evil.

By encouraging and assisting thousands of runaway slaves, boycotting products made by slave labor, tirelessly speaking and organizing international conventions, publishing newspapers, founding political parties, and pressuring politicians, abolitionists brought an end to the most lucrative and dynamic slave system in the history of the world. In terms of both sheer numbers and the fundamental change it wrought in human consciousness, the abolition movement liberated more people than any other in history. And despite the extraordinary violence of the institution itself and the violence used to defend it, the goal of making slavery illegal in every country in the world was accomplished almost entirely without violent revolution.[9]

Like all liberation movements, abolitionism was beset by divisions and differences about tactics and principles.[10] Yet when compared to the violent revolutions of the era, the movement was not only internally consistent, but also externally productive, inspiring other equally important liberation movements. Indeed, a wide range of progressive causes from temperance to a critique of industrialization and the alternative of small-scale socialism can be traced to the Quakers and the inception of the abolitionist movement in England and America. But three bona fide liberation movements sprung from the mid-nineteenth-century effort to analyze and critique slavery. Abolition, the women's movement, and a commitment to nonviolence itself have proved to be the most important and enduring forces of the era. I take each in turn.

From its inception, the American Anti-Slavery Society, operating under the leadership of William Lloyd Garrison (1805–1879), embraced a policy of what would come to be called "non-resistance" to slavery. At the first meeting of the Society in 1833 in Philadelphia, Garrison began his Declaration of Sentiments by referring to the Declaration of Independence, signed fifty-seven years before in the same city. Unlike those early patriots, who wanted to achieve liberty with warfare:

> We have met together for the achievement of an enterprise, without which that of our fathers is incomplete; and which, for its magnitude, solemnity, and probable results upon the destiny of the world, as far transcends theirs as moral truth does physical force. . . . Their measures were physical resistance—the marshaling of arms—the hostile array—the mortal encounter. Ours shall be such only as the opposition of moral purity to moral corruption—the destruction of error by the potency of truth—the overthrow of prejudice by the power of love—the abolition of slavery by the spirit of repentance.[11]

Five years later, in 1838, Garrison convened a Peace Convention that was the occasion for founding the New England Non-Resistance Society. Many members of the American Anti-Slavery Society walked out of the convention because of Garrison's broad condemnation of physical force and his insistence on treating women such as Abby Kelley (1811–1887), as equal participants in the proceedings.[12]

Present at the convention was a Unitarian minister named Adin Ballou (1803–1890), who saw a need to formulate more carefully and specifically what was meant by the term "non-resistance." Perhaps drawing on the attempts of Revolutionary-era Quakers like Dickinson who spoke of a middle way between rebellion and submission ("orderly resistance"[13]), Ballou insisted that non-resistance was a misleading term because it implied passivity. In fact, he argued, non-resistance was active force, a "moral force," or "moral power," which was not only the right but also the duty of every human being to practice in the face of injustice. "In this sense my very non-resistance becomes the highest form of *resistance* to evil."[14] Political action in accordance with non-resistance could even involve physical force and subduing another's will, if that force was not injurious to the person's physical or mental well-being.[15] Arguing that this kind of active non-resistance was a full-fledged alternative to violence, he condemned those who would use violence "in pretended defense" of good ends such as life and liberty.[16] Although not a member of the Society, Henry David Thoreau (1817–1862) was present at meetings where Ballou made his case. A few years later, in the work that popularized the term "civil disobedience," Thoreau offered a secular version of Ballou's non-resistance and a more detailed analysis of how the concept affected an individual's relationship to government. However, Thoreau's version did not disavow violent resistance to injustice.[17]

Like slavery, the subjugation of women reaches deep into history. The story is not one of simple domination and submission. Matrilineal societies were often predominant in the past, and women throughout history have transcended and struggled against the violence and oppression of men.[18] Orlando Patterson argues that the very concept of freedom in the West was likely the invention of Greek slave women.[19] The rape of Lucretia and her willful suicide as an act of resistance is at the heart of the origin story of republican Rome.[20] In the eighteenth century, women property holders in Sweden voted,[21] and women played a critical role in the French Revolution.

However, the women's movement initiated in the mid-nineteenth century by American suffragists was of a different order. The First Wave of feminists tackled a wide range of issues from property ownership to the right to divorce, the right to hold elective office, and the right to vote. Along the way, in their actions and words, they promulgated the radical notion that not only exceptional women but all women were capable of political action and suited for public service. There were some prominent abolitionists who balked at certain aspects of the push for women's rights. Indeed, the early feminist movement was in part inspired by the second-class treatment of female abolitionists by their male counterparts. However, to a remarkable degree the two movements were mutually reinforcing and often one and the same. Susan B. Anthony (1820–1906) and Lucretia Mott (1793–1880) sheltered runaway slaves in their homes. Frederick Douglass (1818–1895) signed the Declaration of Sentiments at Seneca Falls (1848) and spoke forcefully in favor of suffrage for all women.

Like abolitionists, the tactics of feminists have been almost entirely nonviolent, despite the fact that their efforts have often been met with vicious violent resistance by men.[22] From the establishment of domestic violence shelters, to hunger strikes, to demonstrations and speech making, to the organization of political pressure groups, the women's movement has achieved remarkable success without a single violent revolution. If the efforts of feminists to gain full citizenship, equal dignity, equal pay, and reproductive freedom for all of the women of the world are successful, the movement started in Seneca Falls will surpass even abolition in the history of political liberation. It will liberate the better part of humanity.

FREEING THE SLAVES OF ONE'S ENEMIES: WAR AS A CIRCUITOUS
ROUTE TO FREEDOM

In 1893, Leo Tolstoy noted in *The Kingdom of God Is within You* that Ballou's obituary in a Christian publication from three years earlier had not mentioned his life's work on non-resistance. "It seems just as though it did not exist,"[23] he observed. Tolstoy's book, along with Gandhi's reading of it, would revivify the concept. But the reason Ballou's pacifist ideas were seen as less than consequential at the time of his death can be attributed to earlier events. Abolitionists who broke from the American Anti-Slavery Society had long supported violent rebellion among slaves. Although none of them could persuade the mainstream of the movement, John Brown (1800–1859) eventually did, as much with his actions as his words. Susan B. Anthony, Frederick Douglass, Harriet Tubman (1822–1913), and Garrison himself enthusiastically supported Brown's raid on Harper's Ferry in 1859 and the war that it helped to precipitate.

Ballou had to admit that Brown's actions were no "pretended defense" of liberty. To his mind, Brown was "a well-meaning, misguided unfortunate zealot."[24] Nor did Ballou begrudge the abolitionist militants who had supported violent rebellion prior to Brown's actions. But he was deeply troubled that Garrison and so many others abandoned their professed commitment to non-resistance. One of the founding members of the Non-Resistance Society wrote: "The sin of this nation . . . is to be taken away, not by Christ, but by John Brown. Christ, as represented by those who are called by his name, has proved a dead failure, as a power to free the slaves. John Brown is and will be a power far more efficient."[25]

For a brief time, Garrison attempted to argue that the principles of non-resistance were consistent with slave rebellion, visiting Ballou's congregation and his "practical Christian" socialist community in Hopedale, Massachusetts to make his case.[26] Ballou remained steadfast. He wrote:

> Sin is never so dangerous, so tempting, as when it takes on the guise of righteousness and claims to be necessary to some good end—to be indispensable to some noble achievement. The shortsighted souls overlook the evil means and sanctify them for the sake of the end. Deceit, wrath, violence, war, are then deemed right, or at least excusable, because they are for self-defense, justice, liberty or some great humanitarian cause! Away with all such delusions.[27]

Assessing the prospects for what the Civil War might bring, he warned in 1860:

> We weaken our defenses, impair our protection, multiply our enemies, embit-
> ter their hatred, provoke fresh aggression, cheapen human life, aggravate the
> general disposition to resort to violence, and retard the regeneration of our
> race. If we save our own lives or those of our dear friends in doing it, we feed
> a wrathful flame which ultimately causes the destruction of ten, or a hun-
> dred lives, for every one selfishly saved. We transmit a legacy of violence and
> destruction to posterity which must curse unborn generations.[28]

Writing in his autobiography many years later, he was sanguine, if a little sarcastic
regarding his inability to persuade Garrison and the other prominent abolitionist
leaders:

> Scarcely a survivor of the anti-slavery insurrectionary Non-resistants was to be
> found. Had Jesus Christ and His apostles undertaken to abolish slavery and
> other evils in the Roman empire by similar means, we should probably never
> have heard of their doctrine of universal love and good will, nor of them either.
> Their religion and reformatory methods were of a higher order—"not of this
> world."[29]

The Civil War destroyed "non-resistance" as one of the three mutually supporting pillars of the mid-century religious and social movement that defined American
politics. For at least sixty years after the war, the temperance movement appeared to
be the true third pillar of the mid-century revival. The war and its aftermath also
drove a wedge between women's rights advocates and those advocating for full citizenship for African Americans, as the new constitutional amendments for the first
time wrote gendered language into the Constitution.

Although the American Civil War might be considered a second case where
violence led to abolition, it belongs in a special category. First, it was the political
process leading to the passing of the Thirteenth Amendment that brought the end
of slavery in the United States, since the legal status of the wartime Emancipation
Proclamation was somewhat tenuous.[30] Moreover, the Civil War reminds us that
while slaves have hardly ever gained freedom through their own violence, there
have been numerous examples of military forces freeing the slaves of their enemies
in order to gain military advantage by inciting flight and rebellion among them.
When Cinna (d. 84 BC) finally won the consulship from Sulla (138–78 BC) in the
late Roman Republic he did it in part by offering freedom to the slaves of Rome,
who shrewdly waited until he had gathered enough support from others and then

deserted, bringing him to power.[31] In the competition with Britain for control of the Americas, the Spanish colony of Florida offered freedom to any British slaves who escaped, creating the first large free black colony in North America at Fort Mose.[32] During the American Revolution, the British used the same tactic with the rebellious American colonists to great effect. Nearly nine decades prior to Lincoln's wartime maneuver, the British, not the Americans, offered the first Proclamation of Emancipation in November of 1775. The British governor of Virginia raised a battalion of runaway slaves who wore a sash reading "Liberty to Slaves" and fulfilled his promise to grant the "Ethiopian soldiers" freedom even after the British defeat.[33]

BACK FROM THE DEAD: THE PERSISTENCE
OF NONVIOLENCE

After the Civil War, a post-reconstruction backlash to the devastation and occupation of the South, along with resentment of the new freedmen in the North, led most whites to retrench and enforce second-class citizenship for African Americans. Making use of informal customs, legal segregation, a rigged judicial system, lynchings, police brutality, and the rise of white terrorist groups, conservative white elites reasserted their prewar status and power, ensuring that most of Ballou's worst anxieties about the consequences of using violence to end legal slavery came true.

Yet nonviolence survived the retrenchment in two forms. First, the connection between the women's movement and a broader critique of war and violence remained and even grew stronger. Along with highlighting the violence of men toward women—particularly when alcohol was involved—part of the argument First Wave feminists made about the benefit of women participating in politics was that they would be less bellicose and more "civilized" than their male counterparts. Out of the women's movement grew pacifist organizations such as the Women's International League for Peace and Freedom, led by social reformer and eventual Nobel Peace Prize laureate Jane Addams (1860–1935), who along with prominent women's rights advocates such as Sylvia Pankhurst (1882–1960) and Aletta Jacobs (1854–1929) vehemently opposed World War I at the 1915 Women's International Congress at the Hague.[34] Remarkably, even women such as Emma Goldman (1869–1940) who sometimes advocated violence for the purpose of overthrowing capitalism, did not advocate using violent means to achieve political equality for women. (Only with Second Wave feminism did liberal ideas about the integrity of the body and the use of violence to defend oneself come into play, and even then, advocates of violent revolution for women's rights were a distinct minority.[35]) Moreover, because the early women's movement was so closely connected to critiques of violence and warfare, it did not see the necessity of debating nonviolent methods. Instead, both women and men in the movement assumed that they would use means other than violence.

Just as it was assumed that women would achieve liberation through nonviolent means, the Age of Revolutions seemed to demonstrate that men who wished for liberation would use violence. This meant that it was left to men to specifically reject violence by "feminizing" themselves and marking their actions as "nonviolent." This outright rejection took place when the idea of obtaining freedom through non-resistance took an unexpected and circuitous route to South Africa. There the young Mahatma Gandhi (1869–1948), reading Tolstoy and Thoreau, discovered Ballou's pacifism, finding deep resonance between the ideas and practices of abolitionists and those of a particular line of Hindu and Jain traditions.[36] Like the abolitionists of fifty years earlier, the movements Gandhi helped shape were divided on various important issues, with the question of the proper means for confronting injustice foremost among them. One of the main goals of Gandhi's book *Hind Swaraj* (1909), or *Indian Self-Rule*, was to take issue with those expatriate Indians keen to adopt the violent methods of various European revolutionary movements.[37]

Gandhi argued that even if India succeeded in expelling the British and winning complete independence (*purna swaraj*), achieving freedom through violence would mean becoming even more fully colonized. To Gandhi, the embrace of violence as the essential means of political rule was the essence of so-called European "civilization." Alternatively, if Indians took nonviolent steps to begin ruling themselves, they would be free regardless of whether the British stayed or left. The argument was partly that the moral superiority of nonviolence would triumph over violence, but Gandhi also added a critical pragmatic element to it: a hundred thousand British could not rule three hundred million Indians if they simply refused to be cowed.[38]

Drawing on Hindu traditions, Gandhi replaced the term "non-resistance" with "nonviolence," or "ahimsa." Eventually, he would replace this term as well because it failed to capture the active nature of the force he sought to develop.[39] With the advice of others, he finally settled on the term "satyagraha" (holding fast to the truth). By experimenting with this force, he thought he might avoid the purges, terrorism, and civil wars that had plagued previous liberation movements and that were plaguing concurrent liberation movements in Russia and China. Satyagraha included a wide variety of techniques drawn from the labor and women's movements of the nineteenth century (boycotts, civil disobedience, marches, fasting) and encompassed other concepts such as conscious suffering (*tapas*) and the constructive program (promulgating a variety of cottage industries). All of the forms of satyagraha required acting together with others to pursue common purposes beneficial to the nation and humanity as a whole.

Along with picking up the trail of non-resistance, Gandhi shared with mid-century abolitionists a remarkably wide range of concerns that he saw as interrelated. While Lenin and Trotsky contented themselves with parsing loyal and disloyal socialists, each of Gandhi's campaigns seemed to open up onto another. Along with the poetess Sarojini Naidu (1879–1949), he challenged traditional gender roles.[40] He experimented with dietary habits, took a vow of celibacy, and held up subsistence village life as superior to dehumanizing and destructive industrialization. He supported "untouchables" in their struggle against widespread discrimination calling Dalits *harijans* (children of God) and admitting them to his ashram. He organized a campaign using satyagraha to challenge access restrictions to the Vykom Temple Road, which was reserved for upper caste members. In the most potent and famous of all of the satyagrahas, the Salt March to Dandi, he not only initiated acts of civil disobedience that demonstrated the British were incapable of ruling India, but highlighted how colonialism compromised the basic material needs of the poorest Indians. In the heat of India's summers, the salt tax was a tax on the ability to live itself.[41] The material well-being of the poor, the quality of labor, temperance, the end of untouchability, and independence from Britain were all pieces of a whole. By addressing all of these issues at once, Indians could practice swaraj.

By identifying freedom with "self-rule" and making satyagraha the essential means of swaraj, Gandhi recognized that he was offering a challenging new understanding of the very purpose and character of a liberation movement. Writing in 1910 of the struggle by Indians in South Africa against the law requiring them to obtain and carry registration cards, Gandhi pointed to the conservative British politician Lord Hugh Cecil's (1869–1956) definition of liberty: "'Liberty consists in being able to obey your own will and conscience rather than the will and conscience of others.'"[42] In opposing the discriminatory law, he went on to explain, Indians in the Transvaal were "exercising the power to obey their will and conscience rather than the will of the State which is in conflict with theirs. . . . The Asiatic Act imposes slavery on Indians in that it deprives them of liberty, i.e. the ability to obey their conscience."[43]

According to Gandhi, laws cannot make people virtuous. If liberty is the ability to act according to the dictates of our conscience, he argues, we certainly cannot achieve it by force of arms. After all, someone who is compelled by force to do good is "no more to be credited with virtue than a donkey who is compelled to carry a load."[44] By contrast, liberty "is attainable only by suffering in our own persons until our opponents see the error of their ways and cease to harass us by trying to impose their will on us. . . . Any other method of gaining liberty is a usurpation."[45] Liberty obtained through violence is no liberty at all, because the very purpose of liberty is to act in a way consistent with one's conscience. Freedom means resisting violence on two levels: refusing to accept the violence of others and refusing the temptation to do violence to others.

Of all the various issues in the constellation of concerns that comprised Indian swaraj, Gandhi believed the most important was establishing "heart-unity" between Hindus and Muslims. For twenty years, in his personal practices, speeches, and dramatic fasts to rein in religious rioting and violence, he tried to find "points of contact" between Hindus and Muslims.[46] His methods attracted the notice of a young Pashtun Muslim named Ghaffar Khan (1890–1988), who—having witnessed the failure of violent resistance against the British—organized thousands and led dramatic satyagraha campaigns against the British in the Frontier Province. Khan also implemented Gandhi's constructive program, became a leader in Congress, and struck up a friendship and strategic partnership with Gandhi that was a model of Hindu-Muslim cooperation.

Yet just as Lincoln's Emancipation Proclamation was the product of a momentous and tragic conflagration, India's independence from Britain came with the epochal horror of the partition of India. Much as American abolitionists could not resist the temptation to end slavery without abandoning their principles with regard to means, most anti-colonial leaders ended up endorsing religious and political separation in order to finally gain independence from the British. For Muslim League leaders, independence from Britain that included a political stronghold to ensure protection from the majority Hindu population seemed like a safe choice. For Congress, partition was an acceptable price to pay when the long-awaited formal independence from Britain was within grasp. Gandhi and Khan did not waver. To avoid partition, Gandhi recommended offering the position of Prime Minister of India to the would-be leader of a newly formed Pakistan, Muhammad Ali Jinnah (1876–1948). Ghaffar Khan opposed the Muslim League's demand for the partition and encouraged his followers to boycott the referendum that made the Frontier part of Pakistan.[47] But it was not enough. Khan was imprisoned for years and generally harassed by successive Pakistani governments on suspicion of being a traitor to the country and Islam. Gandhi was killed by a Hindu nationalist, who accused him of having worked to undermine the well-being of Hindus in favor of Muslims. (Among the more ironic accidents of history is the fact that Khan worked in the area of Pakistan now understood to be among the most intractable havens for terrorism. Indeed, Gandhi and Khan held perhaps their most important meeting in Abbottabad, where Osama bin Laden was assassinated.[48])

If we think of Gandhi's theory of swaraj as articulating a liberation movement of its own kind, a movement to liberate humanity from violence, it has certainly not yet succeeded. However, the latter half of the twentieth century has proved that Gandhi's campaigns, much like abolition and the women's movement, have begun to extend the range of political possibilities. While the Americans and the Soviets were repelled from Vietnam and Afghanistan with violence, their client states elsewhere fell as a result of nonviolent action and civil disobedience. The end of autocracy in the Philippines (1986), the end of Soviet domination in Eastern Europe, the reunification of Germany (1990), the toppling of Pinochet in Chile (1990), the end of apartheid in South Africa (1994),[49] the end of the reign of Suharto in Indonesia (1998), the ouster of Slobodan Milosevic in Serbia (2000),[50] the Orange Revolution in Ukraine (2004–2005), and, most recently, the overthrow of autocrats in Tunisia (2011) and Egypt (2011) were all precipitated by nonviolence.[51] Empirical studies have convincingly demonstrated that in the last century nonviolent resistance has been more effective than violent revolution, and it has more often led to the establishment of democracies.[52]

Within the United States, the ideas that travelled from Adin Ballou to Gandhi came back around the globe again—to tackle the unfinished business of the abolitionist movement. Finding inspiration in Gandhi's methods, Dr. Martin Luther King Jr. (1929–1968) used direct nonviolent action campaigns to end legal segregation. The civil rights movement brought to the front of the nation's consciousness the still-festering hatred rooted in slavery, the horrific violence used to remove it during the Civil War, the backlash among Southerners that established and enforced Jim Crow, and the myriad forms of discrimination that permeated social, economic, and political life throughout the United States. Like the mid-century abolitionists and Gandhi's campaign for independence, King's first concern opened up into others, namely, the Poor People's Campaign and his dramatic opposition to the war in Vietnam.

A NEW IDEA OF FREEDOM

Liberation movements seek change, and violence seems to directly facilitate change by destroying what exists. By killing people beholden to old ideas, defiling symbols of authority, or destroying extant institutions, violence "clears the table." Some revolutionaries suggest that even if we do not know what should replace the status quo, anarchic freedom is preferable to the oppressive and stifling present. Others hope to offer a constructive set of ideas sufficient to replace what is destroyed. Either way, violence aims to demonstrate that what exists is not historically inevitable or necessary. In this way, it appears to be an expression of human freedom.

Yet the history of revolutions shows us that while the human suffering violence brings is real, the political change it brings is often at best incomplete and at worst reinstantiates tyrannical violence. Nonviolent and violent revolutions alike have resulted in more just, equitable, and less violent institutional arrangements, but the latter have also resulted in horrific conflagrations, internecine killing, purges, and counter-purges. Revolutionary justifications for violence inevitably end up compounding, mimicking, or creating some new form of oppression that still another liberation movement will eventually rise to address. The struggle for freedom has often been successful in the short term and self-defeating over the long term. If liberation means, in part, being free from the violence of another group, using violence in response to violence can only limit freedom. Nonviolent liberation movements— or perhaps the ongoing, centuries-long and worldwide nonviolent liberation movement—provides an alternative. Nonviolent liberation aims to show that violence itself is neither historically inevitable nor necessary.

The last three centuries of liberation movements can be understood as a long conversation about the potential and perils of violence in achieving freedom. Although I have followed violent and nonviolent streams of liberation movements separately in chapters 1 and 2, the streams clearly intersect and intermingle. The ideas of democracy and equality, together with critiques of slavery, tyranny, and economic injustice, have often gained attention through violence, and violent revolutions have ushered in new, more equitable forms of government. Moreover, nonviolent liberation movements have sometimes been derailed by the use of violence or the temptation of tyranny. However, the broad stroke successes of the abolitionist, feminist, and nonviolent liberation movements show that the key factor in achieving liberation is primarily ideas put into action. Theresa Urbainczyk writes of slave rebellions in antiquity:

> [S]lave armies might defeat those of their former masters for a while, even for years, but in the end slavery persisted. There was no abolitionist movement among free people, nor even any text calling for the abolition of slavery. We do not even know that the slaves themselves wanted an end to slavery for other people. It is more likely that, on acquiring their own freedom, they would simply have gone on to become slaveowners themselves.[53]

New ideas about how to live together and the actions of people creatively enacting a world that embodies them are the sine qua non of liberation. We have seen that the idea of using violence as a means to achieve liberation is itself a hindrance to a full-fledged concept of liberation. Without the idea that freedom and violence are antithetical to one another, the very concept of freedom is incomplete or becomes compromised. Nonviolent movements show us that the violent overthrow of people and institutions is not essential to the process and that the idea that violence can be used for liberation is an obstacle to freedom.

Gandhi argued that the "intuition" for violence that Fanon speaks of is no intuition at all. Instead, it represented the final triumph of the oppressor's way of thinking. Chapter 1 showed that Gandhi's skepticism regarding ideas about how to achieve freedom through violence are borne out by much of the historical record. The often-referenced "cycle of violence" and the persistence of "intractable conflicts"—such as the one between India and Pakistan that Gandhi so desperately tried to avoid—suggest that violence is a habit, a cultural norm, and an institution unto itself, despite the outward appearance of chaos. However, we have seen that it would be wrong to suggest that these habits, norms, and institutions cannot be overcome through nonviolent struggle.

Revolutionaries and rebels have long embraced violence as a paramount tool of rebellion and a signal of purified, righteous, and radical frustration. Killing others seems to reflect a special commitment to a cause—a willingness to do anything for freedom. Yet the idea of forcing other people to conform to one's desires is the same idea that underpins the violence of oppressors. In this chapter, I uncovered the trail of a strong—albeit less well-known—nonviolent liberation tradition, one that influenced Gandhi and was decisively influenced by him. Oppressors and the oppressed who resist them violently are not moral equals. However, the modern history of violent political revolutions shows us that the false hope that humanity can be liberated from violence through violence only pushes further into the future the day when all can be free.

PART II

Defending Freedom

Do you intend to issue laws to walls and buildings? Are you ashamed that here in the forum your lictors [bodyguards] virtually outnumber other citizens?

LIVY

3

Plebeian Absences

AMONG THE ROUTINE phrases of contemporary political discourse in the United States is the idea that members of the military are "fighting for our freedom" or "died defending our freedom." Indeed, the pairing of freedom and the state's military prowess is so much a part of American culture that we might assume that freedom and violence were always linked in republican and democratic thought. As I discuss in Part III, this assumption is true in that for the ancient Athenians, the ability to dominate others in warfare was an *expression* of their capacity for self-rule. However, the idea that a republican or democratic government could use violence to *defend* or protect freedom is a relatively recent development.

Similarly, the idea of using violence to defend freedom and the idea of using violence for liberation are historically entirely distinct. In contrast to the revolutionary's claim that violence must be used to destroy the status quo, the idea of defensive violence suggests that it can preserve, protect, and secure us against others. In this way, it betrays a fundamentally conservative line of thinking that connects the use of violence to ethical and political arguments not captured by the liberation tradition. In this Part, I trace the history of the idea that citizens have a right to self-defense as a function of their status as free beings. I find that the three elements I am interested in here—the use of 1) physical violence for the 2) defense of 3) liberty—are brought together into a single coherent concept well after the end of the classical age, only coming to full fruition in modern political thought.

However, before turning to the origins of using violence in defense of freedom, I explore the history of defending freedom in the ancient world, which has been for the most part overlooked, mischaracterized, or forgotten. For the early Romans, defending freedom was not a matter of fighting defensive wars to preserve the state against outsiders or violence toward corrupt patricians within.

In the early Republic, Roman plebs defended liberty by refusing military service in what we would now consider to be acts of civil disobedience. The legendary stories of personal violation that the Romans told to explain these acts gave meaning to the founding of the republic and the creation of the office of the tribunes, the institution that most directly served the interests of the poorest Roman citizens. The secessions involved the plebs withdrawing from the political life of the city, risking their lives, along with the life of the city itself, as they refused to enlist en masse. The stories reflect that these withdrawals in the midst of defensive wars were highly disciplined and moderate, eschewing the killing of political opponents and sometimes even granting them trials. Such principled and coordinated self-sacrifice was thought to be the most suitable means to defend, preserve, and extend liberty in the early Republic.

The founding of the Roman Republic and the expansion of liberty for ordinary citizens over its first centuries established the notion that freedom meant defending one's honor, public reputation, and civic status from those who would compromise them. The defense of life and property was sometimes at issue, since attempts to drive others into slavery involved physical subjection, and since land reforms pulled ordinary citizens out of debt and gave them the necessary means for physical self-sufficiency. But the concept of freedom itself—what it meant to be free—did not consist of having a right to life and property. Instead, freedom often required sacrificing one's life and what little property one had while confronting the patricians who continually encroached upon both. For the least prominent Roman citizens, liberty could only be preserved if they both checked the patricians and avoided internecine violence among themselves. Often, preserving liberty involved a self-conscious willingness on the part of the masses to withdraw support for wars, even if the physical defense of the city was at stake.

In the middle and late Republic, a more complex relationship between defensive violence and freedom emerged. To Roman republicans, the expansion of their republic into Greece was made possible only by the vigor of a self-consciously free people. Indeed, it was only after the invasion of Greece that the idea that expansion could be consistent with "championing liberty" gained currency. In this increasingly imperial context, freedom did not imply that Rome would install a particular kind of government, but rather that it would not interfere with whatever government a Greek city had in place. Moreover, the Romans did not fight in the name of freedom *for Romans*. There is debate among historians about the extent to which Rome understood their early empire as springing from defensive purposes. But there is no question that the idea of fighting to defend the freedom of Rome had little or no significance in the early and middle Republic. Likewise, the Athenian democracy never fought a war to "defend the freedom" of Athens, save perhaps its very last war against the Macedonians. The Roman encounter with the Greeks, along with the conflicts and contradictions of the late Republic brought a nascent idea of fighting to defend freedom that would be picked up in modern thought. For both the Athenian democracy and the Roman Republic, defense as a prominent justification for war coincided with the demise of the hallowed institutions of freedom.

DEFENDING LIBERTY IN THE EARLY ROMAN REPUBLIC: WOMEN, SLAVES, PLEBS

In his analysis of the origins of freedom, Orlando Patterson offers a novel interpretation of Greek tragedy in which Greek women played a critical role in inventing the idea. He suggests that because warring Greek states would often enslave the women of defeated adversaries, women became acutely aware of and invested in distinguishing themselves from slaves.[1] While Patterson's argument is persuasive, it is surprising that he does not cite the origin story of republican Rome where the role of women in creating liberty (and feminizing the concept) is made explicit. The Roman story suggests that the liminal status of women within the household, between slaves and patriarchs, made their position analogous to the position of those men who were neither members of the ruling elite nor without some political resources and status: the plebeians. Historically, Roman women resisted oppression and gained status and influence in a wide variety of ways, including killing men. However, the stories of the Roman Republic emphasize the use of politicized self-sacrifice and refusals to cooperate with existing structures of authority. Moreover, as self-sacrifice is understood as feminine in origin, it is shown to be adaptable for use by men, and plebeian men in particular.

In reading this case, I rely on the admittedly controversial work of the Roman historian Titus Livius (64 or 59 BC—17 AD). Some historians argue that most of Livy's *History of Rome* is either fabricated or based on falsehoods, while others claim much of it is accurate. S. P. Oakley stakes out a middle position, writing in his magisterial commentary that there is a "hard core" of reliable material, which lies buried in the "distortions and literary elaborations which Livy and his annalistic predecessors have superimposed on their material."[2] Like Oakley and another major commentator on Livy, R. M. Ogilvie, I believe that the dramatic secessions of the plebs are among the hard core.[3] (I will say more about why below.)

However, even Livy's distortions and elaborations have value. While his stories surrounding the secessions are too shrouded in mythology to be verified as actual historical events, they are of critical importance for understanding the self-understanding of the Romans. These stories resonated and had meaning for those who thought they were worth remembering. Indeed, while many of the stories may not be true, Livy is reporting from an annalistic tradition, which in turn relies on an oral tradition that handed down the stories of the early Republic. We should also not fail to appreciate the way in which Livy's skill is distinguished by his ability to interweave fact and fiction from multiple sources, creating enduring themes while reflecting his own political perspective.[4]

Tradition has it that the founding of the Roman Republic (c. 509 BC) was sparked by the rape of a noblewoman named Lucretia and her extraordinary response to it. As recounted by Livy, some noblemen were discussing whose wives were more chaste, and after visiting various households they decided that Lucretia was the most virtuous. Later, the Tarquin prince Sextus returns to rape her, but the chaste and willful Lucretia shows a willingness to die rather than submit to him. Sextus threatens to kill her and lay her naked body next to that of a dead slave. To avoid being seen as someone who would debase herself by consorting with the unfree, Lucretia submits.

Yet she devises another way to resist the prince. Calling her father and her brother to her bedchamber, she recounts what has happened and asks them to pledge to punish Sextus.[5] If there is anxiety and uncertainty among the men as to Lucretia's character, it is not expressed. However, to insure that she is above reproach, and to bind the two men to their pledges, Lucretia kills herself. She says "I absolve myself of wrong, but not from punishment."[6] In her response to Sextus, Lucretia demonstrates savvy strategy, preventing the Tarquins from impugning her character either before or after the rape, while also distinguishing her status as a free woman from that of a slave. Most importantly, she sacrifices herself to force action. Lucretia's suicide provides her with enduring and potent political leverage.

Lucius Junius Brutus picks up where Lucretia left off by very carefully managing the political meaning of the rape and the series of events that follow. A nephew of the king and wily observer of the events, Brutus is said to have pulled the knife from Lucretia's body, swearing to drive the king and his family from Rome by whatever means necessary.[7] Yet bloodshed is not required, and in fact is avoided in removing Lucius Tarquinius Superbus. Lucretia's body is carried to the forum and the people of Rome gather to hear Brutus speak. In Livy's report, the speech connects the rape of Lucretia to a wider pattern of exploitation by the king and his family:

> He spoke of the violence and lust of Sextus Tarquin, of the unspeakable rape of Lucretia . . . which was more unworthy and more pitiable than the death itself. He mentioned also the arrogance of the king himself and how the plebs had been forced underground to dig out trenches and sewers: the men of Rome, victorious over all their neighbours, had been turned into drudges and quarry slaves, warriors no longer.[8]

According to Brutus, the king had conscripted plebs to build the temple to Jupiter on the Capitol. He had also demanded military service of them, while transferring many of the workmen to other public projects, including the building of the Great Sewer.[9] The rape of Lucretia is analogized to the plight of the plebs and Brutus places himself in the position of defending the honor and freedom of both.

What distinguishes Brutus's guidance in helping the people defend themselves from the abuses of the king is his assiduous avoidance of violence. His speech inspires the people of Rome to revoke the king's power. Arming a group of select volunteers, he causes the king, who had set out to besiege Ardea, to return to Rome to quell the dissent. However, Brutus and his volunteers leave the city, proceeding to Ardea along a different route in order to avoid battle. When Brutus arrives at Ardea, all of the Roman troops there desert Tarquinius. The first step, declaring that the king should not have power, is the ideological beginning of the Republic. The second step, the detachment of the king from military command, is the pragmatic and strategic use of power that ends his rule. When Brutus and his newly politically active plebeian troops vacate the city, while the king, devoid of power, dwells within, it foreshadows what will become the most dramatic and important means for defending political freedom in the new republic.

Brutus has removed the king by galvanizing the public, but he has not yet demonstrated that his ultimate aim is not to become king himself. An opportunity soon arises for him to show that there is *non acrior vindex liberatis* (no more keen defender of liberty).[10] In effect, he offers his own version of Lucretia's act of supreme self-sacrifice. Livy writes that Rome had expected the exiled Tarquins to threaten liberty from outside the city, but instead the threat came from within. Lamenting that Rome's new liberty and the rule of law serves weaklings (*inopi*) instead of the powerful (*potenti*), Roman nobles, including Brutus's sons Titus and Tiberius, plot to return the exiled king to power.[11] The plot is overheard by a slave, who reports it to the consuls.[12]

Brutus's next move is legendary, not only for ancient Romans but for modern republican thinkers who read the story as it was relayed by Nicolò Machiavelli (1469–1527) in his *Discourses on Livy* (1531). Machiavelli draws our attention to one of the two actions Brutus takes in response to his sons' plot. Specifically, Machiavelli tells how Brutus oversees the flogging and beheading of his own sons, describing the act as part of the necessary renewing of the law that republican-minded rulers must achieve through bloodshed. Yet, Brutus's actions may share more in common with Lucretia's act of self-sacrifice, since the destruction of the family line for a nobleman of ancient Rome would have been viewed as an even greater sacrifice than suicide. Moreover, Machiavelli fails to note Brutus's second and equally stunning action, which is that he oversees the first formal ceremony (*vindicta*) in republican Rome that frees a slave. The *vindicta* frees the slave who betrayed his sons in the interests of the public good. Interpreters dispute whether Livy's reference to Brutus's "fatherly expression" (*animo patris*) in witnessing his sons' execution betrays affection for his children or seriousness at fulfilling his public duty. What is not in dispute is that Brutus breaks the line of succession, destroys his patrimony, frees a slave, and even grants the slave property from the public treasury to affirm his full citizenship.[13] Brutus combines an act of supreme self-sacrifice with an act creating a legal path to political freedom. This origin story is of particular importance because the practice of manumission was a critical feature of republican Rome, allowing a constant stream of new citizens of foreign origin to enter Roman society.[14]

Although they were both nobles, Lucretia and Brutus become exemplars for a century of political advancement by Roman plebeians. The origin story does not show precisely how ordinary citizens can rule without a king, but it suggests some principles. Violence against one's internal political enemies is to be avoided if possible.[15] Self-sacrifice is more likely to win people over than force or fear. The best interests of the plebs are connected to the best interests of women and even slaves.[16] These principles are closely followed and extended through two additional ideas that will be honed and tested in the years that follow: first, that no one can rule Rome if the plebs are united in opposition to them, and second, that innovative institutional arrangements, won by way of self-sacrifice, are the best way to establish and defend freedom.

In the earliest years of the Republic, cooperation among upper- and lower-class Romans works hand in hand with the repelling of external threats and the fortification of their colonies. Beset by neighbors, who are often in alliance with the exiled Tarquins, patricians look to plebeians to help them maintain the city's newfound liberty at home and its growing colonial power abroad. To ensure good will, the patricians make sure the citizens have access to both the grain supply and salt, taking it upon themselves to control the salt supply by removing it from the hands of private entrepreneurs who set exorbitant prices.[17] Through famine and danger, patricians and plebs fight side by side. Colonies that betray Rome are treated brutally and they divide the spoils together.

However, only fifteen years after the exile of the Tarquins, patrician self-sacrifice and plebeian activism are set in opposition to the desire for war and senatorial control. When Tarquin dies in exile, Rome's leading men become confident that the new government is secure and begin to mistreat the plebs.[18] The levying of the war tax combined with time spent fighting away from home has caused many plebs to become destitute, and the elite have taken to putting their plebeian debtors in chains. When the Volsci threaten to attack the city, the plebs demand that the Senate provide relief and protection. Punctuated by a dramatic speech in the forum by an impoverished veteran (who points to the scars on his chest as proof of his honorable service), the plebs refuse to pay the levy or report for duty. Livy writes: "They complained that while fighting in the field for liberty (*libertate*) and empire (*imperio*) they were taken prisoner and maltreated at home by their fellow citizens: the liberty of the plebs was better served in war than in peace and among the enemy than among citizens."[19] Only when Servilius declares that no Roman citizen will be kept in chains and that no one may take their property or harm their children or grandchildren when on active duty are the plebs convinced to enlist.

Freedom from the invasion of outsiders is now at odds with freedom from the encroachments of fellow citizens. Both senators and ordinary citizens lay claim to the defense of Rome and liberty.[20] When the threat grows through an alliance of the Volsci with the Aequi and the Sabines, there is again resistance from below. A dictator is appointed, the plebs relent, and the war is won on all three fronts. Fearing that the plebs might turn on them now that the war is over, the Senate marches the legions out of the city. Some plebs consider killing the consuls to release themselves from their oath of obedience. But since the law stipulates no crime can undo a religious obligation, one Sicinius convinces the plebian forces to secede to the Sacred Mount. Taking almost nothing with them, the plebs fortify their camp and "hold themselves" (*sese tenuere*) from provocation. Back in Rome, the citizens who remain in the city fear violence from the senators, while the senators worry that the city would be undefended in case of an attack. Fear suspends all life (*metuque mutuo suspense errant ominia*). The plebs on the Mount hold sway; the Senate relents; and the office of the plebeian tribunes is created and made sacrosanct.

As Livy's account of the early Republic proceeds, the threat of refusing military service and the war levy is ever-present. But the significance of this form of civil disobedience, its close connection with the republican origin story, and its critical role in defending liberty are most clearly on display in the dramatic second secession of the plebs (c. 450 BC). As the plebs continue to gain strength, they expand the power of the tribunes to include the right of appeal. When envoys return from Athens with laws, the tribunes are eager to craft their own Roman version. Ten men, the decemvirs, are appointed to write the law. With the establishment of the Twelve Tables, the plebs eliminate the consuls and the tribunes, reelect the decemvirs and "in their headlong rush to liberty [fall] into subjection."[21] The decemvirs refuse to call elections and gather young patricians as bodyguards, who are given license to exploit, take property from, and even kill plebs.[22] When the Sabines threaten war, the decemvirs find themselves in need, for the Senate refuses to convene and the plebs follow suit by refusing to enlist. The decemvirs cajole the Senate and the plebs to wage war, but the lack of morale leads to a shameful military defeat.[23]

The story of the toppling of the decemvirs echoes the story of the founding of the Republic, but with important additions and changes. The liberty of
a free woman is once again threatened by the arbitrary rule of a tyrant. The
decemvir Appius Claudius lusts for the daughter of Lucius Verginius, a high-
ranking centurion in camp at Algidus. To conceal his motives, he asks his client
Marcus Claudius to claim that the young woman was born of his slave and to
take possession of her. Three escalating incidents lead to crisis. First, Marcus
tries to take possession of the girl by force in the forum, but her nurse calls to
bystanders, identifying her father and fiancé Icilius as friends of the plebs. The
people gather around and prevent her from being taken. Second, when the girl,
her fiancé Icilius, and her grandfather are summoned to appear in the court of
Appius, the judge summons her father—but rules that in the meantime Marcus
should take possession of her. Icilius puts his life on the line and connects his
cause with the plebeian cause more generally: "You have done away with the
protection afforded by the tribunes and the right of appeal to the Roman people, the two bulwarks in freedom's defense (*duas arces libertatis*)."[24] He continues: "As for me, I will sooner die than fail in my duty to defend the free status
of my betrothed."[25] Finally, Lucius rushes home, moving through the assembled
population of the city in mourning clothes. He tells supporters that he has

> [taken] his place in the battleline every day in defense of their wives and chil-
> dren; no other fighter was reckoned as brave and daring as he. Yet what was the
> use of safeguarding a city in which one's children must suffer the horrors they
> would face had the enemy captured it?[26]

When Appius rules that the girl is Marcus's slave, a confrontation ensues. Women
protect the girl and push Marcus away. Appius brings out armed men, but Verginius
asks for one last chance to meet with his daughter. When Appius gives him permis-
sion he says "I am asserting your freedom (*libertatem vindico*) in the only way I know
how, my daughter."[27] He then stabs her to death.

Even historians who believe there is a "hard core" of truth in Livy and consider
Lucretia to be a historical person doubt that the story of Verginia ever happened.
Yet Livy's masterful telling of the story made it "justly famous in antiquity."[28] The
story tells us that defending liberty can call forth a complex set of relations involving women, slaves, and plebs. Here Verginia, the woman who represents liberty,
is herself a pleb, and her status as a free woman is called into question.[29] Unlike
Lucretia, her words and actions are ignored. Instead of deciding whether or not to
take her own life, her life is taken from her by her own father, who purports to
defend her liberty while protecting other men from the decemvirs. Like the original

republican founding story, her impending subjection is intertwined with the loss of all meaningful legal claims, even for her fiancé and her father.

The story once again holds up self-sacrifice as the critical means for maintaining freedom, and calls upon the people to imitate the actions of the heroes. Verginius combines Lucretia's suicide with Brutus's execution of his sons into a single action. Like Brutus, Verginius uses this dramatic incident to win over the plebeian soldiers. He goes to the soldiers encamped outside the city, pleading that they not blame him (and instead blame Appius) for the death of his daughter. He weeps in public, saying that he would have committed suicide himself, but he must live to avenge his daughter. He also appeals to the soldiers to consider their own freedom (*liberis suis consulerent*).[30] The impending violation of a woman, and her ability to maintain her legally free status, is tied to the liberty of the plebs.

Once again, action is taken by the whole of the people and is associated with, feminine moderation in the name of liberty, in contrast to violence in the service of male desire and license.[31] The soldiers to whom Verginius appeals march to the city and settle on the Sacred Mount where they elect tribunes of the people but take no "extreme actions" (*nulla violenta*).[32] Others on the Sabine front mutiny and retreat to join them. Despite all of this disorder, the Senate remains indecisive, so Marcus Duilius urges the plebs to leave the city.

> [They] pitched camp on the Sacred Mount, following the restraint (*modestiam*) of their ancestors in violating (*violando*) nothing. Every able-bodied civilian followed the army, with wives and children accompanying them for a time, piteously asking what protection there could be for them in a city in which chastity (*pudicitia*) and liberty (*libertas*) counted for nothing.[33]

The senators and the decemvirs are left in an empty city, surrounded only by buildings and their bodyguards.[34] Seeing that there is quite literally noone to rule, the Senate sends envoys to the Sacred Mount. The critical issue for Rome's senators is how to ease the decemvirs out of power while ensuring their own safety. Some plebs want to burn them alive. Others worry about retaliation from the Senate for secession. Yet when an agreement is finally reached, Livy notes the careful, disciplined restraint of the plebs through the voice of the Senate envoys.[35]

The laws introduced as a result of the second secession of the plebs attempt to institutionalize moderation by securing it, paradoxically, with a singular kind of harsh penalty. Although details are disputed by historians, Livy describes how the measures passed by the plebs are made binding upon all of the people: the right of appeal is reinstituted; the tribunes are reintroduced and made sacrosanct; and the laws are to be kept unsuppressed and unaltered. Both the reintroduction of the tribunes and the creation of a public law are associated with feminine liberty, being celebrated by the cult of Ceres, the goddess of motherhood and agriculture, who is honored in a Triad with her two children Liber and Libera. (Some speculate that the temple of Ceres on the Aventine Hill was created as a plebeian response to the patrician's Temple to Jupiter, the god of war.) Anyone who violated the sacrosanct status of the tribunes was made *homo sacer*, which meant that they could be legally killed by any individual and that their worldly goods could be sold at the temple. This remarkable expression of collective enforcement was the only physical threat backing the reforms, and likely originated in an "oath by which plebeians banded themselves as an individual body and dedicated themselves to the goals of self-help and hostility to the patricians."[36] The new public laws would also be kept inside the temple. Laws were no longer to be made by select members of an exclusive group of patricians.[37]

In the immediate aftermath of the secession, the commitment of Rome's plebe-ians to the rule of law and liberty—as opposed to revenge and murder—is tested in the person of Appius Claudius. When Appius is confronted, for his criminal pur-suit of Verginia, this man who had used the pretense of creating a written law to gain power and then flouted it for his own personal aims claims the right of appeal. In his speech against Appius, Verginius contrasts violent male desires (*libidini*) with moderate feminine liberty (*liberis*). Livy summarizes the speech:

> There was no one left in his house to fall victim to Appius' lust: he would defend himself from any other sort of indignity that Appius might inflict in the same spirit he had defended his daughter [i.e. he would commit suicide]. Others should look to what was best for themselves and their children.[38]

Verginius argues that Appius Claudius should be put to death immediately, being the lone person exempt from "the laws and the norms of civilized behavior among citizens and humans (*humani*) everywhere."[39] But despite their love for Verginius, the plebs are unconvinced and grant Appius a trial. Before the trial occurs, the tyrant commits suicide to avoid justice.

Throughout the first century of the Republic, the plebs use the threat of seces-sion and the ever-present possibility of refusing to enlist to great political effect. The plebs continue to worry that the internal threat to liberty is equal to or greater than the external threat. Again and again, the Senate is forced to choose between the victory of foreign enemies or the victory of the plebs.[40] By 444 BC, through block-ing the war levy and gaining passage of a law that allows intermarriage with nobles, Roman plebeians win consular authority for the tribunes.[41] By 433 BC, with the help of a dictator, they institute shorter terms for censors in response to their constant overreach.[42] The plebs also advocate for, and haltingly secure, land reforms and the distribution of territory won in conquest. The defense of liberty within requires a willingness to be vulnerable to outside attack. In their approach, Livy contrasts the plebs of Rome with the less restrained and more violent plebs in other cities.[43]

Some contemporary historians have called into question the historical veracity of the secessions themselves. Yet the evidence they offer could just as easily suggest the opposite conclusion (i.e., that the secessions did in fact occur). For instance, Gary Forsythe writes that the "'revolutionary' explanation for the origin of the plebeian tribunate is quite extraordinary and therefore historically improbable."[44] The first secession "should not be accepted as historical"[45] and the historicity of the second secession "can hardly be defended."[46] He argues that the stories that lead up to the secessions were borrowed from Greece and, in particular, that the overthrow of the decemvirs is modeled on the expulsion of the Thirty Tyrants. Tim Cornell is also not sure that the secessions occurred, arguing that the debt crisis was probably the product of a different century.[47] Cornell agrees with Theodor Mommsen's famous claim, which says that the plebs created a kind of "state within a state," but he points out that they were not hoplites, but acted only in supportive military roles.[48]

Yet the critical feature of the secessions—the withdrawal en masse from the city and the refusal to fight in a defensive war—is strongly supported by the evidence. That such evidence is provided by the skeptics themselves, reveals a tendency to discount the role of nonviolence in history. As Forsythe notes, the Thirty were expelled by exiles through force. Why would Livy, the annalists, or oral tradition fabricate a new method for resisting tyranny when violent expulsion was the main feature of the "original" story? One reason might be the status of the plebs as below the *populus*, or those citizens who could afford to arm themselves and fight as hoplites for Rome. Both Forsythe and Cornell agree on this point. The plebs never raised an army of their own, even as they created robust institutions. Unlike the *populus*, the plebs were organized on the basis of residence rather than according to military units.[49] Skeptical that any new laws were introduced in the era of the second secession, Forsythe writes that the only reason for new laws would have been to ensure that "the enactment of one assembly [the nonmilitary *comitia tribute*] was no less valid than that of the other [i.e. the citizen-soldier assembly]."[50] But this reason is precisely the point.[51] The urban, less wealthy, and not so well armed plebs would have needed an alternative method for achieving their political goals. The plebs were essential to any military effort, but they could not have bested the better-armed citizens in a violent conflict. Even if they could have somehow been victorious, their victory would not have served the interests of Rome as a whole. Instead, their aim was to put themselves on equal footing politically with the thoroughly military and more wealthy class. Withdrawing from participation in the city allowed them to exercise their collective capacities and remind the hoplites of their dependence on plebeian support. It also demonstrated a willingness to sacrifice and a capacity for self-rule. Admittedly, the founding of the Republic and the expansion of the power of the plebs was highly improbable, given their resources and status. Yet no one doubts that they did manage to expand their influence. Thus, the secessions provide a model for how to defend liberty from the encroachments of the powerful.

Importantly, secessions were not a feature of political life at the time when Livy or the annalists were writing. So while some of the issues in dispute between patricians and plebeians may have been anachronistic, it is hard to see what resources the historians would have been drawing upon to inspire stories of dramatic nonviolent action. At the same time, it is possible that Livy's emphasis on liberty of a certain kind (and defended with certain means) did, as Ogilvie writes, contain a "message" for his generation.[52] The idea of defending freedom takes on a much different cast in the middle and later Republic as well as in early imperial Rome. It is not clear why Livy or his sources would invent a different understanding of how the plebs defended freedom if these techniques were not being used in their own time. However, even if they are wholly invented, they can conceivably be seen as a counterpoint to the violent class conflict of the later Republic. Either way, the fact that the history of Rome describes an alternative means for defending freedom is of critical importance, since it is all too frequently overlooked by modern and contemporary interpreters yet was central to the historical imaginary and self-understanding of the poorest Roman citizens.

DEFENDING LIBERTY IN THE MIDDLE ROMAN REPUBLIC: ENCOUNTERING THE GREEKS

In his *War and Imperialism in Republican Rome*, William Harris devotes nearly one hundred pages to exploring the question of whether or not the Romans practiced "defensive imperialism."[53] He notes that historians have long debated the question of whether the defense of Rome required an empire. But he hopes to answer a different question, which is whether the Romans themselves *thought* defense required an empire. What is striking about his answer, wherein he examines nearly every war the Roman Republic fought, is that nowhere in his analysis does he suggest that the Romans thought their empire was necessary to defend Roman freedom. Liberty and freedom were ever-present themes in the debates within the Roman Republic. But as Harris shows, the Romans did not fight wars or gain an empire in order to defend them.

From our contemporary perspective, this seems like a very strange omission. The best way to illuminate it is by exploring the ways in which freedom was connected to warfare and empire in ancient Rome. The tone was set in the early Republic, when the power unleashed by the plebeian defense of freedom through noncooperation was harnessed and repurposed for martial pursuits in the drive for empire. But the earlier defense of freedom is so indelibly connected with the refusal to fight that the connection between freedom and warfare had to be completely redefined. After succeeding in their contests with the Senate, Roman plebeians turned their newfound confidence upon the enemies of Rome, with warfare serving as an expression of freedom rather than a means for defending it. Somewhat paradoxically, the courage and discipline the Roman plebs show in defending freedom through noncooperation at home makes them capable fighters abroad. After the second secession, Verginia's plight is held up as representative of the peril Rome faces from outside enemies,[54] while ceremonies at the Aventine and the Sacred Mount are used to inspire the troops.[55] Yet the point is not that warfare allows the Romans to defend freedom; it is that freedom allows the plebs the courage to fight as they should: as free people.

As the Romans become more adept at war, Livy reports that it begins to compromise the original purpose of defending liberty. By 402 BC, the Senate has offered to pay the plebeians for military service. Although some plebs are skeptical, the proposal is generally welcomed. Long deployments ensue. But when the plebs attempt to refuse enlistment in the face of the war with the Veii, the dynamic shifts decisively. The patricians push back, arguing that "freedom at Rome has come down to this: freedom to scorn the senate, magistrates, and laws, freedom to flout tradition and the institutions of our ancestors, freedom to subvert military discipline."[56] Although morale among plebeian soldiers waxes and wanes over the course of the next three centuries, once the plebeians are on the payroll of the state their refusal to fight is no longer viewed as an act of self-sacrifice. Without the moral authority of voluntarily choosing to fight for Rome without remuneration, the idea of secession becomes less viable and none are reported in the middle Republic.

What, then, were the purposes that brought together patricians and plebeians for the republican conquests? Many centuries of historiography provide us with numerous explanations. Certainly, the potential for plunder, including slaves and land for colonies, played a role.[57] The cultural value of glory, as demonstrated by one's prowess in warfare, undoubtedly spurred on conquest. These factors were combined with institutional incentives to fight wars, particularly the one-year term of the consuls, which encouraged ambitious leaders to take bold action while they had their chance. We also see that the patricians, once they began paying plebs for service, were much more effective in their attempts to quell internal dissent through external distraction. The theory of *metis hostilis*, where fear of foreign enemies ensures domestic

tranquility, was described as early as Polybius.[58] Finally, there were occasions when
the Romans, particularly as the empire expanded, could legitimately argue that further warfare was required for the "defense" of what was already gained, or for the
protection of Rome itself.[59] Yet even when wars were fought to defend Rome, the
idea of defending Roman freedom was conspicuously absent.[60]

This absence is perhaps most apparent when viewed in contrast with the sphere
of Roman influence where they did claim to defend freedom—"the freedom of the
Greeks."[61] Historians of this period agree that Falminius's famous declaration that
Rome was fighting against the Macedonians for the sake of Greek freedom was a slogan they adopted from their experience in dealing with, fighting against, and fighting side by side with the Greeks themselves. This Greek idea of defending freedom
had been circulating as far back as the Peloponnesian Wars (431–404 BC). As understood by the Spartans (and eventually by other powerful cities as well) it was a pledge
to defend others from the encroachments of their erstwhile allies. In the Spartan
sense, freedom could mean a number of things: being exempt from tribute, being
allowed to govern under one's own laws, being allowed certain diplomatic privileges.
Paradoxically, being "free" almost always meant taking on a protector to whom one
owed loyalty, which often translated into providing resources and soldiers in times
of war. For this reason, even historians of the time such as Polybius were skeptical of
the claims of dominant powers to be interested in the defense of freedom. The hege-
monic powers in Greece—whether the Spartans, the Athenians, the Macedonians,
or eventually the Romans—all promulgated "the slogan of freedom" in the name of
defending vulnerable smaller states who were in fact subject to their control.[62]

Nevertheless, even in the Greek context before the arrival of Rome, and certainly
as adopted by the Romans in their wars in Greece, there was little idea that one
would fight to defend one's *own* freedom. The earliest known reference to the idea
is in the speeches of the Greek orator Demosthenes (384–322 BC), whose speeches
attempt, unsuccessfully, to persuade the Athenians to fight Philip of Macedon
(382–336 BC). For the most part, Demosthenes invokes freedom in what would have
been conventional ways, suggesting that Athens should defend the freedom of others, or that freedom is an indication of Athenian superiority.[63] But in one passage he
says: "To begin with ourselves, we must make provision for our defence (*amunom-
enoi*), I mean with war-galleys, funds, and men; for even if all other states succumb
to slavery, we surely must fight the battle of liberty (*eleutherias*)."[64]

DEFENDING LIBERTY IN THE LATE REPUBLIC

Although the idea did not take hold in his own time, speeches modeled on those
of Demosthenes more forcefully articulated the idea of defending freedom nearly

three centuries later in the tumultuous days of the late Republic. The sprawling empire has transformed Roman society. An army of plebs who fought seasonal wars and then returned home to their farms and the forum has been replaced by armies who are in the field for years and are dependent upon individual benefactors. Small farms have been swallowed up by the vast estates of wealthy patricians, which are worked by slave labor. Meanwhile, allied and colonized people are demanding political rights and economic benefits. For instance, Rome had expanded with the help of the Latins, who now demand to play a role in governance, especially in deciding when and whom to fight.[65] Perhaps the most important crack in the old order has appeared with the murder of Tiberius Gracchus. Having introduced land reforms in order to alleviate the poverty of the plebs, help solve recruiting problems, and reduce Rome's dependence upon slave labor, Gracchus is killed by a mob in the Assembly on the day he is to be elected to a second term as tribune (133 BC). Meanwhile, prominent Romans have turned their attendants, clients, and slaves into personal fighting forces.[66] In this context, we find the first clear references to the idea that violence and warfare can be used to sustain and defend republican freedom.

The man who makes the case that violence is the best method for putting this all back together is Rome's greatest orator. In Cicero's (106–43 BC) *Philippics*, he directly appeals to the will of the Roman people, asking them to resist Marcus Antonius (83–30 BC) by whatever means they can. In the second *Philippic* he notes that the Senate has been surrounded by a "belt of armed men," and that Antonius has brought guards from other countries into the forum. But this use of armed guards, he says:

> is no protection . . . a man must be defended by the affection and good will of his fellow-citizens, not by arms. The Roman people will take them from you, will wrest them from your hands. . . . The name of peace is sweet, the thing itself is most salutary. But between peace and slavery there is a wide difference. Peace is liberty in tranquility; slavery is the worst of all evils—to be repelled, if need be, not only by war, but even by death.[67]

Here Cicero transforms the earlier tradition of resisting would-be tyrants with nonviolent withdrawal into violent defense. He says that Antony cannot rule without the consent of the people because they will offer armed resistance. In these same passages, he rewrites the history of the founding of the Republic, saying that "Brutus pursued Tarquinius with war,"[68] a sleight of hand that recalls that Brutus persuaded Tarquin's army to come to his side but papers over the fact he specifically avoided a violent confrontation with Tarquin once he had done so. At the beginning of the fourth *Philippic*, Cicero says he is inspired by the large numbers that have gathered to hear him, and says "I at once have been the leader in the defense of your liberty (*libertatis defendendae fui*)."[69] In the tenth *Philippic*, he observes that four Roman armies have "taken up arms for the sake of the liberty of the Roman people."[70] And when Caius Pansa leads his army against the troops of Marcus Antonius, Cicero congratulates him, saying he "defended the freedom of the Roman people (*libertatem populi Romani defenderit*) with admirable and incredible valor."[71]

Cicero's bold attempt to revivify liberty through violence can be understood as a last-ditch effort to grapple with the contradictions of the late Republic. Indeed, Caesar's civil war is only the last in a long series of wars within the late Republic, all of which relate to the contested meaning of freedom. The Social War of 91–89 BC is fought when the Latins declare an independent confederacy. Rome finally extends citizenship to most Italians in order to win them back, a move that both appeases them and demonstrates that citizenship can be won by force. When the consul Lucius Cornelius Sulla is stripped of his command in Asia in 88 BC, he marches his army on the city, killing many of his patrician enemies and giving their land to his veterans. Three major slave revolts also occur around this time. The first two are fought in Sicily before the turn of the first century; the last is the famous war led by Spartacus and the gladiators from 71 to 73 BC. They are extraordinarily violent, but the ability of their leaders to quickly and spontaneously gather tens of thousands of people together at the risk of their lives suggests they tap into a deep sense of injustice.[72] The manumission of slaves was a frequent practice at the time, and must have had an effect on those left in slavery. At the same time, citizens were arming slaves to fight with them, as when the Italians deployed their slaves against the Romans in the Social War, and the consul Cinna used slave troops whom he drew to his cause with a promise of manumission in 87 BC.[73]

In Rome's dealings with allies and foreign peoples, as well as in the dire condition of its most impoverished citizens and slaves, the meaning and value of Roman freedom were called into question. The wars of the late Republic were not fought because others were striving to achieve an alternative brand of republican freedom. We have no direct evidence that the slave revolts were fought on an ideological basis or for "liberation." But it is clear that the Roman version of republican freedom had become bogged down in a host of contradictions. Typical of these was the difficulty Rome had in suppressing the slave revolts, a difficulty that was a function of, and perhaps exacerbated, recruitment problems and a general lack of morale among Roman soldiers.[74] After two praetors followed by two consuls failed to defeat Spartacus and the gladiator-led revolt, the Romans sent Crassus, one of the richest Romans, to defeat him with no fewer than ten legions. Crassus paid his troops from his personal fortune, but when he perceived severe problems with discipline, he instituted decimation. When he finally defeated Spartacus, six thousand captured slaves were crucified along the Via Appia from Capua to Rome.[75]

Is this what republican freedom had become? The contradictions of a slave-holding republic are on full display in Cicero's orations. Both *Pro Tullus* and *Pro Caecina* examine slavery, the inheritance rights of women, and the management of property. The speeches make two things clear. First, at the time of the orations, it is not a matter of settled law whether or not citizens can arm their slaves to defend themselves and their property. Second, Cicero, for one, clearly believes that anyone who has armed their slaves is in violation of the law, asserting that Caecina's liberty is diminished by those who arm their slaves. Organized, armed resistance is the very opposite of the rule of law.[76] Yet in the *Philippics*, Cicero not only calls upon arms to defend liberty, but also invokes by way of analogy the bravery of slaves who resist their masters. He mentions the courage of gladiators in particular, describing how the plebs felt affinity and affection for them.[77] Thus violence is said to be both entirely anathema to the rule of law in one Cicero oration, and the critical means for preventing tyranny and preserving the Republic in another. As a matter of practice, there is no doubt that violence and the defense of freedom have become linked, and the result is warfare, confusion, and contradiction.

Like Demosthenes, Cicero fails in his call to defend freedom with arms. Nevertheless, the idea that Romans could defend their freedom in such a manner took root for a brief moment. Before freedom receded as a prominent political aim for some twelve hundred years, ironically, the trope was co-opted by the first Roman emperor. In the very first lines of his *Res Gestae*, Caesar Augustus (63 BC–14 AD) claimed to be a *vindex liberatus* for the Roman people, tying his ability to provide safety (*securitas*) and destroy competing factions to *libertas*. Modifying Cicero's emphasis, he links freedom with peace—the peace that came with the dominance of the emperor. As one historian writes, "The *pax Romana*, therefore, became absolute—it covered the entire world, centering on the figure of one person as the champion of freedom and peace; universal freedom and peace now meant universal acknowledgment of his rule."[78] The powers of the tribunes for which the plebs had sacrificed so much are turned over to the emperor, who is tasked with using them to check the ambitions of the patricians in the Senate. Though Cicero had failed politically, he had succeeded rhetorically. The implications of the idea of defending freedom with violence would not become fully apparent or fully developed until the reappearance of freedom in the modern era.[79]

Thus far, I have traced the history of freedom where it intersects with ideas of defense. But the idea of defense, in and of itself, both for individuals and states, has a long separate history. In the next chapter, I will describe how the history of ideas about defense intersect with freedom in modern political thought, but in order to understand where those ideas came from requires a brief discussion of defense, treated separately from freedom. In addition, tracing the history of defense requires examining its origins in the idea that warfare and violence are necessary at all.

In *The Politics,* Aristotle makes a critical distinction between actions that are necessary and those that are good and noble.[80] He places war and violence squarely among those kinds of actions that are merely useful but not good in themselves. Citing the Spartan writer Thibron, Aristotle writes that most men believe that empire leads to material prosperity. But in pursuing war as an end in itself, he observes that the Spartans lost "all that makes life worth living," and risked internal peace through an ethic that implied that any citizen could legitimately capture the government through force.[81]

Holding the line against the slide into despotism and empire, Aristotle develops this distinction in a way that will have a lasting impact on justifications for warfare. Arguing that citizens should be trained to pursue war only when necessary, he sees war as necessary for three interrelated reasons:

> Training for war should not be pursued with a view to enslaving men who do not deserve such a fate. Its objects should be these—first, to prevent men from ever becoming enslaved themselves; secondly, to put men in a position to exercise leadership—but leadership directed to the interest of the led, and not to the establishment of a general system of slavery; and thirdly, to enable men to make themselves masters of those who naturally deserve to be slaves.[82]

The first reason introduces a nascent standard of self-defense. We might be tempted to interpret the passage as advocating a defense of freedom. But a war fought to prevent men "from falling into slavery" is associated with necessity and constraint, and not with the activities characteristic of free men. In fact, when free men are forced to take such actions, they are in danger of being distracted from freedom and the good life.[83] Moreover, to the extent that this passage introduces a standard of self-defense, it is only in the context of a larger theme of order. The key point for Aristotle is that war is necessary to keep men in their proper place and ensure that the hierarchical order that is best for both free men and slaves is preserved. Thus war as a defense against slavery is one part of the bigger issue, which is the use of warfare to dominate some for the benefit of all.

In contrast to Greek political thought, the idea of defensive warfare played a more prominent but still secondary role in Roman thought. Cicero writes in *De Republica* that "no war is undertaken by a well-conducted state except in defense of its honor or for its security." Although individual persons can choose to die when they encounter destitution, exile, or chains, states must do what they can to "endure forever." Distinguishing between just and unjust wars, he also argues that Roman mastery of the world is just because "they defended their allies."[84] In the rituals of the college of fetiales, formal procedures were established that suggested Rome was defending itself from the offense of others.[85] However, as was the case for the Greeks, the idea of defense was not the primary justification for warfare. The pursuit of glory, peace, and (only briefly, in Cicero's *Philippics*) freedom provided intellectual support for warfare.

Early Christian thinkers explicitly reject defending oneself or one's government as a legitimate reason for violence. For some of the most influential of them, the rejection of war and violence is absolute. Christ's willful suffering at the hands of Roman imperial authority serves as exemplary. Origen (184/185–253/254) and Tertullian (c. 155—c. 240) argue that Christian ethics disallow doing violence to another person for any reason, and both recommend conscientious objection to military service.[86] In one passage of Tertullian's *Apology*, he even connects the prohibition of self-defense and military service to a distinctive brand of Christian liberty, pointing out that Christians are sufficiently numerous to best the Romans in warfare, but they refuse to treat them as enemies. "For what war should we not have been fit and ready even if unequal in forces—we who are so glad to be butchered—were it not, of course, that in our doctrine we are given ampler liberty (*libenter*) to be killed than to kill?"[87] Here Tertullian seems to be reconnecting liberty with the refusal to fight, and even raises the idea of secession,[88] albeit with a more thorough prohibition against violence than the early Roman plebs. Later thinkers such as Augustine (354–430) accept only part of this prohibition. Augustine affirms the idea that as individuals, Christians should renounce violence in self-defense.[89] However, Augustine also breaks with pacifists in the Early Church by outlining a position on war that, like Aristotle, describes it as necessary and in conformity with the requirements of temporal (as opposed to divine) law.

Augustine does not explicitly invoke defense. John Langdon writes that the idea that war is necessary means that it "is undertaken, not as a means of self-defense, but as a punitive effort initiated by lawful authority."[90] Admittedly, he assumes that necessity requires that authorities impose peace if rebels violently resist the state.[91] There is some ambiguity here, in that the aim of peace and tranquility is consistent with reestablishing authority and dominance—some might say the "defense"—of the state. The argument is not too far off from the idea of "defending peace," which had some purchase in the Roman Empire and carried through into the Middle Ages, most notably in Marsilius of Padua's (1275–1342) title *Defensor Pacis*.[92] But sensitive to the arguments of the early church fathers, Augustine does not use such phrasing, and does not suggest that war should be used to defend life and property. Instead, he argues that war, and Christian participation in it, are the necessary means for restoring moral order, pursuing the common good, and pacifying the world. The emphasis is on imposing just punishments on wrongdoers.

The defense and preservation of both life and social order as part of the justification for violence emerge more fully in the thought of Thomas Aquinas (1225–1274). Drawing on both Augustine and Aristotle, Aquinas does what neither does explicitly, linking defense and necessity. On the level of the individual, he writes:

[M]oral acts take their species according to what is intended and not according to what is beside the intention, since this is accidental . . . Accordingly, the act of self-defense may have two effects: one, the saving of one's life; the other the slaying of the aggressor. Therefore, this act, since one's intention is to save one's own life, is not unlawful, seeing that it is natural to everything to keep itself in being as far as possible. And yet, though proceeding from a good intention, an act may be rendered unlawful if it be out of proportion to the end. Wherefore, if a man in self-defense uses more than necessary violence, it will be unlawful.[93]

In Aquinas, as in Aristotle, necessity is understood to be a limiting principle, whereby violence in pursuit of anything beyond it becomes dangerous. But in his thinking the connection between necessity and defending oneself from aggressors is unambiguous. The Christian prohibition against violence for the purpose of preserving one's life is transformed into a prohibition against violence with the intention of killing another. In developing the idea of natural law, Aquinas departs from previous Christian thought, saying that the impulse to preserve oneself is legal, beneficial, and necessary.

In the realm of war, Aquinas adopts the Augustinian theory of just war but with a critical exception. Although private individuals should have no part in raising an army or declaring war, rulers have special responsibilities. Like Augustine, Aquinas argues that wars should be fought to stamp out evil. Christians can and should participate in such wars, although there is room for civil disobedience in extraordinary circumstances, as when authorities are egregiously corrupt.[94] Unlike Augustine, Aquinas explicitly connects the pursuit of justice to defense. He writes:

[Since] the care of the common weal is committed to those who are in authority, it is their business to watch over the common weal of the city, kingdom or province subject to them. And just as it is lawful for them to have recourse to the sword in defending that common weal against internal disturbances, when they punish evil-doers, according to the words of the Apostle: "He bears not his sword without cause, for he is God's minister, an avenger to execute wrath upon him that does evil," so too it is their business to have recourse to the sword of war in defending the common weal against external enemies.[95]

Not only is the righteous sword responsible for the internal and external defense of the state, it can also be used to defend the innocent. Here again Aquinas differs from Augustine, who allows that necessity sometimes demands that innocents be killed in prosecuting just wars, and even that innocents be tortured to reveal pertinent information.[96] But for Aquinas, the protection and defense of the innocent are themselves critical components of his just war principle. Thus while both Augustine and Aquinas believe that war is necessary to help one's neighbor and serve the common good in a fallen world, Aquinas is the first major Christian thinker to link these claims to defense.[97] In his thought, we find the first inkling that defense is natural and necessary, and in connecting these concepts he introduces what will become a critical justification for individual violence and state-sponsored war.

Although for the most part Aquinas makes this argument without reference to freedom, some have argued that a brand of apolitical liberty plays a role in the thought of Aquinas. Quoting passages from the *Summa Theologiae,* Eric MacGilvray argues that if the primary political value is justice, the existence of free will

lends a special moral character to right actions . . . because right actions become moral actions only if and insofar as they are done freely—that is to say, willingly or, as we would now say, autonomously. Aquinas emphasizes that actions can be done freely in this sense "even where there is a duty of obedience," that is, even when the threat of legal coercion is present.[98]

If this is true, it would certainly apply in the case of self-defense as well. MacGilvray may be over-interpolating a Kantian vision of the role of the will in relation to ethics, but the apolitical brand of natural liberty Aquinas invokes will be subsequently politicized by the liberals who take up natural law theory. In the next chapter, we will see how the preservation of self and property, understood as an extension of and necessity for the maintenance of the body, are figured as the sine qua non of freedom. The ancient idea that freedom can be defended through self-sacrifice, moderation, and mass civil disobedience is replaced by something altogether different.

[A] FREE-MAN is *he that in those things which by his strength and wit he is able to do is not hindered to do what he has a will to.* But when the words *free* and *liberty* are applied to anything but *bodies,* they are abused.

THOMAS HOBBES

The *power a Conquerour gets* over those he overcomes *in a Just War, is perfectly Despotical:* he has an absolute power over the Lives of those, who by putting themselves in a State of War, have forfeited them.

JOHN LOCKE

4

Liberty as Life

NICCOLÒ MACHIAVELLI IS most famous and most infamous for his work *The Prince* (1532). In that advice book for rulers, he introduces a theory of violence that has been the subject of controversy for five hundred years, asserting that for a prince to ensure the longevity of his rule he must not hesitate to use violence. What is sometimes overlooked by Machiavelli's critics is that he insists violence is used best if it serves the psychological and physical needs of the ruler's subjects. The most adept ruler uses violence to ensure not only that people fear him, but also that they love him, because he uses violence against those who threaten their interests and security.

This overlooked understanding in Machiavelli's theory of autocratic violence sets the table for what is a more important if less well-known work, his *Discourses on Livy.* In the *Discourses,* Machiavelli interprets the history of the Roman Republic in a way that is much different from Livy. Specifically, he is keen to emphasize what he takes to be the most important method for founding and maintaining republics: extraordinary violent acts of exemplary men. On Machiavelli's reading, the critical means for defending freedom against corrupt and ambitious nobles are acts of "unwonted severity" that must recur every five to ten years. The acts are outside the law, but paradoxically they bring "men back to their mark," since violence "reawakens fear" of the law.[1] For Machiavelli, Brutus killing his sons is his most important founding act, so much so that it becomes one of Machiavelli's most frequently repeated phrases. Throughout the *Discourses*, "killing the sons of Brutus" comes to refer to any act of violence conducive to sustaining republican government.

Among political theorists, Machiavelli's work has long been seen as a critical bridge between ancient and modern eras in the history of political thought,[2] and the last few decades have seen an upsurge in scholarship detailing the close connection between Machiavelli and modern republican and liberal thinkers.[3] Indeed, by all but erasing an ancient tradition in which freedom is defended by other means, Machiavelli sets in motion a line of thinking that comes to define much of modern political thought. Thus Machiavelli's work not only provides a bridge between ancient and modern thought, it is a critical part of the early development of an entirely new conception of freedom.

In continuing the story of how we came to associate defensive violence and freedom, I examine three questions. First, when and how does liberty reemerge as an important political aim? Second, how does the idea of defense become a primary justification for war and violence? And finally, when and how do concepts of liberty become attached to justifications for defensive warfare in the modern context and how does this change our understanding of freedom and liberty?

Together, the answers to these questions demonstrate how and why the ancient idea of defending freedom through self-sacrifice and mass action was transformed. Barons and merchants excluded from the inner circles of rule in feudal Europe, or frustrated with the inconsistency of wayward and corrupt kings, looked to the ancient concept of liberty as a way to defend their prerogatives, not so much to participate directly in the rule of states as create protections for their lives and property. The rule of law required defined limitations on sovereign power. A few centuries later, religious thinkers concerned with justifying European colonial projects in the early modern period came upon the idea of self-defense in the natural law theory of the late Middle Ages. While the rulers of Europe did not necessarily feel the need for such niceties in justifying their colonial projects, the principles developed by the Spanish philosopher and theologian Francisco de Vitoria (1492–1546) and the Dutch thinker and jurist Hugo Grotius (1583–1645) would come to the fore when European powers tried to extricate themselves from endemic war among themselves. These streams of thought were brought together in the seventeenth and eighteenth centuries to form the idea that the only legitimate justification for war and violence was the defense of liberty. In the thought of Hobbes, Locke, and the founders of the United States, liberty came to be associated first and foremost with the preservation of life. It was a development that would have surely surprised the architects of just war theory, the framers of the earliest charters of liberty, and the ancients whose republican forms were purportedly being reclaimed.

THE REMERGENCE OF LIBERTY

Liberty and freedom as preeminent, political aims had died with the Roman Republic, but discussions of the concepts had been kept alive in theological treatises on free will and spiritual liberation. It is perhaps not surprising then that when freedom reappears in the political life of Europe more than a thousand years later it is in the form of a promise by Henry I (1068–1135) to "make the holy church of God free," a pledge to respect the property rights of the church upon the deaths of bishops or archbishops.[4] Another, more indirect reference to freedom in Henry's *Charter of Liberties* (1100) harkens back to the decisive issue in the development of freedom in the Roman Republic. As the king, Henry pledges:

> knights who render military service for their lands I grant of my own gift that the lands of their demesne ploughs be free from all payments and all labor, so that, having been released from so great a burden, they may equip themselves well with horses and arms and be fully prepared for my service and the defense of my kingdom.[5]

That Henry makes such promises to the bishops, knights, and barons reflects his acute dependence upon them.[6] Historians tell us that the character of the promises was dictated by the peculiar circumstances of his coming to power. When his eldest brother, King William Rufus (1056–1100), is killed while hunting, Henry moves to capture the throne that rightfully belongs to his older brother Robert, who is fighting in the First Crusade. Henry's pledge to "free" the knights from all payments and labor seems to have been a promise to end the deeply resented war levy for the crusade, a pledge that reminds the knights both of his elder brother's unpopular policies and the rightful heir's participation in the crusade.[7] Henry pledges to rule differently than his brothers. Given his status as a younger brother, it is also particularly important for him to win the support of the church which, in the longstanding coronation tradition, grants the king sovereignty in exchange for his promise to rule with justice and honor.[8] Thus the Charter of Liberties, issued by Henry upon his accession to the throne, springs from his tenuous status as sovereign.[9]

One hundred fifteen years later, using Henry's Charter as a model, a group of barons force King John (1166–1216) to sign Magna Carta (1215). The Great Charter clearly reflects a high degree of self-confidence and awareness on the part of the barons, who take an oath to "stand fast for the liberty of church and realm"[10] and claim "communal liberties" that seem to have been inspired by the existence of free towns and municipalities.[11] In a move surely designed to win the favor of those they depended upon in their efforts against the king, the barons expand the meaning of "free man" to include military tenants holding their lands by knightly service. This expansive use of the term is conspicuous in the most famous provision of the charter: the protection against arbitrary imprisonment and confiscation of property without the judgment of one's peers or the law.[12] In addition, the barons who authored Magna Carta were keen to give liberty the imprimatur of the divine, as seen in the claim that the liberties granted to the barons and knights would be given "in perpetuity." Whereas the earlier Charter of Liberties began with a reference to the liberty of the church, Magna Carta is conspicuous in its attempt to elide the liberties of church and state. As the historian J. C. Holt writes,

> It is as if ecclesiastical liberties infected all the rest, the whole placed within the broader notion of free and perpetual alms, the community of freemen viewed as if it were as permanent and undying as the church itself with all its component institutions.[13]

Although Magna Carta failed to prevent a war and is only adopted partially and haltingly after King John's death, it described a legal basis for limiting the king and distributing divinely sanctioned sovereignty more widely. In the initial attempts to ensconce liberty in the law, we find attempts to co-opt ecclesiastical authority, not remove it.

The very fact that the barons demanded these liberties from the king is indicative of paradoxes that arise in all attempts to implement the rule of law while preserving a conception of sovereign authority. Holt is keen to emphasize that the existence of the Magna Carta, as a document penned and signed by the King, suggests that the barons are not really thinking "outside the terms of reference prescribed by the society in which they lived."[14] The nature of liberties as understood in the thirteenth century is that they had to be *granted*. As Holt explains, monarchs themselves promulgated "acts of self-limitation in which they agreed to restrict their own freedom and initiative, apparently of their own free will."[15] However, Holt believes that the "essential cause" of the crisis of 1215 was that in the King's efforts to regularize the activities of the realm, whether in prescribing weights and measures, assessing property values, or regulating cultivation in the forests, exceptions were offered as a matter of course, whether for expediency or political gain.[16] In large part, Magna Carta was a demand from the barons that the monarch follow his own laws more strictly, and not implement them of his own whim. Holt writes:

> 1215 marked the decision to demand from the Crown that regularity of procedure and treatment which barons, knights and townsfolk had come to expect

and had been led to accept in their dealings with each other. The pupils were now teaching the master the lesson he had taught them.

The liberty and rule of the monarch over and against the irregular and chaotic actions of the people was transformed into the liberty of the subjects over and against an arbitrary monarch. Perhaps the most important example of this transformation is the fact that the King himself had introduced the idea of the communal oath in preparing the national militia when the French threatened invasion in 1205.[17] The barons adopted the idea, taking a communal oath themselves, while inviting all the knights of the realm to take it in order to ensure that the king followed the law.[18] Fifteen hundred years after the secession of the plebs, King John's attempt to arm, regulate, and organize the barons for a defensive war has the unintended consequence of inciting the barons to organize against him and demand liberties for themselves.

The very meaning of "rule," which proscribes and prohibits, seems antithetical to liberty when it is understood as the ability to do as one will. Yet in attempting to regularize the behavior of others with general rules that serve the interests of the monarch, unanticipated outcomes sometimes arise that cause the ruler to change his or her mind. In the circumstances surrounding the creation of Magna Carta, we see that the connection between liberty and the rule of law is twofold: 1) Sovereignty, despite its pretensions, depends upon power gained from the cooperation of others. The king depends on the barons in order to rule and the barons depend upon the knights. Everyone competes for the favor of the Pope and the clergy. 2) Even rules created by sovereigns for the sole purpose of serving their own interests might in fact restrain them to the benefit of others. Liberties are created by careful regulations that carve out areas of noninterference on the part of the sovereign. Just as "grants of liberty" affirm the ruler's sovereignty, they secure cooperation from key constituencies, without which the claim to sovereignty becomes incredible.

THE EMERGENCE OF DEFENSE AS A PROMINENT JUSTIFICATION FOR WAR AND SOVEREIGNTY

The thinkers who made defense a central justification for war and violence in European thought are associated by contemporary political theorists with the genesis of international law. However, as historians of the early modern period note, the term "international law" is applied anachronistically to the dense overlay of laws, customs, authorities, and institutions that existed as European governments emerged from the Middle Ages. Indeed, in the works of Francisco de Vitoria and

Hugo Grotius we find natural law theories that are the basis for the rule of law more generally even though they come to be associated with legal arrangements between governments.

Antony Anghie argues that Vitoria's intellectual project is shaped by two problems, both of them related to colonialism: 1) the desire to free Spain from the authority of the Pope (and the Emperor) and 2) the absence of any legal or religious institutions shared by Spaniards and American Indians. Like Augustine and Aquinas, Vitoria is also concerned with a third issue: to refute what is now the thousand-year-old "problem" of early Christian pacifism. At the very outset of *On the Law of War,* Vitoria quotes Romans 12:19, which states " 'Dearly beloved, defend (*defendentes*) not yourselves, but rather give place unto wrath.' "[19] Vitoria makes headway on all three fronts.

First, Vitoria argues that because natural law applies to everyone, the authority of the Spanish crown cannot be curtailed in its enforcement of it. The "law of the Gospels does not prohibit anything which is permitted by natural law," he writes, which is why it is "called the 'law of liberty.' "[20] While Christians are free to hold themselves to a higher standard by refusing to defend themselves with violence or war, divine law does not demand that we break the natural law. Neither can the Pope deny natural law nor curtail attempts by governments to enforce it.[21] Since natural law is not connected to particular institutions, but rather to the very character of our bodies and minds, both Indians and Spaniards are subject to it. Vitoria disagrees with those Europeans who thought Indians were fundamentally brutish, unreasonable, or inhuman. He denies that Indians can be subjected and their land taken by the authority of the Christian Caesar or the Pope, rejecting the pretexts offered by his contemporaries: because Columbus discovered their lands; as a consequence of their refusal to accept Christ; on the basis of their status as sinners; by the choice of the Indians themselves; or as a special gift from God.[22]

Second, Vitoria argues that the natural law principle of self-defense provides justification for the Spanish subjugation of Indians in America. *On the Law of War* is written as the companion to his *On the American Indians,* which argues that our natural sociability, or "men's free mutual intercourse" gives Spaniards the *"right to travel and dwell in those countries, so long as they do no harm to the barbarians, and cannot be prevented from doing so."*[23] Since it is "inhuman to treat strangers and travellers badly," any resistance by Indians to Spanish trading, traveling, proselytizing, "sharing" their things, or living on their land is construed as an attack.[24] The Spanish government is tasked with protecting Spaniards, any converts to Christianity among the Indians and, more generally, *"the lawful defence of the innocent from unjust death* [so that] *even without the pope's authority, the Spaniards may prohibit the barbarians from practicing any nefarious custom or rite."*[25] Vitoria extends Aquinas's idea that wars to defend and protect the innocent are just, giving the Spanish nearly free rein in the Americas. Indeed, he lays out *jus in bello* criteria whereby innocents may be killed, enemies plundered and enslaved, and enemy combatants slaughtered even after the war is won.[26]

Anghie argues that in Vitoria's justification we find the origins of the modern idea of sovereignty as the all-encompassing authority of a government over a people or territory. The right of self-defense, writes Anghie, "is regarded as a right inseparable from and intrinsic to sovereignty and could even be regarded as the very essence of sovereignty."[27] For Vitoria, he goes on, "law itself is constructed around the core principle of self-defense."[28] Despite his insistence that Indians have their own forms of government, Vitoria formulates his theory so that Indians "are excluded from the realm of sovereignty and exist only as the objects against which Christian sovereignty may exercise its power to wage war."[29] Although no one has to this point credibly claimed that governments in Europe are absolutely sovereign, Vitoria suggests a nascent model whereby national governments, endowed with the legitimacy of "defenders," carry a special right and responsibility to practice violence. By figuring Indians as nonsubjects, the Spanish can claim to be unencumbered by the sovereignty of the Pope. At the same time, they can also establish their absolute sovereignty over the Indians, arguing that it is required for their own defense and to protect the indigenous tribes from themselves.

Anghie's assertion that the principle of self-defense becomes the basis for sovereignty itself is confirmed by Vitoria's own work on the "domestic" context. In his lesser-known *On Civil Power*, Vitoria follows Aristotle and Aquinas in his treatment of the origins of government, but with an additional emphasis on the link between necessity and defense.[30] Vitoria claims to have deduced this primary aim of the state from the physical and mental capabilities of persons—or lack thereof. In a passage that presages Thomas Hobbes, he emphasizes the fragility of the human body compared to other animals:

> In the first place, in order to ensure the safety and defence of animals, Mother Nature endowed them all from the very beginning with coats to fend off the frost and weather; next, she provided each species with its own defence against attack ... so some animals have wings to fly, or hooves to run, or horns, others have teeth or claws for fighting, and none lacks defences for its own protection. But to mankind Nature gave "only reason and virtue," leaving him otherwise frail, weak, helpless, and vulnerable, destitute of all defence and lacking in all things, and brought him forth naked and unarmed like a castaway from a shipwreck into the midst of the miseries of this life ... So it was that, in order to

make up for these natural deficiencies, mankind was obliged to give up the solitary nomadic life of animals, and to live life in partnerships (*societates*), each supporting the other.[31]

In this way, Vitoria articulates the "natural" foundations of both positive law and just war. For inspiration, he draws upon municipal laws of the time, which typically contained rights of self-defense.[32]

That the encounter with American Indians is of critical importance in establishing the idea of sovereignty can be seen in the complexities introduced when Hugo Grotius directly applies the principle of self-defense to Europeans themselves. Grotius draws the principle of self-defense from existing law, where it refers not to a right of governments but to an exception for private individuals to the law against murder. As he explains:

[If] an attack by violence is made on one's person, endangering life, and no other way of escape is open, under such circumstances, war is permissible, even though it involve the slaying of the assailant. As a consequence of the general acceptance of this principle we showed that in some cases a private war may be lawful.

This right of self-defense, it should be observed, has its origin directly, and chiefly, in the fact that nature commits to each his own protection, not in the injustice or crime of the aggressor. Wherefore, even if the assailant be blameless, as for instance a soldier acting in good faith, or one who mistakes me for someone else, or one who is rendered irresponsible by madness or by sleeplessness—this, we read, has actually happened to some—the right of self-defense is not thereby taken away; it is enough that I am not under obligation to suffer what such an assailant attempts, any more than I should be if attacked by an animal belonging to another.[33]

Grotius is keen to say that the right of self-defense is not a right to punish, which is reserved for governments. Instead, the principle of self-defense is a reprieve from just punishment, a right maintained by each individual by virtue of the natural imperative to preserve her or his own life.

Grotius offers a highly detailed examination of this right. He argues that simply being afraid that someone might attack you does not legitimate self-defense.[34] At the same time, he argues that defense of one's chastity is a legitimate reason to kill an assailant, specifically citing examples of women killing men.[35] He also closely examines ancient views on the defense of property. While he finds discussion of defending property as far back as the Law of Moses, he can find only one ancient source who offers an unqualified and explicit argument that the use of violence to defend one's property is justified. (The source is Demosthenes.[36]) He also explicitly argues against those who claim it is dishonorable to not defend one's property, instead upholding the pacifist tradition whereby "the man who endures such an injury shows that in a superior degree he possesses the virtue of long-suffering, and thus rather increases his honour than diminishes it."[37] However, he says that jurists and theologians of his day "teach that we have a right to kill a man in defence of our property," and he accepts the teaching as part and parcel of self-defense.[38]

The significance of Grotius's claim that self-defense can include a defense of property, and that it can be a bulwark against the punishment of governments, will become apparent in the later merging of these concepts of defense with notions of freedom. However, it is important to point out that for both Vitoria and Grotius, self-defense does not have democratic or republican implications. For Vitoria, monarchy is the best form of government, and no less "free" than a republic.[39] Grotius similarly uses the principle of self-defense to support a far-reaching conception of sovereignty even as defense is also simultaneously a justification for exemption from public authority. In contrast to those who argue that sovereignty lies with the people and should be used to restrain and punish kings who make bad policy, Grotius asserts that "no wise person can fail to see" the "many evils this opinion has given rise to, and can even now give rise to if it sinks deep into men's minds."[40] He contends that both individuals and whole peoples can legitimately sell themselves into slavery, or submit to another's absolute sovereignty. They can take such extreme actions for precisely the same reason that self-defense is justified: to preserve their lives and property.[41] In addition, self-defense is a justification not only for private wars, but also for legitimate public wars, i.e., those prosecuted by governments.[42] The private right of self-defense does not apply when one's life is threatened by someone who is "useful to the state."[43] For both men, the right of self-defense is connected to necessity and natural law. They have yet to abandon ancient tradition and continue to maintain that the integrity of one's body and property is basically unrelated to political freedom.[44]

In focusing on the emergence of principles of self-defense in Vitoria and Grotius, I do not mean to exaggerate the importance of the idea in their thought. Neither thinker understands defense as the only legitimate justification for violence and war. For both, governments may fight just offensive wars and employ punitive violence. Moreover, the notion of necessity is not decidedly wedded to the concept of defense—certainly not the defense of life and property—as it will come to be in the sixteenth and seventeen centuries. Machiavelli offers a robust concept of necessity that sometimes references defense and is keen to preserve the existing regime of the state. But his view of political necessity is also entirely consistent with pursuing empire and glory, aims that Vitoria and Grotius reject, at least in principle.[45] Despite the influence of Vitoria and Grotius, recent scholarship suggests that principles of defense play only a small role in the thinking of European proponents of empire.[46] Finally, even among thinkers of the same era who adopt the principles of self-defense, there is disagreement as to its meaning. Inspired by Machiavelli, the Italian jurist Alberico Gentili (1552–1608) for instance takes issue with Vitoria's claim that defense is only justified in response to injuries already committed, arguing that pre-emptive defense is legal and just.[47] Yet there can be no doubt that by placing defense at the center of justifications for war and violence and linking those theories with natural law, Vitoria and Grotius begin to shift the locus of legitimacy, authority, and sovereignty in modern political thought.

TWO STREAMS FLOW TOGETHER: SELF-DEFENSE AND LIBERTY AS COMPLEMENTARY JUSTIFICATIONS FOR VIOLENCE

The story of how early grants of liberty merge with just war arguments about self-defense is complex and circuitous. Although the idea that freedom can be a legitimate preoccupation of government was almost entirely absent among just war thinkers and concepts of liberty and freedom reemerged with little reference to just war theory, the two ideas eventually merge.

The case for an armed citizenry is built on top of a misinterpretation of the history of the Roman Republic put forth by the Italian humanists. As we have seen, the plebs of Rome generally did not take up arms against the patricians to win greater participation and protections. Instead they exercised power by refraining from participation in wars. In the late Republic, assassinations and conflict between classes signaled the end of representative government. Nevertheless, Machiavelli's reading of Livy preaches that citizen militias are the foundation of republican government.[48] A similarly misleading interpretation of the relationship between arms and freedom in Roman history is found in the work of Gentili, who more directly prepares the ground for John Locke's political theory. In the war with King Porsenna after the Tarquins are expelled, Gentili finds "a most just war fought to retain (*retinenda*) . . . freedom."[49] He interpolates this finding into the even more broad and dubious thesis that the Romans typically fought defensive wars for the purpose of maintaining republican forms.[50]

These ideas begin to weave the maintenance of freedom into the understanding that violence is a necessary means for securing material ends. In an apparent diversion from his discourse on republics, Machiavelli gives some advice for would-be princes who wish to satisfy the desires of a democratically minded populace. He writes: "[The] vast bulk of those who demand freedom, desire but to live in security. For in all states whatever be their form of government, the real rulers do not amount to more than forty or fifty citizens." As a consequence, autocratic rulers can subvert democracy by setting up laws, rigorously enforcing them, and not breaking them. "[In] a short time [the people] will begin to live in security and contentment."[51] By eliding the practical difference between autocratic and republican governments, Machiavelli takes a step toward melding freedom and security into a single preeminent political value and aim. A citizen militia is the best way to secure liberty and defend republics, and by the same token, a prince that keeps the people safe is likely to win their support in arms. To be clear, as in Livy, freedom and physical security are two different things for Machiavelli. However, in Machiavelli's claim that physical violence is the best way to maintain and sustain republican laws, the distinction between a public-minded autocrat and an armed citizenry that checks corruption is not obvious: either will suffice, and in practice they might not look very different.

Thomas Hobbes makes the critical innovation of linking freedom and the body. Even the most astute readers of Hobbes sometimes miss this point, and it is not surprising that they do.[52] After all, his entire discussion of liberty in *Leviathan* (1651) is meant to refute its value as a political aim. Against Machiavelli and Gentili, he consistently seeks to diminish the claims of those who "clamour as they do for liberty."[53] However, in his definition of freedom, he makes a break from both ancient and medieval understandings. He writes:

[A] FREE-MAN is *he that in those things which by his strength and wit he is able to do is not hindered to do what he has a will to.* But when the words *free* and *liberty* are applied to anything but *bodies,* they are abused.[54]

Hobbes's break with tradition here is subtle. In his claim that actions of the will "proceed from liberty," as in his frequent references to the will as tied to liberty, there is some consistency between his concept of freedom and Stoic and medieval understandings of the term. It is for this reason that Quentin Skinner, citing Hobbes' contemporary and interlocutor Bishop Bramhall, suggests that his view is a revival of Stoicism.[55]

Yet Hobbes's small step toward a material understanding of freedom marks a decisive moment. By insisting that the body and not the will is the true seat of liberty, he allows for a new line of argument entirely at odds not only with theorists like Seneca (4 BC–65), Epictetus (55–135), and Duns Scotus (1266–1308), but also with ancient traditions of political freedom. For Hobbes, freedom is compromised when persons are either physically prevented from doing something or physically forced to do something against their will. He imputes freedom into the natural law of the just war theorists, saying that "all men equally are by nature free," and that all have a natural right to resist direct physical attacks, even from legitimate authorities.[56] Hobbes is fully cognizant that he is creating a new conception of liberty. He writes that *"Aristotle, Cicero,* and other men, Greeks and Romans, living under popular states, derived those rights, not from the principles of nature, but transcribed them into their books out of the practice of their own commonwealths."[57] When the ancients speak of liberty and freedom, they speak "of the liberty of the commonwealth," a liberty that modern advocates of liberty mistake "for their private inheritance and birth right, which is the right of the public only."[58] Echoing Vitoria, Hobbes stresses that if we are to assess the impact of different forms of government on natural liberty, democracies are just as likely to compromise freedom as monarchies. Conversely, if public liberty is the aim, it bears little relationship to "the liberty of particular men."[59]

The novelty of Hobbes's materialist understanding of liberty can be difficult to see for another reason as well. At first his view seems consistent with Stoicism and ancient conceptions of liberty because he maintains that clear threats of violence, even if they induce extreme fear, and the demands of necessity, even if they are a matter of life and death, do not impinge upon the free will.[60] Such views are consistent with both the ancient association of liberty with courage in the face of tyranny and the medieval understanding of free will operating independently of the demands of public life. But Hobbes is entirely at odds with both traditions when he suggests that liberty can be consistent with fear and necessity in relation to the body. No ancient thinker argues that actions grounded in necessity or driven by fear are consistent with either political or spiritual liberty. The hallmark of ancient freedom is a willingness to sacrifice the preservation of one's individual body—in battle, in the face of deprivation, or in resisting a tyrant—for the sake of liberty. Indeed, as we have seen, such sacrifice is the penultimate expression and embodiment of liberty in the founding stories of the early Roman Republic, second only to participation in collective rule itself.

The differences between ancient and modern understandings of liberty are not simply attributable to Hobbes's reliance on "the principles of nature." Hobbes's understanding of liberty as connected to the body is no doubt influenced by the political claims and legal understandings of his own time—and his desire to put them on more solid foundations. By the seventeenth century, "grants of liberty" to the barons and knights have become the principle of protection from arbitrary physical imposition upon life and property, a cornerstone of the rule of law.[61] Although the Peace of Westphalia (1648) has long been understood as initiating the modern state system, recent scholarship makes the case that it reflected the contested nature of sovereignty. Feudal rights had become territorial rights, as when France claimed to be taking German provinces both to uphold the Emperor's authority and for the purpose of "defending the German estates from an assault on their constitutionally defined privileges and immunities."[62] Nowhere is the word "sovereignty" mentioned in the Westphalia treaties, since there is no Latin word for it (the closest approximation is *supremum dominium*), but it does seem that they reflect a change in emphasis from government rule over people to government rule over territory.[63]

By the time Hobbes writes *Leviathan,* the crisis of sovereignty has come home to roost. Religious and royal authority is eroded by the Reformation and the humanism of the Renaissance. The Thirty Years War (1618–1648) and (of most concern to Hobbes) the English Civil War (1642–1651) further call into question medieval understandings of authority, with the contested nature of liberties and privileges high on the list of unsettled issues. At the same time, the expansion of the colonial enterprise, now deeply implicated in the Atlantic slave trade, raises new moral and material problems. In all of these historical shifts, subject peoples both within and outside Europe, along with intellectuals and contenders for political power, begin to question the wars, orders, and empires of European governments. The violence of kings and queens (as well as popes) lose the veneer of legitimacy, the sanction of true religion, and the pretense of serving the common good. That these issues are on Hobbes's mind is demonstrated by the three examples he uses to prove the existence of the state of nature. The state of nature can be seen 1) in "the savage people in many places of *America*"; 2) in situations where men formerly under government "degenerate into, a civil war"; and 3) in all relationships between "kings and persons of sovereign authority, because of their independency."[64] Locke, who was deeply involved in slavery and the colonial project in America, will adopt the same examples.[65]

Like Vitoria and Grotius, Hobbes claims that the character of sovereignty itself lies in the natural order of things; unlike them, he sees the right to self-defense as the entire basis of sovereignty. Natural freedom is not only compromised by physical attack, it also involves the ability and the right to physically attack others. Hobbes claims that advocates of natural liberty confuse it with the public liberty of sovereigns. He writes that the "*Athenians* and *Romans* were free, that is, free commonwealths, not that any particular men had the liberty to resist their own representative, but that their representative had the liberty to resist or invade other people."[66] However, he himself grounds the liberty of the public sovereign in the natural right of individuals.[67] Whereas natural liberty is only compromised by the actual practice of physical violence, natural liberty also involves the right "to everything, even to one another's body," as long as it is aimed at preserving one's "life against his enemies."[68] In contrast to Vitoria and Grotius but as consistent with

Gentili, Hobbes gives wide berth to do whatever one believes is necessary for self-preservation, so that, because they are grounded in the principle of self-defense, even the most aggressive "anticipatory" actions are encompassed by the principle.[69] This right to everything for the purpose of preserving physical life is what individuals contract to transfer to government.[70] The fact that "all men equally are by nature free"[71] means that government 1) cannot take an individual's liberty without physically restraining or harming them and 2) that sovereignty relies upon liberty being transferred from individuals, which allows any and all means to be used for the purposes of self-defense.

In taking these steps toward a brand of sovereignty grounded in liberty and physical preservation, Hobbes makes an important break with the ancients. However, the natural law principles of self-defense only relate to liberty at the extreme. Hobbes sets an extremely high bar with respect to what it means to physically deprive another of liberty, since liberty is only lost when one is subject to actual physical restraint or violence. At the same time, he sets a very low bar in his estimation of what it means to deprive another of physical security. For Hobbes, even the most minor threat—indeed, the very existence of another person capable of harming another—justifies preemptive action to preserve oneself in the state of nature. In this way, liberty and one's physical safety are set against one another politically, even as they are welded together in natural law. Indeed, the difference between physical threats and physical impositions (i.e., actual attacks amounting to the compromising of one's natural liberty) is the critical point for Hobbes because he aims to show that preserving one's life is more important than maintaining natural liberty.

Hobbes opens the door to the natural law theory of freedom that Locke comes rushing through. In contrast to Hobbes's connection between liberty and the body, Locke perceives a way to fully tie liberty to both the natural law and the right of self-defense. Locke forwards this view by way of a distinction between license and liberty.[72] For Locke, unlike Hobbes, liberty can be taken away by certain threats to life and property, or what he calls declarations of design on another's life. However, even while lowering the bar for what counts as a violation of liberty, Locke raises the bar regarding what is required for sovereigns to justifiably kill or harm others in defense of life and liberty. Instead of a right to everything, self-preservation justifies actions aimed at "*Reparation* and *Restraint*."[73] Locke falls short of returning to the just war principles of Vitoria and Grotius, in that he does not require that actual harm be done before someone can justifiably kill or physically harm another. In these passages, the preservation of life and the protection of liberty become fully consistent with one another.

While much of what Locke says about our natural rights comports with the work of Aquinas, Vitoria, and Grotius, the critical difference lies in his description of

our natural state as one of equality and freedom. In his description of the state of
nature in the *Second Treatise* (1689), Locke suggests that life, health, and property
are closely related to liberty, and that all four together comprise the constellation of
natural rights that reason leads us to respect in others.[74] Arguing for the prohibition
of suicide,[75] he hints at the multifaceted connection between life and liberty, and
goes on to make the point explicit. He writes:

> [He] who attempts to get another Man into his Absolute Power, does thereby
> *put himself into a State of War* with him; It being . . . a Declaration of a Design
> upon his Life. For I have reason to conclude, that he who would get me into
> his Power without my consent, would use me as he pleased, when he had got
> me there, and destroy me too when he had a fancy to do it . . . To be free from
> such force is the only security of my Preservation: and reason bids me look on
> him, as an Enemy of my Preservation, who would take away that *Freedom,*
> which is the Fence to it . . . He that in the State of Nature, *would take away the
> Freedom,* that belongs to any one in that State, must necessarily be supposed
> to have a design to take away everything else, *Freedom* being the Foundation
> of all the rest.[76]

In describing the threatening persons who "declare a design" upon another's
life, Locke suggests that liberty and the preservation of life are mutually supporting aims. The primary means by which one can compromise another's ability to act
freely is by doing something life-threatening. Likewise, only by having the freedom
to follow one's own will[77] can life be reliably preserved. Locke's reference here to
freedom as "the Fence" around physical life is more than just allegory, as he quickly
moves to collapse not only liberty and the preservation of life but also the preservation of property. In arguing that it is lawful to kill a thief, he writes that there is no
reason to believe that he "who would *take away my Liberty,* would not when he had
me in his Power, take away every thing else."[78] The terms "liberty" and "property"
are used nearly interchangeably and both are indelibly linked to life itself.

Yet in proposing that enforcement powers cannot be used for revenge or domination, Locke revivifies the spirit of earlier just war theories.[79] Like Hobbes, he says
that the enforcement powers of governments are precisely the sovereign powers
each subject has in the state of nature. Since he claims that no one ever had unrestrained license, but only lawful liberty, quitting our powers means giving that same
restrained and lawful power to government. Although both Hobbes and Locke
build on natural law principles, Locke goes on to define sovereignty as limited by
natural law. When subjects give up their enforcement powers, government must
use them for precisely the same purposes for which they were intended in the state

of nature. Men create governments "to unite for the mutual *Preservation* of their Lives, Liberties and Estates, which I call by the general Name, *Property*."[80] The sole basis upon which governments can legitimately harm or kill people is the purpose of preserving life and property, which Locke carefully and insistently links to liberty. Thus he welds sovereignty and freedom in two ways: 1) sovereignty is fully identified with the defense of liberty as material bodies and goods, and 2) freedom, as the capacity to justly punish and kill others, is the essence of sovereignty.

Locke transforms the nature of sovereignty in contradictory ways. First, he affirms Hobbes's absolutism in at least one narrow but exceedingly important way. The difference between Hobbes and Locke in their estimations of legitimate sovereignty do not turn on *what* governments can do to bodies, but *when* they can do it. Locke's description of a legitimate government is quite specific, including both the general proposition that its actions must serve the common good and the specific demand that it include institutional features such as a legislature (to express the will of the majority), a judiciary, and a separate executive. Yet in executing the natural and public law, the powers of such a government include not just killing others, but placing them under the government's absolute subjection and slavery. Not surprisingly given the natural law origins of this theory of sovereignty, the purportedly limited circumstances where such violence and domination are permitted are in just wars. Since just wars are fought in conformity with Locke's version of natural law principles, and since states take on the characteristics of individuals in the state of nature, Locke allows that killing those invaders who act like robbers, villains, and pirates is consistent with protecting life and property. He writes: "The *power a Conquerour gets* over those he overcomes *in a Just War, is perfectly Despotical:* he has an absolute power over the Lives of those, who by putting themselves in a State of War, have forfeited them."[81] For the first time in the history of political thought, complete physical domination of others is understood as a potential means for government to defend the liberty of its citizens. In addition, Locke's discussion of "prerogative" suggests there might be instances when executives need to take extraordinary actions in the domestic sphere as well. Although keenly aware of the dangers of unrestricted sovereignty, he says that the law-making power can be too slow, and that "Accidents and Necessities" may require princes take action outside the law for "safety" and the public good.[82]

Second (and in spite of this possibility), Locke suggests that sovereignty remains dispersed among individual persons and communities, even as they give up their capacity to kill and punish to government. We can see the precursors of this transformation in Hobbes's claim that citizens retain certain rights even after they have contracted to create a sovereign.[83] Locke extends Hobbes's claims further, allowing that governments can become the enemies of life, liberty, and property. Predictably, his adoption of just war theory means that aggressors against other governments can "*have no Title to the Subjection and Obedience of the Conquered.*"[84] By the same token, when governments deviate from the natural law with respect to their own people, they have declared war on them. Such governments—not their people—are in rebellion and the people must be at liberty to defend themselves.[85]

While the implications Machiavelli and Gentili draw from the history of the Roman Republic are often questionable, there is one aspect of ancient republican thought that is reflected in liberal ideas about the relationship between violence and freedom. In ancient Rome, a critical guarantee of the plebs' influence in government was the sacrosanct status of the tribunes. In effect, Locke adopts and expands the idea, making every citizen's life and property sacrosanct, so that anyone who kills or harms another in the state of nature is designated *homo sacer*, who "may be destroyed as a Lyon or Tyger, one of those Savage Beasts . . . And upon this is grounded the great Law of Nature, *Who so sheddeth Mans Blood, by Man shall his Blood be shed.*"[86] Whether by influence or an accident of history, the legal right to kill, closely related to divine sanction, is understood as carrying a clear guarantee of freedom.

Locke's thought brings to light the critical features and implications of the idea that freedom must be defended with violence. He is the first to proffer the view that freedom and liberty are entirely coextensive with the survival and well-being of one's body (and by extension one's property), and that this situation provides the essential justification for government and for the use of violence by governments.

DEFENDING THE LIBERTY OF THEIR OWN: CITIZENS IN ARMS

With these ideas circulating, it is not surprising that bourgeois revolutionaries take up arms to pursue liberation in the American and French Revolutions. Once kings are toppled, the question of how to preserve and defend liberty comes to the fore, and the adoption of legal protections for liberty draw on the old charters and social contract theory to create a new brand of liberal sovereignty. Some of the outstanding features of the 1689 English Bill of Rights, the constitutions of the American colonies, and the United States' Bill of Rights may at first appear to undercut the thesis that liberty, by way of defense, is inextricably tied to the well-being of one's body and property. Rights to religion, free speech, petition, and assembly, for instance, are guarantees that individuals and groups can express opinions and hold beliefs. They affirm free action, not physical security.

Yet just as Locke argues that freedom and physical security are mutually support-ive of one another, seventeenth- and eighteenth-century bills of rights tie even these broad freedoms to protection from state-sanctioned violence. The English Bill of Rights makes illegal "all commitments and prosecutions" for petitioning and states that freedom of speech in Parliament "ought not be impeached or questioned in any court or place out of Parliament."[87] The First Amendment to the Constitution says that Congress shall "make no law" regarding religion and will not "prohibit" or "abridge" the rights of speech and assembly.[88] These enumerated rights do not mean that a government cannot issue statements disagreeing with its critics, or that sup-porters of a government are disallowed from assembling.[89] Moreover, no one doubts the human capacity to speak, believe, petition, or assemble. Instead, the political right to believe, speak, petition, or assemble in these texts refers to the ability to do such things without being physically punished, arrested, or harmed. As Carl Schmitt (1888–1985), whose critique of liberalism will be explored more extensively in chapter 6, remarks: "Freedom of speech, freedom of press, freedom of assembly, freedom of discussion, are not only useful and expedient, therefore, but really life-and-death questions for liberalism."[90] This protection against physical punishment is also made apparent by the accompanying rights, which reflect the general spirit and character of legal affirmations of liberty. Protection from cruel and unusual punishment and search and seizure, and the various due process protections, all sug-gest that interference first and foremost means physical violence or confiscation of property. Freedom of speech, religion, and assembly are particularly important enu-merated instances of that overall rule.[91]

In defending such freedoms, one critical right is the right to keep and bear and arms. The Second Amendment right to bear arms goes hand in hand with the Third Amendment protection against the quartering of troops and with the prohibition against the King's power to raise a war levy and fund a standing army in a time of peace in the English Bill of Rights (incorporated into the US Constitution in the form of Congress having the sole power to declare war).[92] Eighteenth-century republicans had long argued that nations cannot remain free with " 'any Souldiers in constant Pay within their cities, or ever suffered any of their Subjects to make War their Profession."[93] The wording of the state consti-tutions from which the Second Amendment was drawn often warned explicitly against standing armies.[94]

However, modern republicans drew a much different conclusion about the right to bear arms than their ancient forebears. Roman citizens (and as Joyce Malcolm observes, most English subjects of the early seventeenth century) understood bear-ing arms as a burden, or at best, as an honorable duty. Military service was under-stood as the price disenfranchised groups paid in order to gain equal treatment and

citizenship. Indeed, participation in the American War of Independence played
a critical role in expanding political participation for rank-and-file soldiers with
little property.[95] Modern republicans transformed bearing arms from a burden
into a right, and a necessary guarantee of freedom.[96] The wording of the Second
Amendment is clear enough in this regard: "A well regulated militia being necessary
to the security of a free state, the right of the people to keep and bear arms shall not
be infringed." Thus an armed citizenry was seen as the best guarantee of material
liberty, an idea that the soldiers who fought the Revolutionary War wholeheartedly
adopted.

Since being proficient in weapons is the essential means of securing liberty, handling them comes to signify self-sufficiency and incorruptibility. As sovereign individuals, each landholder bears arms in defense of his property.[97] Consistent with social
contract principles, the right is also exercised collectively. Richard Price (1723–1791)
writes in his pamphlet *Observations on the Importance of the American Revolution*:

> Free States ought to be bodies of armed *citizens,* well regulated and well dis-
> ciplined, and always ready to turn out, when properly called upon, to execute
> laws, to quell riots, and to keep the peace. Such, if I am rightly informed, are
> the citizens of America.[98]

As in the ancient understanding of freedom, Price and other republicans insisted
that republics require moderate citizens who regulate and discipline themselves. In
stark contrast to the ancient use of civil disobedience in confrontations with one's
fellow citizens, the modern republican use of violence and the threat of violence not
only repels foreign invasion, but also keeps private interests, criminals, and mobs
in check.

Most republican thinkers of the period clearly understood liberty as requiring
the protection of particular bodies—namely, free, white, male property owners.[99]
Despite the broad wording of the Second Amendment, the right to bear arms in
self-defense is conditioned by the ascriptive characteristics of the bearer.[100] African
Americans and American Indians were generally excluded from the state militias.
The 1777 Pennsylvania Militia Act called up "every male white person," and other
states had similar requirements, which made for a "national connection between
whiteness and liability to service in the Continental Army."[101] American citizens
were literally and figuratively located between the spoiled British citizenry and the
unruly American Indian. Price writes that the

> happiest state of man is the middle state between the *savage* and the *refined,*
> or between the wild and luxurious state. [In Connecticut] the inhabitants

consist, if I am rightly informed, of an independent and hardy YEOMANRY, all nearly on a level—trained in arms,—instructed in their rights—cloathed in home-spun—of simple manners—strangers to luxury—drawing plenty from the ground—and that plenty, gathered easily by the hand of industry.[102]

The Second Amendment's reference to a "well-regulated" militia seems calibrated to contrast the ordered violence of American citizens with the corrupt and uncivilized violence of British soldiers and American Indians. In the early history of the United States, Congress went so far as to require citizens to arm themselves, with the Second Militia Act of 1792 specifying exactly what citizens were to purchase. The accompanying First Militia Act gave the President the authority to call up the militias of several states when there was imminent danger from any "foreign nation or Indian tribe."[103]

The armed American landowner is distinguished not only from corrupt British and uncivilized Indian enemies, but also from the effeminate and the enslaved. In July of 1775, the Continental Congress warns their colonial rulers that "men trained to arms from their infancy, and animated by the love of liberty, will afford neither a cheap or easy conquest." This trait is in contrast to the people in another of England's possessions: the "effeminacy [of] the inhabitants of India."[104] In the radical republican rhetoric of the time, carrying weapons becomes the distinguishing characteristic of free men as opposed to slaves.[105] In proposing a constitution for Virginia, Jefferson writes "that no freeman shall ever be debarred the use of arms within his own lands or tenements,"[106] a statement that implies both the exclusion of slaves from the right to bear arms and the right of slave owner to use them with respect to all forms of his property. Jefferson also presages the armed husbandman and frontiersman with his hope that "as long as there shall be vacant lands [*sic*] in any part of America" the United States government can remain virtuous.[107] His own procurement of the Louisiana Purchase both extended slavery and hastened the subjugation and removal of American Indians. The Haitian Revolution, along with other slave rebellions to come, also gave new meaning to the claim that landowners "of necessity" remain skilled and organized in the handling of weapons.

FREEDOM FROM BEARING ARMS?

Amid the general consensus in Anglo-American thought that freedom is secured through the proliferation of weapons among "the people," pacifist thought remained sufficiently influential to require consideration during the debate over the ratification of the Constitution. Throughout the history of just war thinking, there has been some attempt to accommodate the nonviolent teachings of the Gospels even while developing reasons for Christians to use violence in good conscience. Just such an accommodation appears in the amendment James Madison (1751–1836) originally proposed to Congress regarding the right to bear arms. It stated: "A well regulated militia, composed of the body of the people, being the best security of a free state, the right of the people to keep and bear arms shall not be infringed; but no person religiously scrupulous shall be compelled to bear arms." The last clause, or "scruples clause," was based on amendments considered by ratification conventions in Maryland, New York, Virginia, and North Carolina (with only Maryland narrowly voting against recommending the clause to Congress[108]). The Virginia and North Carolina conventions offer the scruples clause as the nineteenth of twenty proposed amendments. The twentieth reads:

> That Religion, or the duty which we owe to our Creator, and the Manner of discharging it, can be directed only by Reason and Conviction, not by Force or Violence, and therefore all Men have an equal natural and unalienable Right to the free Exercise of Religion, according to the Dictates of Conscience, And that no particular religious Sect or Society of Christians ought to be favoured or established by Law, in Preference to others.[109]

Both amendments reflect a desire to shelter conscience from material concerns, while removing religious issues from politics as far as possible. The argument in the twentieth amendment tracks closely to Locke's *A Letter Concerning Toleration* where, echoing a passage from Book 7 of Plato's *Republic*, he says truth "will be but the weaker for any borrowed force Violence can add to her."[110]

The debates in the House of Representatives raise a wide variety of concerns regarding the scruples clause. Elbridge Gerry (1744–1814) worries that it "would give an opportunity to the people in power to destroy the constitution itself. They can declare who are those religiously scrupulous, and prevent them from bearing arms."[111] Others suggest that Quakers and Moravians will free ride while their fellow citizens defend the country from an invading army or, worse yet, that atheists will use it as a pretext to avoid service in a militia.[112] Such concerns lead to attempts to reintroduce language from the New York, Virginia, and North Carolina ratifying conventions, requiring that those with scruples are exempted "upon payment of an Equivalent, to employ another to bear Arms in his Stead."[113] But Roger Sherman (1721–1793) and others argue that it "is well known that those who are religiously scrupulous of bearing arms, are equally scrupulous of getting substitutes or paying an equivalent. Many of them would rather die than do either one or the other."[114]

In the debates that took place on the creation of the Second Amendment, Congressman Elias Boudinot (1740–1821) cites "instances of oppression" during the late War, presumably referring to the massacre of over ninety neutral Moravian Delaware Indians by Pennsylvania militiamen in 1782.[115] Boudinot argues that compelling anyone to bear arms is both foolish and unjust, and worries that striking out the scruples clause will send the message that there is "an intention in the General Government to compel all its citizens to bear arms."[116] (The Militia Acts suggest there was exactly such an intention.) The idea of leaving the question of religions refusing to serve to the states is raised, and Egbert Benson (1746–1833) argues it "may be a religious persuasion, but it is no natural right" to not bear arms and it "is extremely injudicious to intermix matters of doubt with fundamentals."[117] While the scruples clause remained as late as August 24th, 1789, by September 26th it had been removed and was not sent to the states.[118]

The debate over the Second Amendment reflects an understanding of the relationship between religious and material liberty that bears some resemblance to the refusal of the Romans to fight wars in the early Republic. Indeed, even in the practice of warfare itself, liberty, and the preservation of life are only uncomfortably collapsed, if not outright incompatible. Benjamin Franklin (1706–1790) comments before the war that "Massachusetts must suffer all the hazards and mischiefs of war, rather than admit the alteration of their charters and laws by parliament. They who can give up essential liberty to obtain a little temporary safety, deserve neither liberty nor safety."[119] In this sentiment we see that the Roman spirit of sacrifice is not entirely lost. Liberty here means preserving or establishing laws with a certain character, even if the phrase "a little temporary safety" suggests that the result of the war will be the preservation of liberty and life. However, the argument also gives an entirely new cast to the nature of sacrifice. In the context of declaring independence and going to war, the defense of freedom means using violence to keep a government in existence.

Locke preserves an aspect of Hobbesian absolutism even in his advocacy of free government and liberal institutions. Over the course of the next two centuries, the defense of freedom will come to mean not only the right of individuals to bear arms or collectively keep their governments in check, but the duty of citizens to protect the survival or "national security interests" of those governments. The advent of the modern state system and the foundations of liberal conceptions of sovereignty are deeply intertwined. The emergence of self-defense as the primary justification for the legitimate use of violence transformed the meaning of political freedom from self-governance to self-governance in the service of personal and material interests. One way to understand the advent of soldiers "defending freedom"—or prisons that claim to hold enemies of the state for that purpose—is to trace the extension of the individual right to freedom to a collective right, in which the territorial integrity of republican states becomes analogous to the property of the free individual, authorized to use violence to defend its "life" and property.

However, the idea of the "nation" and the claim that a free people might go to war in the name of freedom (either in a self-conscious effort to preserve their own form of government or to impose their brand of freedom on others) taps into themes yet to be explored. Out of the conflicted and self-destructive liberation movements in America, France, and elsewhere emerged the twin ideas of nationalism and socialism. Each places a strong emphasis on providing a route to freedom for the masses of people, even if they often serve different people and different interests. Mass movements of people, taking up arms not to oppose an oppressive state but to support a state that claims to defend, pursue, and spread freedom opens up a whole new set of political possibilities and perils. While these developments finally bring us up to the twentieth century, a full understanding requires that we first look back to the inception of the idea of political freedom in Ancient Greece.

PART III

Freedom to Rule

War is father of all and king of all, and some he shows as gods, others as humans; some he makes slaves, others free.

HERACLITUS

5

Pericles' Ideal

THE FIRST TWO parts of this book explored how violence has been a preeminent *means* to freedom and liberty in the Western political tradition. However, when revolutions become institutionalized and the defense of freedom becomes the primary legitimatization for the use of force by governments, violence serves more than just an instrumental purpose. Throughout the history of the West and especially in the modern period, violence has come to be understood as critical to the exercise and expression of freedom. In the citizen-soldiers of ancient Greece, the republican militias of the seventeenth and eighteenth centuries, and the national armies of the nineteenth and twentieth centuries, the capacity for self-rule is tied to the ability to physically dominate others.

In Parts I and II, I was keen to highlight alternatives to the idea that freedom can be achieved and defended through violence. In this Part, I will also explore alternatives to freedom exercised and expressed through violence that appear in the tradition. However, the idea of nonviolent self-rule requires a more extensive exploration because while various nonviolent forms of freedom are submerged in the Western tradition, the idea of nonviolent self-rule is undoubtedly the least developed of all. Arguably, it is a relatively new, non-Western, idea that challenges the core values of much of modern political thought. However, I do find some attempts to describe nonviolent rule and even, as we will see, in ancient thinkers claimed by the West. At any rate, while there are clearly effective nonviolent means to achieve liberation and there is a well-developed literature and powerful historical examples of nonviolence being used to defend freedom (I will add to the Roman example in the first part of chapter 8), the idea of nonviolent rule is less well developed. Thus, I devote almost the entirety of Part IV to answering the question: How can people rule themselves without violence?

Before answering this question, we must examine why and how people under-stand self-rule as requiring violence. The meanings of freedom that emerged in the fifth and fourth centuries BC in ancient Greece were diverse and contested. However, it was the claim to freedom articulated by the ancient Athenians that eventually came to dominate the political landscape of the period. In Pericles' (495–429 BC) vision of Athenian government and empire, we find the distinctive claim that democratic governance expresses itself in a form of martial courage. This idea of freedom was the preeminent ideological justification for Athens's attempt to best Sparta, and it will become a critical link between freedom and violence from that time to the present day.

When the Peloponnesian War (431–404 BC) ended in defeat for Athens, various challenges to this understanding of freedom emerged from within the city. I exam-ine the radical attempts to overturn and reinterpret Pericles' vision in Aristophanes's *Lysistrata*, Plato's *Menexenus*, and the *Apology*. Women, tragedians, and philoso-phers laid claim to a brand of courage and freedom that involved rejecting warfare or at least placed the courage to resist warfare and violence above martial pursuits. I then show how Aristotle's *Politics* responds to the challenge of philosophers and women to the Periclean ideal by offering a renewed version of patriarchal freedom. Aristotle's claim that slavery and warfare are only necessary means to a brand of political freedom that is distinguished from violence tries to preserve a close rela-tionship between empire, domination, and freedom, while sheltering Pericles' ideal from its critics.

ANCIENT GREEK FREEDOMS

In the fifth century BC, while the plebs of Rome were busy defending their lib-erty through a refusal to fight defensive wars, freedom became a watchword of the Greeks as a critical motivation for war. Kurt Raaflaub's extensive analysis of the meaning and use of the Greek word for freedom (*eleutheria*) tells the story of a fluid concept that was transformed by political dynamics and military posturing over the course of a century or more. The meaning of freedom proceeded through roughly three overlapping stages, eventually becoming a touchstone of political ideology and rhetoric.

First, by playing a critical role in repelling the Persian invasion at the battle of Marathon (490 BC), the Athenians had ensured that Greece would not be enslaved. As early as the *Iliad*, the Greeks spoke of war as "taking away the day of freedom," typically in reference to women being enslaved after defeat.[1] The victory over the Persians demonstrated the strength of Greek character (and the character of the Athenians in particular) because it required resisting the temptation to gain power

and influence as a satellite of the Persian Empire. Freedom and poverty were preferable to submission and riches.[2] As represented in the cult of Zeus Soter (Zeus the
Savior or Deliverer), the Athenians held themselves up as the savior of all of Greece
and on that basis began to build an empire.[3] Although later sources would connect
their victory over the Persians to Athenian civic ideals, the sources of this period do
not suggest that the Athenians had a well-developed sense of what freedom meant
when they repelled the Persians. Certainly, the idea that the Athenians had deliv-
ered freedom for Greece was not connected to a particular form of government,
since the institutions of the city-states of Greece in this period were highly varied.

This first meaning of freedom dovetailed with a second one that implied something more than simple freedom from slavery. The second meaning of freedom,
already in circulation at this time, was that a city had independence or equality.
As used by the Spartans in extending their influence, fighting for freedom meant
saving cities from outside enemies or their own tyrants and oligarchs. In this sense,
freedom was held up in contrast to slavery or severe inequality. Throughout the
Peloponnesian War, the Spartans effectively used the idea that they were the liberators of their fellow Greeks against Athenian demands for tribute and alliance.
Indeed, the Spartans had saved the Athenians themselves from the tyrant Hippias
in 508/7 BC.

However, the Athenians ousted the Spartan leaders in the name of yet another
brand of freedom. The idea of fighting for freedom was eventually transformed by
the Athenians into a third concept of freedom, one explicitly tied to their form of
government. Raaflaub speculates that this third meaning might have been inspired
by the encounter with the Persians. In the vast and unlimited power of the Persian
king, the Athenians may have seen a model of freedom that had an expansive and
positive meaning.[4] The Athenian understanding of freedom was also no doubt a
response to Spartan propaganda—the rhetorical debate over which side in the
Peloponnesian War was truly on the side of freedom.[5] It was almost certainly also
the result of a people with a penchant for deliberation trying to square their distinctive form of democracy with their imperial acquisitions. At any rate, this new meaning of freedom was expressed most forcefully by Pericles (c. 495–429 BC).

THE PERICLEAN IDEAL: POLITICAL FREEDOM
AND MARTIAL COURAGE

After the first year of the Peloponnesian War, the Athenians selected the great
orator, general, and the war's most persuasive champion to lament the loss of
those citizens who had sacrificed their lives in the effort against Sparta. Pericles'
Funeral Oration (431 BC), as recounted by Thucydides, has long been admired for

its loving description of Athenian democracy. From the very outset of the speech, Pericles says that his oration will be different because he will focus on the character of the city:

> I shall say nothing of the warlike deeds by which we acquired our power or the battles in which we or our fathers gallantly resisted our enemies, Greek or foreign. What I want to do is, in the first place, to discuss the spirit in which we faced our trials and also our constitution and the way of life, which has made us great.[6]

From the outset, it seems that Pericles is claiming that battles and war are only tangentially related to Athenian greatness. In this regard, Pericles' oration will be different from other wartime speeches. De-emphasizing Athens's penchant for violence, Pericles will chose to focus on its form of government.

Indeed, much of Pericles' description of Athens conveys a character inconsistent with a militaristic ethos. In contrast to the comingling of war and citizenship among the Spartans, the Athenians do not train for war from childhood. They pride themselves on enjoying the good things in life, the pleasures of the world such as food, games, and festivals, and they respect each other's private endeavors. Each citizen is "able to show himself the rightful lord and owner of his own person."[7] Indeed, the liberality of the city and its openness to foreign observers may at times be a military disadvantage.[8] Here we might expect Pericles to argue that the war is important nonetheless and must be continued because 1) the Athenian form of government makes its people free, and 2) the war is the critical means for preserving—or defending—that government and, thereby, freedom.

But Pericles makes a very different kind of argument, insisting that along with their private endeavors, what truly distinguishes Athenian citizens is their capacity for politics.

> Here each individual is interested not only in his own affairs but in the affairs of the state as well: even those who are mostly occupied with their own business are extremely well-informed on general politics—this is a peculiarity of ours: we do not say that man who takes no interest in politics is a man who minds his own business; we say that he has no business here at all.[9]

In the distinctive Athenian form of direct democracy, nearly every male citizen was tasked with some public duty or office over the course of his life, and all were eligible to vote and participate in the assembly. Pericles reminds his audience that the demands of this democracy reflect a special capacity for political deliberation and judgment.

Here is where the Athenian's capacity for exercising violence and the character of the city come together. The Athenian's political character is not set in contrast to their military prowess. Instead, Pericles argues that it is its essential ingredient. The passage above continues:

> We Athenians, in our own persons, take our decisions on policy or submit them to proper discussions: for we do not think that there is an incompatibility between words and deeds; the worst thing is to rush into action before the consequences have been properly debated. We are capable at the same time of taking risks and of estimating them beforehand. Others are brave out of ignorance; and, when they stop to think, they begin to fear.[10]

A critical theme in Roman and modern political thought is the claim that, in times of emergency, one individual or a very small group must be given decision-making powers in order to act decisively. For the Roman republic, wars required the temporary appointment of dictators. Pericles here refutes the view that democratic rule and decisive action are incompatible. Debate may slow down action, but it also leads to a particular brand of courage.

The brand of courage that emanates from a deliberative body that knows how to rule itself—that self-consciously chooses to fight—is superior to other forms of courage. Moreover, the Athenian enjoyment of the good things in life, while in earlier passages disassociated from militarism, actually contributes to this superior courage.

> There are certain advantages, I think, in our way of meeting danger voluntarily, with an easy mind, instead of with laborious training, with natural rather than with state-induced courage. We do not have to spend our time practicing to meet sufferings which are still in the future; and when they are actually upon us we show ourselves just as brave as these others who are always in strict training.[11]

The Athenians enjoy a good life, yet they are willing to sacrifice that good life if need be. Spartan citizens do not have as much to lose and they do not decide when to fight and what to risk. So in fact both elements of the distinctive Athenian way of life—private liberties and public freedoms—provide the foundation for a special brand of martial prowess.

Pericles is not arguing that courage secures, delivers, or saves the Athenians from slavery. At the height of their empire and only a year into the war, such an outcome was probably not much of a worry for the Athenians. The special brand of courage Pericles is describing is the quintessential exercise and expression of Athenian freedom. The Athenians "do not need the praises of Homer,"[12] he explains, because the war shows their spirit to the world. Pericles says that Athens is an "education to Greece"[13] and that, unlike other empires, "no subject can complain of being governed by people unfit for their responsibilities."[14] The war is proof positive of their greatness, which lies in their ability to dominate others as an extension of their ability to rule themselves.

The connection between Athens's sense of its own freedom and its assertion that it was superior to those they dominated has been much remarked upon in scholarship of this period. To a certain extent, Raaflaub is correct when he says the "only freedom that really counted for Athens was its own. By realizing it in such absolute ways, it turned freedom into tyranny."[15] Yet this formulation obscures the fact that this sense of superiority was not a consequence of simple self-serving behavior or myopia regarding the needs and interests of others. The Athenians understood themselves as superior to other Greeks and non-Greeks and they did not hesitate to exploit them for their own benefit. However, this sense of superiority was not linked—or at least not exclusively linked—with being born Athenian. The very idea that Athens could be an example to others meant that Pericles understood Athens as demonstrating and awakening a brand of freedom that might be imitated. In fact, says Raaflaub, it was an "irresistible model" for other Greek cities.[16]

Courage does not preserve freedom—they are one and the same.[17] Jacqueline de Romilly remarks that Pericles' sense of superior Athenian freedom made ruling over themselves and ruling over others "complementary."[18] Indeed, while Pericles generally focuses on the external expression of freedom, he states in the funeral oration that Athenian freedom also animates the rule of law. Athenians obey those whom they put in positions of power just as those they conquer obey them.[19] One might go so far as to say that the reason Athenians obey themselves is the same reason they are able to elicit obedience among others: because they are free and fit to rule.

Thucydides seems to think that the brand of freedom Pericles describes is sustainable and praiseworthy, and that it was the more explicitly imperious vision of Athenian rule that marked a devolution of the Periclean ideal. Modern republican thinkers were often wary of the Athenian model because it seemed to beget instability and war. Contemporary historians and commentators are divided about the extent to which Pericles' vision can be held responsible for the subsequent downfall of Athens. I only want to point to the fact that the Periclean vision is seductive for good reason. Pericles not only manages to make democracy and empire consistent, he also makes the exercise of self-rule inseparable from ruling over those who have not adopted similar values and practices.

ATHENIAN WOMEN AND FREEDOM FROM WAR

Yet even as waging war on the unfree was seen to be a natural extension of public freedom, the eventual defeat of the Athenians raised hard questions about the Periclean vision from within Athenian society itself. In 415 BC, fifteen years after Pericles commemorated the first year of the war, the Athenians sent a fleet of ships to defend an ally in Sicily, where they suffered a devastating defeat at the hands of the Spartans. The disastrous Sicilian expedition, the toll of years of war, and Athens's eventual defeat produced uncertainty, dissolution, and dissent. The extant sources suggest that dissent took a variety of forms, but undoubtedly much has been lost to time, especially when we consider the written record tends to de-emphasize the role of women and the nearly half of Athenian society that was enslaved.[20] Yet there is some evidence that women undermined the war effort, and sure signs that male authorities feared their efforts to do so.

At the end of Pericles' Funeral Oration, he remarks cryptically that the duty of the widows of slain soldiers is to embody "the greatest glory of a woman," which is "to be least talked about by men, whether they are praising you or criticizing you."[21] Advising someone to avoid being criticized is not particularly noteworthy, but in asking women to avoid being *praised* in response to their husband's deaths, Pericles betrays anxiety about the potential ability of widows to win public sympathy because of their sacrifice. Yet the construction of his advice also reveals just how confident Pericles is of continued male dominance of Athenian culture. He does not consider the possibility that the widows will disrupt the war effort directly. Instead, the only possible way for widows to enter the public sphere is to be talked about by men—and he urges them to be true to their sex by remaining undiscussed in politics. Along with these instructions, he pledges state support for the widows until their children come of age.

In these passages, Pericles may have had in mind the kind of political dynamics portrayed in a tragedy performed ten years prior to open hostilities. In the midst of Athenian efforts to consolidate their empire, Sophocles' *Antigone* figured a strong woman defying a king who fails to pay proper attention to the burial rites of her slain brother. Antigone wins over the people and King Creon loses his son and regrets challenging feminine authority in religious matters and burial rites. Pericles and Sophocles not only served together in positions of military leadership during the suppression of Samos (just after *Antigone* was staged), but Pericles was undoubtedly well aware of the basic themes of the play. The final passages of his Funeral Oration try to preempt the rise of an Antigone. However, Antigone's claims remain firmly in the realm of religious festival and proper rites, the only formal public role for women in Athens. Strikingly, while radically upending male authority and attempting to place limits on the prerogatives of the state, Antigone never claims a right to freedom.

The contrast is startling if we look to the comedies that follow on the destruction of the Athenian fleet three decades later. In *Lysistrata* (411 BC), Aristophanes (446—c. 386 BC) stages what can only be described as a satirical re-founding of Athens. The play is famous for its conceit of a sexual strike whereby the leading women of Greek cities refuse to consort with men until they stop the war. Led by the Athenian Lysistrata and in cooperation with the Spartan Lampito, the women not only withhold sex, but also take possession of the state treasury through the physical occupation of the Acropolis in order to prevent expenditures on war.

The play is a broad indictment of the violence of Greek men. Not only do the women aim to stop the war, they assume that their sexual strike will be met by attempts to rape them. Debating strategies to resist their husbands, they proceed to the Acropolis,[22] where the old men of Athens attempt to burn them alive.[23] The men repeatedly tell the women to be silent, and a magistrate threatens to beat them if they continue to speak.[24] The play suggests that not only is the Peloponnesian War waged at the expense of women, but that men are waging war upon women directly.[25]

While the men of the city constantly threaten violence against the women, the women respond with a combination of action and restraint. The play makes clear that women are just as capable of violence as men.[26] However, in the course of the play they wield power by teasing and taunting, by patience and persistence, and by occasionally threatening violence. They literally douse the old men's attempts to burn them alive with water. They convert many of the magistrate's officers over to their side.[27] For the most part, they show leniency, even as the men act with unbounded violence. The strike and occupation of the Acropolis are successful. Lysistrata finally gets to speak her mind, and she makes the case for ending the war and outlines the peace.

In its description of the attempts of the old men of Athens to remove the women from the treasury, the play recalls the origin of Athenian democracy a century earlier. Sometime around 508/507 BC, the citizens of Athens, acting self-consciously as "a people" (*demos*) founded a new brand of government. It was the first democracy in history, at least among a sizable population. In that revolution, the Spartans had occupied the Acropolis. Cleisthenes would eventually implement the reforms that would make for the first democracy, but the removal of the Spartans from the Acropolis seems to have been done by the people themselves while Cleisthenes was exiled. The play makes reference to the moment when the Athenians acted as a people, showing themselves capable of freedom and self-rule. According to Herodotus, the Athenians removed the Spartans and their leader Cleomenes over the course of a three-day siege and eventually put some of the conspirators to death. However, he also records that Cleomenes was met on the Acropolis by a priestess who warned him not to enter because only Athenians belonged there. There is no record of a battle, military commanders, or even bloodshed in the taking of the Acropolis itself. Instead, a truce allows most of the Spartans to leave unharmed. This is notable in that Cleomenes had taken the Acropolis by force and responded by attempting to raise an army to take it by force again.[28]

By reenacting the founding of democratic Athens, the play undercuts the Periclean suggestion that Athenian men are more capable of self-rule and self-control than Athenian women or non-Athenians. Performing before a war-weary audience, the women who occupy the Acropolis are heroes, while the old men who once founded the democracy are portrayed as now overly enamored with violence and war. The radical edge of the comedy also suggests that Athenian and Spartan women are in cahoots with one another. If Pericles says that the brand of freedom adopted by Athenian men can be imitated, Lysistrata responds by saying that it can be done even better by a cross-section of Greek women.

Aristophanes' female characters explicitly say they are going to reclaim and reform the Athenian idea of freedom. As radical as Antigone's actions are, she is unable to convince others—even her own sister—to act with her. Lysistrata challenges male authority in the public realm directly. She says: "I'm a free woman, I."[29] Her effort to organize the women and keep them from having sex with their husbands is not easy. There is no suggestion in the play that women are generally less desirous of sex than men and there are some defectors. However, the women show themselves more capable of self-control than the men, and they show that the women of many different cities can join together in coordinated action, using peaceful and democratic means to create their Pan-Hellenic alliance.[30] The old men of Athens are not the opponents of tyranny they claim to be.[31] Instead, the assembled women tell them directly that they are frauds because war is not an expression of freedom but a threat to all of their lives.[32]

Lysistrata is a comic rendering of transgressive acts by free women aiming to end a war and overturn the dominance of men in the public sphere. Even if the events in the play are entirely fantastical (and the play itself would have been performed entirely by men), the context in which it was performed—shortly after the worst Athenian losses of the war—would have given the themes unmistakable political and personal relevance for the audience. Indeed, given the assumptions about women's roles reflected in Pericles' oration, the claims the female characters make in the play seem to have been almost unthinkable a generation earlier.

The play may also contain within it a hint of real historical events.[33] On the eve of the Syracuse expedition, all of the herms in the city were vandalized. The herms of Athens were statues consisting of a head (originally of the god Hermes), a stone slab, and an erect penis and testicles. The statues marked the boundaries of public and private spaces. The destruction of the herms was shocking, a bad omen that spread fears of conspirators residing within the city. Alcibiades, an ardent proponent of the war and one of three generals appointed to lead the Athenian expedition, demanded to be put on trial when some accused him of being responsible. The true culprits remained a mystery.

Eva Keuls speculates that *Lysistrata*'s reference to the destruction of the herms, the degree of organization it must have taken to destroy hundreds of statues without being detected, Aristophanes' trilogy of plays depicting female political revolt against war, and the fact that no one was ever put on trial, suggests the women of Athens may have been responsible. When the men appear on stage in *Lysistrata* with erections as a result of the sexual strike, the chorus warns them to cover themselves with tunics lest the herm choppers (Ἑρμοκοπίδης) catch sight of them.[34] Aristophanes's comedy *Thesmophoriazusai*, produced later the same year, again depicted women taking control of the city's governance. Drawing on various forms of textual and archeological evidence, Keuls establishes that the mutilation of the herms must have involved chopping the penises off of the statues. Finally, she argues that prominent male opponents of the war would have been able to register their opposition to the expedition in the Assembly, as was already represented in the well-respected views of Nikias.[35] The women of Athens would not have had this outlet, giving them the motive to carry off the destruction of the herms.

Whether or not Aristophanes's comedies make reference to real events, they articulate a powerful critique and provide a robust alternative to the Periclean ideal. His vision of women united by a disgust for war and capable of self-control and self-rule across political rivalries may have seemed more comedic than realistic at the time. But given Athenian losses, a radical alternative to unending war that included women who were savvy and stalwart in their efforts to subdue the worst desires of men must have had great appeal. When Lysistrata is called upon to give a speech that will encourage a peace treaty with the Spartans at the end of the play, the comedic overtones recede. She reminds the Lacedaemonians that the Athenians saved them from Messenia, and reminds the Athenians that the Spartans once freed them from the tyrant Hippias.[36] She reminds them that they all worship the same gods, and yet go about destroying each other's cities while the barbarians threaten all of Greece.[37]

PHILOSOPHICAL COURAGE AS AN ALTERNATIVE BRAND
OF FREEDOM

There is some dispute about the extent to which Socrates (470/469–399 BC) and Plato (424/423–348/347 BC) can be understood as critics of war. As the progenitor of the Western philosophical tradition, the importance of the Socratic legacy is unquestioned and his philosophic practices are often portrayed as consistent with the martial spirit of Athens. Socrates fought in the Peloponnesian War and his name means Sure Strength.[38] Plato educated tyrants, and both Socrates and Plato point to the faults and paradoxes of democratic regimes and Athens in particular. However, many interpreters also point out that Socrates modeled an early form of civil disobedience in his trial and death, and that his students, Plato in particular, openly questioned Athenian imperial tendencies. Moreover, Socrates's conduct can be understood as deeply invested in bolstering and improving democracy.[39] My aim is to show that both Socrates and Plato offer a resounding critique of war, while also attempting to upend the Periclean ideal of freedom.[40]

Their critique may very well grow out of those offered by women in Ancient Athens. In her analysis, Keuls mentions that Socrates was a friend of women, noted for his "cordial and respectful dealings with priestesses and courtesans," including Pericles' companion Aspasia (c. 470 BC–c. 400 BC).[41] His student Plato would be among the first to write that women were equally capable of ruling as men. The association between women and the origins of philosophy is particularly poignant in Platonic dialogues that offer a critique of war.

The most directly pertinent text in the Platonic corpus is the *Menexenus*. Written in the third decade of the fourth century BC, some two generations after Pericles' funeral oration, the *Menexenus* does something even the most outrageous satirists and comedians of our time would be hesitant to do: it spoofs a funeral for Athenian soldiers. Both the complicity and the ire of women during war time are front and center in the work, because although Socrates recites the oration, he says that he is reciting what he heard from Aspasia. The gender confusion throughout the text—the uncertainty about whether a woman or a man is giving the speech—mirrors the general uncertainty as to whether the speech is praising the virtues of the soldiers of Athens in earnest or indicting their foolishness in fighting a series of unending wars.

There is little doubt that the oration intends to skewer a justification for war grounded in the purportedly superior Athenian character, and specifically in their capacity for political freedom. The speech beings by recounting the previous two centuries of Athenian wars, affirming a core theme of Pericles' oration, that the distinction of the Athenian constitution lies in the fact that each citizen is of equal birth. Plato writes:

> these men themselves, having been nobly born and nurtured in full freedom, showed forth a multitude of beautiful deeds to all men in public and private, considering it necessary to fight in behalf of freedom: to fight with Greeks in behalf of other Greeks and with Barbarians in behalf of all the Greeks.[42]

Yet as the speech recounts the history of wars fought on behalf of freedom, the purportedly great deeds of the Athenians are revealed to be grounded in selfish-ness, short-sightedness, and greed, and they are shown to be altogether inconsistent with the ability to rule themselves peacefully. The speech recounts the war with the Persians, the war with the Spartans, and finally the Athenian civil war.

Through a tongue-in-cheek celebration of their victory at Marathon (490 BC), the speech of Socrates/Aspasia highlights three ways in which the Athenian confronta-tion with the Persians is inconsistent with the Periclean ideal. First, consistent with Raaflaub's theory that the Athenians imitated the Persians, the speech suggests that not only did the Persian King Cyrus attempt to enslave others, but also through his own spirited action "freed his fellow citizens."[43] Even in a war with barbarians, one people's freedom is another's slavery. Second, the Periclean ideal of demo-cratic citizens ruling themselves suggests that the multitude is most capable of self-government. Yet the story of the harrowing victory at Marathon is one where "every multitude and all wealth yields to virtue."[44] The Athenian victory was great because so few defeated so many, suggesting a deeply undemocratic brand of rule. Finally, the example set by the Athenians was not one where freedom is prized over all else. Instead, in the war with the Persians, the Athenians "dared to risk the battles that came afterward in defense of their own safety."[45] To defend one's own safety does not require much courage. Thus the speech suggests that in setting this example for all of Greece, the Athenians sowed the seeds of their own destruction by showing other Greeks how to resist the imperial designs of those who would subdue them.

In the second set of wars, with their fellow Greeks, the Athenians were also fight-ing for freedom—or so the speech claims. Here the speech co-opts the language of the Spartans, trying to erase the Spartan's claim to be the true liberators of Greece with such blatant and overwrought hyperbole that the passages can only be meant as satire of Athenian rhetoric.

> After the Persian Wars, [the Athenians] were the ones who first came to the aid of Greeks against Greeks in behalf of freedom. They were good men, and set free those whom they aided. And they were the first to be honored by the

city and buried in this tomb. After this many wars broke out, and the whole of Greece came in arms against us, ravaging the land and paying ill gratitude to our city.[46]

We know that this depiction is wrong, since the Spartans were more commonly viewed as liberators and the Athenians more commonly viewed as imperialists exacting tribute. But the speech goes even further, suggesting that much of Greece would rather have been ruled by the Persians.[47] In the name of freedom, the Athenians inspired uprisings all over the Greek world. The freedom and so-called virtue of the Athenians set Greek against Greek, filling the graves of the cities with good men.

But the irony of Athenian claims to special virtue in their capacity for freedom and self-rule only comes into full view when the speech lauds the valor of Athenians in their own civil war. Socrates/Aspasia says that only Athenians could have a civil war that was consistent with a deep sense of kinship (and friendship) among citizens. Indeed, "our civil war arose and was fought in such a way that if it were fated for men to stand in party strife, there is no one who would not pray that his own city should suffer such illness in a similar manner."[48] Even as their wars divide barbarian from Greek, Greek from Greek, and eventually Athenian from Athenian, the view that Athenians are virtuous is maintained. In particular, all of these wars, no matter what their cost or result, demonstrate the virtues of Athenians as a free people. The speech takes direct aim at the Athenian orators who will not be dissuaded from upholding the Periclean ideal, irrespective of how many dead soldiers it produces.[49]

The spectacle of a civil war means that the speaker is now confronted with a problem. How can one still be fighting for freedom when the free become enemies of the free? The attempt to recover the Athenian claim to freedom involves recounting a final war against the Spartans that follows immediately on the civil war. In a passage that presages the essentialist arguments of modern nationalism, Socrates/Aspasia makes an argument for Athenian virtues grounded in claims about bloodlines and kinship. Eventually Athenians gave up trying to free their fellow Greeks, because they were too ungrateful. This left the way open for the Spartans to enslave all of Greece.[50] Yet once the Athenians had rebuilt their walls and their navy, they could not stand by and let the Spartans destroy the Parians:

We alone did not dare to swear and betray them, so firm and healthy is the nobility and freedom of this city, hating Barbarians by nature because we are purely Greek and unmixed stock. There dwells among us no stock from Pelops, nor Cadmus, nor Egyptus, nor Danaus, nor the many others who are Greek by law but Barbarian by nature. Greeks ourselves, we live unmixed with Barbarians, whence arises the pure hatred in our city of alien natures.[51]

The Athenian claim is an obvious lie. First, Pericles himself describes how Athens is open to the world and how foreigners mingle among Athenians. Second, Athenians had offspring with their slaves, who were from all over Greece and beyond. Finally, near the end of the Peloponnesian War it seems that many slaves were offered manumission if they served in the army or navy.[52] This was due to the dwindling numbers of freeborn men capable of fighting. In this way, Socrates/Aspasia underscores a critical contradiction in the Periclean ideal: Pericles says that all of Greece should imitate the Athenians, and yet claims that Athenians have a special penchant for freedom. If the Athenians are not a special stock, they have no business subjugating others. If the Athenians are a special stock, their self-destructive exercise of freedom has led to results that complicate and upend the distinction between the free and unfree. In the last line of the speech, Socrates reminds us that Aspasia is a Milesian. Hence we do not even know whether the author of this speech praising Athenian virtues and freedom is Athenian.[53]

Writing *Menexenus* was an act of political courage on the part of Plato. The text itself reflects this bravery when Menexenus and Socrates discuss the speech in the brief postscript. Socrates asks Menexenus not to tell others what he has shared with him, so that he can repeat other speeches of Aspasia at some later date. By highlighting that his is a private recounting of a public funeral oration, that its author may be a woman, and that such a radical expression of dissenting views should be kept secret, Socrates strongly suggests that women and philosophers were operating together in the private sphere to undermine what they thought to be harmful militaristic values.

Historians have sometimes questioned whether *Menexenus* is actually a Platonic text, in part because of its blasphemous content. However, if we think of it as an act of philosophical courage, it is perhaps the text where Plato most directly lives up to the challenge laid down by his teacher Socrates. In the *Apology*, Socrates defends himself from the charges of corrupting the youth and worshiping unsanctioned gods. As Plato recounts it, a critical aspect of his defense is an attempt to co-opt and transform the Periclean ideal.

A direct reference to freedom appears only once in the *Apology*, but it appears at a critical juncture. When he is convicted and sentenced to die, Socrates says that he might have persuaded the jury of his innocence but for his lack of shamelessness, which other citizens in his position often display. He explains:

> I did not then think it necessary to do anything unworthy of a free man because of danger; I do not now regret so having conducted my defense; and I would far rather die with that defense than live with the other. Neither in court of law nor in war ought I or any man contrive to escape death by any

means possible. Often in battle it becomes clear that a man may escape death by throwing down his arms and turning in supplication to his pursuers; and there are many other devices for each of war's dangers, so that one can avoid dying if he is bold enough to say and do anything whatever. It is not difficult to escape death, Gentlemen; it is more difficult to escape wickedness, for wickedness runs faster than death.[54]

In one sense, Socrates upholds the Periclean ideal in this passage by affirming that free men express their worth through a willingness to sacrifice their lives. In another sense, he upends the ideal, strongly condemning his accusers, the jury, and by extension all of Athens for conduct unbecoming of freedom. To Socrates, freedom means telling the truth and acting in a way that is consistent with justice—or at least trying to avoid injustice. Socrates claims that his conscience—his inner voice—has not once "at any point in my argument in anything I was about to say" opposed him.[55] By contrast, he suggests that few Athenians have the courage to speak in a court of law in a way that does not serve their direct interests. If freedom means caring for one's soul, most Athenians seem incapable of this act of caring. By abiding by his conscience, Socrates is free.

That Socrates makes any claims about freedom might be considered surprising given his frequently expressed skepticism about democracy. In the *Apology*, he remarks that a just man will not survive long in a democracy.[56] Moreover, his claim that everyone should be willing to sacrifice their lives to speak the truth and pursue justice can perhaps be made consistent with the idea of fighting a just war. However, as part and parcel of his critique of Athenian orators, Socrates's attempt to refashion the character of freedom, along with his claims about the ways in which it is connected with courage, must be meant to raise questions about the Periclean ideal. The *Menexenus* spoofs Athenian orators for wrapping narrow self-interest, dissention, and death in the cloak of freedom. The *Apology* takes the idea that freedom is more important than physical life seriously, but indicts all of Athens for misunderstanding what freedom really means and failing to live in a way that is worthy of it.

POLITICAL RULE AND SLAVERY: ARISTOTLE'S PATRIARCHAL FREEDOM

While holding up freedom as its preeminent value, Athens was one of the only full-fledged slave societies in the ancient world. Along with a handful of Greek city-states, the other most important slave society in the ancient world was republican Rome. In the modern era, the most prominent slave societies included the United States, Brazil, and the Caribbean states, which drove demand in the transatlantic slave trade.[57] The paradox is stark. Democracies and republics have been the most prominent slavers in the history of the world. Aristotle's explanation for why Athens was a slave society provides the most often cited explanation for this paradox. He claims that in order for a large number of citizens to participate in political rule, another large portion of the population had to be confined to the household. Even strident critics of sovereignty, such as Hannah Arendt, and slavery, such as Karl Marx, affirm that only when some people were forced to tend to the basic needs of the city could others have the leisure required for politics.[58]

Aristotle's arguments for the natural and beneficial aspects of slavery might be considered mature reflections on a society that, for a time, fully embraced the Periclean ideal. Writing in the *Politics*, he claims that some are naturally fit to rule while others are naturally fit to be ruled, and that this fact is a ubiquitous feature of all life. Masters rule slaves, statesmen rule citizens, people rule animals, males rule females, and parents rule children. In each case, if it is done well and accords with the natural abilities of each, ruling benefits both rulers and ruled. In the same way, ruling is also a part of the internal life of each individual person. When reason rules appetite and the soul rules the body, it is to the benefit of the whole person, when the reverse is true the results are "evil and unnatural."[59] Taken together, these dyads of rule make the reasonable male citizen the central figure who guides the household, the polis, and the natural world. Describing the Athenian experience, Aristotle depicts a broadly encompassing patriarchy where free men rule over others for the benefit of all.

Aristotle describes the head of household, citizen, and sometimes statesman as a person for whom ruling is a feature of all of his relationships. Broadly speaking, the distinguishing characteristic of the naturally fit (male) citizen is that he has a greater share of virtue than the women, slaves, children, and animals over whom he rules. (Aristotle draws direct parallels between slaves, animals, and the needs of the body: "We may thus conclude that all men who differ from others as much as the body differs from the soul, or an animal from a man . . . are by nature slaves."[60]) Higher natures are associated with reason and manliness. Lower orders are associated with the body, femininity, and animals. Consistent with Pericles' view, the most important activity of the free man comes in his dealings with other free men. Just as Pericles argues that what distinguishes Athenians is that each citizen takes part in politics, Aristotle's model citizens are designed by nature for political rule. Some eight decades after Pericles' Funeral Oration, Aristotle transforms his effort to laud the "peculiar" feature of Athenian citizens into the human quality par excellence. Indeed, Aristotle—perhaps not surprisingly given that he was not an

Athenian—suggests that the Greek penchant for believing barbarians are only "well born" relative to their own context, is myopic and parochial.[61]

However, Aristotle reformulates the connection between being free and ruling over others. Unlike Pericles, he claims that a man's ability to fight wars and enslave inferior people is not a natural extension of or way of exercising *political* rule. Although "ruling" is a feature of all of the free man's relationships, different kinds of ruling are qualitatively different from one another. That is, in ruling one's fellow citizens, women, slaves, children, and animals, each requires something different. Political rule is distinguished from all the others by the fact it is not a relation of dominance or necessity. Aristotle writes:

> There is rule of the sort which is exercised by a master; and by this we mean the sort of rule connected with the necessary functions of life. . . . But there is also a rule of the sort which is exercised by those who are similar in birth to the ruler, and are similarly free. Rule of this sort is what we call political rule.[62]

When masters rule slaves, they do not need knowledge of how slaves labor. Meeting the basic needs of the household only requires that masters provide direction to slaves. However, political rule requires knowledge of both how to rule and how to be ruled. Political rule involves equal citizens taking turns ruling and being ruled by one another, and when ruling, exercising practical reason.[63] This reciprocal relationship, says Aristotle, is freedom.[64] The rule of masters over slaves is for the purpose of the "necessary functions of life," while the rule of citizens over other equal citizens is an expression of the highest form of human togetherness (a flourishing life of reasonable and free men).

This contrast between slave rule and political rule at first may appear to offer a stark challenge to the Periclean ideal. It would seem that dominating others with violence and ruling others reasonably and freely are two very different kinds of activities, and not the natural extension of each other that Pericles describes. Indeed, Aristotle denigrates the rule of masters over slaves, along with the acquisition of slaves through warfare. Although a master's virtue is what makes him fit to rule over slaves, the specific knowledge required for such rule "is something which has no great or majestic character: the master must simply know how to command what the slave must know how to do."[65] In fact, "the life of a free individual is better than that of the master of any number of slaves. There is nothing very dignified in managing slaves . . . and giving orders about menial duties has nothing fine about it."[66] Aristotle also joins Plato in critiquing the bellicose Spartan constitution for confusing acquiring goods (including slaves) with goodness. They "did not know how to use their leisure," he says of the Spartans, once they had an empire.[67] Aristotle says that when it "comes to politics most people appear to believe that mastery is the true statesmanship; and they are not ashamed of behaving to others in ways which they would refuse to acknowledge as just, or even expedient, among themselves." However, Aristotle avers that a just and free constitution might in theory do away entirely with military pursuits, which although they are "one and all to be counted good" are "not the chief end of man, transcending all other ends: they are [only] means to his chief end."[68]

Moreover, in an apparent effort to encourage better treatment of slaves, Aristotle tries to further distinguish the rule of slaves from their acquisition in warfare. He writes that the "task of producing in the slave the sort of goodness we have been discussing belongs to the master of the household ... This is why those who withhold reason from slaves, and argue that only command should be employed, are making a mistake: admonition ought to be applied to slaves even more than it is to children."[69] (Aristotle worries that children will be corrupted by slaves and recommends corporal punishment as a way of setting them straight when they use any of the slaves' bad language.[70]) This distinction may also be a concession to Plato, as the dialogue *Meno* demonstrates that a slave has the capacity for reason. The rule of masters over slaves, according to Aristotle, is best conducted not by "legal sanction or superior power,"[71] but by goodness and natural capacity for rule.

Aristotle's arguments are not meant to do away with the Periclean ideal. They are an effort to respond to the proto-feminist and philosophical challenges described above as well as another challenge to Pericles' vision of freedom. There is no evidence that there were thoroughgoing critics of slavery in ancient Greece. But Aristotle's work is perhaps the best indication that questions were being raised about its legitimacy, at least in certain cases. Whereas previous thinkers rarely broach the topic, the first books of the *Politics* are preoccupied with arguing that slavery is natural and just. Aristotle writes that, contrary to nature's intention, slaves can sometimes have a freeman's soul.[72] The fact that noble souls are occasionally enslaved is due to the fact that it is "not as easy to see the beauty of the soul as it is to see that of the body."[73] Not only does Aristotle uncouple slave rule and political rule, he also acknowledges that on some occasions the wrong people might be enslaved.

Yet it turns out that the distinction between ruling slaves and acquiring slaves provides the key to how one might ensure that those who are naturally slaves take their rightful place. Aristotle says that someone is "a slave by nature if he is capable of becoming the property of another."[74] There is one way to discover whether or not someone is so capable: warfare. He writes:

[A]ll animals have been made by nature for the sake of men. It also follows that the art of war is in some sense a natural mode of acquisition. Hunting is a part of that art; and hunting ought to be practiced, not only against wild animals, but also against human beings who are intended by nature to be ruled by others and refuse to obey that intention, because this sort of war is naturally just.[75]

When those who are naturally slavish refuse to obey, justice requires making war upon them. Political rule, reason, and freedom are distinguishable from the rule of slaves, but they are also founded on a bedrock of physical domination, whereby those who are naturally less fit are placed in their subordinate position. Previously, Aristotle has said that tame animals are more gentle than wild animals, and that the tame get the benefit of being preserved through man's stewardship.[76] The same is true of unruly people who refuse to be guided by more virtuous people. Even here, Aristotle is quick to compare animals and slaves and make a distinction between the two modes of acquisition. Suggesting a kind of *jus in bello*, he reminds his readers that although slaves are like animals, people should not be hunted "to furnish a banquet or a festival." Only wild animals—not slaves—are to be eaten.[77]

I mentioned above that political rule is distinguished from all of the others because it is not a relationship of dominance. However, at times Aristotle suggests that the rule of men over women is in a similar category. He says that female citizens must be taken into account by the laws because they comprise half of the free population,[78] and because the relationship of a man to his wife is like that of a statesman to a citizen.[79] That is (perhaps under the influence of his teacher Plato), Aristotle at least takes into consideration the possibility that free women have the same capabilities as free men.

However, over the course of the *Politics* it becomes clear that while offering Pericles' Athenian critics some concessions, the primary aim of Aristotle's effort is to recover the main elements of the Periclean ideal. In the following passage, we see him taking on Socrates and Plato—and specifically singling out their understanding of the proper role of women—in an effort to reconstruct a vision of freedom linked to a brand of patriarchal courage.

It is thus clear that while moral goodness is a quality of all those mentioned [slaves, children, women], the fact still remains that temperance—and similarly courage and justice—are not, as Socrates held, the same in a woman as they are in a man. One kind of courage is concerned with ruling, the other with serving; and the same is true of the other forms of goodness.... To speak in general terms, and to maintain that goodness consists in "a good condition of the soul," or in "right action," or in anything of the kind, is to be guilty of self-deception. Far better than such general definitions is the method of simple enumeration of the different forms of goodness, as followed by Gorgias. We must therefore hold that what the poet said of women "A modest silence is a woman's crown" contains a general truth—but a truth which does not apply to men.[80]

Here the core of the Periclean ideal is restated in a way that responds to the robust challenge of women and philosophers. The courage of free women is not like the courage of free men. When women are silent, it is a virtue, and if they were to have the courage to speak as a man, they would be considered a gossip.[81] The souls of men and women are not the same.[82] Moreover, it is Socrates who forwards the mistaken view that there is one sort of virtue and therefore one sort of (sexless) soul that can be rightly understood as free and courageous. That Socrates, a Platonic dialogue, and the issue of the status of women are all connected in this passage confirms that Aristotle perceived his teachers and women as allied in opposition to the values he seeks to defend.

One might argue that Aristotle's version of patriarchal courage is not the same as that of Pericles because for Aristotle the courage of free men consists of speaking and ruling with other free men as opposed to a brand of martial courage. Yet the distinction becomes increasingly tenuous when Aristotle says that the "relation of the male to the female is permanently that in which the statesman stands to his fellow citizens."[83] Despite the fact that the very essence of political rule is the practice of both ruling and being ruled, it turns out that the so-called political rule of husband and wife is more like that of the Egyptian king Amasis over his subjects. Women will naturally desire to be equal to their husbands (as true political rule demands), but the husband must "establish a difference, in outward forms, in modes of address, and in titles of respect" that places him permanently above the wife.[84] In keeping with his arguments establishing the foundation of political rule in dominance and warfare, and with the fact that most slaves would have been women, Aristotle is brought much closer to Pericles than it might at first appear. We can put it this way: Aristotle's technical distinctions between different kinds of rule avoid some of the pitfalls of the Periclean ideal. He describes a notion of political rule that does not find its ultimate expression and proper exercise in violence or martial courage. Yet at the same time, he attempts to stabilize and more firmly establish the connection between political freedom and dominance, warfare, and subjugation.

Two final points underscore the fact that Aristotle is well aware that he is pushing back against the proto-feminist challenge to the Periclean ideal, while also offering his own distinctive brand of patriarchal freedom. First, Aristotle is less enamored with the Athenian brand of democracy than Pericles. Pericles mentions in the funeral oration that Athenians "do not get into a state with [a] next-door neighbor if he enjoys himself in his own way."[85] By the middle of the fourth century, it seems that the idea that freedom involves not only political rule but "living as you like" is more firmly established. Yet whereas Pericles portrays private freedom in a favorable light, Aristotle associates such freedom with slaves, women, and children being allowed more leeway in an extreme form of democracy similar to tyranny.[86] Second, Aristotle associates the increasing political influence of women with overly militaristic societies. In a sense his argument affirms the story I have tried to tell in this chapter, that women come to political power as a result of overly bellicose men. But for Aristotle it is not the bellicose men who are in the wrong, but the women coming to rule. Using Sparta as an example, he says that while men are away fighting for their city, women begin to take over the city. "Even in the matter of courage, which is useless in all life's ordinary affairs and only of use, if it has a use, in time of war, the women of Sparta have had a most mischievous influence."[87] He goes on to say, that the Spartan women refused to submit to the law of Lycurgus in contrast to the more disciplined men returning from war. One cannot help but wonder if it is Athens that Aristotle has in mind in his diagnosis of a city that has become too licentious and too free in a particular way.

We might be tempted, as many have, to excuse Aristotle's attempt to associate patriarchy and slaveholding freedom as anachronistic or as the best possible way of conducting politics given the material and social constraints of his time. However, we have the benefit of knowing that proto-feminist and philosophical challenges to public and patriarchal authority preceded him. Aristotle's patriarchal freedom is not originary, but reactionary. His magisterial and misguided attempt to diminish and disassociate warfare and slaveholding from freedom while also justifying and requiring them is an effort to save patriarchy and empire from its challengers.

Aristotle attempts to reclaim freedom from the ruins of the Periclean ideal. On the one hand, he offers serious concessions to the critics of militarism. He posits that there is a basic division and important qualitative distinction between political rule and other kinds of rule, and suggests that true freedom is political rule without violence. On the other hand, he justifies slavery and the acquisition of slaves through warfare as the essential foundation upon which freedom is built. The strange paradox that haunts democratic thought, whereby freedom and claims of necessity are mutually supportive of one another, begins with Aristotle.

We might also interpret Aristotle's *Politics* as finding a middle way between the Periclean ideal and the challenges to it. He holds up the rule of free people as fundamentally different from the conduct of war or the practice of slavery, while also maintaining that warfare and slavery provide fundamental supports for political freedom. Slavery and war are justified by and essential to creating the space for political freedom, but as forms of rule they are qualitatively different from and inferior to political freedom. Masters and victorious warriors are naturally more courageous and virtuous than slaves and the defeated. Women, children, and animals are also of lesser capabilities, and therefore benefit from the rule of men. But war and slavery are not the highest expressions of free persons' courage or a free state's capacity for freedom.

The overall effect of Aristotle's efforts is to recover, revivify, and shelter the Periclean ideal from its critics. By at least one measure, his efforts were a resounding success. The idea that the use of violence and domination is not an expression of freedom, but only a means to it, sets a course for political thought and practice that sees violence as a route to liberation and the critical means for defending freedom. Aristotle's basic distinction, whereby the Periclean ideal is submerged in an argument from necessity, as we have seen, will become a defining feature of the violence and empire of modern democracies and republics. However, something akin to the Periclean ideal would reemerge in in the modern era in the nationalist and socialist movements of the nineteenth and twentieth centuries. Indeed, in their sweeping historical impact and broad intellectual underpinnings, these movements provide full-fledged and wide-ranging articulations of the idea that freedom can or must be expressed and exercised through violence.

We can take two other important things from Aristotle's analysis. First, the effort helps us make sense of many of the contradictions that appear in the liberal and republican traditions that would follow him. The idea of defending freedom with violence becomes one of the preeminent justifications for war and slavery in modern thought. Yet the vestiges of the idea that the collective self-rule of freemen can and should operate apart from the relations of the household and the vagaries of international affairs are very much apparent in modern thought as well. Aristotle's reformulated version of Periclean freedom echoes in the speeches of modern democratic political leaders who will not say directly that our freedom enables and justifies our rule over others and yet are often willing to say that the values of a free society are superior to all others. Second, Aristotle's description of political rule can be disentangled from patriarchy. He holds up virtue and moderation as the critical features of freedom and begins to describe the complex relationship between individual self-rule and collective self-rule. In Part IV, I will show how Gandhi and a nonviolent conception of freedom can recover this claim while at the same time upending the idea that warfare and slavery are necessary for political rule and freedom.

But the aim for which the [First World] War was fought was the most sublime and the most overpowering which man is able to imagine: it was the freedom and independence of our nation. . . . [N]ations without honor usually lose their freedom and independence, which, in turn, corresponds only to a higher justice, as generations of scoundrels without honor do not deserve freedom.

ADOLF HITLER

We are determined that before the sun sets on this terrible struggle our flag will be recognized throughout the world as a symbol of freedom on the one hand and of overwhelming force on the other.

GENERAL GEORGE C. MARSHALL

6

Workers of the Nations

CONTEMPORARY CONCEPTS OF collective freedom attempt to describe the character and practices of free nations, free workers, free states, and free peoples. But what does it mean for free people to rule themselves? In this chapter, I explore various answers to this question. Although I limit my analysis to the somewhat narrow issue of the role of violence and nonviolence in self-rule, as will become apparent, the issue is a decisive one.

Let us return briefly to the two signs at Guantánamo and Auschwitz that opened the book. Chapter 4 described how the collapsing of liberty and physical life in conjunction with the principles of defense endows the modern liberal state with sovereignty. By capturing and torturing the bodies of those who purportedly[1] threaten the lives and liberties of Americans, the prison at Guantánamo puts into practice the idea that a free people can delegate to their government extraordinary powers. The defense of life as liberty is today widely understood to be necessary and just.

Yet this understanding does not seem to capture the full significance of the sign at Guantánamo. The sign reads: "Honor Bound to Defend Freedom." The word "honor" connotes military tradition and values, while the notion of "binding" suggests that it is the duty of the Joint Task Force at Guantánamo to create the prison. The notion that free states are obligated to do violence to others (and the idea that the militaries and police forces of democratic states have a responsibility to carry out that violence) adds something significant to the notion that violence is a means to the end of preserving and defending freedom. Though one would be hard-pressed to find anything courageous or honorable in the prescribed duties of the soldiers at the prison camp at Guantánamo, the motto of the Task Force echoes Pericles' ideal in linking core military values with freedom. In certain versions of nationalism and socialism, we find similar close connections between collective freedom and collective violence, and even more elaborate justifications for those connections.

The sign on the gate at the entrance to Auschwitz claims that work can make you free. On its face, it is an ironic and cruel aphorism aimed at the prisoners entering the camp. The purpose of the "work," which was typically forced labor under grueling conditions, was to isolate and destroy each individual prisoner. Nothing in the camp system encouraged a collective sense of achievement or solidarity. The idea that the prisoners could somehow free themselves from the camp, let alone achieve freedom through work in it, was farcical.[2] In this way, the reality of the camp set in contrast to the sign highlights the ways in which it upends the core aims of workers' and peoples' movements, turning the redeeming values of socialism and nationalism on their head.

Yet, the sign might also be interpreted as accurately describing the implementation of a perverse concept of violent freedom. That is, the camp itself may be an attempt to show that work makes those who designed and operated the camp free. Hannah Arendt argues that philosophers dating back to Plato dreamed of creating governments and political orders on the model of work—the skills of craftsmen, doctors, or those who are knowledgeable and talented manipulators of the material world. She notes that work always requires some sort of violence with respect to the material world in order to create its products. In this way, the claim of *Arbeit Macht Frei* can be interpreted as an aphorism aimed not so much at the prisoners, but at the Nazi regime or even the German people. The sign can be read as stating: "Here, we will work on bodies—indeed, manufacture dead bodies—and, in doing so, make freedom for ourselves."

The different concepts of freedom and the historical echoes that reverberate in the two signs do not necessarily work at cross-purposes. The idea of defending freedom can work in conjunction with the patriotic nationalism that motivated the creation of the prison at Guantánamo (and for that matter, the entire project of the so-called War on Terror). Likewise, the bureaucratic aspects of the death camps worked in conjunction with freedom as understood in the mass movement of fascism as the exercise and expression of superiority through violence. Yet the understandings of collective freedom reflected in the signs at the two camps have distinctive and complex histories that we have yet to fully explore.

In this chapter, I explore those histories by asking two key questions. First, to what extent is freedom a central preoccupation of nationalist and socialist theories of politics? While freedom is certainly a prominent theme among the theorists and practitioners of nationalism and socialism, many of the thinkers and political figures associated with these ideologies are also deeply critical of liberal understandings of freedom. These differences have been the subject of many extensive studies, perhaps most famously, in Isaiah Berlin's influential analysis of what he calls positive and negative freedom. The second question is a bit more narrow: How do nationalist and socialist concepts of collective freedom differ from freedom as described by earlier liberal thinkers? Liberal, nationalist, and socialist traditions each argue that rule requires violence. Yet each of these traditions is critical of the extent to which the others endorse certain forms of violent rule.

Finally, these two questions push us to ask a third, more fundamental one: To what extent does the rule of free nations, workers, and peoples require violence? We will not find a uniform answer to this question among socialist and nationalist thinkers. Instead, in this chapter I want to give some sense of the variety of answers to this question, point to some of the more challenging and persuasive arguments endorsing violence, while also highlighting what I take to be glaring and irreconcilable contradictions. At the same time, I will try to recover aspects of collective freedom in the ideas and practices of prominent socialist and nationalist thinkers and actors that allow us to rule with as opposed to over one another. The labor movement in particular has had a vexed and complex relationship to violence. However, its most important legacy has been to innovate and develop nonviolent forms of rule. Applying methods of direct action and voluntaristic forms of governance, the international labor movement has achieved remarkable success over a long period of struggle. This aspect of working people's movements, operating parallel to and sometimes in conjunction with the abolitionist, women's rights, and anti-colonial movements covered in earlier chapters, help inform Part IV, where I develop a more full-fledged understanding of nonviolent rule and political freedom.

NATIONALISM, POPULAR SOVEREIGNTY, AND THE STATE

According to the *Oxford English Dictionary*, the Sanskrit Indo-European base of the word "free" is *priya*, which means beloved or dear. The Old English *Frīg* refers to a goddess and the Old Saxon *frī* refers to woman or wife. It has been conjectured that the base means "one's own," from the Greek *peri* (περί), which means round or around. "Free" in the sense of "not in servitude" is peculiar to Germanic and Celtic usage, but it is not difficult to see the connection between the base and the Germanic and Celtic meanings. The dictionary says that this sense of the word "perhaps arose from the application of the word as the distinctive epithet of those members of the household who were 'one's own blood', i.e. who were connected by ties of kinship with the head, as opposed to the unfree slaves."[3] We can deduce four points from these origins of the word "free." First, it is consistent with the idea that concepts of freedom were either invented by or closely associated with the status of women. Second, in referencing the head of the household in contrast to slaves therein, the word "freedom" implies a hierarchy where the free rule over the unfree. Third, the word reflects a sense of deep affection, sentimental attachment, or love among those who are free. Fourth, these sentiments and the collective sense of being free as opposed to enslaved were typically connected to one's association with a family, kin, or blood relations.

Each of these aspects makes reference not to individual liberty but to collective freedom, as a relationship with other people. At its very origin, the word "freedom" implies both a collective feeling of fellowship and the exclusion, oppression, and rule of others. Over the course of the nineteenth and twentieth centuries the defense of freedom came to mean not only the right of individuals to bear arms or collectively keep their governments in check, but the duty of citizens to protect the survival or "national security interests" of democratic or republican states. The idea of the nation, along with the claim that a free people might go to war in the name of freedom, either to preserve their own form of government or to impose its brand of freedom on others, grew out of the conflicted and self-destructive liberation movements in the Americas, France, and elsewhere. Eventually, such movements became the model for the creation of new independent states around the globe. Mass movements to oppose an oppressive state or colonial power were transformed into mass movements to capture or create a new state that claimed to defend, pursue, or spread freedom. This process opened up a whole new set of political possibilities and perils.

The definitions of nation and nationalism are hotly disputed topics among social and political theorists. Whether or not a nation requires a definite relationship to a particular language, religion, culture, ethnicity, race, or territory—or some combination of these factors—is an unsettled issue. Some have introduced the concept of "civic nationalism" to suggest that a nation does not require that people have any particular ascriptive characteristics, but instead share a desire to live a common way of life.[4] Most seem to agree that in order for a nation to exist it must involve a group of people who are self-conscious with respect to their status as a "nation" or a "people." This self-consciousness is something that most scholars accept as socially constructed, even if it is based in certain common historical experiences, religious principles, cultural affinities, or kinship ties. Likewise, most scholars of nationalism, as well as most nationalists themselves, have argued that in order for a nation to be free, its people must govern themselves.

Typically, this understanding has meant that a nation or people is attached to or governs a state of their own. In modern and contemporary political thought this proposition brings us to yet another contested concept: popular sovereignty. Let us start with an examination of the origins of the concept of popular sovereignty, then move to liberal conceptions of the idea, and finally, to nationalist and socialist ideas of popular sovereignty that go beyond or directly challenge liberal ideas of popular rule. Like nationalism itself, the history and character of popular sovereignty are widely disputed. For our purposes, the concept is important to the extent it encourages or facilitates violence in the name of collective freedom. Joan Cocks points out that it was not inevitable that sovereignty would come to be associated with freedom and that both Jean Bodin and Thomas Hobbes, two of the most important modern theorists of sovereignty, disassociate it from freedom.[5] Moreover, even some contemporary thinkers—most notably Hannah Arendt—argue that freedom and sovereignty are at odds with one another. Nevertheless, Jean-Jacques Rousseau's (1712–1778) idea that the general will of the people could and should be expressed in a way similar to the sovereign power accorded to monarchs has come to be the dominant meaning of collective freedom in modern political thought. Cocks describes the transition from an understanding of sovereignty as divinely inspired to one grounded in humanist principles:

> The self who is liberated from divine authority is free to desire and will and do exactly what he wishes instead of what some metaphysical entity dictates that he *should* desire and will and do. The self who is liberated from a divinely invested human authority can command himself politically as he sees fit, being no longer morally compelled to bow down to a human superior, even if he chooses to bow down to what he sees as his sovereign God. In either case, however, the secular self enjoys sovereign freedom only theoretically. In practice, he can determine himself freely only if he gains control of all the worldly conditions that otherwise would condition or limit him.[6]

Here is the difficulty for thinkers such as Cocks and Arendt. If popular sovereignty and collective freedom are one and the same, it must mean that freedom involves a great deal of violence. To gain control over "all the worldly conditions" that would limit the people must mean attacking the condition of human plurality and making the will of the people uniform—only in this way, could a so-called free will of this type be made a reality.[7] Recall that Kurt Raaflaub speculates that freedom as an expansive and positive force along the lines of Pericles' ideal might have been inspired by the encounter with the vast and unlimited power of the Persian king.[8] This sort of freedom is what Orlando Patterson calls, somewhat anachronistically when applied to the ancients, sovereignal freedom or "the freedom to exercise complete power over another person in the group, to do with them as one pleased."[9]

For this reason, Rousseau's general will has often been accused of being the taproot of totalitarianism. In *The Social Contract*, Rousseau writes that civic freedom paradoxically involves forcing people to be free.[10] Yet Rousseau strenuously works to distinguish the will of a tyrannical majority, or even the combined "will of all," from the general will. Indeed, the will of the majority (even if ensconced in the rule of law), and the will of all (even if it takes into account the will of each individual in the collective), can overextend themselves and threaten freedom and equality.[11] Ideally, those who pursue private interests at the expense of everyone will be forced by the general will to be free of personal dependence. Freedom is comprised of 1) the moral will to act with an eye toward the interests of everyone, combined with 2) the physical ability to do so, or respectively, the legislative and executive powers. Genuine sovereignty then is only an expression of the general will.[12] Rousseau says the general will rarely comes into play in routine governance, checks the will of the majority, and is supported by a general sense of empathy for and identification with one's fellow citizens.[13] Nonetheless, in connecting a collective expression of the will with the absolutism of monarchical sovereignty, Rousseau weds two concepts into one. "Popular sovereignty" becomes a paradoxical term in the modern political lexicon.

Strangely, despite the effort of republicans and liberals to strike at the heart of justifications for monarchy, there are no great modern critics of sovereignty.[14] Indeed, with the exception of Arendt's critique and recent work by Giorgio Agamben, most modern and contemporary political theorists have failed to turn a critical eye toward sovereignty itself. In particular, many liberals who might otherwise take exception to Rousseau's version of the social contract accept the necessity and validity of popular sovereignty. Indeed, the conventional wisdom among liberal thinkers seems to be that popular sovereignty can be made consistent with liberalism. Liah Greenfeld argues that the terms "country," "commonwealth," "empire," and "nation" all became synonymous in sixteenth-century England. The term "nation" in particular had been associated with the cultural and political elite, but now became associated with the people (the Country as opposed to the Crown). She argues that the nation was comprised of "free and equal individuals" who were assumed, in the humanist tradition, to possess reason. Because of this distinguishing human quality, they were entitled to participate in collective decision-making and possess all sovereign powers.[15] Brendan O'Leary argues that even Ernest Gellner's critique of nationalism as philosophically unfounded can be made consistent with liberalism. He explains:

Consistent liberal nationalists hold that all nations should be free, free to express themselves, culturally and politically, and that this freedom is constrained by other nations' rights to the same cultural and political freedom. [This assumption includes the principle that] nations have the right to determine their form of self-government and, relatedly, that all nations have the right to self-determination.[16]

Likewise, what Michael Billig refers to as "banal nationalism," or the everyday reminders of national identity, which are often a subtle subtext unless activated by a crisis, helps to explain nationalism as supporting and giving life to collective sensibilities in liberal democratic orders.[17]

In each of these descriptions of the relationship between liberalism and sovereignty, it is assumed that the creation and maintenance of a state are required to implement liberal principles and realize national freedom. Even among scholars who emphasize the socially constructed and historically specific character of nationalism, the state plays a critical role. Gellner writes that it

> seems to be the case that nationalism emerges only in a milieu in which the existence of the state is already very much taken for granted. The existence of politically centralized units, and of a moral–political climate in which such centralized units are taken for granted and are treated as normative, is a necessary though by no means a sufficient condition of nationalism.[18]

Building on the thought of Max Weber (1864–1920), Gellner closely associates the state with a monopoly on legitimate violence, although he later provocatively suggests that the "monopoly on legitimate education is now more important, more central than the monopoly on legitimate violence."[19] Likewise Benedict Anderson, whose analysis of nationalism is notable for its emphasis on developments in print technology and the social aspects of nationalism, maintains that "the gage and emblem of [national] freedom is the sovereign state."[20] The work of both Gellner and Anderson was presaged by the anarchist Rudolf Rocker's (1873–1958) *Nationalism and Culture*, which argues that nationalism is a product of the state as opposed to the state being an expression of nationalist desires. Moreover, Rocker claims that national identities are inculcated and cultivated in ways similar to religious identities.[21]

Scholars of nationalism are often dismissive of the intellectual contributions of nationalists themselves. However, it is worth examining the actions and words of certain prominent actors, if only to get a sense of the extent to which freedom and violence are rhetorically connected to one another. For instance, the importance of Napoleon Bonaparte (1769–1821) and his creation of the political and military institutions of post-revolutionary France can hardly be overestimated when considering the connection between freedom, nationalism, and violence. In the coup d'état of 18 Brumaire that brought Napoleon to power and the events that followed, one could easily see the principles of the revolution being compromised, as Napoleon made himself Emperor and dictator (1804), creating a new hereditary monarchy, and reinstituting slavery in the West Indies. Yet drawing on Roman traditions and besieged on all sides by European monarchs, he also instituted his famous civil code and established rights for minority groups in the countries France invaded. In a context where many liberal and republican thinkers endorsed arming all capable citizens, he positioned himself as an advocate for freedom against the restoration of monarchs and raised an army of the people by drawing on the *levée en masse.* At first calling himself First Consul (1799), he accumulated for himself the accoutrements of sovereign power in the name of "the people."

The extent to which Napoleon was truly committed to liberal principles, as opposed to winning glory for himself and France, is somewhat beside the point.[22] What is important is that in practice it was possible to institutionalize unleashing the extraordinary violence of the masses in the name of freedom. We should note too that Napoleon described himself as leading the French people in defending themselves and their newfound freedom against the various coalitions of monarchs who opposed them. In this way, his efforts were consistent with liberalism's defense of freedom. However, Napoleon's efforts involved something more than self-defense. A free people rallying around a charismatic leader in the name of freedom called forth claims of military honor and glory. In reviving these aspects of the Greek and Roman traditions, this expression of freedom through violence also resuscitated patriarchy in a new form. Combining liberal themes of self-defense with a version of masculine nationalism led to a mythology whereby the nation (along with liberty itself) was figured as a woman in need of protection.[23] As David Bell has argued, there was a pervasive sense that a liberated French people, mobilized against the monarchs of Europe and their professional armies, would have special qualities: as Bell describes their philosophy, the Girondins such as Jacques-Pierre Brissot (1754–1793) believed that "freedom made men into supermen capable of 'prodigious, supernatural efforts.'"[24] Despite being purged by the Jacobins, Brissot's ideas were part of the sensibility behind Napoleon's grand effort to simultaneously subdue and liberate Europe.

Of course, in the philosophical and practical attempts to square liberalism with popular sovereignty, as in the domination of other people, we see conundrums and contradictions. Critics as diverse as Edmund Burke and Karl Marx argued that "the people" of France were simply being used by the bourgeoisie to overthrow the monarchy and the feudal system.[25] I mentioned above Greenfeld's argument demonstrates that nation and empire become synonyms when the nation becomes associated with "the people." Cocks points how this idea of popular sovereignty becomes exclusivist:

> [Popular sovereignty is an] expansive democratic ideal when set against the foil of monarchical sovereignty and an exuberant democratic ideal when set against the foil of an impersonal liberal legal system [but becomes] a negative, exclusivist ideal as soon as there is a reason to ask who counts as belonging to "the people" and who does not.[26]

I already demonstrated in chapter 4 the extent to which liberal ideals undergirding sovereignty as implemented in the United States were closely tied to the rule of whites over African Americans and American Indians. There is now a burgeoning literature on the relationship between liberalism and the British Empire,[27] where none other than John Stuart Mill (1806–1873) declared that certain barbarous people would require autocratic governments until they reached a certain stage of development.[28] O'Leary's claim that nations have a right to determine their own form of "self-government" runs into problems if that form of government violates liberal principles. If some forms of government are not truly free, or if some people are thought to be ill-equipped for self-determination, it opens up the possibility of governments "liberating" others from their own governments. Indeed, the Spartans did exactly that, and it was a frequent refrain among the superpowers in the Cold War era that they were intervening on behalf of freedom and self-determination in countries around the world.[29] Finally, while nationalism may be a banal background condition at times, we have seen liberal democracies consumed by nationalism jettison core liberal principles in times of crisis. All of these difficulties can be seen in the justifications for the invasion of Iraq and the prosecution of the so-called War on Terror.[30]

Such contradictions were repeatedly played out as Napoleon sought to conquer Europe, and as newly formed governments and coalitions fought back. In Germany, for instance, there was an upsurge in nationalism among intellectuals and philosophers (perhaps most notably Johann Fichte [1762–1814]), along with a general effort to craft a vigorous national identity that would support wars of liberation and collective freedom. The result was that the character of "the German people" came to be described in contrast to others. Commenting on the situation following the expulsion of the French, Ludwig Börne (1786–1837) describes the process:

> Amongst the Germans who blamed Napoleon alone for all the tyranny under which they suffered . . . The urge to freedom and hatred for the French united in one sentiment. And as man misunderstands or despises the good that

enemies offer, so what was worthy of respect brought by French legislation into Germany was misunderstood or despised. Thus after the expulsion of the French, the civil freedom of the Jews, granted by the French, began here and there to be looked on as something dangerous. In addition, the Jews were considered friends of the French rule because, though they were no less oppressed than other Germans, they found some recompense for their hardship.[31]

Here we see how inspired by the French invasion the desire for German "freedom" in turn inspired hatred of, and eventually violence against, both the originators of freedom—those outside the nation—and a minority group within, who are also understood to be other than "German."[32]

Intellectuals and politicians in country after European country examined their histories, claimed a connection to certain lands and territories, theorized or created racial or ethnic lineages, and more generally worked to cultivate collective sensibilities that encouraged each citizen—particularly each male citizen—to understand themselves as distinctively capable and free. Though not exclusively connected to the raising of popular armies, nationalism became deeply entangled with wars involving masses of people in the nineteenth and twentieth centuries. Moreover, colonialism and imperialism served as proving grounds for newfound conceptions of freedom. Racialists such as Frieda von Bülow (1857–1909) viewed the experience of colonizing others as critical to the development of freedom. For instance, historians have noted that

> One of the features of German colonization most frequently remarked upon by travelers to the colonies was the ubiquitous nature of whips. State Secretary Bernhard Dernburg noted in 1908 that in German East Africa, most white men—officials and private persons—would not go out without one. To the dismay of many metropolitan officials, the central state had relinquished part of its monopoly of violence to citizens in its overseas territories, with few effective limitations. The privilege to flog had become a kind of birthright for colonial Germans, an exercise of citizenship. Sovereignty—freedom—was thereby becoming associated with the brutalization of the bodies of racial others. The idea of popular governance that emerged in the colonies was therefore a democracy of terror, in which a racial underclass was a necessary component of a people's exercise and expression of real power.[33]

We have already noted that liberalism was thought to be consistent with the domination of racial others, often in the name of "defending" the freedom of European colonizers. However, this illiberal understanding of collective freedom reflects a willingness to use violence that is in some ways more honest and direct because it is not wrapped in the pretense of human equality. Of course, in response to the collective freedom of colonialism, those who were colonized asserted their own right to self-determination and claimed their own capacities for freedom—often, by mimicking the European penchant for violence.

Many have commented on the contradiction between the specific values of nationalism and the universal values of liberalism. This contradiction has led some to conceive of nationalism as a force that is counter to the liberal state. Conversely, others have argued that the universal claims of liberalism should be jettisoned in favor of a more specifically nationalistic brand of democracy. On the first score, John Breuilly argues that for liberals, the state was to be regarded as an association of the citizens, which meant that freedom was in some sense embodied in the state. Yet freedom was also defined as limitations on state power and sovereignty. "Having accepted the absolute nature of sovereignty and invested it in the state, liberals faced an impossible theoretical task in seeking to limit state power."[34] For the influential German jurist Carl Schmitt, these contradictions led him to conclude that liberal freedoms such as freedom of speech, religion, and the general valuing of open discussion only encouraged ineffectual and corrupt government that avoided the critical aspects of political rule.

In an attempt to revive the ancient meaning of dictatorship, Schmitt highlights the fact that those who believe in democratic principles are often in the minority. Democratic rule—instituting "the people's will"—in practice means that someone must form the people's will, which at least temporarily means that the rule of the few or even a single individual must prevail. Schmitt would eventually join the Nazi party, and although he was a much more careful and perspicacious thinker than most of the party leaders, his ideas clearly resonated with the party. As Hitler (1889–1945) writes in *Mein Kampf*:

> A nation's chance of reconquering its independence is not absolutely bound up with the integrity of a State territory, but rather with the existence of a never so small remnant of this nation and State which, having the necessary freedom, has it in its power to be not only the bearer of the spiritual communion of the entire nationality, but also the preparer of the military struggle for freedom.[35]

That is, far from being inconsistent with democracy and freedom, a dictator who can decide and rule with the interests of the people as a whole in mind is much more consistent with democracy than a committee of ineffectual bourgeoisie representatives, who tend to serve their own interests and have difficulty making decisions as they get bogged down in petty disputes. Schmitt is particularly keen to point out that a hallmark of liberal democratic theories of governance is education and consciousness-raising, which implies that a select few must educate the people as a whole.[36] In addition, Schmitt argues that the most difficult questions of rule typically do not conform to our expectations, and therefore are not easily anticipated by existing law. The very meaning of sovereignty is to be able to decide the exception, to make decisions without the guidance of the law, particularly in times of emergency. Considering his view that the distinguishing characteristic of politics is the human capacity and tendency to treat others as either friends or enemies,[37] it is not difficult see how the exercise of violence is central to his understanding of democracy.

Other prominent nationalists forwarded ideas that on their face viewed violence as a necessary means to expanding and preserving freedom. The prominent Italian nationalist Giuseppe Mazzini (1805–1872) organized insurrections in an attempt to unite Italy and create a new republic. Yet he viewed liberation movements as a necessary step on the way to creating a community of democratic and republican governments that would live in peace with one another. Wars of liberation and self-determination might eventually lead to the end of war itself.[38] Likewise, Ernest Renan (1823–1892) in his influential essay on nationalism writes: "Historical inquiry, in effect, throws light on the violent acts that have taken place at the origin of every political formation, even those that have been the most benevolent in their consequences. Unity is always brutally established." Yet he argues that "the nation" does not consist of a race, a language, or a religion, and must not be beholden to military necessity. Indeed, Renan argues that racial philosophies will lead to "the destruction of European civilization. To the same degree that the right of nations is just and legitimate, the primordial right of races is narrow and full of danger for true progress." Instead, the nation "is a soul, a spiritual principle" where "great aggregation of men, in sane mind and warm heart, created a moral conscience." Like Mazzini, Renan contemplates the possibility of a United States of Europe. But he says that in the current political circumstances the existence of independent nations "is the guarantee of liberty, a liberty that would be lost if the world had only one law and one master."[39]

Despite their diverse views, these thinkers share the idea that nationalism as associated with collective freedom requires the possession and maintenance of a state with the capacity to enforce the "will of the people" through violence. As Cocks writes, "the idea of self-rule was swept under the sovereignty rubric."[40] Observing the drive for the unification of Italy, the English historian and politician

Lord Acton (1834–1902) saw freedom as coming into direct conflict with national-ism. Indeed, he disputed any definition of freedom that was connected to the collec-tive exercise of sovereign power, writing:

> [T]he liberal doctrine subjects the desire of freedom to the desire of power, and the more it demands a share of power, the more it is averse to exemptions from it. This is the aspiration of nations which know not what freedom is. Where the people is sovereign, it wishes to exercise its sovereignty, not to be restrained in the exercise of it.[41]

Acton feared a combination of absolutism and democracy, whereby individuals such as Louis Napoleon (1808–1873) would be elected by the people but then (as with the establishment of the Second Empire [1852]) become dictators. Such abso-lute rulers, having won the consent of the people to rule, would become the sole arbiters of the meaning of the will of the people. Moreover, they would consolidate and centralize their rule, while sowing destruction and disorder through warfare in order to "liberate" other nations.

SOCIALIST EXPERIMENTS WITH AND WITHOUT VIOLENCE

Class conflict has been the subject of political theory throughout history. However, the origins of modern socialism are typically located in a wide variety of philo-sophical and practical responses to the Napoleonic Wars (1803–1815), the Industrial Revolution, and the reappearance of democratic ideas in Europe in the eighteenth and nineteenth centuries. Indeed, if we take the inception of modern nationalism as born of the French Revolution and Napoleon's France, then from its very origins, nationalism was intertwined with socialism.[42]

In what the socialist historian Ernest Belfort Bax (1854–1926) called the "last epi-sode of the French Revolution," insurrectionaries such as François-Noël (Gracchus) Babeuf (1760–1797) and Philippe Buonarroti (1761–1837) attempted to restore the Constitution of 1793, which had promised greater social and economic equality. Creating a Secret Directory, Babeuf and his allies, who perhaps eventually num-bered in the thousands, formed what they called the Society of Equals and hatched a plan whereby those "who usurp sovereignty ought to be put to death by free men." Though he claimed in the call to insurrection that "[a]ll opposition shall be sup-pressed immediately by force. Those opposing shall be exterminated," once impris-oned by the government and foiled by internal dissension within the Society, Babeuf disavowed his reputation for being bloodthirsty. Writing of the Society from prison he says: "They wish to walk in other paths than those of Robespierre. They desire no blood."[43] Instead, the aim of the Society was to "found the REPUBLIC OF EQUALS, this great home open to all men." In this new government, would "[d]isappear at last, revolting distinctions between rich and poor, great and small, masters and servants, *rulers* and *ruled*."[44]

Unlike Babeuf and Buonarroti, many of the early-nineteenth-century socialists were less enamored with capturing the state than establishing new forms of community and experimenting with more equitable social and economic organizations. Robert Owen (1771–1851) began a series of such experiments in his own textile mills. Emphasizing a basic standard of living for workers in the mill, Owen sacrificed short-term profits to provide affordable necessities. Hoping to inspire similar efforts among other industrialists, he expressed his views in four essays titled *A New View of Society* (1813), where he emphasized the malleability and possibilities of the human character. Owen believed that even the most lowly had the capacity for reason, if only they were given the opportunity to develop it. He also believed that all persons deserved a basic standard of living, achieved through a humane job, which he hoped the government would not have to provide, but thought it should provide if necessary. He advocated restrictive laws to prevent drinking, reform of the Poor Laws, and compulsory public education to transform the lowest classes into productive members of society. His argument was as much utilitarian as humanitarian, emphasizing that the British Empire would benefit greatly if those who were currently poor and unproductive became conscious of their own abilities. Inner transformation and consciousness-raising would take some time. But he thought that in order to avoid the resistance of capitalists, the "prospect of freely enjoying [the] rational liberty of mind" could not come about too suddenly.[45]

Owen set about to create examples that he hoped would demonstrate how his ideal economic and social structure would work. In his mills in New Lanark and in the experimental community of New Harmony, Indiana, Owen thought that he might be able to design a self-sustaining Community of United Interest whereby the needs of everyone would be met in an equitable manner. Once such communities were established, he thought they would be self-evidently superior to the horrors of industrialization as it currently existed.

> None must suffer in person, property, or comfort; all will be soon reconciled to the change, and lend a helping hand. The instructors of the endless, varied, and existing creeds or faiths, which have deluged the world with blood and rendered it a curse and desolation, will all become of the unresisting teachers of *Charity*. . . . A change of the most extensive magnitude the world ever contemplated will be accomplished without violence or confusion, or any very

apparent opposition. The feelings and the interests of mankind imperiously demand this change. THE WORLD APPROVES—AND NONE CAN RESIST.[46]

In these passages, we see Owen's belief in the power of experimentation, his strident secularism, and his self-confident paternalism that sometimes belied his efforts at making society more equitable. Instead, from the standpoint of ruling, it is clear that Owen believed only the enlightened—and he was unsure of who exactly this might be—could instruct the poor sufficiently. His experiments in America hoped to draw from a pool of citizens who were already well-versed in self-governance. However, he soon found himself disappointed, rescinding a Constitution that called for direct participation in the governance of New Harmony and never implementing a system of collective land ownership. While promoting improvements in working conditions at the national level in Britain, actively participating in trade union organizing, and sinking much of his personal fortune into his experimental communities, he also came to have a deep skepticism of the readiness of those who had not yet been properly educated to participate in ruling themselves. However, unlike other social reformers, his confidence in his own vision did not translate into a willingness to do violence to those who opposed him, or to a brand of rule that was imposed imperiously.[47]

In a similar fashion, but with an entirely distinctive anthropology, the French philosopher Charles Fourier (1772–1837) inspired his followers to found what he called phalanxes in Great Britain and the United States. He propounded a *Theory of Four Movements* (1808), which held that labor was inherently pleasurable if only industry were set up in such a way as to draw upon natural human desires and inclinations. Fourier was particularly concerned with the gendered aspects of property relations. Offering a complex history of the world, along with a detailed projection of what the future might bring, he called gender relationships the critical "pivot" on which the first eight stages of human development depended. Although he recommended a wide range of social and economic reforms in his detailed plan for self-sufficient communities, he proposed that more free and open sexual relations were critical in creating more productive and happy societies. He explained:

The reason why God has given amorous custom so much influence over the social mechanism and the transformations it undergoes is because he abhors violence and oppression. It was his will that the happiness or unhappiness of human societies should be proportionate to the degree of constraint or liberty they allowed. But God only acknowledges freedom that encompasses both sexes, not merely one, and therefore he decided that those seed-beds of social atrocity, savagery, barbarism and Civilization, should only have a single pivot, the subjection of women; and that all the periods which produce social well-being, like the sixth, seventh and eighth periods, should have no pivot, no point of orientation, except the progressive liberation of the weaker sex.[48]

His ideal community included an Areopagus, or supreme industrial council. But even here, the Areopagus could not enforce its rules, but only give recommendations and counsel to the larger community. Instead of relying upon Enlightenment principles of universal reason, Fourier thought that the passions of each man, woman, and child should be developed and expressed as fully as possible. Freedom and an equitable society were fundamentally at odds with violence and central governance. Disillusioned with Owen's New Harmony, thinkers such as the anarchist Josiah Warren (1798–1874) became involved in communities set up on the basis of Fourier's ideas in places such as Utopia, Ohio and Brook Farm, Massachusetts. (Later, on the basis of widely divergent philosophies, John Ruskin's Guild of St. George and Zionist kibbutzim in British Palestine were created with the aim of demonstrating that there was a viable alternative to for-profit capitalism.)

Despite their differences, both Owen and Fourier believed that fundamental social transformations could take place without violence. Instead, freedom depended upon establishing exemplars of new ways of living that were entirely voluntaristic. Drawing inspiration from both thinkers, French politician and pioneer of anarchist thought Pierre-Joseph Proudhon (1803–1865) developed a revolutionary philosophy that he called "scientific socialism." As Russia, Great Britain, and his own France were obsessed with capturing territory, Proudhon maintained that once the revolution in social relations had happened, it would spread by emulation. Wars, national boundaries, and colonies would all become obsolete and irrelevant. Skeptical of representative government as a bourgeois institution, he believed that "[c]ollective power, the principle of **WORKMEN'S ASSOCIATIONS** [would replace] *armies*" and that centralized government of any sort, particularly those established through insurrection, amounted to "[reestablishing] despotism by metaphysics" and would only destroy "all who speak in favor of liberty and local sovereignty."[49] His critique extended to a wide-ranging polemic against forms of violent punishment by the state, which were typically aimed at the lower classes in favor of defending property rights.

Much of Proudhon's philosophy, including his claim to have discovered a science of economic and social relations, influenced Marx. But there remained a critical difference in their approach to the proper means to collective freedom. For Proudhon:

> Absolutists, doctrinaires, demagogues and socialists, all incessantly turn their regard to authority, as if towards their shared magnetic pole. From this comes the aphorism of the radical faction, which the doctrinaires and absolutists assuredly would not disavow: *The social revolution is the goal; the political revolution* (that is to say, the change of authority) *is the means.* This means: "Give us the right of life and death over your persons and your belongings, and we will make you free!" . . . For more than six thousand years the kings and priests have been repeating that line!

Despite his emphasis on politics and law as nothing but superstructure built upon the base of economic relations, Marx believed that the state was a necessary means, at least in a transitional phase, to achieving a revolution in human affairs. Bakunin forwarded a view of power and social revolution similar to Proudhon's, but he rejected the notion that history was scientific or that reason was universal. Proudhon held that social and economic relations would be transformed without violence and that the state is merely an epiphenomenon of power.

The outbreak of the 1848 revolutions stemmed from a wide variety of causes, but seemed to confirm the view that a revolution could be spontaneous, would transcend national boundaries, and did not require raising formal armies. Yet the harsh and generally effective response of reactionary forces convinced others that only a highly organized and violent revolution that would capture the state and use all of its tools could bring about the desired economic and social equality. The rise and fall of the Paris Commune (1871) similarly encouraged diverse interpretations from communists, socialists, and anarchists.

Perhaps the most cogent expression of what would become the dominant view of the relationship between violence and collective freedom among communists is expressed by the British Marxist Christopher Caudwell (1907–1937) in his essay "Liberty: A Study in Bourgeois Illusion" (1938). Stating bluntly: "I am a Communist because I believe in freedom," Caudwell excoriates Bertrand Russell (1872–1970) and others as "champions of unfreedom":

> What, to the proletarian, is liberty—the extermination of those bourgeois institutions and relations which hold them in captivity—is necessarily compulsion and restraint to the bourgeois, just as the old bourgeois liberty generated non-liberty for the worker. The two notions of liberty are irreconcilable.

Once the proletariat is in power, all attempts to re-establish bourgeois social relations . . . will therefore be repulsed as fiercely as men repulse all attacks on their liberty. This is the meaning of the dictatorship of the proletariat, and why with it there is censorship, ideological acerbity, and all the other devices developed by the bourgeois in the evolution of the coercive State which secures his freedom.[50]

Caudwell, like Marx, did not believe that this phase, which was currently happening in Russia, would last long. Instead, the state would wither away as a classless society made hierarchical relationships unnecessary.

Caudwell also introduces a novel theory of freedom, which attempts to square economic determinism with free will. He contends that freedom means being conscious of necessity. Drawing on Sigmund Freud (1856–1939) and Marx, he argues that freedom requires the proletariat to become conscious of the necessity of violent revolution and the causal relationship between one's material conditions and one's mental state. Caudwell writes: "Thus freedom of action, freedom to do what we will, the vital part of liberty, is seen to be secured by the social consciousness of necessity, and to be generated in the process of economic production. The price of liberty is not eternal vigilance, but eternal work."[51] Consciousness free of the illusions of the bourgeois notion of liberty is poised for free action. Liberals regard collective social action as a threat to liberty but this individualistic view of freedom is the freedom of animals or an "unconscious brute." For people, institutions make the difference. Those who have an understanding of the iron laws of necessity can bring about a new world where material relationships and the social and economic order facilitate freedom.[52]

Though Caudwell certainly would have stood aghast at the sign on the gates of Auschwitz, we see something quite close to the idea that "work makes one free" in his thinking. In his wide-ranging critique of liberalism and socialism, Schmitt calls to task those who would reject the state, suggesting they are either utopian or hypocritical. Whether or not they were literally influenced by Schmitt, many communists forwarded a brand of collective freedom quite consistent with Schmitt's vision. Lenin, Stalin, and Mao among others embraced the state, dictatorship that was meant to represent the people, the selective use of nationalism, and propaganda that lauded the working man. They generally associated labor and rule with centralized industrialism as opposed to domestic labor or small-scale production. Writing in 1945, the English historian and international relations theorist E. H. Carr (1892–1982) could proclaim that

"Planned economy" is a Janus with a nationalist as well as the socialist face; if its doctrine seems socialist, its pedigree is unimpeachable and nationalist. A few years ago "socialism means strength" would have seemed, even to socialists, a paradoxical slogan. To-day when a nation determines to exert its utmost strength in war, it resorts without hesitation to policies of out-and-out socialism. Now that *laissez-faire* has succumbed to the joint onslaught of nationalism and socialism, its two assailants have become in a strange way almost indistinguishable in their aims; and both have become immensely more powerful through the alliance.[53]

Carr claims that for all intents and purposes, all of Western civilization—and indeed, nearly the entire world—had embraced both nationalism and socialism in the interwar years. Governments did so specifically to muster the extraordinary violence that culminated in the Second World War. His claims ring true, at least if we focus on those socialists who embraced the idea of popular sovereignty and the necessity of the state.

THE LABOR MOVEMENT AND THE STRIKE

The wide and deep embrace of the state belies a counter-tradition whereby novel and voluntaristic people's organizations played a critical role in shaping the character of the political, social, and economic world over the past two centuries. Unlike the abolitionist movement and the women's rights movement, the labor movement has not historically been wedded to what we would now call nonviolence. This characteristic is particularly true if we consider what is perhaps its most important public expression of power: the strike. Instead, the strike is associated with violence by many of its most prominent advocates and detractors alike.[54] Without downplaying the coercive force of the strike, and without papering over the many instances where strikes were closely related to violent revolutions or individual acts of violence and sabotage, I want to argue that the strike is fundamentally a nonviolent form of power. The insight I wish to convey is that, while bourgeois revolutionaries required violence to achieve their aims due to the incompatibility of their universalist ideology and their particularist interests, the indispensability of labor combined with the sheer numbers involved when people take direct action makes violence unnecessary. One might go so far as to assert that the litmus test for whether or not a revolution is truly one of the people, as opposed to a vanguard that claims to be representing "the people," is the degree to which the movement relies upon violence.

A fully adequate rendering of the history of the labor movement, and strikes in particular, would reveal tremendous diversity in tactics and strategy, particularly regarding the use of violence. Such an analysis would be highly useful, but it is beyond the scope of what I want to do here. I maintain that on the whole, milestones such as the eight-hour workday, child labor laws, and industrial health and safety standards were achieved (where they have been achieved) with relatively little violence, particularly in comparison to the organized violence of corporations and states resisting such change.[55] This assertion may hold true even if we focus on those labor organizations ideologically predisposed to support and sometimes engage in acts of violence.[56] However, three of the most dramatic events pressing governments to respond to the needs of working people in the history of the West—the 1848 uprisings, the Paris Commune, and the Bolshevik Revolution—all involved mass violence. Peoples' uprisings around the world, sometimes directly influenced by these events, have likewise often embraced at least some degree of violence. Moreover, while there are many instances where violent actions on the part of labor unions have alienated the public and hurt recruitment, more moderate unions have often benefited from the violence or threat of violence of less moderate ones. Finally, to the extent that the achievements of national and international labor movements involve passing laws that will be physically enforced, one might say that the collective freedom of working people is maintained through the violence of a co-opted state.

Yet despite these facts, I will maintain that strikes are at their core nonviolent. Instead of attempting a comprehensive history, I will lay out the arguments of those thinkers who forward the claim that the basic logic behind strikes is violent, then turn to those who argue otherwise, adding additional arguments of my own. Walter Benjamin (1892–1940) writes:

> The critique of violence is the philosophy of its history—the "philosophy" of this history, because only the idea of its development makes possible a critical, discriminating, and decisive approach to its temporal data. A gaze directed only at what is close at hand can at most perceive a dialectical rising and falling in the lawmaking and law-preserving formations of violence.[57]

I take Benjamin to mean here that a philosophical approach to history means that we do not have to accept that what has been will always be. In particular, a historical critique of violence means reframing and pulling back from the extraordinary influence of violence on past and current political formations and seeing it as a development as opposed to a necessity. In that spirit, I take up the thought of Georges Sorel (1842–1922), Rosa Luxemburg (1871–1919), Benjamin, and Hannah Arendt on the issue of the strike and other forms of "direct action."

Georges Sorel's *Reflections on Violence* (1908) attempts to articulate a brand of socialism that, influenced by Proudhon, relies upon the ability of ordinary workers to establish an alternative to a bourgeois parliamentarian and centralized state. At the core of this revolution from the ground up are the syndicates, or self-organized collections of labor unions working to reorganize social and economic relations in a more equitable manner by taking possession of the means of production. Like Proudhon, Sorel thought that political revolution was secondary to these alternative institutions and arrangements. Yet in direct contradiction to Proudhon, he believed the destruction of the bourgeois state would not happen through education or example. Thus he condemned those

> *wise men*, the democrats devoted to the cause of the rights of man [who] think that violence will disappear when popular education becomes more advanced; they recommend, therefore, a great increase in the number of courses and lectures; they hope to drown revolutionary syndicalism in the saliva of professors.[58]

According to Sorel, the revolution could only be achieved through a general strike. The syndicates had already learned how to "intimidate the prefects by popular demonstrations, which have the potential for serious conflict with the police, and they commend riotous behavior."[59] In doing so, they put pressure on the state, which in turn put pressure on their capitalist allies.

In advocating for this "*direct and revolutionary method*," which he thought had already proven its "enormous efficacy" in France,[60] Sorel draws upon two analogous moments in history, while attempting to distance syndicalism from a third. First, just as the martyrdom of the early Christians was hardly worth noting among pagan historians, yet ended up transforming Western civilization, so it may take only a few scattered incidents of violence (barely noticed by the bourgeoisie) to spark the idea of a general strike and the proletarian revolution.[61] Second, the syndicates will need to rely upon the power of myth. Quoting Friedrich Nietzsche (1844–1900) on the ancient Greeks, Sorel admires "'that audacity of noble races, that mad, absurd and spontaneous audacity ... their indifference and contempt for all security of the body, for life, for comfort.'" He associates this "full freedom from all social constraint" with Pericles in particular, who in turn invokes Achilles.[62] According to Sorel, the early Christian martyrs and the ancient Athenians show us that the general strike is nothing like the bourgeois revolution. He condemns the Jacobins of the French Revolution for their excesses, but at the same time faults the bourgeoisie for forwarding the idea that "violence is a relic of barbarism which is bound to disappear under the progress of enlightenment." In the place of liberal rationalism and natural law theory, the "aim must be to acquire *habits* of liberty with which the bourgeoisie are no longer acquainted."[63]

Sorel's analysis is both perceptive and deceptive, as well as strategically blind. On the one hand, he traces the lineage of Pericles' ideal, updating his vision of collective freedom and embracing a brand of liberty consistent with the love of honor

and glory. He does so in order to devolve and decenter power from the state, and
to embolden local cooperative organizations to take direct action and express their
freedom collectively and spontaneously. He reclaims an ancient conception of
liberty, re-appropriating it and contrasting it with the prioritizing of bodily security and comfort in liberal rationalism. On the other hand, his description of the
Christian martyrs entirely misses the point that what made their actions distinctive and inspired a movement against paganism was their wholesale rejection of the
heroic war ethic celebrated in ancient Greece and Rome.

Sorel's portrayal of bourgeois attitudes toward violence is equally misleading.
Far from offering an alternative, he endorses one of the most pernicious distinctions in liberal thought. He argues that the violence of the liberal state should
be called "force," whereas the violence of socialist revolutionaries is the only true
"violence."[64] In part, we can attribute his rhetorical move to the early-twenti-
eth-century reaction against a growing consumer and leisure culture, which was
thought to encourage corruption and effeminacy. Prior to the First World War,
across a wide swath of the ideological spectrum, it was thought that violence
would renew and reinvigorate freedom. Sorel wishes to reserve for revolutionary
syndicates the antidote to slavish comfort.

Sorel's thought, like that of many socialists and communists of the day, mirrors bourgeois and liberal ideology in this attitude toward violence. In fact, while
he insists early in *Reflections* that his revolutionary syndicates will not replicate
the bourgeois revolutions, he later betrays his admiration for the republican ideal,
which holds that participation in warfare contributes to molding "free men."[65]
Of course, neither revolutionary liberals nor revolutionary socialists are keen to
embrace too much violence. Liberals in the coming decades would claim to be
against war by arguing that World War I was the "war to end all wars." In adopting the liberal distinction between force and violence, Sorel ignores the glaring
contradiction between the practice of liberal violence and the theory that violence
is on its way out.

This contradiction between theory and practice is also reflected in Sorel's thought
regarding the unfolding of the new socialist order. It appears most acutely in his
rejection of the dictatorship of the proletariat and his endorsement of the Bolshevik
Revolution. In theory, he claims that the dictatorship of the proletariat is nothing
more than a dangerous outcome of the political general strike, which aims to capture the state.[66] Yet when Lenin comes to power, he favorably compares him to Peter
the Great (1672–1725) and argues that even if he fails in the short term

the ideology of the new form of proletarian State will not perish; it will survive
by merging with the myths which will take their substance from the popular

accounts of the struggle undertaken by the Republic of *soviets* against the coalition of great capitalist powers.[67]

Sorel believes that the Bolsheviks have replaced violence from the top down with violence from the bottom up. He says that historians will no more lament the destruction of the bourgeoisie than the Romans lamented the destruction of Carthage. The soviets will prevail because they represent the new sort of voluntaristic self-governance that others will imitate when they see their heroic actions. Lenin is just the sort of pragmatic and intelligent leader such a movement requires.

As it happens, the other major theorist of the strike and advocate of mass spontaneous action as the critical expression of and means to socialist revolution articulates precisely the reverse position. Rosa Luxemburg, the German philosopher and activist of Polish-Jewish descent, endorses the dictatorship of the proletariat, but saw Lenin as a threat to genuine socialist freedom. Critiquing Lenin and Trotsky for what she believes is their "ready-made formula" for revolution, Luxemburg argues that impositions upon free association and free speech, along with their attempts to centralize control of the soviets, will quickly drain vitality from the revolution. She writes that "[f]reedom only for the supporters of the government, only for the members of one party—however numerous they may be—is no freedom at all. Freedom is always and exclusively freedom for the one who thinks differently."[68] Luxemburg is not opposed to dictatorship in theory. She argues that tearing down the capitalist and bourgeois order, redistributing property, and resisting the violence of the state will undoubtedly require organized violence. Yet she was deeply concerned that such violence might compromise the building up of a new world where ordinary workers and laborers can control their own lives. She writes:

> From the uppermost summit of the state down to the tiniest parish, the proletarian mass must therefore replace the inherited organs of bourgeois class rule—the assemblies, parliaments, and city councils—with its own class organs—with workers' and soldiers' councils. It must occupy all the posts, supervise all functions, measure all official needs by the standard of its own class interests and the tasks of socialism. Only through constant, vital, reciprocal contact between the masses of the people and their organs, the workers' and soldiers' councils, can the activity of the people fill the state with a socialist spirit.[69]

She argues that Lenin has a deep appreciation for the spiritual transformation required for the true raising of the consciousness of the proletariat. But his means— of terror and dictatorial force—to these ends can only demoralize that spirit.

More than Sorel, Luxemburg engages in a vigorous critique of nationalist bour-geois violence, which she specifically identifies as an illegitimate form of collective freedom. At the same time, she persistently works to distance herself from utopian socialists and peace activists. Drawing on interpretations of Marx and Kautsky, her opposition to the First World War, colonialism, and imperialism are not based on the claim that violence is immoral or unnecessary. Instead, she argues that nation-alism is a tool that the bourgeois use to divide the proletariat while mustering its collective power. She writes that

> the development of the bourgeoisie has proved unequivocally that a modern nation-state is more real and tangible than the vague idea of "freedom" or national "independence"; that it is indeed a definite historical reality, neither very alluring nor very pure. The substance and essence of the modern state comprise not freedom and independence of the "nation," but only the class dominance of the bourgeoisie, protectionist policy, indirect taxation, milita-rism, war, and conquest.[70]

Luxemburg also perceived that the freedom of some was typically achieved at the expense of others, and that it often required a particularly virulent form of violence, writing that "[p]olitical discrimination against a particular nationality is the stron-gest tool in the hands of the bourgeoisie, which is eager to mask class conflicts and mystify its own proletariat."[71] Given her perceptive critique of nationalist under-standings of freedom, it is not entirely surprising that she was killed by the German right-wing militia group whose members called themselves the Freikorps.

Yet it is in her writings about the relationship between economic and political strikes that Luxemburg distinguishes herself as a thinker. Reflecting upon the tur-moil in Russia in 1905, where most perceived a failure in the general strikes, she argues that the grievances of the bricklayers, sailors, metalworkers, oil workers, sugar workers, and others laid the groundwork for the mass general strike, and that the general strike in turn raised the consciousness of workers who were finally able to perceive their exploitation, be emboldened to organize, and act in their own locali-ties. Instead of lamenting the challenges democratic socialists face, she embraces the potential power of labor:

> This is a gigantic, many-coloured picture of a general arrangement of labour and capital which reflects all the complexity of social organisation and of the political consciousness of every section and of every district; and the whole long scale runs from the regular trade-union struggle of a picked and tested troop of the proletariat drawn from large-scale industry, to the formless

protest of a handful of rural proletarians, and to the first slight stirrings of an agitated military garrison, from the well-educated and elegant revolt in cuffs and white collars in the counting house of a bank to the shy-bold murmurings of a clumsy meeting of dissatisfied policemen in a smoke-grimed dark and dirty guardroom.[72]

Whereas others viewed the failure to overthrow the czar as demonstrating the ineffectiveness of the general strike, Luxemburg saw it as achieving something of vital importance. First, she is not above celebrating "*a general raising of the standard of life of the proletariat*, economic, social and intellectual."[73] The capturing of the state is not the be-all and end-all of the revolution. Second, leveraging her argument to make the case that German trade unions ought to join together in a mass strike of their own, she castigates those who worried that the trade unions would "fall in pieces in a revolutionary whirlwind like rare porcelain" in the face of government crackdown.[74] Instead, she argues that the crackdown in Russia produced a proliferation of trade union organizing that was previously thought to be impossible.

Luxemburg is relentlessly pragmatic in her approach to violence and its place in the strike. The infighting between socialists, communists, and anarchists regarding the usefulness of violence, together with the relative prioritizing of the economic, social, and political are issues that Luxemburg elides by claiming they are all interrelated:

Political and economic strikes, mass strikes and partial strikes, demonstrative strikes and fighting strikes, general strikes of individual branches of industry and general strikes in individual towns, peaceful wage struggles and street massacres, barricade fighting—all these run through one another, run side by side, cross one another, flow in and over one another—it is a ceaselessly moving, changing sea of phenomena. And the law of motion of these phenomena is clear: it does not lie in the mass strike itself nor in its technical details, but in the political and social proportions of the forces of the revolution.[75]

The different kinds of strikes are part of a historical progression, which she does not so much recommend as a strategy as perceive as the natural course of events. She argues that highly disciplined, nonviolent strikes are necessary in specific industries during the early stages of resistance to capitalism. However, once these strikes inspire a general strike, she expects a rapid escalation of violence due to what will surely be a vigorous attempt on the part of the bourgeoisie to hold on to their property and political power. At this stage, the workers must arm themselves and the bourgeoisie must be disarmed. Like Sorel and the liberals supporting World War

I, she is not entirely immune from arguments that the proletarian general strike and violent revolution would usher forth a period of perpetual peace, equality, and prosperity.[76]

In her insistence on the importance of maintaining vibrant public cooperative associations, Luxemburg presages many of Hannah Arendt's arguments about the role of power in strikes. However, before turning to Arendt, we must examine Walter Benjamin's 1921 essay "Critique of Violence," because it sets the stage for Arendt's unique conception of power. It is also quite possibly the first socialist tract to argue that the strike—or rather, a certain kind of strike—is fundamentally nonviolent. To begin, Benjamin offers an assessment of the natural law tradition that amplifies and crystallizes Sorel's critique of liberal rationalism and resonates strongly with Schmitt's critique of parliamentary law. But instead of distancing the liberal state from violence, he makes the bold claim that all violence is either lawmaking or law-destroying, and that all law, even that which results from parliamentary deliberations, is violent.[77] The natural law tradition, he argues, prevents us from discriminating "within the sphere of means themselves." Instead, it portrays "violent means to just ends [as] no greater problem than a man sees in his 'right' to move his body in the direction of a desired goal."[78] Benjamin says that the law is essentially the human attempt to intervene in fate. Instead of allowing factors beyond our control to determine who lives and dies, the law deigns to make that determination.[79]

What, then, of human attempts to act outside of formal institutions, to act outside of the law? What of human action outside of the natural law tradition, which might allow us to take a critical approach to means regardless of their ends? Like Sorel, Benjamin begins his discussion by postulating that strikes are violent. The collective refusal to work contains an element of extortion whereby the employer is coerced into concessions. Likewise, Benjamin maintains Sorel's distinction between the political general strike and the proletarian general strike, with the former retaining the extortive element of violence. But in a remarkable attempt to turn Sorel's analysis on its head, and in contradiction to much of the socialist tradition, Benjamin maintains that the proletarian general strike is not only nonviolent but is the prime example of what he calls "pure means." He writes:

Against this deep, moral, and genuinely revolutionary conception, no objection can stand that seeks, on the grounds of its possibly catastrophic consequences, to brand such a general strike as violent. Even if it can rightly be said that the modern economy, seen as a whole, resembles much less a machine that stands idle when abandoned by its stoker than a beast that goes berserk as soon as its tamer turns his back, nevertheless the violence of an action can be assessed no more from its effects than from its ends, but only from the law of its means.[80]

It may very well be that a general strike will lead to a great deal of violence, as the state lashes out at those who refuse to participate in the continuation of capitalism. Yet by introducing the idea of "pure means," Benjamin suggests that both violence and nonviolence can be cut loose from the logic of means and ends altogether and be judged, finally, in their own right. Some violence is a form of expression (this is Sorel's mythic violence[81]) and would fall under the category of what I have been calling an expression or exercise of collective freedom. The pure means of the nonviolent general strike is essentially an antidote to this mythic violence, which Benjamin believes can break "this cycle maintained by mythical forms of law, on the suspension of law with all the forces on which it depends as they depend on it, finally therefore on the abolition of state power, a new historical epoch is founded."[82]

At one point, Benjamin quotes the pacifist and early gay rights activist Kurt Hiller (1885–1972): "If I do not kill I shall never establish the world dominion of justice . . . that is the argument of the intelligent terrorist. . . . We, however, profess that higher even than the happiness and justice of existence stands existence itself."[83] Benjamin offers a qualified endorsement of Hiller's claim, maintaining it is true only

> if existence, or, better, life (words whose ambiguity is readily dispelled, analogously to that of freedom, when they are referred to two distinct spheres), means the irreducible, total condition that is "man"; if the proposition is intended to mean that the nonexistence of man is something more terrible then the (admittedly subordinate) not-yet-attained condition of the just man.[84]

What Benjamin is saying here is that a pacifist argument grounded in the claim that physical life is sacred (and therefore should never be destroyed under any circumstances) is invalid. The sanctity of physical life can easily justify violence by the state, as the liberal tradition demonstrates and even the Kantian categorical imperative allows.[85] However, if by life and existence one means the character of the human condition more broadly, then the pacifist argument holds: on these grounds violence can be absolutely prohibited, or at least a purely nonviolent means discovered. Benjamin suggests that the difference between prioritizing physical life over the human condition is quite similar to the prioritizing of one kind of freedom over another.

In her magnum opus entitled appropriately *The Human Condition*, Hannah Arendt suggests that the question of prioritizing physical life over the human condition (or vice versa) is not analogous to that of divergent meanings of freedom, but identical to it. Following Benjamin's logic and situating the labor movement in the context of her theory of action, freedom, and politics, Arendt sees the possibility for a new brand of collective freedom:

> Just as the modern masses and their leaders succeeded, at least temporarily, in bringing forth in totalitarianism an authentic, albeit all-destructive, new form of government, thus the people's revolutions, for more than a hundred years now, have come forth, albeit never successfully, with another new form of government: the system of people's councils to take the place of the Continental party system, which, one is tempted to say, was discredited even before it came into existence.[86]

Arendt associates the appearance of this "system of people's councils" with places and societies that are experiencing the early development of capitalism, arguing that early trade unions joined together to briefly create this new form of government. For a time, people were "not led by official party programs and ideologies, [but] had their own ideas about the possibilities of democratic government under modern conditions."[87] These moments were fleeting because states eventually adapted to the appearance of such groups by granting suffrage to citizens without property.[88] In doing so, trade unions and laborers were elevated to the status of interest groups that could form political parties and press for particular demands within the confines of the nation-state.

Where Arendt differs from Sorel, Benjamin, and much of the socialist tradition is that she sees these developments in the early response to capitalism as "purely" political:

> The enormous power potential these movements acquired in a relatively short time and often under very adverse circumstances sprang from the fact that despite all the talk and theory they were the only group on the political scene which not only defended its economic interests but fought a full-fledged political battle. In other words, when the labor movement appeared on the public scene, it was the only organization in which men acted and spoke *qua* men— and not *qua* members of society.[89]

In this way, Arendt further upends Sorel's insights. While Benjamin claims the general strike is nonviolent, Arendt says it is nonviolent and political. All three thinkers lament the devolution of the general strike into interest groups, parties, or calcified ideologies. Yet each interprets its value and distinctiveness differently: for Sorel, the general strike is characterized by its rejection of politics and embrace of

respect to the expression and exercise of collective freedom, the labor movement and strikes as described by Benjamin and Arendt sketch a historically grounded model with appealing if somewhat ill-defined features. In the final Part of this book, I will try to draw together these ideas and actions to describe what freedom from the perspective of nonviolence means.

violence; for Benjamin, it is unique because it directly transforms economic and social relations through nonviolence; for Arendt, the general strike is novel because it weds political power and freedom.

In fact, even though they are clearly referring to many of the same events, Arendt simply calls the general strike a revolution. Citing the period from 1848 to the 1956 Hungarian Revolution (the latter unfolding even as she wrote *The Human Condition*) Arendt writes:

> If for a time it almost looked as if the movement would succeed in founding, at least within its own ranks, a new public space with new political standards, the spring of these attempts was not labor—neither the laboring activity itself nor the always Utopian rebellion against life's necessity—but those injustices and hypocrisies which have disappeared with the transformation of a class society into a mass society and with the substitution of a guaranteed annual wage for daily or weekly pay.
>
> The workers today are no longer outside of society; they are its members, and they are jobholders like everybody else. The political significance of the labor movement is now the same as that of any other pressure group; the time is past when, as for nearly a hundred years, it could represent the people as a whole—if we understand by *le peuple* the actual political body, distinguished as such from the population as well as from society.[90]

Despite their differences, there is a remarkable similarity between Arendt's "pure politics" and Benjamin's "pure means." Both might seem peculiar, nostalgic, and somewhat ahistorical in comparison to Luxemburg's more subtle appreciation of the interaction between economics and politics, and between violence and nonviolence. We might ask: What is at stake for Benjamin and Arendt in identifying these purportedly more "pure" associations, interactions, and events? Why insist upon these peculiar and particular distinctions, when the reality surely reflects that the economic, social, and political are all deeply intertwined?

For Arendt, the answer is clear. She is casting around for a brand of freedom that neither denies the individual nor shortchanges the power of the collective, while distinguishing itself from freedom expressed or exercised through violence. This theme carries through in *The Human Condition, On Revolution*, her essay "On Violence," and especially her essay "What Is Freedom?" In her essay devoted to freedom, she offers a historical narrative that helps explain the explosive violence that has surrounded two thousand years of attempts to pursue it. The Greeks and the Romans were the first to experience public freedom (a redundant phrase for Arendt), but it was so closely tied to the domination of slaves and barbarians that philosophers such as Epictetus and Augustine thought freedom must be found elsewhere. Yet in locating freedom in our inner life, and specifically in the capacity to freely express our will, philosophers framed government and public life as either irrelevant to or the enemy of freedom. In an attempt to reclaim a brand of public freedom, Rousseau created the general will. But just as the will of an individual requires unanimity within in order to act, the general will as the animating force of government requires unity and singularity as opposed to a plurality and difference. For Arendt, freedom cannot mean imposing one's will upon another, cannot mean sovereignty, and cannot be practiced alone. Instead, power, action, and freedom all require others, and all imply that human beings reveal their uniqueness in the presence of others.[91]

When Martin Luther King Jr. gave his famous "I Have a Dream" speech at the March on Washington for Freedom and Jobs (1963), standing nearby and part of the lineup of speakers was the United Automobile Workers union leader Walter Reuther (1907–1970). Reuther was a veteran of numerous sit-down strikes. Opposed to communist organizing of trade unions, Reuther had helped to organize the International Confederation of Free Trade Unions. In the many struggles leading up to the March, as in the struggles that would follow, Dr. King frequently used the phrase "direct action," borrowing the idea that the masses of people could act without the mediation of formal institutions to achieve economic, social, and political change. But of course, as Dr. King deployed the term, it meant strictly nonviolent action.

If Arendt attempts to describe a brand of freedom that neither falls prey to liberalism's collapsing of freedom with physical life, nor endorses nationalism's claim that freedom requires capturing state sovereignty, nor abides by the socialist and communist elevation of economic need over politics as the litmus test for freedom, it would seem that the development of the practices and theories of nonviolence over the past two centuries provide the closest model. The abolitionist movement aimed to end the most pernicious form of economic domination human beings have invented. The women's movement highlighted the ways property rights and the inequitable valuing of different kinds of labor have been used to oppress women. Most recently, the Arab Spring was touched off by the mistreatment and subsequent self-immolation of a street vendor in dire economic straits. Painstaking organizing of labor unions set the stage for the massive antigovernment protests which followed. In Gene Sharp's catalog of 198 methods of nonviolence, nearly one-fourth (49) involve economic noncooperation or strikes. Economic need is often inseparable from the politics of nonviolent action. However, the politics of nonviolence typically cannot be reduced to demands for physical or material well-being. With

I, she is not entirely immune from arguments that the proletarian general strike and violent revolution would usher forth a period of perpetual peace, equality, and prosperity.[76]

In her insistence on the importance of maintaining vibrant public cooperative associations, Luxemburg presages many of Hannah Arendt's arguments about the role of power in strikes. However, before turning to Arendt, we must examine Walter Benjamin's 1921 essay "Critique of Violence," because it sets the stage for Arendt's unique conception of power. It is also quite possibly the first socialist tract to argue that the strike—or rather, a certain kind of strike—is fundamentally nonviolent. To begin, Benjamin offers an assessment of the natural law tradition that amplifies and crystallizes Sorel's critique of liberal rationalism and resonates strongly with Schmitt's critique of parliamentary law. But instead of distancing the liberal state from violence, he makes the bold claim that all violence is either lawmaking or law-destroying, and that all law, even that which results from parliamentary deliberations, is violent.[77] The natural law tradition, he argues, prevents us from discriminating "within the sphere of means themselves." Instead, it portrays "violent means to just ends [as] no greater problem than a man sees in his 'right' to move his body in the direction of a desired goal."[78] Benjamin says that the law is essentially the human attempt to intervene in fate. Instead of allowing factors beyond our control to determine who lives and dies, the law deigns to make that determination.[79]

What, then, of human attempts to act outside of formal institutions, to act outside of the law? What of human action outside of the natural law tradition, which might allow us to take a critical approach to means regardless of their ends? Like Sorel, Benjamin begins his discussion by postulating that strikes are violent. The collective refusal to work contains an element of extortion whereby the employer is coerced into concessions. Likewise, Benjamin maintains Sorel's distinction between the political general strike and the proletarian general strike, with the former retaining the extortive element of violence. But in a remarkable attempt to turn Sorel's analysis on its head, and in contradiction to much of the socialist tradition, Benjamin maintains that the proletarian general strike is not only nonviolent but is the prime example of what he calls "pure means." He writes:

Against this deep, moral, and genuinely revolutionary conception, no objection can stand that seeks, on the grounds of its possibly catastrophic consequences, to brand such a general strike as violent. Even if it can rightly be said that the modern economy, seen as a whole, resembles much less a machine that stands idle when abandoned by its stoker than a beast that goes berserk as soon as its tamer turns his back, nevertheless the violence of an action can protest of a handful of rural proletarians, and to the first slight stirrings of an agitated military garrison, from the well-educated and elegant revolt in cuffs and white collars in the counting house of a bank to the shy-bold murmurings of a clumsy meeting of dissatisfied policemen in a smoke-grimed dark and dirty guardroom.[72]

Whereas others viewed the failure to overthrow the czar as demonstrating the ineffectiveness of the general strike, Luxemburg saw it as achieving something of vital importance. First, she is not above celebrating "*a general raising of the standard of life of the proletariat*, economic, social and intellectual."[73] The capturing of the state is not the be-all and end-all of the revolution. Second, leveraging her argument to make the case that German trade unions ought to join together in a mass strike of their own, she castigates those who worried that the trade unions would "fall in pieces in a revolutionary whirlwind like rare porcelain" in the face of government crackdown.[74] Instead, she argues that the crackdown in Russia produced a proliferation of trade union organizing that was previously thought to be impossible.

Luxemburg is relentlessly pragmatic in her approach to violence and its place in the strike. The infighting between socialists, communists, and anarchists regarding the usefulness of violence, together with the relative prioritizing of the economic, social, and political are issues that Luxemburg elides by claiming they are all interrelated:

> Political and economic strikes, mass strikes and partial strikes, demonstrative strikes and fighting strikes, general strikes of individual branches of industry and general strikes in individual towns, peaceful wage struggles and street massacres, barricade fighting—all these run through one another, run side by side, cross one another, flow in and over one another—it is a ceaselessly moving, changing sea of phenomena. And the law of motion of these phenomena is clear: it does not lie in the mass strike itself nor in its technical details, but in the political and social proportions of the forces of the revolution.[75]

The different kinds of strikes are part of a historical progression, which she does not so much recommend as a strategy as perceive as the natural course of events. She argues that highly disciplined, nonviolent strikes are necessary in specific industries during the early stages of resistance to capitalism. However, once these strikes inspire a general strike, she expects a rapid escalation of violence due to what will surely be a vigorous attempt on the part of the bourgeoisie to hold on to their property and political power. At this stage, the workers must arm themselves and the bourgeoisie must be disarmed. Like Sorel and the liberals supporting World War

PART IV

Nonviolent Freedom

[The] greatest difficulty in reaching an understanding of what freedom is arises from the fact that a simple return to tradition, and especially what we are wont to call the great tradition, does not help us.

HANNAH ARENDT

Political theory derives justice from the undiscussed value of spontaneity; its problem is to ensure, by way of knowledge of the world, the most complete exercise of spontaneity by reconciling my freedom with the freedom of others. . . . [But] freedom discovers itself murderous in its very exercise.

EMMANUEL LEVINAS

7

The Capacity for Freedom

WE HAVE SEEN that the attempt to achieve, defend, and exercise freedom over the last twenty-five hundred years of the Western political tradition has unleashed extraordinary violence and suffering. It seems that the more radical our commitment to freedom and the more extreme our measures in pursuing it, the further it recedes from our grasp. These investigations might lead us to conclude with Hannah Arendt that, after two millennia of trying to achieve, preserve, and express it, we still have very little idea of exactly what freedom is. Or we might conclude with Emmanuel Levinas that political theory's preoccupation with freedom has been wrongheaded. If it is true that freedom is inherently "murderous," perhaps we should abandon the attempt to achieve, practice, or cultivate it.[1]

However, we have also uncovered a submerged but discernible counter-tradition, in which freedom is achieved, defended, and exercised through nonviolence. In the last part of this book, from that submerged tradition I will develop a theory of nonviolent freedom. Does such a thing exist, and if so what are its critical features? As I have indicated throughout, the most difficult aspect of this question is: what does nonviolent self-rule look like?

The claim that freedom is something that inheres in individuals despite their social, economic, or political circumstances has often been used by advocates of authoritarianism, apologists for various forms of oppression, or those who argue

that freedom is antithetical to politics. Feminists have offered particularly persuasive critiques of concepts of freedom that are overly reliant upon understandings of
individual autonomy at the expense of social and political context.[2] A perverse form
of pacifism extending from the Stoics to Hobbes insists that peace is best achieved
by submissive subjects who defer to the authority of whatever government they live
under for the simple reason that as individuals they are free, in their wills, their
bodies, or both. However, despite these dangers, strong philosophical arguments
support the claim that the capacity for freedom exists and endures, even if it is sometimes atrophied, suppressed, or turned against itself.

In fact, if the capacity for freedom is not a quality of every individual, then the
advocates of violence must be right that violence is an unavoidable and precondi-
tioned action or reaction on certain occasions. In this chapter, I want to establish
that individual freedom, or more precisely the capacity for freedom in every individual, means that violence will always be possible and at the same time is never necessary. Establishing these claims, will take us on a journey through controversial and
difficult issues surrounding the nature of the free will and free thought. Through
a critique and reconstruction of Hannah Arendt's work on freedom, I will argue
that we are all spontaneous and separate beings in dialogue with one another and
ourselves. That is, I will discuss the value of what Levinas claims goes unspoken of in
political theory. Understood in this way, the capacity for freedom in each individual
is indeed potentially murderous; however, it also has a fundamentally egalitarian
and anti-authoritarian aspect to it, protecting against some of the dangers of con-
ceiving of freedom as an individual quality. This capacity for freedom also means
that violence is never necessary in the sense that there is always an opportunity for
a different response to the violence or threat of violence from others. Our lack of
awareness of this aspect of our fundamental capacity is perhaps the greatest obstacle
to its full, public, and political realization.

In the next chapter, I argue that despite this innate individual capacity for
freedom, nonviolent political freedom is always to some degree a collective enterprise. This argument may seem paradoxical because if freedom inheres in each
individual it would seem that we do not need others to realize it. However, I will
argue that political freedom means not only being free from the physical violence
imposed by others on individuals, but also collectively understanding the possibilities of exercising power through nonviolence in response to violence. We
can never be absolutely certain that we will be free from the violence of others. If
being completely secure in one's person was the meaning of freedom, then freedom surely does not and never will exist in this world. Instead, freedom requires
liberating ourselves from the delusion that the ever-present possibility of violence
demands that we respond with physical violence in kind. Drawing on a wide

variety of thinkers, I show that liberation from the so-called necessity of violence requires rejecting it both as a necessary means and an adequate expression of freedom.

Taken together, these two chapters describe the dimensions of a certain brand of self-control and self-rule. Although related to moral virtue and perhaps best expressed when individuals and collectives act with virtue and virtuosity, nonviolent political freedom demands something less stringent than we typically associate with principled action. Minimally, it requires an awareness of our individual capacity for freedom and recognizing this capacity in others and interacting with them on that basis. Although the examples of extraordinary and memorable action that I have often referred to and that we typically associate with nonviolence are demonstrative of the facts of freedom, nonviolent political freedom does not require a brand of self-sacrifice indicative of extraordinary self-control or self-abnegation. Instead, awareness of the facts of freedom can be expressed in extraordinarily subtle habits and actions that we might take little notice of and yet instantiate and cultivate nonviolent freedom. We can think here, for instance, of Václav Havel's paradigmatic example of the greengrocer who lives under a totalitarian government that demands obedience on the most minute level and yet one day decides not to display the "Workers of the World Unite!" sign in his store.[3]

However, in another way, our typical understandings of moral virtue fail to incorporate this minimalist recognition of our own capacities and the capacities of others. Instead, ideas about moral virtue often turn upon ideas about human development, which inevitably end up suggesting that certain people are less developed or less capable of freedom. This is true of the theory of nonviolent political freedom in the sense that some collective bodies have become more aware than others of their capacities and therefore have begun to exercise and cultivate the habits of freedom to a greater extent. However, there is a critical difference between this theory of freedom and self-rule and other theories of moral virtue. The concept of nonviolent political freedom can never justify ruling over those who are "less developed" because it would negate or further push back the time when they become aware of and begin to practice their own freedom.

WHAT GUIDES A FREE WILL?

In our discussion of freedom, we have explored ancient Greece, ancient Rome, and various expressions and ideas about freedom in the medieval, modern, and contemporary periods. However, we have said relatively little about the nearly thousand years when it seemed as if freedom had disappeared from political life. In Hannah Arendt's essay "What Is Freedom?" she argues that after the fall of the

Roman Republic, a wide variety of thinkers disillusioned with the possibility of political freedom turned inward in search of freedom. For Epictetus, the Stoics, and Augustine the issue of freedom was transformed from a political claim into a debate about the nature of the human soul and its relationship to God, nature, and fate.

We have already seen the influence of this disillusionment in debates about public freedom carried out by natural law theorists. Thinkers such as Thomas Aquinas were concerned not only with issues of justice and violence, but also with questions of determinism and free will. We saw in chapter 4 that when John Locke draws from this tradition, grounding sovereignty in the natural freedom to preserve one's life, he breaks from the previous discussions of the free will and offers a new concept of public freedom. But he also brings along an argument about self-defense that was slowly developed over the period when freedom was in hiding. Likewise, when Rousseau introduces the concept of the general will as the only legitimate basis for sovereignty, he is both bringing freedom back into the realm of public activity and drawing from a philosophical tradition that figured the will as a self-sufficient, individual, and apolitical (even anti-political) capacity.

The question of the very existence of free will, as well as its dimensions and critical features if indeed it does exist, has been the subject of philosophical and theological inquiry for at least fifteen hundred years, with precursors rooted in thought at least a thousand years earlier. I will not attempt a comprehensive overview of these discussions, but will instead highlight what I think are some of the most promising portrayals of free will as it relates to the capacity for self-rule and nonviolence. At the same time, I will show how other depictions of free will seem to encourage violence. Typically, depictions of free will by a particular thinker contain aspects of both nonviolence and violence, providing opportunities for both inspiration and critique.

Among the most influential commentators on free will, a critical issue is what aspect of the soul, or the internal life of an individual, must be followed in order for the will to be properly called free. Immanuel Kant (1724–1804), for instance, argues that freedom only manifests itself when one follows the strictures of reason. Autonomy means being free from personal desires and cognizant of a universal moral law, which despite its universal characteristics is nonetheless given by each individual, through reason, to oneself. By contrast, Nietzsche (1844–1900) argues that the will is only free when it follows desire. The distinguishing feature of human will is its capacity to will to power, which involves rejecting the moral sensibilities that are propagated by political and theological authorities. True freedom can be had for the will that instead imposes itself upon others.

In each of these portrayals of free will we see both the possibility for violence and an attempt to describe freedom as inconsistent with it. Thus, Kant's rule of reason involves treating every individual person as an end in and of her or himself. This anti-utilitarian view of humanity makes murder among free people impossible. Yet Kant endorses the death penalty by arguing that appropriately calibrated retribution is consistent with reason and treating individuals as ends.[4] (I discuss this further in the next chapter.) Nietzsche on the other hand argues that punishment is never grounded in reason, and is instead a formalistic attempt to legitimize revenge. The death penalty and other forms of punishment reflect our failure to accept that we cannot will things in the past, and that suffering is an inexorable part of life.[5] Yet Nietzsche's critique of punishment is grounded in an embrace of cruelty and violence in which "giving the law to oneself" means displaying a will to power that overwhelms and destroys all other moral, ethical, and legal systems.[6] The very conception of "conscience" is rejected as nothing but inculcated guilt and a slavish mentality reflecting a weak and overrun will.

So we see that the will as directed by reason or desire can be both a harbor against and an encouragement to physical violence. Yet these portrayals of what makes the will free do not tell us exactly what the will is. Instead of offering yet another in the long line of philosophical attempts to define the will, I will instead describe a cluster of capacities, which I call the "facts of freedom." Establishing the existence of these so-called "facts" relies upon the reader's intuition with regard to her or his experience and whether or not the reader finds the examples I invoke convincing. Moreover, as I will argue below, awareness of these facts of freedom is itself a critical step in bridging "inner" and "outer"—or private and public—freedom.

THE CAPACITY FOR FREEDOM

Arendt's narrative history of freedom in the West describes how the experience of freedom began in the public spaces of Athens and Rome. She says the concept was of little interest to philosophers, until the collapse of those public spaces. Then came the Stoics and Augustine, who figured freedom as something within individuals that could be cultivated away from communal life. Yet the will as Augustine and other Christian thinkers saw it was free because of its capability for negating itself. Just as the freedom of public spaces could be frustrating and stultifying, the idea of free will split the internal life of the individual into two. It was not so much the mortification of the body that was necessary but the disciplining of an impotent and yet at the same time omnipotent will. This led to a deeply repressive and retrenched attitude toward freedom.[7] For Arendt, it is this domineering and tyrannical will that then returns to politics, through the general will in Rousseau and the will to power in Nietzsche with horrifying results.[8]

Arendt herself says there is no going back to ancient public freedom for both practical and ethical reasons. However, she does maintain that a resuscitation of political freedom is possible and I will follow in her footsteps in the next chapter. I will also try to avoid what I take to be her missteps by drawing upon a number of other thinkers that both complement and critique her vision. First, though, I will describe what I take to be the inner life of human freedom. The danger here is that I will simply redo a version of liberalism that starts with the "sovereign individual" with certain rights and then extrapolates to governments and states. However, I think Arendt's description of the inner life helps to mitigate against this danger.

As I will discuss in the next chapter, Arendt's "What Is Freedom?" makes a distinction between sovereignty and rule, in which sovereignty destroys freedom but politics and rule are part and parcel of it. A cursory reading suggests that as part of this effort she is interested in using freedom to drive a wedge between public and private life. However, I want to maintain that through a more careful reading of her essay on freedom and in the work she undertook toward the end of her life we can discern dimensions of "inner" freedom that assist us in *linking* thinking and willing to political action. Arendt's most ambitious intellectual projects are structured by conceptual distinctions. *The Life of the Mind* describes and contrasts thinking, willing, and judging; *The Human Condition* describes and contrasts labor, work, and action; and the separation between the two works is meant to indicate the distinction between the active and contemplative life (*vita activa* and the *vita contemplativa*). In most of her work, our view of freedom is refracted through the lenses of these major conceptual distinctions. We might say that the lost opportunity of her essay "What Is Freedom?" is to show how an overarching concept of freedom might repair some of the breaches between individual and community, thinking and action, and the will and politics that characterize her work. I will attempt to recover that opportunity here.[9]

Arendt tells us that the discovery of the will was the discovery of its impotence by Paul and Augustine. The will is broken: when it tries to control itself, it finds that "'it is resisted'" by the will itself.[10] The result was an attempt by Christians to liberate themselves by "willing to be free"—not so much to be free from sin or temptation, but to be free from the brokenness of the will, thereby gaining self-control. However, when we move to vanquish the resistance of the will to itself, it becomes unified, and (far from becoming free) becomes oppressive. Indeed, according to Arendt, willing ends up destroying the freedom that can really only be had when the will is broken. Only in the moment when we feel that we can do a thing or not do it is our will free.[11] In this way, feeling free involves doing nothing but doing something destroys freedom. The very possibility of self-rule appears hopelessly paradoxical.

Of even greater concern for Arendt is what this paradox does to the possibility of public freedom. In "What Is Freedom?" she does not say exactly how the development of "Christian will-power" becomes a threat to political freedom, but it seems to involve two divergent calamities. First, Christian philosophy repeated and affirmed Epictetus's notion that strengthening the will required withdrawal from public life. At a minimum, Christian theologians, by making the will so central to their analysis, kept the focus of attention on our inner life. Second, a preoccupation with the will was subsequently imputed into public life by Rousseau in his theory of sovereignty. Rousseau's general will attempts to conceive of political power on the model of undivided "individual will-power."[12] In this way, Arendt suggests, the idea of the general will is inherently unpolitical because it denies plurality. Thus the "equation of freedom with the human capacity to will" has had "fatal consequences for political theory."[13] Indeed, the equation has been quite literally fatal for many millions of people because the "famous sovereignty of political bodies" is an "illusion" that is "maintained only by the instruments of violence, that is, with essentially nonpolitical means."[14]

As useful and important as this warning is for a nonviolent conception of freedom, the will cannot be entirely separate from politics. Free will and political freedom must share some connection, even if we maintain the idea that one is an "internal" experience and the other is an "external" one. Arendt is loath to admit this point, but despite her indictment of the will in "What Is Freedom?" it seems that *The Life of the Mind* reopens the issue of how the free will is related to politics. Arendt says therein that the will is the "spring of action" and "prepares the ground on which action can take place."[15] This assertion is startling, since action is the lifeblood of politics for Arendt. Even more surprising is that she makes only a halting effort to further describe the link between willing and action.[16] The overall significance of these passages (and whether or not they represent a change in her thought) has been the source of much consternation in Arendt scholarship.[17] I will try to spell out the connection between free willing and political freedom more clearly.

Technically, the *free* will disappears the moment it is enacted—the moment the will is resolved to itself and appears in the world. Arendt identifies the inner experience of indeterminacy as the moment when the will is free. "[T]he human will is indetermined, open to contraries, and hence broken only so long as its sole activity consists in forming volitions; the moment it stops willing and starts to act on one of the will's propositions, it loses its freedom. . . ."[18] This is the case because once the will is resolved to itself and is exercised, it appears to us as though it was *necessary*.[19]

The notion that "what I just did was necessary" is an understandable mental habit among beings who want to make sense of experience, but "the will I just exercised" is not an illusion. Arendt writes that the power of the will "as a mental potency . . . does not consist, as in Epictetus, in shielding the mind against reality but on the contrary, inspires it and endows it with self-confidence."[20] The view of the free will offered by the theologian Duns Scotus (1266–1308) is critical here. Arendt says that Scotus has Aristotle in mind as he formulates his theory of the will, suggesting that his conception of free will is like "sheer activity." In "What Is Freedom?" Arendt provocatively suggests that Augustine's concept of the free will contains within it an attempt to understand the will as the capacity to begin something new and unexpected. She goes so far as to say that Augustine believes the free will gives us the power to perform non-supernatural miracles. History is made by interrupting the natural course of events.[21] Moreover, to perform such "miracles" requires virtue and virtuoso performances.[22]

Herein lies the connection between free will and political freedom. The will, once enacted and no longer free from the standpoint of the individual reflecting on the past becomes, under the right conditions, politically free in the same instant. Although Arendt never says it, the conclusion is unavoidable that the only possible source of political action is a free will. With Kant, Duns Scotus, and Augustine, Arendt says that the will is not only the condition of *liberum arbitrium* (having a range of choices), but also the power to begin something new.[23] She writes that "freedom of spontaneity is part and parcel of the human condition. Its mental organ is the Will."[24] By the end of the volume on willing she has begun to refer to "free acts." From the standpoint of spectators of politics, the exercise of the will appears as the arrival of the newcomer and the disclosure of the unique person, the "who."[25] Furthermore, the will "freely designs ends that are pursued *for their own sake*, and of this pursuance only the will is capable."[26] In the next chapter, I explore Arendt's use of the Greek concept of *archien*, which means both to rule and begin something new. The creative exercise of free will must be how we distinguish ourselves from (and compete with) others.[27] Since political action proper is not concerned with material things or the achievement of particular ends, its source cannot be desire or even practical reason, it must be free will itself.[28]

What are the right conditions under which the exercise of the will can be politically free? Arendt's public sphere must consist of wills exercised freely in the presence of one another. Only free wills made manifest with other free wills could instantiate the condition of plurality that is necessary for politics, because only people capable of acting spontaneously could create such a diverse field. Individual free wills prepare the ground for action but, when each acts, it is no longer free. However, if the will is exercised in the presence of others who are likewise freely resolving broken wills, the resulting actions can constitute political freedom. The public sphere consists (one is tempted to say exclusively) of the exercise of free and creative wills and it is *the possibility of public freedom that saves us from losing the experience of freedom once the will becomes manifest.*

A critical aspect of the connection between the free will and political freedom is Arendt's discussion of the I-can. What is important to note here is that being willing to do something is different than being able to do something.[29] As Harry Frankfurt writes, "to deprive someone of his freedom of action is not necessarily to undermine the freedom of the will."[30] The sense that I can do something involves the free will in the means/ends relationship of fabrication.[31] Yet Arendt means fabrication in a very particular sense. The will has in mind here itself as a causal agent that creates an "external object." The free will is not concerned with the work of *homo faber*; instead, its "product" consists of doing something. The mental experience of "I-can," a "mental potency" that "inspires and endows [us] with self-confidence," is the internal experience that corresponds to action in the public realm. The I-can when actualized either is affirmed and "saved" by others or is stifled by other wills rejecting it. Yet in either case, the will is rescued and free because it is precisely the separation and the necessarily dialogical quality of being in the public realm with others that gives action meaning, as others reject or accept such actions.

Two other thematic parallels between willing and action suggest such a connection. First, the notion that once a free will is exercised it becomes paradoxically "determined" is consistent with Arendt's description of political action. In *The Life of the Mind* she writes:

> [A]n act can only be called free if it is not affected or caused by anything preceding it and yet, insofar as it immediately turns into a cause of whatever follows, it demands a justification which, if it is to be successful, will have to show the act as the continuation of a preceding series, that is, renege on the very experience of freedom and novelty.[32]

Our mental propensity to demand justification and make sense of the world in terms of causal chains makes it *seem* as though the previous mental experience of indeterminacy and freedom was an illusion. By the same token, Arendt emphasizes in *The Human Condition* that political action—the quintessentially "free" act—has endless consequences and is irreversible. Political action is both unpredictable and cannot be undone.[33] Our propensity for thinking that free actions done in the past were "necessary" may be the cause of such irreversibility, or irreversibility may be the cause of our propensity for thinking things were necessary. Either way, the irreversibility of political action and the apparently determined quality of the free will are closely related.

We can think of many examples where a single individual acts spontaneously without regard for the long-term consequences, with results that nonetheless reverberate in the public sphere and make history. We can think of Lucretia's suicide or the speech of the veteran debtor in the forum described in chapter 3. In our own time, the most enduring image from the Tiananmen Square uprising in China in 1989 is the figure of a lone individual standing in the way of a tank. In Tunisia in 2011, 26-year-old Mohamed Bouazizi, a street vendor frustrated by his inability to make a living due to the harassment of government officials, set himself on fire, sparking mass demonstrations which toppled the government and led to the Arab Spring. When Rosa Parks was arrested in December 1955 for refusing to give up her seat for a white passenger on a bus in Montgomery, Alabama, it galvanized a boycott that would propel the civil rights movement. In Primo Levi's memoir describing his time in Auschwitz, he tells the story of a prisoner who is hung before a gathering of his fellow prisoners for being part of a plot to blow up the crematoriums. Levi writes that just before his execution the man cried out: "Comrades, I am the last one!" His words "pierced through the old thick barriers of inertia and submissiveness, it struck the living core of man in each of us."[34] One doubts that the "last one" imagined his words would appear in a memoir read by millions.

Such examples do not show us that freedom always means political success. However, they do demonstrate that even in conditions of extreme repression, free action remains a possibility. These actions demonstrate that Arendt's description of the political character of the human condition hold even when her ideal conditions for public life are not in place—indeed, even when we are actively working to deny or suppress the political character of humanity. In each instance, the individual is not simply choosing to take a particular action among various options, but is instead initiating creative words and deeds that change the character of the world.

THE BROKEN WILL AND FREE THOUGHT

Political freedom revivifies in public our private experience of the free will. Yet the exercise of political freedom is not exactly the same thing as the exercise of the free will. Arendt maintains that the inner experience of the broken will is not dialogical—the will comes up against itself but does not "discuss" anything with itself.[35] The experience of political freedom, on the other hand, is a matter of doing and speaking with one another, so even while such actions may be impelled by a free will, the internal experience of having a free will does not really feel like the external experience of political freedom. Willing may be more or less exhilarating than action, but it is not the same thing. However, even here there are similarities. Arendt emphasizes that willing involves the internal experience of "impotence," and action involves the external experience of "frustration."

Also, the brokenness of the will inspires thinking,[36] and thinking—or what I will call free thought—involves an internal experience that is similar to what Arendt describes as external political freedom. As with willing, she is loath to admit to connections between internal thinking and external action. She suggests that thinking is impossible when one is acting, and (more plausibly) that thinking brings action to a halt or slows it down. The thinking versus acting distinction is the most important nexus of the larger *vita contemplativa–vita activa* split. Thinking is not "real" because it does not exist anywhere—it is homeless and tends toward generalizations.[37]

Arendt says that philosophers were not interested in freedom until its public collapse. However, two Greeks with whom she is very well acquainted disprove that claim. First, while the "two-in-one" of thought is not the same as the two-in-one of the free will, there is no doubt that Socratic thinking bears some kind of relationship to freedom. If the invention of the free will is taken from the public life of debate and deliberation, then surely the invention of thinking borrows something from the public life of Athens. Socrates strenuously argues that the methods he uses are counter to and different from (even an antidote to) the brand of public freedom that Athenians so prize. The rhetoricians and orators are the anti-philosophers. But even from a cultural standpoint, it is typically understood that the rise of philosophy took place in conjunction with democracy, in large part because it was possible to experiment with different forms of free and frank (*parrhesia*) discussion.[38] Second, while in her early essays Arendt attributes her concept of public freedom to Augustine, her later works demonstrate that it is Aristotle who is a primary inspiration. While it may be too strong to claim that Aristotle was preoccupied with freedom, he certainly offers a conception of it that is integral to his overall theory of politics.

Arendt must not believe political theorizing is an oxymoron. Even if not a "real" conversation, she says that Socrates discovered "that we can have intercourse with ourselves, as well as with others, and that the two kinds of intercourse are somehow interrelated."[39] She allows that thinking can be a kind of backstop against evil, and famously condemned the Nazi bureaucrat Adolf Eichmann for his thoughtlessness.[40] Some have suggested that Arendt is attempting to integrate the practices of thinking, judging, and acting.[41] There is substantial evidence for this claim. She connects the "discovery" of the two-in-one with Aristotle's remark that " '[t]he friend is another self' "[42] and in *The Human Condition* states that thought "is still possible, and no doubt actual, wherever men live under the conditions of political freedom."[43] Thinking is an activity that "is its own end,"[44] which is something she often says about politics and political freedom. Political freedom is frustrating because one's freedom is checked by the freedom of others, which can mean nothing is accomplished and we are prevented from acting together. Likewise, free thought can produce paralysis and disable our capacity to act as individuals. Speaking in the presence of others is risky because one's opinions might be refuted. Free thought can destroy one's assumptions and previous understandings.

Both free thought and political freedom are creative. Despite the fact that it is sometimes frustrating, acting together with others also holds the potential for power. Although she is willing to admit that the free will prepares the ground for action, we have to add something to Arendt to delineate the ways in which free thought facilitates the free will. We know from C. S. Peirce (1839–1914) (and perhaps Duns Scotus as well) that thinking not only comes from our experience of a broken will, but also can repair it and, to borrow Arendt's phrase, prepare the ground for the will.[45] Socrates says he is a midwife that brings forth new opinions, and although Arendt is correct that he finds many of these ideas to be "wind-eggs" as opposed to "real" children, he certainly sees thinking as not exclusively a destructive exercise, but a creative exercise as well.[46] Indeed, while Arendt suggests that Socrates the gad-fly stimulates only the Athenian's internal "feelings" of being alive,[47] both the plain and the sensible meanings of the passage in *The Apology* suggest that he believes his questioning will lead Athens to have a more active intellectual life, which in turn, he hopes, will make it act more justly.[48] Indeed, one wonders why the Athenians would have bothered to bring to trial and kill Socrates if thinking and questioning were only tangential to the character of political life.[49]

At the very least, then, we can say that thinking with oneself in private has a lot in common with discussing things with others. It probably also sets the table for political freedom. For example, consider the writings and life of Frederick Douglass, who describes in *My Bondage and My Freedom* his devastating realization that his grandmother and the cabin in which she lived were owned by someone else, his struggle to learn to read and write when it was illegal for slaves to do so, and his sense that his thinking about his circumstances both made him miserable and ultimately inspired him to try to escape them.[50] We might also point to a line in his famous speech on "The Meaning of July Fourth for the Negro" where he states that "Oppression makes a wise man mad."[51] Wisdom is the result of thinking about one's experience, and it changes the experience of oppression, creating internal pressure that can lead in many directions.

Epictetus argues that freedom can be had even if one is a slave, as long as one orders the inner life with equanimity. In a sense, we can see this as an utter abandonment of the value of public freedom, and even as an apology for slavery. We can also see it as a precursor of the perverse post-Augustinian Christian "pacifism" that advocates obedience to the state under almost every circumstance. On the other hand, this notion of inner freedom opens up extraordinary political possibilities.

Arendt's essay on freedom discusses self-control extensively. Self-control often ends up being mobilized for politics, as seen in Buddhist monks in Burma and Tibet, liberation theology in Latin America, and Christian resistance to Rome. Arendt overlooks how inner freedom can be externalized in ways that are not tyrannical and domineering, but instead in precisely the kind of action she is interested in cultivating.

I have tried to show that free will, free thought, and political freedom hold certain qualities in common. Free thought, free willing, and political freedom are all characterized by a capacity for creativity and spontaneity, which can bring something new into the world and which carries potential for destroying the old. Free thought can prepare the ground for free willing, and free willing can prepare the ground for political action. In turn, a public life characterized by the plurality of free wills appearing to one another saves the will from its deterministic tendencies. Free discussion in the public realm shares some connection to free thought and philosophical conversation. Free thought, free willing, and political freedom are all activities that are their own ends. The critical facts of freedom inhere in the character of subjective and intersubjective reality. We are spontaneous beings with creative capacities that allow us to begin something new. We are separated from one another and from ourselves in the sense that there is sufficient space between us to ensure that our very existence, with and without others, is dialogical. In this sense, everyone is free.

AWARENESS OF THE FACTS OF FREEDOM

In the last chapter, I mentioned that nationalist thinkers and scholars of nationalism emphasize the socially constructed and educative aspects of becoming "a people." Likewise, socialists of all varieties, but especially those interested in creating model communities and cultivating self-rule, claim that educating people in their capacity for self-rule must precede a new brand of more equitable politics. In addition, a vast scholarship claims that free thought, free will, and political freedom were "discovered." The historians of Ancient Greece, Buddhist thinkers, Arendt, and Mahatma Gandhi all emphasize that freedom involves becoming aware of one's capacity for freedom. Freedom, even on an individual level but certainly on a political and collective one, requires a brand of self-awareness.

In Arendt's work, the idea of awareness appears in conjunction with all three valences of freedom explored above: free thought, free willing, and political freedom. Arendt says that the only adequate metaphor for free thinking is "the sensation of being alive,"[52] recalling Socrates's belief that "the wind of thinking [awakens] you from your sleep."[53] In her descriptions of free will, she says that the "Will's freedom consists in freely affirming or negating or hating whatever confronts it. It is this freedom of the will mentally to *take a position*."[54] The key word for my purposes is "mentally," because it indicates that the will is free when it is conscious of its freedom. Arendt writes (citing Scotus) that "the willing ego in performing [either the will or the nil] is aware of being free to perform its contrary also."[55] Finally, in politics, our imagination is engaged in judgment, which involves cultivating an "enlarged mentality" where we can see things from the standpoint of others and hence formulate more expansive conceptual categories. Indeed, Linda Zerilli, citing Kant in an effort to clarify Arendt, persuasively argues that in the moment we embrace our capacity to imagine something new, "we *feel* our freedom" (italics mine).[56]

Historians who disagree on a wide variety of issues describe the Athenian "discovery" of political freedom (or Greek discovery, there is dispute on that matter as well) as a matter of becoming aware. Raaflaub writes that the significance of the discovery lies in "a new political awareness" and "a vast leap in the consciousness of freedom."[57] Likewise, Josiah Ober argues that the "episteme-shattering-and-creating-moment of revolution"[58] occurred when the Athenian people, by besieging a Spartan king for three days on the Acropolis, first understood themselves and acted as " 'I, the people.' "[59] This understanding, in turn, was made possible by a nascent "demotic self-consciousness"[60] that prepared the way for the moment when they had become "sufficiently self-conscious to act in concert."[61]

Similar themes also appear in the Buddhist conception of freedom. Although many scholars interpret karma as a kind of fatalism, others argue that it does not deny that we have free will, but only that the consequences of our actions are irreversible and long-lasting. Karma, which literally means "action," is a "form of self-expression."[62] Freedom lies in awakening to and fully accepting the ways in which action is frustrating, troublesome, and implicated in the cycle of suffering and rebirth. Emphasizing that each person "must think for themselves and test the truth of things,"[63] Buddha (as The Awakened One) frees himself of this cycle by no longer feeling attached to the achievement of particular ends.[64] Arendt sounds more like the Buddha than Homer or Pericles when she says that judging political action requires setting aside "motives and intentions on the one hand, and aims and consequences on the other."[65]

Finally, Gandhi's concept of freedom—swaraj (self-rule)—also contains the theme of awareness. Again and again, he urges Indians to accept freedom as something they already have, as opposed to something that must be achieved or won. Each person, like the community as a whole, needs to become aware of their own capacities. Arguing that whether or not the British are expelled from India has little bearing on whether or not India is free, he says: "[I]f we become free, India is free. And in this thought you have a definition of Swaraj. It is Swaraj when we learn to rule ourselves. It is, therefore, in the palm of our hands. Do not consider this Swaraj to be like a dream."[66] If the British left and Indians adopted their repressive government structures, they would not be free. If the British stayed but Indians became aware of and exercised their capacities, they would be free.

Swaraj is a particularly useful term because it indicates that both individuals and communities rule themselves. Gandhi writes:

> In this age of democracy it is essential that desired results are achieved by the collective effort of the people. It will no doubt be good to achieve an objective through the effort of a supremely powerful individual, but it can never make the community conscious of its corporate strength.[67]

At the same time, he argues that a single individual, if sufficiently practiced in creative nonviolence, can keep all violence at bay.[68] The crucial thing was for India and Indians to become free by realizing they already were free. For Gandhi, freedom also meant taking responsibility for one's actions, and being guided by duty.

A wide variety of thinkers identify freedom with awakening to, becoming aware of, or realizing the facts of freedom. As I noted from the outset, Levinas points out that our separation from one another, together with our creativity and spontaneity, makes violence among us possible. Almost all of the conceptions of freedom explored in this book argue that one must become aware of freedom in order to be free, and that gaining such awareness is sometimes connected to violence. For instance, liberals such as John Stuart Mill argue that people who have yet to develop their capacity for reason require despotism. Communists and anarchists argue that when false consciousness plagues the proletariat, the "propaganda of the deed," which for many thinkers included acts of violence, may be the best route to shaking the oppressed from their slumber. Many nationalists argue that a collective sense of identity—awareness of one's status as a community member—can be forged by making war on others and is critical to exercising freedom. Even more disturbing, we might say that certain individual creative acts of violence might express freedom as well. Arendt, for instance, is enamored with Achilles' distinctive actions even though she generally contrasts violence and action.[69] Even in the examples of individual, creative history-making action I offered above, we might see an element of violence in the self-sacrifice or outright suicide of individuals attempting to change their political circumstances.

Yet Levinas's description of spontaneity maps unevenly on to the facts of freedom. Freedom is realizing and fully embracing the implications of the fact that we are separate beings. From the standpoint of the individual, this realization means becoming aware of the fact that I am a spontaneous and creative being in dialogue with myself and with other creative and spontaneous beings. From the standpoint of community, freedom is realizing and fully embracing the implications of the fact that we are spontaneous and creative beings in dialogue with one another and ourselves.

The facts of freedom as I have described them here cannot be secured or promoted by acts of physical violence. Neither can physical violence help us become aware of the facts of freedom. The phrase "creative acts of violence" contains an element of self-contradiction, given that any creative aspects of violence are always but accoutrements to the distinguishing feature of violence: the destruction of bodies. In his magisterial effort to describe "the rebel," Albert Camus grapples with precisely the paradox presented by our separation, creativity, and freedom in an attempt to recover freedom from advocates of revolutionary violence on one hand and perverse pacifism on the other:

> The moment that we recognize the impossibility of absolute negation—and merely to be alive is to recognize this—the very first thing that cannot be denied is the right of others to live. . . . In actual fact, this form of reasoning assures us at the same time that we can kill and that we cannot kill. It abandons us in this contradiction with no grounds either for preventing or for justifying murder, menacing and menaced, swept along with a whole generation intoxicated by nihilism, and yet lost in loneliness, with weapons in our hands and a lump in our throats.[70]

Camus's description of the rebel rejects liberal, communist, and nationalist attempts to square the valuing of the right to life (or certain lives) with murder that aims to protect it. Freedom also aims to find a way out of this contradiction. Acts of physical violence, even if made possible by freedom, compromise freedom by destroying the spontaneity and creativity of other individuals and denying that we are in dialogue with others.

If we follow Arendt's understanding of conscience as the two-in-one of thinking, doing physical violence may also amount to a denial that we are in dialogue with ourselves. Arendt posits that being in active dialogue with oneself leads some to conclude that they do not want to live with a murderer (i.e., oneself).[71] Recall Gandhi's claim that liberty is "[the] ability to act according to the dictates of our conscience," which means "we certainly cannot achieve it by force of arms, i.e., by physical violence."[72] Gandhi posits that liberty means recognizing this in ourselves and living with others who recognize this. This conception of freedom bears a resemblance to one of Montesquieu's definitions of liberty, as "the power of doing what we ought to will, and in not being constrained to do what we ought not to will."[73] These concepts are political in the sense that being prevented from acting according to our conscience depends upon how those around us act. Both concepts in turn relate to Kant's concept of freedom as having moral autonomy, and both imply that certain forms of collective organization are more or less conducive to freedom.[74] But for now we should note that, by limiting the free play of others and making them conform to our wishes, physical violence not only ends dialogue with others but potentially denies the existence of our internal dialogue, or free thought. Conversely, recognition and awareness of free thought and its implications sets us on the road to freedom and in a certain way brings it to fruition.

By incorporating "rule" into his conception of freedom, Gandhi attempts to resolve the critical issue we must now address. If people are not really free until they become aware of the facts of freedom, then what are the consequences of this awareness? If physical violence undermines the freedom that makes it possible, how then can we rule one another or ourselves? Is there a brand of rule that does not practice physical violence? Can ruling account for the fact that we are spontaneous beings in dialogue with ourselves and others? Liberalism is tasked with explaining how freedom is preserved by executing thieves and criminals, or by putting them in jail. Communism tries to convince us that freedom can be achieved by confiscating a rich person's property or killing the bourgeoisie who resist the destruction of private property. Nationalism attempts to implement freedom by showing the superiority of "the people" by excluding or destroying those who are not part of that group. In a similar way, advocates of nonviolent freedom face the problem of how to preserve freedom without compromising it. However, the problem of freedom and rule for a conception of nonviolent freedom is greater than all of these other ideologies because it tries to avoid the use of violence altogether.

Little quarrels of millions of families in their daily lives disappear before the exercise of this force. Hundreds of nations live in peace. History does not and cannot take note of this fact. History is really a record of every interruption of the even working of the force of love or of the soul.

MAHATMA GANDHI

[States] that are today nominally democratic have either to become frankly totalitarian or, if they are to become truly democratic, they must become courageously nonviolent.

MAHATMA GANDHI

8

Nonviolent Political Freedom

THROUGHOUT THIS BOOK I have discussed social and political movements whose work remains unfinished. The labor movement, the women's rights movement, the attempt to abolish slavery, the efforts of those attempting to overthrow or democratize repressive, authoritarian regimes, and the peace movement all remain active. Other movements, which I have only briefly touched upon, also take the pursuit of freedom to be their animating force, whether it be minority groups striving for recognition and political power, the worldwide struggle for LGBT rights, efforts to resist violent incursions by great powers in the affairs of countries beyond their borders, the prison abolition movement, or the animal liberation movement. Despite the similarities between many of these movements, there is still significant disagreement among these groups as to the meaning of freedom and self-rule, especially when it comes to the issue of violence. I have suggested throughout that freedom sought through violence typically results in internecine conflict, and self-rule that ends up looking more like domination. In Part I, I argued that historical and empirical analysis demonstrates that nonviolence is a more effective and more consistent means to liberation than violence.

In this final chapter, I wish to accomplish two things. I suggested that the secessions of the plebs provide an alternative to the modern idea that freedom must be defended with violence; however, I have yet to give a full account of how free societies can defend themselves without resorting to violence. The first task of this chapter is to show that overlooked philosophical arguments, other historical examples, critiques of the prison-industrial complex, and a well-developed literature on nonviolent civil defense all suggest that defending extant institutions, combating crime and corruption, and even repelling violent invaders can be achieved with nonviolent means. In fact, only a self-conscious and collective capacity to exercise power without resorting to violence, can secure political freedom.

The second task and final argument of the book is to show how expressing and exercising freedom are inescapably linked to nonviolence. I begin by examining some preeminent if flawed attempts to separate the exercise of freedom from violence. Hannah Arendt, Isaiah Berlin, Immanuel Kant, and Mahatma Gandhi each attempt to describe a kind of self-rule that either marginalizes or eliminates the need for violence. I point to the strengths and weaknesses of their approaches and argue that they correct and complement one another in important ways. This argument leads me to a conception of nonviolent political freedom, which brings together all of the various movements examined in this project under the banner of human freedom. By rejecting the tyrannical and violent aspects that have so long accompanied conceptions of freedom, we can describe a brand of self-rule that resists violence even while drawing upon the submerged practice of nonviolence, which has quietly accomplished so much.

ÉTIENNE DE LA BOÉTIE AND THE DEFENSE OF FREEDOM

Making the case for nonviolence as the superior means for defending freedom is a bit more complicated than making the case for nonviolence as the best means for liberation, in part because it has less frequently been tried. As I have argued, the defense of freedom as associated with the preservation of liberal or republican states is indelibly tied to the state's capacity to kill criminals and invaders, which in turn draws its legitimacy from its so-called "natural enforcement powers." While liberation movements the world over have experimented with and shown the effectiveness of nonviolence in toppling governments and achieving political, social, and economic change, the idea that freedom can be preserved or that tyranny and criminal violence can be deterred with nonviolence requires recovering lost histories, examining marginalized alternatives to violent defense, and resuscitating frequently overlooked philosophical arguments.

I will begin with an examination of Étienne De La Boétie's (1530–1563) *Discourse on Voluntary Servitude (or Anti-Dictator)* (1548). La Boétie's essay is a strident defense of freedom against tyranny, which at first may seem to undermine the entire line of argument I make in chapter 4. Well before Thomas Hobbes and John Locke, and reaching back into ancient history, La Boétie argues that the Spartans defended Greece and their own city against the Persians in the name of preserving freedom. He recounts a story from Herodotus wherein the Spartans send two emissaries to Xerxes as penance for killing two of the Persian ruler's messengers. When Xerxes' representative offers great power to the emissaries if they submit to his rule, they reply:

> By such words, Hydarnes, you give us no good counsel . . . because you have experienced merely the advantage of which you speak; you do not know the privilege we enjoy. You have the honor of the king's favor; but you know nothing about liberty, what relish it has and how sweet it is. For if you had any knowledge of it, you yourself would advise us to defend it, not with lance and shield, but with our very teeth and nails.[1]

Here we seem to have the modern concept of defending freedom with violence. Moreover, Herodotus refers to the Athenians as defending freedom both in their efforts to repel the Persians[2] and (less surprisingly) in their last-ditch effort to stop the incursions of Alexander the Great.[3]

However, neither the ancient histories upon which he relies nor the spirit of La Boétie's essay conveys the modern sense of defending freedom. First, we should note that Herodotus does not use the term "freedom" to refer to a particular type of government, in a way that approximates a concept of natural rights, or in relation to bodily integrity. It is telling that emissaries from Sparta, no democratic regime, claim to be interested in defending freedom. Indeed, Herodotus refers to Cyrus, the founder of Persia, as having "won the Persians their freedom."[4] While the efforts of the Athenians are associated with democratic figures such as Themistocles, they are said to have defended the freedom of Greece—not Greek democracy. As the example of the Spartans suggests, some Greeks may have materially benefited by replacing their own rulers with Persian rule, and Herodotus indicates that many Greek cities were divided as to whether or not to resist or become acolytes. So if defending freedom here does not mean preserving a particular regime type or defending one's physical well-being, it must mean something along the lines of "independence," or simply not being "enslaved" to a foreign power.

Second, contrary to the modern conception of defending freedom, La Boétie offers an understanding of how freedom can be defended without violence. Written when he was only 18 years old, the essay at times makes contradictory claims. For instance, while the entire thrust of his argument suggests that freedom means resisting the absolute power of an individual, he reserves judgment on whether or not monarchy is the best form of government. Similarly, while roundly criticizing historical tyrants and contemporary autocrats such as the Grand Turk, he expresses loyalty and admiration for the French King.[5]

Yet the clear through-line of the essay is an argument about the nature of oppression and the role of consent and obedience in sustaining it. La Boétie expresses wonder and amazement that people so frequently "suffer plundering, wantonness, cruelty, not from an army, not from a barbarian horde, on account of whom they must shed their blood and sacrifice their lives, but from a single man; not from a Hercules nor from a Samson, but from a single little man."[6] He posits that this suffering is made possible not through simple cowardice, which is not an adequate explanation for the degradation of so many by a single person. Instead, what makes tyranny possible is the failure to realize the nature of political power:

> Obviously there is no need of fighting to overcome this single tyrant, for he is automatically defeated if the country refuses consent to its own enslavement: it is not necessary to deprive him of anything, but simply to give him nothing; there is no need that the country make an effort to do anything for itself provided it does nothing against itself. It is therefore the inhabitants themselves who permit, or, rather, bring about, their own subjection, since by ceasing to submit they would put an end to their servitude.[7]

He details multiple ways in which people provide for the well-being and power of tyrants:

> You sow your crops in order that he may ravage them, you install and furnish your homes to give him goods to pillage; you rear your daughters that he may gratify his lust; you bring up your children in order that he may confer upon them the greatest privilege he knows—to be led into his battles, to be delivered to butchery, to be made the servants of his greed and the instruments of his vengeance; you yield your bodies unto hard labor in order that he may indulge in his delights and wallow in his filthy pleasures; you weaken yourselves in order to make him the stronger and the mightier to hold you in check.[8]

Well before liberal and republican arguments suggesting that governments should be based upon the consent of the governed, La Boétie makes a much more far-reaching claim. He argues that the consent of the governed is the lifeblood of government—that it simply cannot function without it. Well before Marx's theory of surplus labor, he argues that those intent upon domination extract labor from others and then receive gratitude from the oppressed for anything the oppressor gives back.[9]

In contrast to both of these later traditions, however, La Boétie argues that violence is completely unnecessary to correct laws that allow for exploitation and check rulers who do as they please. People can defend and preserve their freedom, which he associates with natural right, without revolution, assassination, or any violence whatsoever:

> But if not one thing is yielded to them, if, without any violence they are simply not obeyed, [tyrants] become naked and undone and as nothing, just as, when the root receives no nourishment, the branch withers and dies. To achieve the good that they desire, the bold do not fear danger; the intelligent do not refuse to undergo suffering.[10]

Some short-term sacrifice may be necessary in order to defend one's natural right and freedom. However, La Boétie goes so far as to say that freedom can be had even without taking political action. It is simply a matter of the will: "From all these indignities, such as the very beasts of the field would not endure, you can deliver yourselves if you try, not by taking action, but merely by willing to be free. Resolve to serve no more, and you are at once freed."[11]

Recall that this is the very moment when free will and the concept of natural right are emerging from the Middle Ages, concepts that will undergird sovereignty in the works of Vitoria and Grotius. La Boétie introduces the possibility that the will alone, because of its capacity for *refusal*, is sufficient for political freedom. Here is a different understanding of what it means to defend freedom. Instead of the will and natural right as the foundation of sovereignty, he posits them as the rock upon which sovereignty both relies *and founders*. One is reminded here of Gandhi's claim that swaraj is in "the palm of our hands."

Yet La Boétie does not forward a positive understanding of self-rule. Certainly, he suggests that human beings are basically equal, and he briefly portrays our natural state as one of mutual interest and capabilities.[12] But once he asserts that the simple refusal of the will to cooperate is sufficient bulwark against tyranny and exploitation, he turns to the great puzzle that the essay seeks to solve, which is why people fail to realize this fact. He offers many reasons, including initial terrifying acts of violence by rulers, the habit of obedience cultivated over generations by those who live under the rule of tyrants, the stifling of speech and communication among those who yearn for freedom, the use of magic, religion, and other symbols of power, and the ability of savvy rulers to co-opt language and titles that suggest their actions serve the people and the public welfare.

However, the primary targets of his ire are the government functionaries who make the rule of tyrants possible. Here he begins by arguing that while most would conclude that rulers are protected by physical means, displays of force are really only for show:

> I come now to a point which is, in my opinion, the mainspring and the secret of domination, the support and foundation of tyranny. Whoever thinks that halberds, sentries, the placing of the watch, serve to protect and shield tyrants is, in my judgment, completely mistaken. These are used, it seems to me, more for ceremony and a show of force than for any reliance placed in them.[13]

Instead, the true source of domination is an organizational structure in which each individual is dependent upon other individuals, all of whom are driven by a desire for some perceived or real gain. For instance, if six people are close advisers who have the ear of the tyrant, and each control six hundred others who profit from their association with the advisor, and those six hundred offer offices and rank to six thousand more, we find that the "consequence of all this is fatal indeed . . . [for] whoever is pleased to unwind the skein will observe that not the six thousand but a hundred thousand, and even millions, cling to the tyrant by this cord to which they are tied."[14] He describes both the lives of tyrants and their functionaries as pitiful. Anticipating the arguments of Montesquieu, he argues that tyrants constantly live in fear, since those around them cannot afford to be honest due to their unequal relationship. The petty functionaries who surround the tyrant live their lives trying to anticipate the needs of the tyrant in order to win favor or keep it. Moreover, the usually wealthy and influential functionaries who expect to gain from their relationship with the tyrant are eventually fleeced of everything, if not by the first tyrant they serve, then by the next. In this way, La Boétie makes the argument for maintaining and defending one's liberties, since no matter how much wealth or favor one may gain from a tyrant, it can be taken away upon a whim.

La Boétie's essay was not well known until the eighteenth century, because his friend Montaigne was worried that it would be misinterpreted as a call to violent revolution.[15] If it had circulated more widely when it was written, the entire history of modern freedom might have a different cast. On the one hand, his critique of overly submissive courtiers and functionaries can be seen as one of many arguments in favor of aristocratic and bourgeois rights. Given his emphasis on the dependency of rulers, perhaps it might even be interpreted as an argument in favor of power-sharing arrangements with monarchs. On the other hand, the essay does something much more radical. Whereas contemporaneous thinkers such as Machiavelli, Gentili, Vitoria, and Grotius tend to focus on how violence is managed and legitimized by regimes (or usurped by those who oppose them), La Boétie argues that violence itself is a distraction, a ruse that masks the true source of political power.

GENE SHARP AND CIVILIAN-BASED DEFENSE

It is only in contemporary political theory that this argument has been revived. The foremost proponent of a similar conception of power is Gene Sharp. Although Sharp's work has been largely ignored by academic political theorists he is one of the most influential political thinkers of the twentieth century, if the impact of his work on world events is considered. From his small office in Boston and in various academic positions, Sharp has consulted for decades with activists from around the world.[16] In his most comprehensive and ambitious work, *The Politics of Nonviolent Action*, he offers a view of power that accounts for factors such as authority, human resources, skills and knowledge, material resources, and sanctions (including physical violence), pointing out that exercising these aspects of power always relies upon the cooperation of others. Identifying four groups in particular (the general population, the ruler's agents, foreign governments, and foreign peoples),[17] Sharp offers almost two hundred examples of resistance techniques that can be employed by them, listing a startling array of examples that involve not only withdrawing consent (as with strikes, boycotts, or resignations) but also creative political action (as in setting up alternative governments, mobilizing demonstrations, and staging critical theater productions).

Although his thinking is mostly known for its implications for resisting existing governments (and especially for toppling dictatorships and authoritarian regimes), Sharp has written extensively on the possibility of using nonviolence to defend existing governments. In *Civilian-Based Defense: A Post-military Weapons System*, Sharp and his coauthor Bruce Jenkins methodically make the case for alternatives to military defense. Realizing that their arguments are likely to be met with skepticism, the authors begin their discussion with four remarkable contemporary examples of what they call "improvised struggles" against internal usurpation and foreign invasion.

With respect to coup d'états, they offer examples from Germany in 1920 and France in 1961. When Dr. Wolfgang Kapp and the right-wing Freikorps successfully ousted the existing government in Berlin, it directed all local governments to refuse cooperation. A general strike led by the Social Democratic Party and widespread noncooperation from civil servants and conservative government bureaucrats led to harsh repression. However, when the Berlin Security Police demanded Kapp's resignation, he fled. Amidst violent skirmishes, the Freikorps once again acknowledged the legal government. The Weimar Republic had "withstood its first frontal attack by the use of popular and governmental noncooperation in defiance against its internal attackers."[18]

The French case is even more dramatic. In April 1961, President Charles de Gaulle signaled that he would abandon the effort to hold on to Algeria. The French First Foreign Legion Parachute Regiment rebelled and took control of Algiers. The rest of the military in Algeria soon followed. With half a million French troops in Algeria, and with two other French divisions in Germany of doubtful reliability, the rebels quickly became a threat to the government in Paris. Political parties and trade unions called for a one-hour symbolic general strike and de Gaulle and Prime Minister Régis Debré appealed to the French people and military in radio broadcasts to resume loyalty to the legal government. De Gaulle's broadcast was heard in Algeria and copies of it were distributed widely. Ten million workers participated in the symbolic general strike. Most French troops in Algeria acted in support of the legal government, removing transport and fighter planes from Algeria. The Algiers police, who had at first supported the coup, were thwarted by civil servants and local government officials who resisted by hiding documents or not showing up for work. When some leaders of the revolt contemplated a violent response, de Gaulle ordered loyalists to violently resist them. The leaders of the revolt soon surrendered or went into hiding, and the coup was defeated with less than a handful of casualties.[19]

With respect to foreign invasions, Sharp and Jenkins offer the examples of Germany in 1923 and Czechoslovakia in 1968. In January 1923, France and Belgium invaded the Ruhr to secure World War I reparations and separate the Rhineland from Germany. Both the German government and trade unions urged adoption of a policy of noncooperation with the occupiers, with the government helping to finance the effort. Although not planned in advance, noncooperation was widespread and diverse, including

the refusal of mine owners to serve the invaders; massive demonstrations at courts during trials of resisters; the refusal of German policemen to salute foreign officials; the refusal of German workers to run the railroads for the French; the dismantling of railroad equipment; the refusal of shopkeepers to sell to foreign soldiers; the refusal of ordinary people, even when hungry, to use occupation-organized soup kitchens; defiant publication of newspapers in spite of many bans; posting of resistance proclamations and posters; and refusal to mine coal.[20]

The occupiers responded with severe repression including the execution, imprisonment, whipping, and seizing of money and personal property of resistors. Resistance to the occupation inspired acts of sabotage, which tempered international support and produced divisions among those resisting the invasion. Eventually, the

noncooperation campaign was called off, but support for the operation within
Belgium and France waned. Occupation forces were withdrawn, with Britain and
the United States intervening to restructure reparations payments. The occupiers
had achieved none of their main objectives.

The final example employed by Sharp and Jenkins is the infamous invasion of
Czechoslovakia by Soviet forces in 1968. Typically understood as a failure of nonviolence in the face of overwhelming military force, Sharp and Jenkins highlight
how the unexpected improvised civilian defense dramatically complicated and pro-
longed what the Soviets expected would be a short operation. When half a million
troops entered Czechoslovakia and the KGB kidnapped or detained all of the key
leaders of the reform-minded regime led by Alexander Dubček, they met with no
military resistance. Instead, they were confronted by a concerted effort by high-level
officials and ordinary citizens to refuse cooperation. The government news agency
refused to issue statements, a radio defense network helped organize the Fourteenth
Party Congress and a one-hour general strike, and rail workers slowed the transfer
of Russian communications tracking and jamming equipment. The upshot was to
make it simply "impossible for the Soviets to find sufficient collaborators to set up
their puppet regime."[21] Facing plummeting morale among their troops, the Soviets
called Czech President Svoboda to Moscow for negotiations, whereupon he immediately demanded that the rest of the Czechoslovak leaders be present. A compromise was worked out, which Sharp and Jenkins argue was "probably a major strategic
mistake."[22] For a week, the general population did not accept the compromise. From
August to April of 1969 there was tentative acceptance of some reforms. However,
anti-Soviet rioting served as a pretext for replacing the reform group and this time
the Soviets had lined up collaborators. Sharp and Jenkins point out that despite the
failure of civilian defense, a military response would have certainly been crushed
more quickly, and the civilian resistance delayed the achievement of Soviet political
objectives for eight months, requiring them to "shift from their initial use of military means to gradual political pressures and manipulations."[23]

Sharp and Jenkins argue that these examples demonstrate the extraordinary
potential of nonviolent civilian-based defense, particularly because in each case
the noncooperation strategy involved very little preparation, planning, or training.
The authors spend a substantial portion of the rest of the volume explaining what
a civilian-based defense system might look like if it was planned in advance and if
existing governments or civil society institutions devoted sufficient resources to its
implementation. They place much emphasis on civil society, its strength or weakness, and relative willingness to act independently in the face of repression. They
argue that a well-publicized training program in civilian-based defense can offer
a credible deterrent to foreign invaders or aspiring dictators. As with traditional

military preparations, a grand strategy of civil resistance—training in diverse tactics as well as developing the capacities of various formal and informal institutions—is required for success.

Since the publication of *Civilian-Based Defense*, others have expanded on the theme and even experimented with the idea. The Dutch government appointed a committee to make recommendations for implementing civilian-based defense systems, which eventually lost funding. Interestingly, considering La Boétie's focus on government functionaries, one aspect of this effort involved cataloging and identifying key persons in the civil service for civilian-based defense training.[24] Other authors have found additional examples of noncooperation as a response to invasion or attempts to usurp governments from within. Perhaps the most dramatic come from the resistance to Nazi occupation, which sometimes proved remarkably effective.[25] Another author has offered powerful arguments against traditional military justifications for self-defense.[26] Jonathan Schell has argued that the growing awareness on the part of the peoples of the world as to the power of noncooperation may have made the world "unconquerable."[27] While these arguments deserve serious consideration, most governments and ordinary people remain committed to the idea that military means are required for defense.

We might ask why governments have not been particularly eager to explore civilian-based defense despite its promise. At the same time, we might also ask how alternatives to traditional methods of defense affect our conceptions of freedom. In theory, a dictator or monarch who maintains the loyalty and favor of the people might use civilian-based defense against an outside invading force, or even against those within who wish to install a democratic government. Yet there are good reasons why rulers might be hesitant to do so. Sharp and Jenkins claim that their analysis is closely related to and encourages freedom because:

> The degree of liberty or tyranny in any political society is ... largely a reflection of the relative determination of the subjects to be free, of their willingness and ability to organize themselves to live in freedom and, very importantly, their ability to resist any efforts to dominate or enslave them. In other words, the population can use the society itself as the means to establish and defend its freedom. Social power, not technological means of destruction, is the strongest guarantor of human freedom.[28]

To fully grasp the significance of this passage requires turning to the arguments Sharp makes in an earlier work, titled *Social Power and Political Freedom*. Although his unassuming tone and patient analysis encourage readers to overlook the polemical aspects of his arguments, Sharp's work strikes at the heart of liberal and republican arguments about the necessity of violent defense, at foundational justifications for sovereign prerogative in modern democratic theory, and at the idea that freedom first and foremost involves the protection of lives and property.

Sharp's argument is complex, but two important points stand out. First, he maintains that freedom requires the maintenance of numerous "loci of power." Against those who argue that certain features of a constitution (i.e., particular institutional structures, the enumeration of rights, or regular elections) create democratic control and freedom, Sharp argues that the character of social power—how it is distributed and how it is generated—is the critical factor in maintaining free societies. The ability to replace a ruler or rulers tells us very little about the extent to which ordinary people are capable of limiting, checking, or guiding those rulers. Without independent groups and institutions willing to take responsibility for making decisions, rule themselves and their local communities, and sacrifice when the state tries to usurp such powers or responsibilities, societies are structurally vulnerable to tyranny, irrespective of their formal institutions or laws.[29]

Second, Sharp argues that the means deployed in political conflicts bear a close relationship to whether power is consolidated or, alternatively, devolved and voluntaristic. The use of violence tends to consolidate the diverse locations of power. Preparations for military conflict generally involve creating hierarchical power structures that require centralized control. During warfare or revolution, the ability to efficiently apply physical violence, quash dissenters, and destroy competing institutions in the name of emergency measures is typically considered paramount. If the outcome of the military conflict is successful, the leaders of the violent struggle often retain these structures. If they have conquered an already existing state, then they will add to its existing powers. Moreover, the example set by the conflict will encourage rulers to use violence to defend themselves from internal or external enemies. All of this contributes to a feeling of dependency and overall helplessness on the part of ordinary citizens, who come to "regard violence as the only kind of effective power and the only real means of struggle."[30]

The use of nonviolent means tends to have the opposite effect. Sharp notes that although strong leadership often plays an important role in nonviolent struggle, leaders are frequently jailed or killed, so that sustaining nonviolence requires members of the movement to plan and strategize on their own. Moreover, as nonviolent movements proceed, those in leadership positions do not depend upon an ability to apply violence or physically enforce discipline, but instead rely upon the perception of those in the movement that the leaders are skillful and trustworthy. Successful nonviolence requires that rank-and-file members of the movement actively and enthusiastically participate of their own accord. In this way, nonviolent movements tend to strengthen and increase the locations of power. Creating, strengthening, and drawing upon a wide variety of social, religious, and civic groups are the hall-marks of nonviolent campaigns, which typically teach people to work together, to be self-sufficient, and to assert themselves even in the face of violent repression.[31]

We should be careful about overdrawing the distinction between nonviolent and violent campaigns. Sharp himself refers to nonviolence as deploying "weapons," while also requiring strategy, discipline, and courage to be effective. In making the case for the primacy of social power, he cites thinkers such as Machiavelli[32] and Marx,[33] arguing that while both thinkers are preoccupied with capturing and hold-ing states, they also advocated forms of decentralized violence which they thought were essential for ordinary people to effectively pursue freedom. Here, the primary significance of Sharp's insights is to challenge the idea of the citizen militia or the armed proletariat as the guarantor of freedom. Instead, he highlights the primacy of social power, even when it is "unarmed." (We can think here of socialists such as Proudhon, Owen, and Fourier as paving the way for this line of thinking.) Sharp points out that if ordinary citizens are properly trained, united in their purpose, and self-sufficient in their capacities, they do not need to use physical violence to wield power. Moreover, when citizens do deploy physical violence in the name of freedom, it introduces special dangers, which tend to undermine whatever political purposes they set out to achieve. Liberation movements that rely upon violence often implode in internecine violence or raise up tyrants; defensive violence meant to protect free-dom often subverts democratic institutions and destroys the bodies and properties they aim to defend; violence used to express and exercise freedom has resulted in some of the most horrific conflagrations in history. While these dangers are not neatly captured by the overarching claim that violence tends to centralize power and strengthen the state, they do suggest that violence intended to liberate, defend, or exercise freedom often ends up handing power to the few instead of the many.

CRIME, PUNISHMENT, AND RESTORATIVE JUSTICE

Before moving to describe a brand of self-rule consistent with nonviolent concep-tions of power, we should explore one more aspect of the claim that violence is nec-essary to defend freedom. As I have argued, liberal and republican arguments for defending freedom are closely related to state sovereignty, which means they are implicated in our most basic understandings of the rule of law, the role of the police, and the proper role of punishment in society.

The rise of liberal and republican ideas and governments in the seventeenth and eighteenth centuries initiated the first large-scale prison building projects in human history. While prisons have been part and partial of punishment since ancient times, an emphasis on confining criminals—as opposed to inflicting pain upon them—coincided with the idea that the primary purpose of government was to pre-serve and protect bodies and property. The death penalty, torture, forced labor, and other forms of punishment have not disappeared under liberal regimes, but their location, justification, and relationship to the public at large have been transformed over the last two centuries,[34] as emphasis upon confinement became the dominant understanding of the appropriate punishment for abusing natural-born freedom.

In contemporary times, there is great variance across countries in the number and percentage of people incarcerated or killed by their governments.[35] A number of criminologists have tried to explain the differences among industrialized countries, looking to cultural, economic, and political structures.[36] Empirical work has been done to test whether regime type (particularly if countries are relatively authoritar-ian or democratic), affects whether they are more likely to incarcerate their citizens.[37] However, the fact that the United States has far and away the highest incarceration rate of any sizable country suggests that violent punishment can be made consistent with democratic institutions.[38] Recall that Thomas Hobbes warns that democratic governments are more likely than those ruled by one or a few to compromise the freedom of its citizens, assuming that freedom is understood as the ability to move about as one pleases. Although there is not sufficient evidence to support his broad claim, the example of the United States certainly demonstrates how the logic of defending freedom as assuring bodily integrity and protecting property against crime can go wrong in democracies.

In the United States, police brutality and the militarization of local police forces, poor prison conditions and draconian policies such as solitary confinement, col-lateral sanctions such as felon disenfranchisement, and the infusion of the profit motive as a consequence of privatization have all contributed to creating a criminal justice system that has had devastating effects on communities.[39] Combined with the historical legacy and present reality of institutional racism and classism, these factors have led some to call for the outright abolition of the vast prison-industrial complex. At the same time, the militia tradition and the democratization of fire-arms ensconced in the Second Amendment have grown into Stand Your Ground and concealed carry laws as well as a general resistance to legislation regulating the sale or purchase of firearms. This reliance upon formal and informal physical vio-lence has not only failed to eliminate crime but contributes to generating criminal acts by reinforcing the equation of violence and power. Indeed, neither the prison-industrial complex nor the proliferation of firearms does a very good job of preserv-ing life and property, and both in very direct and obvious ways increase citizens' physical vulnerability to one another and to the state.[40]

The existence of societies founded upon liberal and republican principles that are not as severely afflicted by these problems demonstrates the possibility and potential for prison reform, a change in emphasis toward rehabilitation over punishment, and a departure from attitudes advocating the necessity or desirability of ubiquitous gun ownership. However, even more radical departures have been proposed, which broadly fall under the heading of "restorative justice" and share much in common with the underlying philosophical principles of nonviolence.

There are many different examples of restorative justice occurring in various parts of the world. An important aspect of the concept is an attempt to move away from reliance upon the laws of the state and toward reliance upon those directly affected by the crime. Different communities have developed different ways of dealing with the fallout from criminal acts, offering diverse solutions in their attempts to repair wrongdoing and take responsibility. One model is referred to as "circle sentencing." Originating in aboriginal communities in Canada, the process usually involves the formation of a Community Justice Committee. Although restorative justice programs can take place entirely outside the formal justice system, "the circle" typically includes a judge, lawyers, police officers, the victim and offender, and family and community members affected by the crime. All of the stakeholders face one another in a circle. The offender usually admits guilt in advance. Victims and others in the circle are permitted to directly ask questions about the crime, and offenders and their families actively participate in the process. The circle builds consensus among all the participants as to the appropriate measures for reconciliation, restitution, and/or reparation.[41]

Typical criminal courts rely heavily upon professionals, encourage competing views of reality, and focus on determining the guilt or innocence of the offender. They see the sentencing process as resolving all issues related to the crime. Gandhi offers a devastating critique of the British legal system in *Hind Swaraj*, arguing that Indians should try to avoid it as much as possible. In a seemingly uncharacteristic endorsement of violence he says that: "Truly, men were less unmanly when they settled their disputes either by fighting or by asking their relatives to decide upon them. They became more unmanly and cowardly when they resorted to the courts of law."[42] But it is not so much that Gandhi is here promoting violence as emphasizing the extent to which reliance upon formal institutions creates dependency. "The chief thing ... to be remembered is that, without lawyers courts could not have been established or conducted, and without the latter the English could not rule. ... we love quarrels and courts, as fish love water."[43] Community circles regard the criminal incident as a small part of a larger dynamic, focus on the present and future conduct of the offender, and emphasize the importance of the process of conflict resolution in shaping and healing relationships among the parties.[44] We might recall Carl Schmitt's observation that no laws can anticipate every particular circumstance, which he argues requires the need for executive prerogative and sovereignty to decide the exception. Circle sentencing reverses this logic by suggesting that only equitable relationships and consensus building among all the concerned parties can adequately address the complexities that face a particular community in a time of rupture and crisis.

Restorative justice programs emphasize both peacemaking, or the resolution of specific ongoing conflicts, and peace building, which aims to address underlying problems such as poverty and drug and alcohol abuse that promote conditions conducive to crime.[45] In this way, such programs approach defending freedom in an entirely different fashion than conventional courts. Presently, restorative justice programs are limited and not designed for widespread use. But if further developed, they hold the promise of being expanded. Instead of relying upon the state and its contractually instituted enforcement powers, the responsibility for those who break the law is understood to be held by the community as a whole, including both formal and informal institutions. Just as invading forces or an attempted coup d'état can be repelled by citizens who self-consciously refuse to cooperate, the harmful actions of criminals can be addressed and corrected by citizens who self-consciously rule themselves. We might also note that corrupt officials and imperious police officers can be held accountable through the same mechanisms and that citizens are less vulnerable to them in the first place since they themselves are in charge.

No society has ever managed to eliminate crime and injustice, irrespective of its willingness to use violent enforcement measures. Likewise, no law is enforceable unless most citizens actively abide by its demands or conform to its prohibitions. In place of the prison-industrial complex and the never-ending and futile effort to defend freedom with violence in a domestic context, we might pursue and further develop restorative justice programs, which are premised upon an acceptance of human plurality, the difficulty of living with other human beings, our fundamental dependence upon one another, and our capacity for collective rule.

NONVIOLENT SELF-RULE

Throughout this project, I have maintained that the most difficult problem with fostering nonviolent freedom is imagining how we might rule ourselves without violence. I have argued that an awareness of certain capacities and facts of freedom in ourselves and others moves us some ways toward nonviolent self-rule. I have described historical events, radical experiments, and theoretical propositions that give us some sense of what nonviolent self-rule might look like. The secessions of the plebs, the general strike as described by Benjamin and Arendt, and the communities inspired by Owen, Fourier, Ruskin, and Proudhon all give us clues in this regard. However, these examples lean heavily upon the idea of withdrawal—either withdrawing consent to a particular decision or withdrawing from larger society with the hope of providing a model for novel forms of governance.

In the remainder of this chapter I will draw upon a number of thinkers who try to construct a more positive vision of what nonviolent self-rule entails (although even in these thinkers there is sometimes a tendency to define freedom as what it is not). With the exception of Gandhi, whose work I will use to draw together these thinkers, these sources are not self-consciously attempting to describe nonviolent self-rule, or at least they do not employ the term "nonviolence." However, the problem of the relationship between ruling and the use of violence is central in the approach of each.

ISAIAH BERLIN AND NEGATIVE LIBERTY

We begin with the Russian-born British philosopher and historian of ideas Isaiah Berlin (1909–1997) and his famous distinction between positive and negative liberty. Berlin attempts to solve the problem of how to be free and at the same time rule one another by arguing that they are fundamentally different from one another. Rejecting the notion that freedom is a matter of "self-direction and self-control,"[46] Berlin argues that it is primarily a matter of personal liberty, which means that a range of choices is preserved for each individual. While acknowledging that certain positive physical conditions are required for the enjoyment of negative liberty (and may be desirable goals for governments to pursue in their own right), whether one has shelter or food, for instance, is not related to preserving negative liberty itself.[47]

Berlin's route has some redeeming qualities. First, in his attempt to solve the problem of ruling by arguing that freedom is unrelated to it, Berlin elucidates some implications of the facts of freedom. The idea of negative liberty suggests that we have an obligation to acknowledge and respect the fact that others are creative and spontaneous beings, thereby giving them as much free play as possible in their activities. Second, taking up the principle that I will not interfere with others (or we will not interfere with one another) leaves some room for another fact of freedom: that we are in dialogue with each another. Although not a point of emphasis for Berlin, the liberal tradition is particularly well-suited to emphasize and cultivate discussion, debate, and dialogue as ways of negotiating our status as separate and spontaneous beings. One of the central purposes of Mill's *On Liberty*, for instance, is to describe how protecting a space for free-thinking individuals enlivens and improves our dialogue with one another.

Yet Berlin's solution does not really achieve its aim. Instead, while the idea of negative liberty on its face only describes a realm of free play that cannot be trespassed upon by others, it implies an amorphous but far-reaching set of duties and obligations for members of society. Berlin suggests that negative liberty does not really require that we do much for others. However, if liberalism in its strong form demands that we preserve "a maximum degree of noninterference compatible with the minimum demands of social life,"[48] negative liberty must place on everyone the burden of doing whatever we can to refrain from interfering with the lives of others. At its worst, liberalism becomes a pact wherein we isolate ourselves to our private lives, agreeing not to do much with or in the presence of others because to do something might limit the range of choices others have. To truly give each individual the widest range of choices would mean that no one ever exercises their choices in public or in a way that interferes with everyone else's range of choices. Far from being a concept of freedom that solves the problem of self-rule, it requires a high degree of discipline and self-rule.

Offering a vision of self-rule that places stringent requirements on conscientious citizens is not necessarily a bad thing. Perhaps preserving negative liberty requires awareness with regard to how our actions can impede those of others, thereby encouraging us to embrace responsibility for our actions and empathize with how they might affect others. Yet Berlin does not seem to be offering a vision of liberal citizens who take responsibility for preserving negative freedom, or at least not in a way that avoids violence. In practice, liberal governments do not simply rely upon their citizens to preserve negative liberty, except perhaps by encouraging them to retreat to their private lives. In a variety of ways, the state enforces the principle of noninterference. For instance, laws against murder, trespassing, eavesdropping, stalking, stealing, and the destruction of property are meant to preserve and protect negative liberty. Since Berlin does not offer any alternative to such laws, we can assume that states that enforce them are ones that preserve negative liberty.

It is understandable that Berlin, who witnessed the horrors of Nazi Germany and Stalinist Russia, sees "positive" rule and collective freedom as less legitimate and more dangerous than negative liberty. Certain brands of socialism can lead to a denial of individual creativity and spontaneity in favor of ideological unity and conformity. Nationalism tends to weave narratives that encourage violence against insiders who are insufficiently like us, and against outsiders who are purportedly nothing like us at all. Certain forms of both socialism and communism encourage quashing all dissent. In their worst manifestations, authoritarian and totalitarian governments attempt to create utterly predictable people, stripped of their individuality and working as part of an "organic" whole. The most strident advocates of positive freedom suggest we must sometimes act together, even if it ends up trampling individuals, crushing spontaneity and creativity.

However, Berlin's solution introduces new dangers. Liberals tend to place a primary emphasis on the individual, in spite of the fact that our unique individuality and our shared sociality are both irreducible. As a wide variety of theorists of freedom tell us, the only choice we do not have is whether to have choice.[49] The communal corollary of this one "necessary" aspect of freedom is that we cannot avoid taking action in the presence of other spontaneous and creative beings, and therefore must decide what to do together. The most strident advocates of negative liberty argue that our spontaneous individuality trumps our inherent sociality. This approach threatens to deny, splinter, and atrophy the public world.

Ideologies that attempt to escape the paradoxical facts of freedom by denying either individuality or sociality often turn to physical violence. On the liberal side, an overemphasis upon individualism can lead to a nihilistic rejection of all communal obligations. For instance, certain versions of liberal individualism celebrate the creativity of entrepreneurs and capitalists to such a degree that they argue that no regulation of trade or industry is justified. Our individual freedom means that the unlimited accumulation of property is not only permitted, but must be enforced by the state. Exploiting, harassing, and sometimes killing workers who resist the demands of such individuals is perfectly acceptable in order to protect free enterprise and the free market. For those liberals who are more critical of the use of the state, an overemphasis on negative liberty can that invite us to arm and isolate ourselves on whatever property we have, encouraging physical resistance and violence to any government or communal encroachment on our lives.

Conceptions of freedom that describe it as secured by a particular kind of government demand that we fight for it, preserving particular institutions and structures so that it is not "lost." Freedom as awareness, however, cannot be reduced to living under particular governments. Instead, freedom is spread and secured through an educative process. This process may be more or less formal and require different sorts of activities attentive to cultivating free thinking, free willing, and political freedom. Examples of cultivating each of these include, for instance, Socrates' elenchus, Gandhi's satyagraha, and the US Constitution. Such historical developments and innovations help us become more free by sparking awareness of certain facts of being and living together with ourselves and others.

HANNAH ARENDT AND THE ARCHEIN OF THE ANCIENTS

Whereas Berlin tries to distance freedom from rule, Hannah Arendt takes aim at sovereignty. As mentioned previously, Arendt suggests a historical connection in the development of political thought between the discovery of the individual will and sovereignty. As soon as Augustine found the will was "an organ of self-liberation . . . the will-to-power turned at once into a will-to-oppression."[50] This had "fatal consequences for political theory" because Rousseau adapted this theory of the will into a theory of sovereignty. Arendt writes:

The famous sovereignty of political bodies has always been an illusion, which, moreover, can be maintained only by the instruments of violence, that is, with

essentially nonpolitical means. . . . Where men wish to be sovereign, as individuals or as organized groups, they must submit to the oppression of the will,
be this the individual will with which I force myself, or the "general will" of
an organized group. If men wish to be free, it is precisely sovereignty they must
renounce.[51]

I argued in the last chapter that we can discern parallel internal and external
processes between the free will and political freedom. In this light, the idea of a
general will denies the facts of freedom—it denies that we are spontaneous and
creative beings in dialogue with ourselves and others[52]—and claims that we can all
act together as one, like an individual. The theory of individual willing led political theory astray by emphasizing the capacity to escape the brokenness of the will
instead of remembering that it is in its very brokenness that freedom lies. When we
debate and discuss things together in public and take action in politics, the experience of collective indecision—with an unknown outcome—makes public life akin
to our private experiences of the facts of freedom. Arendt writes: "It is as though
the I-will immediately paralyzed the I-can, as though the moment men *willed* freedom, they lost their capacity to *be* free."[53] The theory of a general will is even more
dangerous because it transposes the idea of a powerful, actualized, unified individual will into community. It probably does not actually exist and only through
the violent enforcement of "consensus" can it be made to appear that it does.

In these passages, Arendt offers her most damning critique of communitarian
and republican theories of government. Given the similarities and connections
between free willing and political freedom, we can see why Arendt argues that sovereignty and freedom are opposed to one another. Just as the broken will is no longer
free from the standpoint of the individual when it is healed and is put into action,
political freedom disappears the moment it is exercised as a singular general willing.
Arendt's argument that sovereignty—even so-called "popular sovereignty"—is antithetical to freedom closely parallels her distinction between violence and power.[54]

In Arendt's demand that we stay focused on the "I-can," it might at first appear
as though she sides with liberalism in a way quite similar to Berlin's insistence that
freedom consists in preserving a range of opportunities for choice.[55] However, unlike
Berlin, Arendt tackles the question of rule head-on, arguing that ruling must be
part and parcel of what it means to be free and has little to do with choice. Instead,
she says that freedom relates to the capacity to begin something new in conjunction
with others. She writes that for the ancient Greeks

Freedom, as we would say today, was experienced in spontaneity. The manifold
meaning of ἄρχειν [*archein*] indicates the following: only those could begin

something new who were already rulers (i.e. household heads who ruled over slaves and family) and had thus liberated themselves from the necessities of life for enterprises in distant lands or citizenship in the polis; in either case, they no longer ruled, but were rulers among rulers, moving among their peers, whose help they enlisted as leaders in order to begin something new, to start a new enterprise; for only with the help of others could the ἀρψων [*archōn*], the ruler, beginner and leader, really act.[56]

Here Arendt suggests that there is a way of acting which accounts for the facts of freedom. Unlike sovereignty, *archein* indicates both that ruling relates to our capacity to begin something new *and* a recognition that (some) others have this capacity and we therefore must rule together. Since all other citizens were spontaneous and creative, power must consist of action in concert with others. We know from Aristotle that such "political rule" must be closely connected to deliberation among equals—the dialogical fact of freedom.

However, we must keep in mind that Arendt does not think the Greek model is viable for contemporary politics. Arendt is not arguing that she has found a nonviolent form of self-rule. In the passage cited above, she remarks that only those who "ruled over slaves and family," and who had "liberated themselves from the necessities of life," could partake of the kind of rule consistent with freedom. As we have seen, the relationship between slavery, empire, and the Athenian conception of rule was even more direct than Arendt lets on. Among the aims of *archein*, was the achievement of *autarkeia*, or "absolute self-sufficiency," something that was only fully accomplished by Athens in Pericles' time. Raaflaub says that the word as used in the funeral oration "presupposes both the polis's freedom and its domination over others."[57] He argues that absolute self-sufficiency, in turn, must be coupled with absolute sovereignty and "the explicit causal linkage of freedom and rule over others."[58] Thucydides combined "the domestic rule of the Athenian citizens (in democracy) with their external rule (in the empire) to create a comprehensive 'hyperconcept' of power and rule, and [connected] this with freedom under the same double perspective."[59] Only in this way do we get an adequate sense of the abstract noun that appeared and became the ascendant value in Greek politics (*eleutheria*)—a noun perhaps best understood in its superlative form: "superior freedom" (*eleutherôtatê*).[60] For the Athenians, the utter brutality of slavery and warfare did not just make political freedom *possible* as Aristotle would later argue. Freedom was expressed through warfare and domination. The Athenians's capacity to dominate and enslave others demonstrated that they were self-sufficient.[61]

In this light, it is hard to see why Arendt thinks the distinction between sovereignty and ruling has much importance, at least as far as violence and oppression are concerned. It fact, the distinction raises hard questions about the concept of self-rule. The concept of self-rule appeared (perhaps for the first time in history) among a people who were self-consciously and collaboratively exercising their capacity for spontaneity in order to employ extraordinary physical violence. If sovereignty refers to a unified and homogenizing political will, and self-rule refers to a pluralistic exercise of free wills in power, neither seems any more or less predisposed to violence. Blind obedience to a single ruler and the exercise of a unified will have extraordinary potential for violence. They also deny the facts of freedom by suggesting that only one person is capable of or ought to have the right to spontaneous and creative action. Such a regime must use violence in the place of and for the purpose of devaluing and crushing dialogue. However, what could be more dangerous than a whole people becoming fully aware of one of the undeniable implications of the facts of freedom, that we are free to dominate others. Together, with one another, we can rule everyone else. Empire and slavery cannot be disconnected in the political freedom and rule of Athens because it was precisely the invention of political freedom that created their collective power and capacity to unleash violence on vast numbers of subject peoples.

Arendt's focus on what went on between Athenian citizens, and not between Athenians and their slaves, is not entirely unjustified. After all, Athens was not unique because it dominated and enslaved other peoples; it was unique in its form of government. Moreover, we have seen that Arendt has a model of self-rule in the early labor movement, which supplements her description of *archein*. But, for the moment let us consider Arendt's attempt to distinguish between sovereignty and freedom to be a seemingly promising route that leads us down a blind alley in a way similar to Berlin's attempt to separate freedom and ruling.

IMMANUEL KANT'S MORAL SELF-RULE

Any discussion of the relationship between freedom and self-rule would be incomplete without considering the work of Immanuel Kant. Kant begins with the premise that each individual human being is autonomous in a way similar to my claim that our separation from one another is a fact of freedom. However, as mentioned previously, Kant insists that we are only truly free when we follow the dictates of reason. "Only freedom in relation to the internal lawgiving of reason is really a capacity; the possibility of deviating from it is an incapacity."[62] In every action we take there is an underlying volitional principle called a maxim, which posits a means/ends relationship. That is, the will creates an action in a circumstance that intends to produce a result. Reason assesses the moral viability of any maxim—and in particular, the viability of the means. Individuals, if led by reason, can give the moral law to themselves, ruling themselves and being free.

Kant is specific in his description of how reason assesses our actions. He posits that some maxims formulated by the will fall under what he calls the categorical imperative. He describes the categorical imperative in a number of different ways, but perhaps most famously as 1) I must act only in accordance with a maxim that could become a universal law,[63] and 2) I must treat other human beings as ends and never exclusively as a means to some other end. In these formulations we see both an individual and social element. Kant argues that if our actions cannot be universalized—that is, if everyone cannot act according to the same means/ends proposition of a particular autonomous will—then it will be apparent to us that the maxim is immoral. Stronger still, he suggests that when a particular action violates the categorical imperative, a reasonable person will see that if their will was universalized it would lead to utter destruction. For instance, if I lie or kill in order to achieve a particular end, a reasonable person will see that if everyone acted in a similar way, human living together would become impossible.

At the heart of this idea is the notion that no one can force us to act in accordance with the moral law, that no one can force us to be free. Neither natural law nor prior experience is a cause of the will or freedom. Instead, the will is solely a first cause grounded in reason. Kant says in his discussion of radical evil that no one directly rebels against their own moral predisposition. Yet at the same time we often fail to abide by reason. This failure is due to the fact that we all love ourselves. Self-love is not a bad thing in and of itself, but when placed above the moral law it tends to corrupt the ground of all maxims. Our regard for ourselves cannot be extirpated from human powers. It is not an outside influence or the result of our sensuous nature. To love oneself is consistent with and originates in our freedom. The evil that results from it is therefore "radical."[64]

What are the implications of this view of freedom for the use of violence? This question is a matter of dispute among Kant interpreters.[65] In setting the stage for his discussion of radical evil, Kant indicts those who dismiss the idea of a league of peoples and a world republic as a "wild fantasy."[66] Against those such as Rousseau who find morality in the "state of nature," he sees examples of "barbarity" among the native peoples of North America and New Zealand. However, the so-called civilized nations are worse because each strives for universal autocracy, which produces constant warfare. Quoting a forgotten ancient thinker, he says that "'war creates more evil men than it destroys.'"[67] These passages have led many interpreters to claim that Kant is a pacifist in the sense of decrying all war as unjust, while some have argued that one can discern a just war theory in his writings. Not surprisingly, the main proponent of the just war view argues that Kant believes that self-defense is consistent with freedom.[68]

Given his anti-consequentialist approach to morality, it would seem that being free and ruling oneself means never practicing physical violence. Although Kant does not say so directly, physical violence is often a quintessential example of radical evil. Physical violence uses another human being as a means to one's own will with the purpose of subduing or destroying another's will. Not only does the perpetrator of physical violence violate the categorical imperative and demonstrate an unwillingness for self-rule, but the victim of physical violence finds the very source of their own freedom (the autonomous will) attacked by way of their body. Self-rule as described by Kant is the reverse of physical violence, and it often springs from self-love.

However, there is no question that Kant believes freedom and moral duty are consistent with physical violence in certain circumstances. Most notably, he argues that the death penalty is consistent with justice and morality. At its core, it would seem that Kant's concept of freedom challenges the idea that punishment could ever assist in making one free. Even if others observe someone failing to abide by reason, intervening with physical punishment cannot substitute for that individual giving the law to her or himself. Moreover, those who mete out the physical punishment would seem to be in violation of the categorical imperative by attempting to use another's body in order to control or dominate the will. Yet Kant insists that when persons commit murder, it is consistent with treating them as ends in themselves to punish them by death.[69]

GANDHI'S SWARAJ

We now turn to Gandhi's concept of freedom, or swaraj, which translates as "self-rule." Gandhi believes that freedom is fundamentally and irreducibly an individual quality. However, swaraj is not Berlin's negative liberty, even though the practice of swaraj would lead to all of the rights championed by liberal individualism. Swaraj is an individual quality in that no group can reduce or take it away. As Ronald Terchek writes, Gandhi's "life as a member of colonial India reveals a person who thinks he is not formally free but also thinks he is autonomous and acts that way."[70] In a way similar to Kant, Gandhi rejects utilitarianism and consequentialism and holds that every individual retains the capacity to be free irrespective of external circumstances, including the direct violence of others. However, unlike the Stoics or Indian ascetics, who saw freedom as an apolitical or unpolitical capacity, Gandhi claims there is nothing more relevant to politics and economics than swaraj.[71] Collective swaraj is possible and desirable, but can only be built on a foundation where each individual rules her or himself.

How does the irreducibly individual and inner quality of swaraj translate into public action? While everyone is capable of swaraj, very few have become fully aware of or practice it. This means that the quality of public life is constantly degraded by people who fail to rule themselves. This raises two multi-part questions. First, how can one demonstrate self-rule to others in such a way that it inspires them to rule themselves and hence gain freedom? More specifically, how can we do so without taking over or trying to dominate or mold the will of another—that is, without losing our own freedom? We might even go so far as to say that Gandhi was not sure whether he himself had attained swaraj, so that his experiments in public were a way of testing the degree of self-rule he had attained. Second, how was individual swaraj connected to collective self-rule? And what would collective swaraj look like?

Gandhi develops robust answers to each of these questions. Although to some extent he worked on both questions throughout his life (as is consistent with his view that the distinction between means and ends was typically overdrawn, misleading, or outright dangerous[72]), he devoted most of the first part of his career to the first question and then later focused more heavily on the second. Given the paucity of swaraj among individuals in the world, it is perhaps not surprising that Gandhi first worked to develop the means for expressing individual swaraj in public (and trying to inspire others to practice it). Only then could he envision in any detail the "end" of collective freedom, or what it might look like if some greater number of people were to exercise swaraj together.

After variously applying the terms "ahimsa," "nonviolence," and "soul force," Gandhi eventually settled on the term "satyagraha," or "holding fast to the truth," to describe his method of exercising swaraj in public. Like Kant, Gandhi seems sure that there is a moral law, which he often referred to as being like Euclid's geometry. Even if we might not be able to see or grasp it perfectly in experience, Gandhi was sure that it existed and that it was worth trying to approximate. Kant's categorical imperative provides us with some clarity here—a way of understanding what Gandhi means when he says that liberty means being able to follow one's conscience.[73] Although Kant is less apt to emphasize it, both suggest that following the moral law may require self-sacrifice. Given that others often fail to practice self-rule, the immediate consequences of doing so may be physically harmful to the person who acts according to their duty. Gandhi was more clear about how this public demonstration of self-sacrifice might affect others. By holding fast to the truth and refraining from destroying or attacking others, the satyagrahi would offer a model of self-rule and moderation that might change others.

Indeed, swaraj cannot be reduced to Kantian autonomy because it offers a much more robust anthropology. Gandhi does not have an understanding of the free will that relies solely upon reason. Instead, he suggests that the heart, or our affective disposition and emotions, are equally important in guiding our behavior. Unlike Kant, Gandhi works to develop a form of self-rule that specifically addresses the needs of others. Reason alone is an insufficient basis for self-rule.[74] Love is required as well. When it works properly, satyagraha appeals to the heart of one's opponent by highlighting the suffering of the least among us.

However, satyagraha does not rely upon moral suasion, or appeals to reason and emotion alone. Instead, it also shares qualities similar to *archein* as described by Arendt. Gandhi's swaraj helps us understand what are otherwise somewhat cryptic passages in "What Is Freedom?" Where Arendt writes that "self-control has remained one of the specifically political virtues . . . where I-will and I-can must be so well attuned that they practically coincide."[75] Consider, for instance, the Great Salt March to Dandi. Walking over 200 miles, with throngs growing along the way and officials associated with the British regime resigning in his wake, Gandhi and many thousands of supporters decided to make salt for themselves at the seaside. Doing so meant breaking British law and highlighted the ways in which those laws directly interfered with ordinary Indians meeting their basic physical needs. The March cannot be reduced to "a choice." Instead, it involved the creation of something new, spontaneous, and distinctive. Just as Arendt details in her description of *archein*, Gandhi's unique and creative action enlisted the help of others and inspired them to exercise power with him. Unlike the brand of self-rule practiced by the Athenians, however, this exercise of power was not made possible by forcing others to meet the basic needs of the rulers so that they could be free. Instead, it was specifically premised upon considering the needs of the poorest of the poor, and involving them in self-rule as well. Exercising freedom meant creating an activity that allowed everyone to combat the British tax laws that prevented them from attaining salt at a reasonable price—a matter of survival in India's climate.[76]

Arendt worries that the I-can will be engulfed by and overwhelmed by the I-will as soon as the broken will is healed. But in emphasizing that freedom is a matter of self-rule, where one remains perpetually in control of oneself, Gandhi suggests we can act and at the same time preserve our sense of "I-can." The March opened up new possibilities, such as the nonviolent raids on salt processing factories, which were led by others such as the poetess Sarojini Naidu when Gandhi was imprisoned. In addition, since swaraj refers in one and the same word to the self-rule of the individual and the self-rule of India, ruling oneself is unmistakably a matter of ruling with others at the same time. If we recall Rousseau, collective self-rule may very well be the expression of a kind of general will, but it must be entirely voluntary and nonviolent in its exercise in order to be swaraj. In addition, against Rousseau, even as we rule ourselves, we remain in constant dialogue, aware of our potential to change our minds, make mistakes, or create something new—a we-can is preserved in the midst of a we-will. Gandhi's swaraj constitutes an emboldened and expansive endorsement of Arendt's assertion that "[o]nly where the I-will and the I-can coincide does freedom come to pass."[77]

If satyagraha involves attempts to use political means that demonstrate self-rule in the midst of violence and oppression, what does collective swaraj look like? That is, what does Gandhian self-rule look like if a large portion of a given society (or even humanity) were to adopt it? In his *Constructive Programme* (1941), Gandhi spells out a vision for India grounded in a system of decentralized cottage industries based on the idea that small villages could become self-sufficient if they rejected Western industry. Instead, they would rely upon traditional lifeways such as home-spun cloth, agriculture, animal husbandry, and informal and interpersonal governance. Placing a strong emphasis upon the most menial labor and the maintenance of good hygiene, Gandhi envisions villages where everyone contributes to cleanliness, health, the provision of basic needs, and conflict resolution.

Unlike other theorists of freedom, Gandhi is deeply committed to the idea that politics and economics are inseparable, and that freedom means self-rule and self-reliance in both realms. However, against those socialists and communists who attempt to build upon the productive innovations of capitalism, Gandhi insists that all innovations are useless unless they serve human need. Frequently criticizing Western mechanized industry, Gandhi clarified that it was not machinery per se that bothered him:

> Village Swaraj is man-centred non-exploiting decentralized, simple village economy providing for full employment to each one of its citizens on the basis of voluntary co-operation and working [to achieve] self-sufficiency in its basic requirements of food, clothing and other necessities of life.[78]

To the extent that machinery produces more goods but compromises the well-being of individuals by creating poverty and unemployment, it is contrary to self-rule. This claim does not require that the government provide jobs for everyone. It is an argument calling for economic systems with certain kinds of values. Instead of relying upon a centralized state and encouraging consumerism,[79] each individual should work to the best of their ability to provide for their own needs and the needs of the community. Likewise, every community should be structured in such a way as to draw upon and cultivate the capacities of each individual. Without full employment, without utilizing the abilities of the impoverished masses to the fullest extent, swaraj would be fleeting.

Although Gandhi articulates the constructive program as a return to Indian and Hindu tradition, it rejects the caste system, challenges the division of gender roles, and models religious harmony among all faiths.[80] In the tradition of experimental communities like those of Owen and Fourier, and directly inspired by the thought of John Ruskin and Leo Tolstoy, he established Tolstoy Farm in South Africa and the Sabarmati Ashram in India. But his constructive program envisions an expansive and interconnected (as opposed to small and isolated) form of self-rule:

> In this structure composed of innumerable villages, there will be ever-widening, never-ascending circles. Life will not be a pyramid with the apex sustained by the bottom. But it will be an oceanic circle whose centre will be the individual always ready to perish for the village, the latter ready to perish for the circle of villages, till at last the whole becomes one life composed of individuals, never aggressive in their arrogance but ever humble, sharing the majesty of the oceanic circle of which they are integral units.[81]

In this way, swaraj is premised upon an expansive notion of communal equality. Consistent with Aristotle's concept of political rule as distinctive because it involves simultaneously ruling over others and being ruled, Gandhi emphasizes taking responsibility and submitting oneself to the judgment of others. There is an obvious way in which civil disobedience seems to violate the principle that political rule involves allowing oneself to be ruled by others. However, civil disobedience also requires that one be willing to accept consequences imposed by others. In both satyagraha and the constructive program, swaraj demands give and take. In fact, while expecting individuals and communities to exercise extraordinary power as a consequence of newfound awareness of their capacity for freedom, power is always exercised in a way that leaves open the possibility for correction and a change in direction.

In both the practice of satyagraha and the constructive program, Gandhi indicates that he is very much aware that majority rule can be potentially destructive to the well-being of minorities.[82] Thus he develops strict rules and works to describe in detail when collective power can be legitimately exercised. With respect to the constructive program, freedom depends upon a majority of people possessing a certain attitude toward the whole:

> Swaraj can be maintained, only where there is [a] majority of loyal patriotic people to whom the good of the nation is paramount above all other considerations whatever including their personal profit. Swaraj means government by the many. Where the many are immoral or selfish, their government can spell anarchy and nothing else.[83]

Gandhi realizes that liberty is often confused with license. But instead of offering a solution whereby each individual recognizes the rights of others, he draws upon and modifies a form of nationalism. He gets to the heart of what is required, a point that Berlin and other liberals are hesitant to embrace, when he says that swaraj means "self-rule and self-restraint, not freedom from all restraint which 'independence' often means."[84]

This puts Gandhi's thought in a complex relation to Kant's thought as well. On the one hand, both maintain that freedom means doing one's moral duty, and that rights are the result of the performance of duty. Both also place a strong emphasis on the truth, and decry lying as corrosive, immoral, and unreasonable. However, while both are certain that moral truth exists, Gandhi is less sure of its parameters, and therefore argues that public experimentation and dialogue with others are required to move us closer to genuine self-rule.[85] Thus he could never endorse the death penalty.

> True democracy or the swaraj of the masses can never come through untruthful and violent means, for the simple reason that the natural corollary to their use would be to remove all opposition through the suppression or extermination of the antagonists. That does not make for individual freedom. Individual freedom can have the fullest play only under a regime of unadulterated ahimsa [nonviolence].[86]

Here Gandhi sounds much more like Berlin, in his aim of giving each individual "the fullest play." However, with his concepts of satyagraha and the constructive program, he details a more positive vision of public life than the liberal idea that freedom means not doing violence to or interfering with the lives of others.

Indeed, despite his emphasis on the individual as the foundation of swaraj, Gandhi offers a resounding critique of liberal individualism:

> [Man] is as much self-dependent as inter-dependent. When dependence becomes necessary in order to keep society in good order it is no longer dependence, but becomes cooperation. There is sweetness in co-operation; there is no one weak or strong among those who co-operate. Each is equal to the other. There is the feeling of helplessness in dependency. Members of a family are as much self-dependent as inter-dependent. There is no feeling of either mine or thine. They are all cooperators. So also when we take a society, a nation or the whole of mankind as a family all men become co-operators.[87]

While swaraj lies in the hands of each individual, Gandhi believes so firmly in the interdependence of human beings that his notion of freedom has much in common with Arendt's view that freedom is an inherently public capacity. As with Arendt's definition of *archein*, Gandhi's idea of freedom requires that each must recognize the freedom of everyone else, working with others on a voluntary basis to achieve self-rule both individually and collectively. However, Gandhi has more confidence in the possibilities of a free will than Arendt.[88] He incorporates, integrates and embraces a strong will in his definition of freedom, and relies on the will to elicit the self-control required for us to work with others. A reasonable, active, moral will can freely rule over the self for the specific purpose of ruling with others.

His vision of vigorous, communal, voluntaristic self-rule means that Gandhi imagines a distinctive approach to enforcing the law, based in large part on simply outnumbering or overpowering criminals nonviolently. For instance, if a given village contained "five or seven" criminals and seven hundred people fully cognizant of their capacity for self-rule, the criminals would either "live under the discipline of the rest or leave the village."[89] To the extent that a police force might be necessary, it would be composed of

servants, not masters, of the people. The people will instinctively render them every help, and through mutual co-operation they will easily deal with the ever decreasing disturbances. The police force will have some kind of arms, but they will rarely be used, if at all. In fact the policemen will be reformers. Their police work will be confined primarily to robbers and dacoits. Quarrels between labor and capital and strikes will be few and far between in a non-violent State, because the influence of the non-violent majority will be so great as to command the respect of the principal elements in society.[90]

Since he cannot claim to have discovered a form of rule that would entirely do away with punishment, prisons, and police, Gandhi thought his system was incomplete. However, he maintains that this shortcoming is a personal failure as opposed to a weakness of nonviolence and he is confident that eventually alternatives to violent forms of enforcement would arise through experimentation and the continued pursuit of creative nonviolence.

Arendt, Berlin, and Kant each attempt to advance an understanding of freedom disconnected from violence. Arendt does so by distinguishing freedom from sovereignty and willing. Berlin does so by distinguishing negative liberty from ruling and action. Kant does so by tying the free will to reason. All three thinkers make progress in describing conceptions of freedom that are not reducible to violence, but they also downplay the ways in which their conceptions of freedom and liberty have close practical and historical ties to physical violence. Gandhi's concept of swaraj helps us sort through some of the thorny issues each thinker presents. In his concept of self-rule, he rejects neither the will nor ruling, but instead tries to describe a kind of will and a kind of rule that are nonviolent. Our question has been whether or not it is possible to rule ourselves without violence. Gandhi shows us that finding ways to rule ourselves without violence, both individually and collectively, is what freedom means.

Freedom understood in this way involves the practice of a certain kind of love as well. Gandhi's and Martin Luther King Jr.'s treatment of love finds surprising resonance in Arendt's discussion of Duns Scotus. While in her early essays Arendt worries about the "I-can" being overwhelmed by the oppressive "I-will," in her later work she says that it is the I-can that limits the I-will.[91] She goes on to suggest that love can perpetuate the "delight" of the mental experience of willing—and in particular the feeling of "I-can."[92] Love seems to be connected to willing for Arendt because willing involves accepting or rejecting what our desires, reason, or nature presents to the will. Love involves an unconditional acceptance of what is. When the will is transformed into love, it rejects ruling and domination. Arendt says that the kind of willing Scotus describes is expressed in the phrase: "'*Amo: Volo ut sis*,' 'I love you; I want you to be'—and not 'I want to have you' or 'I want to rule you.'"[93] Yet she argues in *The Human Condition* that love cannot be political.[94] In King's "beloved community," however, and Gandhi's explicit assertion that nonviolence or ahimsa is similar in meaning to Pauline love, we see how precisely the same phenomenon Arendt is discussing can manifest itself in politics.[95]

Gandhi's observation that violence is always antithetical to self-rule seems to be true because acts of physical violence are almost always an attempt to prevent someone from doing something or being as they are. Physical violence rejects things as they are—and specifically rejects the facts of human freedom. We say that violence "forces" people because when we take up or destroy another person's body, we attempt to deny them the capacity to exercise their will as they sees fit—and potentially to deny the fact of their existence. This effort implies both that we are attempting to make their actions more predictable—less spontaneous and creative—and that we are no longer in dialogue with them. Instead of ruling with others, physical violence suggests we are now ruling over others. In one and the same movement, violence broadly denies the facts of freedom; it is both anti-individual and antisocial.

Having free will means that we can reject the facts of freedom. Using physical violence can seem to destroy those facts; however, ultimately, the facts of freedom remain. Slavery can convince some people for some amount of time that they are not creative and spontaneous. Rulers and slave masters may come to believe that they are entirely self-sufficient and disconnected from the fate of others. Yet freedom is ultimately inescapable. Property rights can only be protected if we rule together. No amount of physical violence can crush the spontaneous and creative actions of slaves and workers. Regimes that demand utter conformity stagnate or crack when confronted with the new ideas of free-thinking individuals and the new actions of free willing people. The possibility of love as the acceptance and affirmation of such facts remains as perhaps the highest expression of the free will.

This is not to say that awareness of the facts of freedom is inevitable or widespread. To the contrary, such awareness is uneven. For this reason, Gandhi is constantly educating us as to our capacity for political action and the likelihood that this will require some form of self-sacrifice. Freedom is most vibrant where the paradoxical characteristics of the facts of freedom are constantly at play, where nearly every political issue comes down to a debate over the extent to which the demands of the public constrain individuals or the conscience of individuals requires challenging existing power structures. Freedom is most vibrant in societies where the common fate of everyone is taken for granted, as is the frustration and inefficiency of politics, since our common fate is yet to be written by us and is beholden to the mysterious whims of our deep plurality.[96]

A pacifist conception of freedom ought not assume any historically necessary progress toward nonviolence.[97] However, we can note that at different times and places in history, people have been more or less attentive to the facts of freedom, and thereby more or less free. The facts of freedom suggest that even if physical violence is not necessary, the possibility of physical violence will always be with us. People will always be free to ignore or reject our possibilities and the pluralistic quality of reality. At our present moment in history, most people estimate that violence is necessary on certain occasions. But the very fact that we can bring something new and unexpected into the world suggests that violence never is necessary. Gandhi was perhaps the most politically creative person of the twentieth century. The twenty-first century has already seen extraordinary and unexpected expressions of nonviolent freedom in every part of the world.[98] The nonviolent movements of the last two centuries and the brief but always remarkable appearances of freedom over the last two thousand years assure us that freedom without violence exists. While there is no guarantee of historical progress, there is some solace in the idea that the facts of freedom remain as a constant challenge to the idea of necessary violence.

Our future is not written, it is not certain: we have awakened from a long sleep, and we have seen that the human condition is incompatible with certainty. No prophet any longer dares to reveal our tomorrow to us, and this, the eclipse of prophets, is a bitter but necessary medicine. We must build our own tomorrow, blindly, gropingly; build it from its roots without giving in to the temptation to recompose the shards of old shattered idols and without constructing new ones.

PRIMO LEVI

Conclusion

AS A WAY of exploring and testing out ideas for this book, I offered an upper-level undergraduate course on freedom at LSU on two occasions over the last few years. As part of a section of the course devoted to the issue of free-thinking, I showed the students Errol Morris's documentary *Standard Operating Procedure*, which includes interviews with key players in the abuses at the Abu Ghraib prison in Iraq. I also had them read one of the memos from the Justice Department's Office of Legal Council offering grounds for "enhanced interrogation techniques."[1] We discussed whether or not those who participated in torture, or those who meticulously crafted legal justifications for it, were "thinking" when they did so and what kind of thinking they were doing. We discussed Hannah Arendt's idea that thinking involves having a conversation with oneself, and that this kind of thinking may help in the development of one's conscience, which could be a backstop against participation in evil.

A few weeks after the end of the first semester I taught the class, one of the students from that class came to my office. He told me that he had been stationed at Abu Ghraib after the worst abuses had occurred. He wanted to give me something. He and a few other soldiers had found some boxes at the prison with hundreds of blank ballots from the first nationwide Iraqi elections. Although some of his fellow soldiers were not interested, he was struck by their historical significance and took a few of them home. He wanted me to have one of them. As ballots go, the broad thin paper he handed me was particularly striking and even beautiful. Arabic script flanked by colorful symbols representing dozens of candidates and parties unfold into a near-poster-sized sheet. I got the message. He clearly wanted to show

194 Conclusion

me that the results of the United States' invasion and occupation were not all bad, and were connected to opportunities for Iraqis to collectively express their will and form their own government. We might have done some bad things, but we had freed Iraqis from a tyrant and introduced political freedom.

One way to interpret the historical evidence I have presented in this book is as a critique of the often-cited aphorism by Winston Churchill (which he attributed to an unknown source) "that democracy is the worst form of government except for all the others that have been tried." If the claim to freedom is the hallmark of democratic governance, it may be responsible for more violence, warfare, and oppression than any other reason except perhaps religion. Yet I do not wish to abandon the idea that political freedom is a valuable aim. Instead, in order to maintain that it should be a preeminent aim of politics, I have tried to show that freedom must mean something very different from what liberal democratic thinkers say it is, and from what my well-intentioned student assumes it to be.

Gandhi writes that "[as] every country is fit to eat, to drink and to breathe, even so is every nation fit to manage its own affairs, no matter how badly."[2] The claims of necessity that liberal democratic thinkers employ in arguing that violence is required to achieve and defend freedom do not hold up in light of the historical record or under close philosophical analysis. Nationalism and socialism, when wedded to the idea that the violence of states is required to exercise and express freedom, fare just as poorly. Violence used to defend or exercise freedom typically undermines it. Although sometimes a route to political freedom, it is the worst of all the available options. As one author puts it: "How you fight determines who you will become when the battle is over."[3] Using the methods of domination and violence in order to resist domination and violence rarely succeeds in removing domination and violence.

Earlier I mentioned Baron de Montesquieu's definition of freedom as "the power of doing what we ought to will" and connected this to Gandhi's claim that liberty is the ability to act according to the dictates of our conscience. These definitions suggest that violence can only impede freedom because the use of another's body to force their will denies them the chance for self-rule. This sort of freedom depends upon our individual moral orientation and capacity for moderation and self-control. It depends, as well, on living in a social and political order that acknowledges and makes space for these individual capacities. When we do not live in such a context, freedom means relying upon our capacity for creative political action, which draws upon the aspect of the will connected with acceptance and love. Such action always holds the potential for inspiring others to join with us in such action.

The US invasions and occupations of Afghanistan and Iraq, like all violent efforts, retain an element of creative political action, and violence can sometimes rally people to exercise power. However, aside from the fact that the results of such violence, like all political action, have a strong element of unpredictability, the use of physical violence works against and attempts to deny the character of freedom. Killing other people belies the Pauline, Buddhist, and Gandhian form of love in that it rejects reality. By eliminating certain people, it hopes to narrow the possibilities of human relationships. Typically, violence is framed as an attempt to eliminate the possibility of others doing violence. But violent political action cannot eliminate our paradoxical freedom to do violence.

We have seen such efforts as a search for fool's gold. The reason for the collapse of great empires has been a source of dispute among historians. However, the reason the most "successful" democracies and republics lost their freedom is less mysterious. The ancient Athenians introduced the idea that a group of equals might rule with one another, but when Pericles tied this to martial courage it sowed the seeds of disaster. Instead of broadly affirming equality, freedom meant that a particular class of people could express their superiority through warfare and oppression. Freedom figured as the capacity to dominate others proved to be a practical primer for raising up tyrants who claimed to be representing the people as superiors among equals. In the case of the Romans, the vast imperial project that grew from a self-confident and free people eventually collapsed under the weight of its own contradictions. The methods that had won freedom for the plebs were abandoned when the oligarchs began to pay ordinary soldiers for their services, undermining the idea of self-rule and the moral viability of refusing to fight wars. The demands of the empire and the violence required to maintain it eventually superseded freedom. The instability of Athenian democracy and the collapse of the Roman Republic had many causes, but it was the practice of violence that eroded their political freedom.

When liberty and freedom reappeared in modern Europe, liberal republican thinkers were anxious to correct the problems of the past. These thinkers saw the horrific potential for violence in the collectivist understandings of freedom, and drawing on just war and natural law theory, they argued that liberty should be wedded to life and property. They hoped that by linking liberty and freedom to material things, it would limit collectivist visions and protect the rights of individuals. However, this attempt to value physical life and property above all else unleashed extraordinary violence, as the idea of defensive violence came to undergird all the trappings of sovereign rule. The advocates of freedom who did not address the problems of the ancients quickly fell into the same trap as their forebears. The major strands of socialism and nationalism picked up the banner of violence as an expression of freedom. The Napoleonic Wars, the Bolshevik Revolution, Nazism, and other manifestations of collective freedom advocating the superiority of one people, class,

or race over another resulted in tyranny, and in combination with modern bureaucracy and innovations in the technologies of violence, the result was totalitarianism.

Most current democracies and republics contain some elements of the liberal and
the collectivist understandings of freedom. The mainstream of Western political
thought and history is defined by attempts to obtain, secure, and exercise freedom
with violence. Yet throughout this history, the practices of nonviolence and theories
of freedom that are not linked to violence have at times appeared. I have tried to
bring these moments and theories to the forefront, describing how we can find in a
variety of thinkers a fairly coherent vision of nonviolent freedom.

In addition to the definition offered above, Montesquieu also has a second definition of freedom. As distinguished from the philosophical liberty of the will,
Montesquieu argues that *political* liberty "consists in security, or, at least, in the
opinion that we enjoy security."[4] At first such a definition might seem in line with
the liberal idea that liberty means a lack of imposition upon one's physical body and
property. But Montesquieu's addendum—that political liberty involves the *opinion* that we enjoy security as opposed to actual security—is of critical importance.
Indeed, for Montesquieu the best route to political liberty is the development of
criminal law that is fair and just. If the "spirit of the laws" is such that the people
find them reliable, they have political liberty even if they are "condemned to be
hanged." For instance, victims of the death penalty in just regimes have "much more
liberty than a pasha enjoys in Turkey,"[5] since he is likely to live in constant fear of
assassination or subversion. This peculiar claim suggests that it is not the violence of
a state per se that guarantees freedom but how states use violence. Against the liberal tradition, which holds that a violent state is the best route to security because it
keeps criminals and would-be invaders in check through fear, Montesquieu emphasizes that under a just regime those who are not criminals or invaders will be free of
fear (and even those who are criminals or invaders can be certain of just treatment).
Political freedom is not actual physical security, but a sense of trust in one's fellow
citizens and government.

But is the fair administration of the death penalty and other punishments really
the best route to cultivating a collective sense that we are safe? Gandhi offers a different route. Gandhi is directly critical of the idea that physical well-being should
be a preeminent political value.[6] Instead he emphasizes self-sacrifice—and physical
self-sacrifice in particular—as crucial to the practice of nonviolence in satyagraha
campaigns as well as the constructive program. So it might at first seem that that
he would reject Montesquieu's definition of political liberty, as well as his route for
attaining it. However, if we think of Montesquieu's definition of political freedom
as living with a sense of peace and togetherness, then it is very much consistent with
what Gandhi expects will result from swaraj.

Gandhi rejects the idea that we can have certainty as to our physical well-being and security. Instead, he suggests embracing our vulnerability, deploying it for good political use and attending to it through collective efforts, which meet the bodily needs of those who are most vulnerable. Speaking of nonviolence in relation to defense, he writes:

> Non-violence affords the fullest protection to one's self-respect and sense of honour, but not always to possession of land or movable property, though its habitual practice does prove a better bulwark than the possession of armed men to defend them. Non-violence, in the very nature of things, is of no assistance in the defense of ill-gotten gains and immoral acts.[7]

Such claims directly invert a long history of political thought when it comes to freedom. Liberalism promises that by giving over our enforcement powers to government we will be more secure in our lives and property. The means may be unsavory but the end will be good. Advocates of collective freedom through state violence demand the sacrifice of individual lives and property, but always for the good of all and the freedom of the people. Although some may not feel secure, most will because they will have the power to collectively exercise violence. Gandhi rejects both approaches. He points out that self-sacrifice is part and parcel of human living together, and that when we accept this fact and properly orient ourselves to it, it preserves both individual and collective physical well-being. Nonviolence works directly to foster the opinion that we are secure in the company of others. This is true despite, or perhaps because of its de-emphasis on physical security.

I opened the book by asking how it is that the word "freedom" could become emblazoned on a prison camp and a death camp in two different political contexts and times. Our investigation found that the dominant ideologies of Western political thought have been unable to disentangle the striving for freedom from the practice of violence. The US response to 9/11 was not a consequence of a liberal democracy turning away from its values, but a manifestation of the logic that freedom can be defended through violence. While liberal arguments can certainly be used to suggest that the wars in Iraq and Afghanistan were wrongheaded, or that Guantánamo and the use of torture were unjustified, the basic premise that freedom can be defended through the violence of the state continually regenerates such "excesses." Moreover, the militarization and securitization of the United States and the world that have gone hand in hand with these excesses are a greater threat to freedom than terrorism. This is not to minimize the extent to which terrorism undermines freedom by denying the facts of human togetherness. Indeed, state violence and terrorism share much in common.[8]

The idea that freedom can be expressed through violence lies just below the surface and at times bubbles up into our current discourse. Even if arguments for violence on the international stage are more likely to turn on the themes of necessity and defense, nationalism, socialism, and the parochialism of particular identities are not passé. These themes are usually expressed in the trappings of ritual, tradition, and formality. (In the United States, for instance, crowds cheer as a stealth bomber flies over a football game during the national anthem.) People the world over still fall prey to nationalistic appeals to violence on the basis of the idea that we are free and therefore superior to others. Some are not free, or do not act sufficient to the standards of freedom, and therefore are thought to be legitimately subject to the violence of those who are. Despite all of the work in democratic theory that has been done since the inception of liberal democracy, it is hard to imagine a form of rule without some form of violence, punishment, and subjugation. In recovering some of our lost histories and in describing a novel brand of freedom, I have tried to show how people might resist this tradition and liberate, defend, and rule themselves without violence.

NOTES

INTRODUCTION

1. Karen J. Greenberg and Joshua L. Dratel, *The Torture Papers: The Road to Abu Ghraib* (New York: Cambridge University Press, 2005); US Select Committee on Intelligence. *Findings and Conclusions*, Committee Study of the Central Intelligence Agency's Detention and Interrogation Program (Washington, DC: US Senate, 2014); Dan Lamothe, "US Judge Permits Pentagon to Force-Feed Guantánamo Prisoner but Issues Rebuke," *The Washington Post*, May 23, 2014; Jane Mayer, *Dark Side: The Inside Story of How the War on Terror Turned into a War on American Ideals*, 1st ed. (New York: Doubleday, 2008).

2. On the always-contested nature of purportedly coherent traditions see: Farah Godrej, *Cosmopolitan Political Thought: Method, Practice, Discipline* (Oxford; New York: Oxford University Press, 2011).

3. The meaning of violence in the Western tradition is unstable. However, for the purposes of this book, I define violence as "the use of bodies in order to subdue or destroy the will of another for some purpose." I hold the meaning of violence stable in order to track how various concep-tions of freedom relate to this particular phenomenon. For an exploration of various meanings of violence and an argument for the political usefulness of this particular definition see: Dustin Ells Howes, *Toward a Credible Pacifism: Violence and the Possibilities of Politics* (Albany: State University of New York Press, 2009), chapters 1–4.

CHAPTER 1

1. I do not mean to suggest that these are the only common themes among liberation movements and literatures. There are many others. For instance, liberators often propose a

consciousness-raising program whereby the downtrodden are educated to the injustice of their circumstances and made aware of the possibility of freedom. The purpose of this program is to mobilize large numbers of people to take collective political action that resists and overturns the present order. Common problems in undertaking such a project include a) the contradictions of a revolutionary vanguard educating people to their own degradation, b) how to deal with reactionaries among the oppressors and the oppressed, c) the extent to which sympathizers among the oppressors can be trusted, d) whether or not to accept accommodation and gradual progress or demand the complete overturn of the extant order, e) whether or not to demand ideological purity from group members or maintain a big tent with a plurality of views on the nature of liberation and f) how to deal with other, concurrent liberation movements.

2. Against the idea that the tactics of American Indians were disorganized, amoral, and ineffective, Starkey writes: "European soldiers brought the new weapons and techniques associated with [the military revolution in Europe] with them to North America and by 1675 had provoked a military revolution of a sort among Native Americans, a revolution that for 140 years gave them a tactical advantage over their more numerous and wealthier opponents." Armstrong Starkey, *European and Native American Warfare, 1675–1815* (London: UCL Press, 1998), 134–135.

3. Woody Holton, *Forced Founders: Indians, Debtors, Slaves, and the Making of the American Revolution in Virginia* (Chapel Hill: Published for the Omohundro Institute of Early American History and Culture, Williamsburg, Virginia, by the University of North Carolina Press, 1999).

4. See William N. Fenton, *The Great Law and the Longhouse: A Political History of the Iroquois Confederacy*, The Civilization of the American Indian Series (Norman: University of Oklahoma Press, 1998); Daniel K. Richter and Institute of Early American History and Culture (Williamsburg Va.), *The Ordeal of the Longhouse: The Peoples of the Iroquois League in the Era of European Colonization* (Chapel Hill: Published for the Institute of Early American History and Culture, Williamsburg, Virginia, by the University of North Carolina Press, 1992); Donald A. Grinde and Bruce E. Johansen, *Exemplar of Liberty: Native America and the Evolution of Democracy*, Native American Politics Series (Los Angeles: American Indian Studies Center, University of California, Los Angeles, 1991). Skeptics include Elisabeth Tooker, "United States Constitution and the Iroquois League," *Ethnohistory* 35, no. 4 (1988): 305–336. American Indians also influenced the colonial law and constitutions. See Vicki Hsueh, *Hybrid Constitutions: Challenging Legacies of Law, Privilege, and Culture in Colonial America* (Durham, NC: Duke University Press, 2010).

5. On the complex relationship between the Quakers and the revolution see Arthur J. Mekeel, *The Relation of the Quakers to the American Revolution* (Washington, DC: University Press of America, 1979). Although a minority of Quakers were loyalists, most were not. All who were true to the "peace testimony" refused to assist both the American and British militaries. Those who participated in the war effort in any way were disowned.

6. In this way, the Declaration harkened back to Roman traditions whereby specific conditions were stated by the war making party prior to the initiation of hostilities, which in turn anticipated how the war could be brought to a close in legal terms. See Brien Hallett, *Declaring War: Congress, the President, and What the Constitution Does Not Say* (Cambridge: Cambridge University Press, 2012).

7. Thomas Paine, *Common Sense*, ed. Isaac Kramnick, 2nd ed., Pelican Classics (Harmondsworth: Penguin, 1976), 72, 80.

8. Ibid., 82.

9. The extent of the demonstrators' "disorder" is still a matter of dispute among historians. For two views see Albert Soboul, *The French Revolution, 1787–1799: From the Storming of the Bastille to Napoleon* (London: NLB, 1974), 225; and Louis Madelin, *The French Revolution*, The National History of France (London: W. Heinemann, ltd., 1928), 198–199.

10. Maximilien Robespierre, *Virtue and Terror*, ed. Slavoj Zizek, Revolutions (London; New York: Verso, 2007), 89.

11. Edmund Burke, *Reflections on the Revolution in France*, ed. J. C. D. Clark (Stanford, CA: Stanford University Press, 2001).

12. Robespierre, *Virtue and Terror*, 65.

13. His support for the American Revolution was also accompanied by a strong warning against the Royal governor of Virginia's policy of freeing slaves for British military advantage. Seymour Drescher, *Abolition: A History of Slavery and Antislavery* (Cambridge; New York: Cambridge University Press, 2009), 120–121.

14. Sara E. Melzer and Leslie W. Rabine, *Rebel Daughters: Women and the French Revolution*, Publications of the University of California Humanities Research Institute (New York: Oxford University Press, 1992).

15. Anticipating that he would be taken to task for subversion because of his stance against the Constitution, Paine says in his speech to the French National Convention on July 7, 1795: "Citizens, a great deal has been urged respecting insurrections. I am confident that no man has a greater abhorrence of them than myself, and I am sorry that any insinuations should have been thrown out upon me as a promoter of violence of any kind. The whole tenor of my life and conversation gives the lie to those calumnies, and proves me to be a friend to order, truth and justice." Thomas Paine, "The Constitution of 1795," in *The Complete Writings of Thomas Paine with a Bibliographical Essay, and Notes and Introductions Presenting the Historical Background of Paine's Writings*, ed. Philip Sheldon Foner (New York: Citadel Press, 1945), 593.

16. Thomas Jefferson, "French Revolution," in *Thomas Jefferson Encyclopedia* (Monticello, 1773), http://www.monticello.org/site/research-and-collections/french-revolution.

17. Leonard L. Richards, *Shays's Rebellion: The American Revolution's Final Battle* (Philadelphia: University of Pennsylvania Press, 2002).

18. Thomas Jefferson, "To William Stephens Smith," in *The Works of Thomas Jefferson, vol. 5 (Correspondence 1786–1789)*, ed. Paul Leicester Ford (New York; London: G. P. Putnam's Sons; The Liberty Fund, 1787 [1905]), 362, http://oll.libertyfund.org/titles/802#lf0054-05_head_086.

19. Machiavelli argues that the laws of republics must be renewed with bloodshed every five or ten years. Niccolò Machiavelli, *The Discourses of Niccolò Machiavelli*, trans. Leslie J. Walker (London: Penguin Classics, 1970), III: 1.

20. Jefferson tried to convince Lafayette that the expansion of slavery into the West would "dilute the evil everywhere, and facilitate the means of getting rid of it." Lafayette replied that the more he thought about Jefferson's argument, the less convincing it became. Marie Joseph Paul Yves Roch Gilbert du Motier Lafayette and Thomas Jefferson, *The Letters of Lafayette and Jefferson*, ed. Gilbert Chinard, The Johns Hopkins Studies in International Thought (Baltimore, MD; Paris: The Johns Hopkins University Press, 1929), 356–357.

21. James writes that although in normal times the workers and peasants of one country are not likely to take an interest in the slavery of others, the Paris masses came to detest "no section of the aristocracy so much as those whom they called 'the aristocrats of the skin.'" Cyril Lionel Robert James, *The Black Jacobins* (New York: The Dial Press, 1938), 95.

22. Merrill D. Peterson, "Thomas Jefferson and the French Revolution," *Tocqueville Review—La Revue Tocqueville* 9 (1987), 15–25.

23. In the same letter supporting Shays' Rebellion, Jefferson had written from France: "You ask of S. America? Not a word. I know that there are combustible materials there, and that they wait the torch only. But this country will join the extinguishers." Jefferson, "To William Stephens Smith," 362–363.

24. For months, slaves on the island had been organizing for a rebellion using voodoo as a way of communicating and planning. On August 22, 1791, the leaders of the revolt gathered on a mountain overlooking the city of Le Cap. After voodoo incantations and the sucking of the blood from a pig, the high priest Boukman spoke a prayer in Creole that ended with the words "Our god who is good to us orders us to revenge our wrongs. He will direct our arms and aid us. Throw away the symbol of the god of the whites who has so often caused us to weep, and listen to the voice of liberty, which speaks in the hearts of us all." James, *The Black Jacobins*, 67. San Domingo was a notoriously brutal slave colony and the anger of the slaves was unleashed with extraordinary ferocity. For three weeks, the slaves systematically rampaged the plantations, killing masters, raping women, and burning plantations to the ground. The response of the French authorities was equally brutal. In the Roman tradition they lined the streets with the heads of killed slaves placed on pikes, and killed free mulattos, who generally hated slaves, on suspicion of fomenting the rebellion. The effect of the attempt at suppression was to galvanize the slave population. In a few weeks the insurgents numbered 100,000. Ibid., 75.

25. "The slaves destroyed tirelessly. Like the peasants in the Jacquerie or the Luddite wreckers, they were seeking their salvation in the most obvious way, the destruction of what they knew was the cause of their sufferings; and if they destroyed much it was because they suffered much. They knew that as long as these plantations stood their lot would be to labour them. From their masters they had known rape, torture, degradation, and, at the slightest provocation, death. They returned in kind. For two centuries the higher civilisation had shown them that power was used for wreaking your will on those whom you controlled. Now that they held power they did as they had been taught. In the frenzy of the first encounters they killed all, yet they spared the priests whom they feared and the surgeons who had been kind to them. They, whose women had undergone countless violations, violated all the women who fell into their hands, often on the bodies of their still bleeding husbands, fathers and brothers. 'Vengeance! Vengeance!' was their war-cry, and one of them carried a white child on a pike as a standard. Yet they were surprisingly moderate ... They did not maintain this revengeful spirit for long. The cruelties of property and privilege are always more ferocious than the revenges of poverty and oppression." Ibid., 68.

26. In part this showed that unlike the French tribunals, which refused to punish even the most sadistic whites, there were some limits to what rebel leaders would accept. Ibid., 73. On Jeannot killing former slaves for perceived loyalty to whites, see Laurent Dubois, *Avengers of the New World: The Story of the Haitian Revolution* (Cambridge, MA: Belknap Press of Harvard University Press, 2004), 112, 123.

27. Toussaint was born a slave but through the moderation of his owners and his own talents had accumulated education, a managerial position on the plantation, a small amount of land and money, and at least a second-class status. James writes: "An important thing for his future was that his character was quite unwarped. Since his childhood he had probably never been whipped as so many slaves had been whipped. He himself tells that he and his wife were one of the fortunate few who had acquired a modest competence and used to go hand in hand

very happy to work on the little plot of land which some of the slaves cultivated for themselves." James, *The Black Jacobins*, 71. See also Philippe R. Girard, *The Slaves Who Defeated Napoleon: Toussaint Louverture and the Haitian War of Independence, 1801–1804*, Atlantic Crossings (Tuscaloosa: University of Alabama Press, 2011), 13.

28. Ibid., 19–20. Sonthonax, the white republican, was a greater supporter of racial equality than Toussaint and he threatened death for any former masters who returned to the island. But Toussaint authorized the return of his former master Bayon de Libertat. Suspicions that the French might rescind abolition led leaders such as Villate to attack Toussaint and the French governor, but he routed them. In 1798, Britain and America tried to persuade Toussaint to declare independence from France, but he refused as long as the abolition of slavery remained in place. When Napoleon came to power in 1799, he tried to prevent Toussaint from invading the eastern, Spanish, half of the island. But Toussaint, determined to abolish slavery there, invaded anyway. See Dubois, *Avengers of the New World*, 199–201.

29. However, "when Libertat returned from exile, Louverture refused to embrace him and reminded him curtly that 'there is today more distance between you and me than there was in the past between me and you.'" Girard, *The Slaves Who Defeated Napoleon*, 25.

30. Ibid., 17–19, 22–23.

31. The experience of slave and Indian rebellions left many creoles so fearful that they felt their own protection required independence from the Spanish crown, which often had a more liberal attitude toward the majority populations. See John Lynch and R. A. Humphreys, *Latin American Revolutions, 1808–1826: Old and New World Origins* (Norman: University of Oklahoma Press, 1994), 18–24, 38.

32. As was the case in Haiti, the meaning of abolition was contested and even when slavery was formally made illegal it was a "slow and partial process." Ibid., 381.

33. The meaning and significance of the Haitian Revolution was deeply contested in the run-up to the American Civil War. See Matthew J. Clavin, *Toussaint Louverture and the American Civil War: The Promise and Peril of a Second Haitian Revolution* (Philadelphia: University of Pennsylvania Press, 2010).

34. On the influence of indigenous American rebellions on the rebellion of creoles in South America and the effects of independence on native peoples see Lynch and Humphreys, *Latin American Revolutions, 1808–1826*, 381–384.

35. "The error arises from the learned jurists deceiving themselves and others, by asserting that government is not what it really is, one set of men banded together to oppress another set of men . . . [History] shows that from Caesar to Napoleon, and Napoleon to Bismarck, government is in its essence always a force acting in violation of justice, and that it cannot be otherwise. Justice can have no binding force on a ruler or rulers who keep men, deluded and drilled in readiness for acts of violence—soldiers, and by means of them control others. And so governments can never be brought to consent to diminish the number of these drilled slaves, who constitute their whole power and importance." Leo Tolstoy, *The Kingdom of God Is within You*, trans. Constance Garnett (Rockville, MD: Wildside Press, 2006), 98.

36. Marx writes that the Critical Utopian Socialists endeavor to "deaden the class struggle and to reconcile the class antagonisms. They still dream of experimental realization of their social Utopias . . . and to realize all these castles in the air, they are compelled to appeal to the feelings and purses of the bourgeois. By degrees they sink into the category of the reactionary conservative Socialists . . . differing from these only by more systematic pedantry, and by

their fanatical and superstitious belief in the miraculous effects of their social science." Karl Marx, "Manifesto of the Communist Party," in *The Marx-Engels Reader*, ed. Robert C. Tucker (New York: Norton, 1978a), 499.

37. On Locke's use of the word "violence," see also Dustin Ells Howes, "Terror in and out of Power," *European Journal of Political Theory* 11, no. 1 (2012b): 36.

38. Marx writes: "In bourgeois society capital is independent and has individuality, while the living person is dependent and has no individuality. And the abolition of this state of things is called by the bourgeois, abolition of individuality and freedom! And rightly so. The abolition of bourgeois individuality, bourgeois independence, and bourgeois freedom is undoubtedly aimed at." Marx, "Manifesto of the Communist Party," 485.

39. John Locke, "The Second Treatise of Government," in *Two Treatises of Government*, ed. Peter Laslett (New York: Cambridge University Press, 1988), IX, 127.

40. Disputing Bakunin's worries about his embrace of the state for revolutionary purposes, Marx writes: "during the time of struggle to destroy the old society the proletariat still acts on the foundation of the old society and therefore still gives its movement political forms that more or less belong to the old society, in this time of struggle it has not yet attained its final organization and uses means for its liberation which will fall away after the liberation." Karl Marx and Friedrich Engels, "After the Revolution: Marx Debates Bakunin," in *The Marx-Engels Reader*, ed. Robert C. Tucker (New York: Norton, 1978), 547.

41. A "society is conceived without government—harmony in such a society being obtained, not by submission to law or by obedience to any authority, but by free agreements concluded between the various groups, territorial and professional, freely constituted for the sake of production and consumption, as also for the satisfaction of the infinite variety of needs and aspirations of a civilized being. . . . [If] society were organized on these principles, man would not be limited in the free exercise of his powers in productive work by a capitalist monopoly, maintained by the state; nor would he be limited in the exercise of his will by a fear of punishment, or by obedience towards individuals or metaphysical entities, which both lead to depression of initiative and servility of mind. . . . He would thus be able to reach full *individualization*, which is not possible either under the present system of *individualism*, or under any system of state socialism in the so-called *Volkstaat* (popular state)." Petr Alekseevich Kropotkin, *The Conquest of Bread and Other Writings*, ed. Marshall Shatz, Cambridge Texts in the History of Political Thought (Cambridge; New York: Cambridge University Press, 1995), 233–234.

42. Bakunin writes: "The predominance and the abiding triumph of force—that is the real core of the matter, and all that is called *right* in the language of politics is only the consecration of fact created by force. It is clear that the people, longing for emancipation, cannot expect it from the theoretical triumph of abstract right; they must win liberty by force, for which purpose they must organize their powers apart from and against the state." Yet when it comes to the form this force will take he says "Socialists will not be able to prevent the people in the early days from giving vent to their fury by doing away with a few hundreds of the most odious, the most rabid and dangerous enemies. But once that hurricane passes, the Socialists will oppose with all their might hypocritical—in a political and juridical sense—butchery perpetrated in cold blood." Mikhail Aleksandrovich Bakunin et al., *The Political Philosophy of Bakunin: Scientific Anarchism* (Glencoe, IL: The Free Press, 1953), 376, 413.

43. "Now the question is: How could such a monstrous ratio ever come into existence? How is it that 200,000 are capable of exploiting 70,000,000 with impunity? Have those 200,000

people more physical vigor or more natural intelligence than the other 70,000,000? It is enough to pose this question to have it answered in the negative. Physical vigor is of course out of the question, and as to native intelligence, if we take at random 200,000 people from the lower strata and compare them with the 200,000 exploiters in point of mental capacity, we shall convince ourselves that the former possess greater native intelligence than the latter. But the latter do have an enormous advantage over the mass of people, the advantage of *education.*" Ibid., 353.

44. Trotsky writes: "[T]he first condition of salvation is to tear the weapons of domination out of the hands of the bourgeoisie. It is hopeless to think of a peaceful arrival to power while the bourgeoisie retains in its hands all the apparatus of power. Three times over hopeless is the idea of coming to power by the path which the bourgeoisie itself indicates and, at the same time, barricades—the path of parliamentary democracy." Leon Trotsky, *The Defence of Terrorism*, new ed. (London: G. Allen & Unwin ltd., 1935), 35.

45. Karl Marx, "The Possibility of a Non-violent Revolution," in *The Marx-Engels Reader*, ed. Robert C. Tucker (New York: Norton, 1978b), 523. Despite the "concession" on the issue of violence, the speech clearly reflects Marx's conviction that material force is superior to moral force. Though he was able to persuade the membership to expel the anarchists, it still bothers him that the International Working Men's Association is based solely on the cooperation and consent of its members: "Does the General Council have a bureaucracy and an armed police to compel obedience? . . . Under such conditions—without an army, without police, without courts—on the day when the kings are forced to maintain their power only with moral influence and moral authority, they will form a weak obstacle to the forward march of the revolution." Ibid., 523. These arguments are anticipated by Engels in the *Anti-Dühring*, where he describes his "force theory." Friedrich Engels, *Herr Eugen Dühring's Revolution in Science (Anti-Dühring)*, ed. C. P. Dutt (New York: International Publishers, 1966), 176–203.

46. Hubert Kennedy, "Johann Baptist Von Schweitzer: The Queer Marx Loved to Hate," *Journal of Homosexuality* 29, no. 4 (1995): 90.

47. Mikhail Aleksandrovich Bakunin, *Marxism, Freedom and the State* (London: Freedom Press, 1950), 26.

48. Marx and Engels, "After the Revolution: Marx Debates Bakunin," 542–548.

49. Trotsky, *The Defence of Terrorism*, 60. Robert Tucker provides what is still perhaps the most careful analysis of Marx's arguments regarding the state, arguing that both Kautsky and Trotsky exaggerate their positions and that his view was somewhere in between. See Robert C. Tucker, *The Marxian Revolutionary Idea*, 1st ed. (New York: Norton, 1969), Chapter 3. See also Karl Kautsky, *The Dictatorship of the Proletariat* (Westport, CT: Greenwood Press, 1981); Vladimir Il'ich Lenin, *State and Revolution: Marxist Teaching about the Theory of the State and the Tasks of the Proletariat in the Revolution* (Westport, CT: Greenwood Press, 1978).

50. Mao's attitude toward violence was keenly attentive to winning popular support. On the one hand he laid down strict rules of decorum for the Red Army, which included no confiscation of peasant property, a prohibition on harassing women, and a rule against mistreating prisoners. On the other hand, the strategy of the Army was to make examples of particular local officials and nationalist sympathizers. In response to worries about "going too far" in humiliating these officials and landlords Mao writes: "To put it bluntly, it is necessary to create terror for a while in every rural area, or otherwise it would be impossible to suppress the activities of the counter-revolutionaries in the countryside or overthrow the authority of the gentry. Proper limits have

to be exceeded in order to right a wrong, or else the wrong cannot be righted." Tsetung Mao, *The Selected Works of Mao Tsetung*, 5 vols., vol. 1 (Oxford: Pergamon Press, 1965), 29.

51. The number of Vietnamese casualties is a matter dispute but most agree it was at least one million. For an examination of some of the issues of calculating the death toll, see Guenter Lewy, *America in Vietnam* (New York: Oxford University Press, 1978), Appendix I.

52. Frantz Fanon, *The Wretched of the Earth* (New York: Grove Press, 1963), 147.

53. Mohandas K. Gandhi, *Hind Swaraj and Other Writings*, ed. Anthony Parel, Centenary ed., Cambridge Texts in Modern Politics (Cambridge; New York: Cambridge University Press, 2009), Chapter XIII, 115–116.

54. "Thousands of practical forms and methods of accounting and controlling the rich, the rogues and the idlers should be devised and put to a practical test by the communes themselves, by small units in town and country. Variety is a guarantee of vitality here, a pledge of success in achieving the single common aim—to cleanse the land of Russia of all sort of harmful insects, of crook-fleas, of bedbugs—the rich, and so on and so forth. In one place half a score of rich, a dozen crooks, half a dozen workers who shirk their work (in the hooligan manner in which many compositors in Petrograd, particularly in the Party printing shops, shirk their work) will be put in prison. In another place they will be put to cleaning latrines. In a third place they will be provided with "yellow tickets" after they have served their time, so that all the people shall have them under surveillance, as *harmful* persons, until they reform. In a fourth place, one out of every ten idlers will be shot on the spot." Vladimir Il'ich Lenin, "On Revolutionary Violence and Terror," in *The Lenin Anthology*, ed. Robert C. Tucker (New York: Norton, 1975), 431–432.

CHAPTER 2

1. Recent historians have suggested that while there was real sexism within the black freedom struggle, women were nationally known as "theorists, leaders, strategists and organizers." This suggests that sexism has defined the historiography of the movement as much as it did its practice. Dayo F. Gore, Jeanne Theoharis, and Komozi Woodard, eds., *Want to Start a Revolution? Radical Women in the Black Freedom Struggle* (New York: New York University Press, 2009), 6.

2. At the same time, identifying groups of oppressors and the oppressed often overlooks and minimizes the reality of the privileged position of certain group members. Gays and lesbians who live in accepting subcultures have a very different experience than gay kids in conservative enclaves. Free blacks and Creoles in New Orleans owned slaves. Bourgeois intellectuals who support the Communist Party may have little in common with the workers they hope to inspire to revolution. Many powerful and influential women guided history while most men lived in squalor.

3. In ancient times, Aristotle (384–322 BC) wrote that slaves are "animate instruments" that meet the material needs of the household. In perhaps the most influential modern description of slavery, Friedrich Hegel (1770–1831) wrote that masters use the threat of death so that the slave's "whole being has been seized with dread." For Hegel, the experience of slavery emboldens the slave and instantiates a dialectic of resistance that produces self-consciousness for both slave and master. Unfortunately, Hegel was wrong in his assertion that physical subjugation and an atmosphere of fear necessarily produce a violent dialectical response and, eventually, mutual recognition. Aristotle, 1998, I:4. Georg Wilhelm Friedrich Hegel, *Phenomenology of Spirit*, trans. Arnold V. Miller (Oxford: Oxford University Press, 1977), para. 194, 117.

4. Finley writes that it is "'a fallacy to think that the threat of rebellion increases automatically with an increase in misery and oppression. Hunger and torture destroy the spirit; at most they stimulate efforts at flight or other forms of purely individual behavior (including betrayal of fellow victims), whereas revolt requires organization and courage and persistence.'" Moses I. Finley, cited in Theresa Urbainczyk, *Slave Revolts in Antiquity* (Berkeley: University of California Press, 2008), 4. As I discuss below this statement is somewhat misleading in that flight can be organized and an effective weapon against slavery, as was the case with the Underground Railroad.

5. Urbainczyk, *Slave Revolts in Antiquity*, 112.

6. Orlando Patterson, *Slavery and Social Death: A Comparative Study* (Cambridge, MA: Harvard University Press, 1982), 112. This claim turns on accepting slavery as an institution different from indentured servitude or alienated labor. The condition of slavery, according to Patterson, is distinguished from other economic systems not by the degree of deprivation or physical maltreatment of slaves but by the experience of "social death." Its three features involve the fact that slavery is 1) a substitute for death, 2) natal alienation, or alienation from all claims of "rights" from birth, and 3) being dishonored in a general way. Ibid., Introduction.

7. "In both North and South America all such attempts ended unsuccessfully, although they lasted much longer than is generally acknowledged. The decimation of the Indian populations throughout the Americas following attempts to enslave them or force them into encomienda relations and reservations is well known; it is the extent of the genocide that has been fully appreciated only in recent years." Ibid., 112.

8. To be clear, slavery has not ended as a matter of practice. Millions of people are still held in slavery, including the international sex trade of millions of (mostly) women and girls. Kevin Bales, *Disposable People: New Slavery in the Global Economy*, Rev. ed. (Berkeley: University of California Press, 2004). A new generation of abolitionists has much work to do, often working with governments and international organizations.

9. Slave rebellions and the Haitian Revolution in particular, did play an important role in the debates between abolitionists and proslavery forces. However, even those histories that try to establish the importance of slave rebellions in contributing to abolition show that the violent rebellions were as much a liability as an asset to the movement. See Gelien Matthews, *Caribbean Slave Revolts and the British Abolitionist Movement* (Baton Rouge: Louisiana State University Press, 2006). For a work arguing for a larger role for violent slave revolts in some cases see Paul E. Lovejoy and Jan S. Hogendorn, *Slow Death for Slavery: The Course of Abolition in Northern Nigeria, 1897–1936*, African Studies Series (Cambridge, UK; New York: Cambridge University Press, 1993). Genovese argues that the case of the Haitian Revolution is of such singular importance as to have driven the entire dynamic of abolition, but he also suggests that the interchange of ideas played a crucial role in inspiring slave revolts. See Eugene D. Genovese, *From Rebellion to Revolution: Afro-American Slave Revolts in the Making of the Modern World*, The Walter Lynwood Fleming Lectures in Southern History, Louisiana State University (Baton Rouge: Louisiana State University Press, 1979). For a comparative analysis of various post-emancipation situations see Eric Foner, *Nothing but Freedom: Emancipation and Its Legacy*, The Walter Lynwood Fleming Lectures in Southern History (Baton Rouge: Louisiana State University Press, 1983). On insurrections aboard slave ships, which were sometimes successful, see Eric Robert Taylor, *If We Must Die: Shipboard Insurrections in the Era of the Atlantic Slave Trade*, Antislavery, Abolition, and the Atlantic World (Baton Rouge: Louisiana State University Press, 2006).

10. For an excellent history with particular attention to debates within the abolition movement regarding the proper use of violence see Valarie H. Ziegler, *The Advocates of Peace in Antebellum America*, 1st pbk. ed. (Macon, GA: Mercer University Press, 2001).

11. William Lloyd Garrison, "Declaration of Sentiments of the American Anti-Slavery Convention," *Selections from the Writings of W. L. Garrison* (1852), http://utc.iath.virginia.edu/abolitn/abeswlgct.html. A year later, a member of the Society named Charles K. Whipple published a short tract entitled *Evils of the Revolutionary War*, which outlined how a program of civil disobedience (not yet so named) and conscious suffering (not yet so named) in the face of the repressive violence of the British government could have accomplished the goals of the revolution with less blood and treasure and greater moral purpose. "Our fathers might have accomplished this object, great as it was, merely by taking the course which the society of Friends took to maintain their rights, and by which, though a small and despised body of men, they compelled the English and American governments to recognize and protect those rights. This course consisted of three things. 1st. A steady and quiet refusal to comply with unjust requisitions; 2nd. public declarations of their grievances, and demands for redress; and 3rd. patient endurance of whatever violence was used to compel their submission." Charles K. Whipple, *Evils of the Revolutionary War* (Boston: New England Non-Resistance Society, 1839), 3–4.

12. The Declaration of Sentiments for the new organization stated: "we cordially adopt the non-resistance principle; being confident that it provides for all possible consequences, will ensure all things needful to us, is armed with omnipotent power, and must ultimately triumph over every assailing force. . . . But, while we shall adhere to the doctrine of non-resistance and passive submission to enemies, we purpose, in a moral and spiritual sense, to speak and act boldly in the cause of GOD; to assail iniquity, in high places and in low places; to apply our principles to all existing civil, political, legal and ecclesiastical institutions; and to hasten the time when the kingdoms of this world will have become the kingdoms of our LORD and of his CHRIST, and he shall reign for ever." William Lloyd Garrison, "Declaration of Sentiments Adopted by the Peace Convention" (1838), http://teachingamericanhistory.org/library/index.asp?document=564.

13. James Jasinski, "Constituting Antebellum African American Identity: Resistance, Violence, and Masculinity in Henry Highland Garnet's (1843) 'Address to the Slaves'." *Quarterly Journal of Speech* 93, no. 1 (2007): 42.

14. Adin Ballou, *Christian Non-Resistance*, ed. Lynn Gordon Hughes (Providence, RI: Blackstone Editions, 2003), 4.

15. "[The] generic meaning of the term force is 'strength, vigor, might,' whether physical or moral. Thus we speak of the force of love, the force of truth, the force of public opinion, the force of moral suasion, the force of non-resistance. . . . Or in relation to the muscular force of human beings, we may speak of benevolent force, kind force, uninjurious force; meaning thereby various applications of muscular strength for the purpose of preventing human being committing on themselves or others some injury; in which no prevention no personal injury is inflicted by real kindness and benefit done to all parties concerned." Ballou, *Christian Non-Resistance*, 6.

16. "The almost universal opinion and practice of mankind has been on the side of resistance of injury with injury. It has been held justifiable and necessary, for individuals and nations to inflict any amount of injury which would effectually resist a supposed greater injury. The consequence has been universal suspicion, defiance, armament, violence, torture and bloodshed. . . . [They] who could inflict the greatest amount of injury, in pretended defense of life, honor,

rights, property, institutions, and laws, have been idolized as the heroes and rightful sovereigns of the world." Ibid., 5.

17. On the influence of Ballou and the Society on Thoreau, see Raymond Adams, "Thoreau's Sources for 'Resistance to Civil Government,'" *Studies in Philology* 42, no. 3 (1945): 640–653.

18. Mary Ritter Beard, *Woman as Force in History: A Study in Traditions and Realities* (New York: Persea Books, 1987), 275–278.

19. Patterson, *Freedom in the Making of Western Culture*, Chapter 7.

20. Livy, *The Rise of Rome*, I:57–60.

21. Michael Roberts, *The Age of Liberty: Sweden, 1719–1772* (Cambridge, UK; New York: Cambridge University Press, 1986), 70.

22. This is not to say that women have not actively participated in violent liberation movements and sometimes struggled within those movements for equality. For instance, women played important roles in the American, French, and Haitian Revolutions. For an ambitious account of the role women have played in revolutions more generally see Sheila Rowbotham, *Women, Resistance and Revolution: A History of Women and Revolution in the Modern World* (New York: Vintage Books, 1974). On various forms of resistance, including armed revolt, by slave women in the French colonies see Bernard Moitt, *Women and Slavery in the French Antilles, 1635–1848*, Blacks in the Diaspora (Bloomington: Indiana University Press, 2001), Chapter 7. This is also not to say that women have never used violence against men. Women have occasionally used violence, sometimes in organized fashion, to upend patriarchal norms and masculine privilege. See Janet Saltzman Chafetz, Anthony Gary Dworkin, and Stephanie Swanson, *Female Revolt: Women's Movements in World and Historical Perspective* (Totowa, NJ: Rowman & Allanheld, 1986), Introduction.

23. Leo Tolstoy, *The Kingdom of God Is within You*, trans. Constance Garnett (Rockville, MD: Wildside Press, 2006), 19.

24. Ballou, *Autobiography*, 421.

25. Wright, 1859, 9.

26. Ballou's autobiography contains the lengthy, public correspondence between himself and Garrison on the matter. See Adin Ballou, *Autobiography of Adin Ballou, 1803–1890. Containing an Elaborate Record and Narrative of His Life from Infancy to Old Age*, ed. William Sweetzer Heywood (Lowell, MA: The Vox Populi Press, 1896), 416–422.

27. Ballou, *Christian Non-resistance*, 179.

28. Ballou, *Christian Non-resistance*, 178.

29. Ballou, *Autobiography*, 422.

30. Also, some have argued that slavery did not end until the civil rights movement, which I discuss below. See Douglas A. Blackmon, *Slavery by Another Name: The Re-enslavement of Black Americans from the Civil War to World War II*, 1st Anchor Books ed. (New York: Anchor Books, 2009). For a comparative analysis of various post-emancipation situations see Foner, *Nothing but Freedom: Emancipation and Its Legacy*.

31. Urbainczyk, *Slave Revolts in Antiquity*, 107.

32. Jane Landers, *Black Society in Spanish Florida*, Blacks in the New World (Urbana: University of Illinois Press, 1999).

33. "There are no reliable statistics for slaves who freed themselves through flight but extant evidence suggests they numbered in the tens of thousands. Contemporary estimates suggest that South Carolina lost over 20,000 slaves and Georgia perhaps 10,000, either as a result of

flight or by death from smallpox or camp fevers in British military camps. Even if Jefferson's estimate of 30,000 slaves lost by Virginia in the year 1781 alone is exaggerated, the slave exodus during the war years was, by any measure, extraordinary, in terms of its impact on the South's productive capacity, on the wealth and power of the southern plantocracy, and on the spread of the revolutionary ideological seed scattered by Dunmore's Ethiopian soldiers." Sylvia R. Frey, "Resistance and Rebellion in American Slave Societies," in *Slavery, Abolition and Social Justice* (Adam Matthew Digital).

34. Addams writes: "I became gradually convinced that in order to make the position of the pacifist clear it was perhaps necessary that at least a small number of us should be forced into an unequivocal position." Jane Addams, "Personal Reactions during War," in *Nonviolence in America: A Documentary History*, ed. Staughton Lynd and Alice Lynd (Maryknoll, NY: Orbis Books, 1995). On Sylvia's split with her mother and sister, both of whom supported the war, see Adam Hochschild, *To End All Wars: A Story of Loyalty and Rebellion, 1914–1918* (Boston: Houghton Mifflin Harcourt, 2011), 106–108. On WILPF see Catia Cecilia Confortini, *Intelligent Compassion: Feminist Clinical Methodology in the Women's International League for Peace and Freedom*, Oxford Studies in Gender and International Relations (New York: Oxford University Press, 2012).

35. See, for instance, Valerie Solanas, *SCUM Manifesto* (London; New York: Verso, 2004).

36. See Anthony Parel, *Gandhi's Philosophy and the Quest for Harmony* (Cambridge, UK: Cambridge University Press, 2006); Farah Godrej, "Nonviolence and Gandhi's Truth: A Method for Moral and Political Arbitration," *The Review of Politics* 68, no. 2 (2006).

37. Mahatma Gandhi, *Hind Swaraj and Other Writings*, ed. Anthony Parel. (New York: Cambridge University Press, 1997), xxv.

38. On the realist element in Gandhi's thought see Karuna Mantena, "Another Realism: The Politics of Gandhian Nonviolence," *American Political Science Review* 106, no. 2 (2012); James Tully, *Public Philosophy in a New Key*, Ideas in Context (Cambridge, UK; New York: Cambridge University Press, 2008), II: 308–309.

39. Farah Godrej, "Ascetics, Warriors, and a Gandhian Ecological Citizenship," *Political Theory* 40, no. 4 (2012): 437–465.

40. On the complexity of Gandhi's views toward women see Madhu Kishwar, "Gandhi on Women," *Economic and Political Weekly* 20, no. 40, 41 (1985): 1753–1758.

41. Chadha, 1997, 288. See also Thomas Weber, *On the Salt March: The Historiography of Gandhi's March to Dandi* (New Delhi: HarperCollins Publishers India, 1997).

42. Gandhi, *Collected Works*, Vol. 10, 379.

43. Gandhi, *Collected Works*, Vol. 10, 379–380.

44. Gandhi, *Collected Works*, Vol. 10, 380.

45. Gandhi, *Collected Works*, Vol. 10, 380.

46. "The 'points of contact' referred to by me is a phrase intended to cover all social, religious and political relations alike as between individuals and masses. Thus, for instance, instead of accentuating the differences in religion, I should set about discovering the good points common to both. I would bridge the social distance wherever I can do so consistently with my religious belief. I would go out of my way to seek common ground on the political field." Gandhi, *Collected Works*, Vol. 28, 184.

47. Easwaran Eknath, *Nonviolent Soldier of Islam: Badshah Khan, a Man to Match His Mountains*, 2nd ed. (Tomales, CA: Nilgiri Press, 1999), 184–185.

48. Amitabh Pal, "Gandhi Was in Abbottabad, Too," http://www.progressive.org/news/2011/05/161838/gandhi-was-abbottabad-too.

49. On the complex story of the use of violence and nonviolence in opposition to apartheid see Kurt Schock, *Unarmed Insurrections: People Power Movements in Nondemocracies*, Social Movements, Protest, and Contention (Minneapolis: University of Minnesota Press, 2005), chapter 3.

50. On the Otpor movement and the NATO bombing see Peter Ackerman and Jack DuVall, *A Force More Powerful: A Century of Nonviolent Conflict*, 1st ed. (New York: St. Martin's Press, 2000), 478–488.

51. For further analysis and examples, see Adam Roberts and Timothy Garton Ash, *Civil Resistance and Power Politics: The Experience of Non-violent Action from Gandhi to the Present* (Oxford; New York: Oxford University Press, 2011); Sharon Erickson Nepstad, *Nonviolent Revolutions: Civil Resistance in the Late 20th Century* (New York: Oxford University Press, 2011).

52. Erica Chenoweth and Maria J. Stephan, *Why Civil Resistance Works: The Strategic Logic of Nonviolent Conflict*, Columbia Studies in Terrorism and Irregular Warfare (New York: Columbia University Press, 2011). Amid success, nonviolent techniques (like many violent uprisings) have failed spectacularly, in the sense that those using them have not always achieved the goal of liberation. Yet, even when nonviolence has failed, it has had important effects on politics. For instance, the protestors in China in 1989 spotlighted human rights abuses in that country, the participation of many millions in the anti-violence movement in Colombia in the late-90's continues to influence the government and the various insurgent groups, and the 2009 Green Wave in Iran complicated the Obama administration's policy of engagement with the existing leadership while emboldening liberal forces within the country.

53. Urbainczyk, *Slave Revolts in Antiquity*, 1.

CHAPTER 3

1. Orlando Patterson, *Freedom: Vol. 1: Freedom in the Making of Western Culture* (New York: Basic Books, 1991), chapter 7.

2. S. P. Oakley, *A Commentary on Livy, Books VI–X*, 4 vols. (Oxford; New York: Clarendon Press; Oxford University Press, 1997), viii.

3. Robert Maxwell Ogilvie, *A Commentary on Livy, Books 1–5* (Oxford: Clarendon Press, 1965), 310, 489.

4. Of particular value in this regard are "stock motifs," such as the rape of Lucretia. Scholars generally believe that when these motifs appear, the events have been fabricated. But these stories have had enduring influence, in part due to their repetition. By tracing these mythologies to modern thinkers and noticing their influence (or lack thereof) we get a better sense of how the ancient and modern understandings of freedom differ. As I discuss below, I also find the incredulity of contemporary historians for events others consider to be in the "hard core" to be equally revealing.

5. Livy's account suggests that Lucretia's body is the property of her father and husband, which she reports has now been defiled, but also that the three of them agree that there is a distinction between Lucretia's soul and her body—that the guilt should be fixed "not upon the

victim but the transgressor." Livy, *The Rise of Rome: Books One to Five*, trans. T. James Luce, New ed., Oxford World's Classics (Oxford; New York: Oxford University Press, 2008), 1:58.

6. Ibid., 1:58.

7. Ibid., 1:59.

8. Ibid., 1:59.

9. Ibid., 1:56. Brutus also reminds the people that the previous king, Servius Tullius, had curtailed the influence of the aristocracy and expanded plebeian participation in government. Tarquinius had married his daughter and, with her help, murdered him.

10. Ibid., 2:1.

11. Ibid., 2:3.

12. As with the description of Lucretia, Livy describes the slave as being a savvy strategist in that he waits until an incriminating letter is in the proper hands before revealing the plot.

13. On the significance of both freeing a person from slavery *and* granting them citizenship see Ogilvie, *A Commentary on Livy, Books 1–5*, 241–243.

14. Gary Forsythe, *A Critical History of Early Rome: From Prehistory to the First Punic War* (Berkeley: University of California Press, 2005), 220.

15. Livy writes that the plebeians would not have been ready for freedom in previous years because they were shepherds and strangers (*conuenarumque*) who did not have a sufficiently mature attachment to their families and their property. Only through the moderate rule of previous kings had they gained a sensibility that would mitigate against them attacking the senators of a city that was not originally their own. Livy, *The Rise of Rome: Books One to Five*, 2:1.

16. The use of Lucretia's story and her act of self-sacrifice as a way to gain freedom for Roman men could be understood as a cynical double move, whereby the raising up of the plebs reinforces the second-class status of female citizens and makes male and female slaves more vulnerable than ever. After all, Lucretia is dead and Brutus is left to rule, along with her husband, as the first consuls. However, there are a number of indications in Livy that the women of Rome see their interests being served by the establishment and maintenance of the Republic. For instance, he notes that the matrons mourned Brutus's death for a full year because he had so championed the cause of a woman and he recounts the story of the heroic Cloelia who leads an escape of Roman women who were hostages of King Porsenna. Ibid., 2:9, 2:13.

17. Ibid., 2:9.

18. Ibid., 2:21.

19. Ibid., 2:23.

20. "When none responded to his name, the multitude came crowding around as if at a meeting and declared that the plebs could be duped no longer; not a single soldier would step forth unless the state made good on a solemn pledge; it must guarantee every single individual his freedom before issuing him his weapons, for men would fight for country and countrymen, not for people who owned them." Ibid., 2:28.

21. Ibid., 3:37.

22. Ibid., 3:37.

23. When the Sabines attack, even the nobles are ready to use noncooperation against the "ten Tarquins." Needing money and soldiers, the decemvirs reluctantly call the Senate into session, but the senators retreat to their estates. The plebs, following suit, refuse recruitment. The decemvirs respond by levying a fine for nonattendance and sending men to the estates to

demand attendance. Attendance is good but the decemvirs' attempt to stifle the speech of the senators fails, as they denounce them anyway. Ibid., 3:42.

24. *Arces* means to "enclose" or "shut away." Ibid., 3:45:8.

25. *Me vindicantem sponsam in libertatem vita citius deseret quam fides.* Literally: "I assert that my wife has liberty, my life forfeited in trust." Ibid., 3:45:11.

26. *Quid prodesse si incolumi urbe quae capta ultima timeantur liberis suis sint patienda.* Literally: "What use is an unimpaired city, whose own final liberty is feared to live and suffer." Ibid., 3:47.

27. Ibid., 3:50.

28. Ogilvie, *A Commentary on Livy, Books 1–5*, 487.

29. She was originally portrayed as a noblewoman and it is likely that the story was changed to heighten her identification with the plebs. Ibid., 477.

30. Livy, *The Rise of Rome: Books One to Five*, 3:50:9.

31. Livy's emphasis on libido in conjunction with tyranny is an addition from the version told by Dionysius of Halicarnassus. Ogilvie, *A Commentary on Livy, Books 1–5*, 478.

32. Livy, *The Rise of Rome: Books One to Five*, 3:50:14.

33. Ibid., 3:52.

34. Horatius and Valerius ask the Senate: "Do you intend to issue laws to walls and buildings? Are you ashamed that here in the forum your lictors virtually outnumber other citizens?" Ibid., 3:52.

35. "But continue to show the same restraint in entering the city that you have shown hitherto; for you have violated no man's property despite the need of this great throng for so many basic necessities." Ibid., 3:54.

36. Ogilvie, *A Commentary on Livy, Books 1–5*, 313.

37. For an extensive discussion of Ceres as indelibly linking the women of Rome and the plebs, see Barbette Stanley Spaeth, *The Roman Goddess Ceres*, 1st ed. (Austin: University of Texas Press, 1996). The site of the secessions themselves is sometimes placed on the Aventine Hill; the hill is also associated with non-Romans residing in Rome, and the *lex sacrata* and the secessions may have been Italian in origin. Ogilvie, *A Commentary on Livy, Books 1–5*, 313–314.

38. *Non esse iam Appi libidini locum in domo sua: ab alia violentia eius eodem se animo suum corpus vindicaturum quo vindicaverit filiae: ceteri sibi ac liberis suis consulerent.* Livy, *The Rise of Rome: Books One to Five*, 3:50:9.

39. Ibid., 3:57.

40. *apparebat aut hostibus aut ciuibus de uictoria concedendum esse.* Ibid., 4:6:6.

41. Ibid., 4:6.

42. Ibid., 4:23.

43. Ibid., 4:9.

44. Forsythe, *A Critical History of Early Rome: From Prehistory to the First Punic War*, 176.

45. Ibid., 175.

46. Ibid., 230.

47. Tim Cornell, *The Beginnings of Rome: Italy and Rome from the Bronze Age to the Punic Wars (C. 1000–264 BC)*, Routledge History of the Ancient World (London; New York: Routledge, 1995), 267.

48. Ibid., 257.

49. Forsythe, *A Critical History of Early Rome: From Prehistory to the First Punic War*, 181.

50. Ibid., 232.

51. Establishing the legitimacy of nonmilitary institutions is also consistent with the plebeian association with unarmed women and slaves.

52. Ogilvie, *A Commentary on Livy, Books 1–5*, 478.

53. William V. Harris, *War and Imperialism in Republican Rome, 327–70 bc* (Oxford; New York: Clarendon Press; Oxford University Press, 1979), 163–254.

54. The incident with Verginia is recounted and the internal conflict is remapped onto the external conflict: "It was shameful to show more courage fighting against citizens than foreign foes and to have greater fear of enslavement at home than at the hands of victorious enemies. In peace time it had been only Verginia's purity that had put her in danger, only Appius' lust that had endangered her; but if the fortunes of war should so incline, everyone's child would be in danger from thousands of triumphant foes." Livy, *The Rise of Rome: Books One to Five*, 3:61.

55. The Sabines raid Roman territory when the decemvirs take power because the Romans had "lost their spirit" and "those who had lost their liberty were unworthy holders of imperial power." Ibid., 3:38. Eventually, the Aequi and the Volsci join the attack. But after the secession, the consul Valerius turns the tide. He bids the plebs to think of "the Aventine and Sacred Mount: where liberty had been won a few months before, there they should return with Rome's power undiminished. They should show that the nature of the Roman soldier was the same after the expulsion of the decemvirs as before their entry into office, and that with the establishment of equal rights the courage of the Roman people had not been impaired." Ibid., 3:61. The Romans rout the Aequi and the Volsci, which in turn inspires the defeat of the Sabines ("Men, I think you have heard how the fight went at Algidus. The army behaved as the army of a free people should." Ibid., 3:62.) For the first time, a triumph is celebrated by the order of the people without the sanction of the Senate. Ibid., 3:64.

56. Ibid., 5:6.

57. Harris is skeptical of those who argue that the plebs were opposed "to the more aggressive kind of Roman imperialism." Harris, *War and Imperialism in Republican Rome, 327–70 BC*, 42.

58. Ibid., 260.

59. Harris argues that the case for defensive war is most strong for the Second Punic War. Ibid., 200.

60. Although in retrospect, the Romans sometimes adopted Greek language to explain the expansion of the Republic. See Sviatoslav Dmitriev, *The Greek Slogan of Freedom and Early Roman Politics in Greece* (Oxford; New York: Oxford University Press, 2011), 272–274.

61. On the very few references to *libertas* with regard to external affairs prior to the invasion of Greece, see Erich S. Gruen, *The Hellenistic World and the Coming of Rome*, 2 vols. (Berkeley: University of California Press, 1984), II:143.

62. See Dmitriev, *The Greek Slogan of Freedom and Early Roman Politics in Greece*; Gruen, *The Hellenistic World and the Coming of Rome*.

63. Philip himself claimed to be fighting for the freedom of the Greeks and used the rhetoric quite effectively. Indeed, he subdued very few cities by force. Dmitriev, *The Greek Slogan of Freedom and Early Roman Politics in Greece*, 354.

64. Demosthenes, *Phillipics*, trans. J. H. Vince (London: Harvard University Press, Perseus Digital Library, 1930), 9:70.

65. These problems were present as early as the mid-second century. Astin describes the situation for plebs as follows: "men were recruited under a system designed to raise armies for short

local wars and very little adapted to the new conditions. They were still treated as a citizen militia; a contribution toward the cost of equipment and food was deducted from their not very substantial pay; and no regular provision was made for them upon discharge. In earlier times the peasant had returned to his farm after an absence of a few months, or possibly only a few weeks; but these men were away for years on end, at a time when the pressures upon the peasant farmer were in any case great and the threat of dispossession very real." A. E. Astin, *Scipio Aemilianus* (Oxford: Clarendon Press, 1967), 169.

66. Ibid., chapter 15.

67. Cicero, *Phillipics*, trans. C. D. Yonge, The Orations of Marcus Tullius Cicero (London: George Bell & Sons, Perseus Digital Library, 1903), 2:44:112–113.

68. Ibid., 2:44:114.

69. Ibid., 4:1:1.

70. Ibid., 10:7:15.

71. Ibid., 14:14:36.

72. This is perhaps further reinforced by the religious callings and spiritual aura of leaders like Eunus and Spartacus. See K. R. Bradley, *Slavery and Rebellion in the Roman World, 140 b.c.–70 b.c.* (Bloomington; London: Indiana University Press; B. T. Batsford, 1989), 55, 93.

73. Ibid., 90.

74. On problems with desertion, leading to mass public punishment in the wars to win back modern-day Spain and Portugal from Quintus Sertorius, see Astin, *Scipio Aemilianus*, 167. Harris believes the recruiting problems stretched back into the second century: "Though the people's direct power declined somewhat after the Hannibalic War, ordinary citizens in the category of *assidui* came to exercise an important influence over external policy in the second century by means of their willingness or unwillingness to serve in person in particular wars. From the 160s at least, recruiting considerations must have entered into senatorial thinking." Harris, *War and Imperialism in Republican Rome, 327–70 BC*, 142.

75. On troop discipline problems in the war and the possibility that some Romans even deserted to the Spartacus cause, see Bradley, *Slavery and Rebellion in the Roman World, 140 B.C.–70 B.C.*, 95, 97, 99. His army also contained many free Italians from the south.

76. In *Pro Caecina* he says: "It is not right for me to be summoned together on account of a dispute about possession; it is not right for a multitude to be armed for the sake of preserving a right; nor is there anything so contrary to law as violence; nor is there anything so irreconcilable with justice as men collected together and armed (*convocati homines et armati*)." Cicero, *For Aulus Caecina*, trans. C. D. Yonge, The Orations of Marcus Tullius Cicero (London: Henry G. Bohn, Perseus Digital Library, 1856), 33.

77. "You know the insolence of Antonius; you know his friends, you know his whole household. To be slaves to lustful, wanton, debauched, profligate, drunken gamblers, is the extremity of misery combined with the extremity of infamy. And if now (but may the immortal gods avert the omen!) that worst of fates shall befall the republic, then, as brave gladiators take care to perish with honor, let us too, who are the chief men of all countries and nations, take care to fall with dignity rather than to live as slaves with ignominy. There is nothing more detestable than disgrace; nothing more shameful than slavery. We have been born to glory and to liberty; let us either preserve (*teneamus*) them or die with dignity." Cicero, *Phillipics*, 3:14:35–36.

78. Dmitriev, *The Greek Slogan of Freedom and Early Roman Politics in Greece*, 375.

79. A notable feature of the history examined thus far is the extent to which the defense of freedom from enemies outside the Republic is almost indistinguishable from (and indelibly intertwined with) the defense of freedom from enemies inside it. When the Tarquins are sent into exile, former insiders are now in alliance with outsiders. The plebs refuse to fight wars against these outsiders in order to gain leverage over those who threaten liberty at home. Demosthenes asks the Athenians to defend their freedom from the outsider Phillip. Cicero strikes the same theme in his condemnation of the homegrown Marc Antony. These same dynamics would reappear as the idea of defending freedom is developed in the modern world, but the idea of territorial integrity and national sovereignty combine to tip the balance toward a notion of defending freedom that is largely externalized. The original Roman idea of defending freedom, where the use of civil disobedience against one's fellow citizens takes precedence over the physical defense of the city from outsiders, is all but lost in the modern era.

80. "[I]n the sphere of action we may ... distinguish acts which are merely necessary, or merely and simply useful, from acts which are good in themselves." Aristotle, *Politics*, trans. Ernest Barker (New York: Oxford University Press, 1998), VII:14 1333a31–32.

81. Ibid., VII:14 1333b15–32.

82. Ibid., VII:14 1333b38–1334a2.

83. Put another way, slavery and, by extension, warfare are associated with the demands of the physical body, which free men must of necessity use war to meet. It is not hard to see how this theory springs from practice, given that war is a primary means for acquiring slaves in the ancient world.

84. Marcus Tullius Cicero, *On the Commonwealth*, trans. George Holland Sabine and Stanley Barney Smith (New York: Macmillan Publishing Company, 1976), III:23.

85. Embassies were sent to would-be enemies on the pretense or reality of making a deal. Rome's enemies were forced to accept or reject those representatives and when they rejected them hostilities were initiated as a "reply." See Harris, *War and Imperialism in Republican Rome, 327–70 BC*, 166–174, 267–268. Others suggest an even more direct connection, in that the "*jus fetiale* held that only attacks upon Roman territory or violations of treaties or of the immunities of ambassadors would serve to legitimize the taking up of arms in defense or retaliation." M. A. Weightman, "Self-Defense in International Law," *Virginia Law Review* 37, no. 8 (1951): 1095.

86. See Jean Michel Hornus, *It Is Not Lawful for Me to Fight: Early Christian Attitudes toward War, Violence, and the State*, Rev. ed., A Christian Peace Shelf Selection (Scottdale, PA: Herald Press, 1980).

87. Tertullian, "Apology," in *Apology, De Spectaculis*, ed. T. R. Glover, et al. (London, New York: W. Heinemann, G. P. Putnam's Sons, 1931), XXXVII:5.

88. "Why! without taking up arms, without rebellion, simply by standing aside, by mere ill-natured separation, we could have fought you! For if so vast a mass of people as we had broken away from you and removed to some recess of the world apart, the mere loss of so many citizens of whatever sort would have brought a blush to your rule—yes, that it would, and punished you, too, by sheer desertion! Beyond doubt, you would have shuddered at your solitude, at the silence in your world, the stupor as it were of a dead globe. You would have had to look about for people to rule." Ibid., XXXVII:6–7.

89. As Hartigan remarks, for Augustine "whatever it is that the attacker might take away, whether life or property, is not really very important because the individual does not wholly own

these things anyway [in that they belong to God]." Richard Shelly Hartigan, "Saint Augustine on War and Killing: The Problem of the Innocent," *Journal of the History of Ideas* 27, no. 2 (1966): 196.

90. John Langan, "The Elements of St. Augustine's Just War Theory," *The Journal of Religious Ethics* 12, no. 1 (1984): 22.

91. Quoting from Augustine's Letter 189 to Boniface in 418 BC, Langdon writes: "Augustine reminds Boniface that war is waged for the sake of peace and that he is to wage war as a peacemaker. Violence is appropriate in dealing with rebels who reject peace. War is 'the result of necessity,' and therefore 'let it be necessity, not choice, that kills your warring enemy.'" Ibid., 26.

92. Marsilius of Padua, *Defensor pacis*, trans. Alan Gewirth (Toronto: University of Toronto Press, Medieval Academy of America, 1986).

93. Aquinas Thomas, "Summa Theologica," in *On Law, Morality, and Politics*, ed. William P. Baumgarth and Richard J. Regan (Indianapolis: Hackett, 1988), II-II:64:7.

94. Scholz argues that Aquinas only sanctions civil disobedience when an entire system is corrupt and when it is not in the self-interest of persons to disobey. Disobedience is an evil, but it may be a lesser evil if an entire government is corrupt. Presumably, this might involve refusing to fight an unjust war. See S. J. Scholz, "Civil Disobedience in the Social Theory of Thomas Aquinas," *The Thomist* 60, no. 3 (1996). Also on this topic see Charles P. Nemeth, *Aquinas and King: A Discourse on Civil Disobedience* (Durham, NC: Carolina Academic Press, 2009).

95. Thomas, "Summa Theologica," II-II:40:1.

96. In Augustine "the requirement to vindicate justice obviates all other considerations, and though he recognizes that the innocent may accidentally suffer in the process, he consigns this to necessity and is resigned to it." Hartigan, "Saint Augustine on War and Killing," 202.

97. As Reichburg writes: "Thomas explains not only how the military function is rightly exercised by . . . religious knights for the occasional protection of civilians who have fallen victim to ambush or other criminal violence, but also they may avail themselves of arms even for the defense of the entire commonwealth (*totius reipublicae defensio*) against the onslaught of its enemies. This they do, not in view of any 'worldly purpose,' but rather 'to support the neighbor and in the service of God.'" Gregory M. Reichberg, "Thomas Aquinas between Just War and Pacifism," *Journal of Religious Ethics* 38, no. 2 (2010): 235.

98. Eric MacGilvray, *The Invention of Market Freedom* (Cambridge, UK; New York: Cambridge University Press, 2011), 61.

CHAPTER 4

1. Niccolò Machiavelli, *The Discourses of Niccolò Machiavelli*, trans. Leslie J. Walker (London: Penguin Classics, 1970), III:1, 387–388.

2. Leo Strauss, *Thoughts on Machiavelli* (Chicago: University of Chicago Press, 1978); Harvey Claflin Mansfield, *Taming the Prince: The Ambivalence of Modern Executive Power*, Johns Hopkins pbk. ed. (Baltimore: Johns Hopkins University Press, 1993).

3. Margaret Michelle Barnes Smith, "The Philosophy of Liberty: Locke's Machiavellian Teaching," in *Machiavelli's Liberal Republican Legacy*, ed. Paul Anthony Rahe (New York: Cambridge University Press, 2006), 36–57; Gisela Bock, Quentin Skinner, and Maurizio Viroli, eds., *Machiavelli and Republicanism*, Ideas in Context (New York: Cambridge University Press, 1990); J. G. A. Pocock, *The Machiavellian Moment: Florentine Political Thought and the Atlantic Republican Tradition*, 2nd pbk. ed. (Princeton, NJ: Princeton University

Press, 1975). Critics include John P. McCormick, "Machiavelli against Republicanism: On the Cambridge School's 'Guicciardinian Moments'," *Political Theory* 31, no. 5 (2003).

4. Henry I, "Charter of Liberties," *Medieval Sourcebook* (1100), http://www.fordham.edu/halsall/source/hcoronation.asp. On the antecedents of the charter and its probable derivation from borough charters see Henry L. Cannon, "The Character and Antecedents of the Charter of Liberties of Henry I," *The American Historical Review* 15, no. 1 (1909).

5. Henry I, "Charter of Liberties." The Latin does not bear out the use of the word "free" here but the sense of the passage is mostly captured by the translation. For the Latin, see James Clarke Holt, *Magna Carta*, 2nd ed. (Cambridge, UK; New York: Cambridge University Press, 1992), 426.

6. He also made many additional individual deals reflecting his need to build up "as much support as possible" in the wake of a hasty coronation. Judith A. Green, *Henry I: King of England and Duke of Normandy* (Cambridge, UK; New York: Cambridge University Press, 2006), 49.

7. "It appears that what was going on here was a promise that traditional exemptions, which had been ignored in the great four-shilling levy of 1096 taken to raise money for the First Crusade, were to be restored." Ibid., 49.

8. On the "potent, even intoxicating" coronation ritual, see ibid., 48.

9. His tenuous status is also his reason for distributing it widely, so as to gather as much support as possible. Green writes that while Henry was "not breaking new ground in promising to redress grievances . . . [what] was different in 1100 was the way Henry's coronation charter was widely disseminated and soon copied into compilations of law." Ibid., 44.

10. Danny Danziger and John Gillingham, *1215: The Year of Magna Carta*, 1st Touchstone ed. (New York: Simon & Schuster, 2004), 248. The Great Charter and the circumstances surrounding its creation reflect an even more far-reaching crisis of authority than faced Henry I. The barons openly threaten rebellion against King John as a consequence of his taxes and failed wars, but there is no clear alternative heir. The barons thus seem to imagine that they can severely delimit his rule by way of the Charter. They even send competing envoys to the Pope, who is unimpressed and mostly sides with the king. Green, *Henry I: King of England and Duke of Normandy*, 49.

11. Holt, *Magna Carta*, 56–57. In article 61, the King agrees to allow a committee of 25 barons to confiscate the monarch's property and hold him and his family alive if he fails to abide by the Charter. The article is removed in the version that goes into law in 1225. For the wording of the article, see ibid., 471.

12. "Charter, cap. 39, erected defences against arbitrary imprisonment and disseisin by the king which it applied not to any one social grade or even to an enumeration of them, but to the free man. . . . Cap. 9 of the Articles . . . covering the amercement of free men still applied to all non-baronial tenants, and hence to military tenants holding their lands by knight service. This broad generic use of the term 'free man' is not matched in any other similar concessions or statement of laws and liberties." Ibid., 277–278.

13. Ibid., 518.

14. Ibid., 24.

15. Ibid., 24.

16. Ibid., 35.

17. Ibid., 57.

18. This was also contained in the controversial and later removed article 61. "And anyone in the land who wishes may take an oath to obey the orders of the said twenty-five barons in the execution of all the aforesaid matters." Ibid., 471.

19. Francisco de Vitoria, *Political Writings*, ed. Anthony Pagden and Jeremy Lawrance, Cambridge Texts in the History of Political Thought (Cambridge, UK; New York: Cambridge University Press, 1991), 296. The word "defend" here comes from the Latin Vulgate version. The authorized King James version would translate this passage as "avenge not yourselves."

20. Ibid., 297. Vitoria here quotes the Book of James 1:25, 2:12.

21. Anghie writes: "Natural law administered by sovereigns rather than divine law articulated by the Pope becomes the source of international law governing Spanish-Indian relations." Antony Anghie, "Francisco De Vitoria and the Colonial Origins of International Law," *Social & Legal Studies* 5, no. 3 (1996): 325.

22. Vitoria, *Political Writings*, 252–277.

23. Ibid., 278.

24. Ibid., 277–285.

25. Ibid., 288.

26. Ibid., 314–321. Vitoria argues that innocents can only be killed if it is "by accident," and plundered and enslaved only if the property or people are being used to fight against those who are waging the just war. While it is not always lawful to execute all enemy combatants for the sole purpose of avenging injury, it may be lawful if it is expedient.

27. Antony Anghie, "Rethinking Sovereignty in International Law," *Annual Review of Law and Social Science* 5(2009): 293.

28. Ibid., 293.

29. Anghie, "Francisco De Vitoria and the Colonial Origins of International Law," 330.

30. "Since, therefore human partnerships arose for the purpose of helping to bear each other's burdens, amongst all these partnerships a civil partnership (*ciuilis societas*) is the one which most aptly fulfills men's needs. It follows that the city (*ciuitas*) is, if I may so put it, the most natural community, the one which is most conformable to nature. The family provides its members with the mutual services which they need, but that does not make it whole and self-sufficient (*una sibi sufficiens*), *especially in defence against violent attack*. This seems to have been the chief reason which induced Cain and Nimrod to compel the first men to live together in cities (Gen. 4:17, 10:11)." Vitoria, *Political Writings*, 9, emphasis mine.

31. Ibid., 6–7.

32. "Thus the law of nations, while a separate discipline, derived like municipal law from natural law. Since the two were aspects of the same thing, i.e. human law, it is not difficult to understand why scholars leaned heavily upon the codified and comprehensive municipal law in speculating upon the law of nations. The right of self-defense was well-established in municipal law. The so-called naturalists transferred it bodily into the law of nations." M. A. Weightman, "Self-Defense in International Law," *Virginia Law Review* 37, no. 8 (1951): 1096.

33. Hugo Grotius, *The Law of War and Peace De Jure Belli Ac Pacis Libri Tres*, trans. Francis W. Kelsey, Essay and Monograph Series of the Liberal Arts Press (Indianapolis: Bobbs-Merrill, 1962), II:I:III, p. 172–173.

34. Those "who accept fear of any sort as justifying anticipatory slaying are themselves greatly deceived, and deceive others." Ibid., II:I:IV, p. 173.

35. Ibid., II:I:VII, p. 175.

36. Grotius cites Demosthenes in a speech against Aristocrates as saying "'In the name of the gods is not this a hard and unjust thing, contrary not only to written laws but also the law common to all men, that I am not permitted to use force against the man who, in the manner of an enemy, seizes and carries off my property?'" Ibid., II:I:XI, p. 179.

37. Ibid., II:I:X, p. 178.

38. Ibid., II:I:XIII, p. 182.

39. "[U]nless anyone is so mad as to believe himself a slave when he obeys one wise king, and fancy himself free when he is subject to a barbarous mob." Vitoria, *Political Writings*, 20.

40. Grotius, *The Law of War and Peace De Jure Belli Ac Pacis Libri Tres*, I:III:VIII, p. 103.

41. "In truth it is possible to find not a few causes which may impel a people wholly to renounce the right to govern itself and to vest this in another, as, for example, if a people threatened with destruction cannot induce any one to defend it on any other condition; again, if a people pinched by want can in no other way obtain the supplies needed to sustain life." Ibid., I:III:VIII, p. 103.

42. Interestingly, Grotius suggests that the reason for this is that our individual lives and property are *not* the highest or only value. Instead, consistent with ancient tradition, we are sometimes guided by our love for others—and our regard for sovereign officials in particular. Ibid., II:I:XVI, p. 184.

43. Ibid., II:I:IX, p. 176.

44. Although they do not connect freedom to self-defense, both Vitoria and Grotius are not without interest in the subject. Vitoria's affirmation of the Spanish "right to travel and trade" and Grotius's work *The Free Sea* portend how the claim to certain rights of movement will be combined with justifications of self-defense in the service of empire. Hugo Grotius et al., *The Free Sea*, Natural Law and Enlightenment Classics (Indianapolis: Liberty Fund, 2004); Vitoria, *Political Writings*, 278. For a nuanced description of how Grotius departs from and affirms classical understandings of the natural law see Mark Rigstad, "The Grotian Moment," in *Penal Practice and Culture, 1500–1900: Punishing the English*, ed. Simon Devereaux and Paul Griffiths (New York: Palgrave Macmillan, 2004), 187.

45. See Dustin Ells Howes, "Creating Necessity: Well-Used Violence in the Thought of Machiavelli," *symplokē* 20, no. 1–2 (2012a): 145–169.

46. Anthony Pagden, *Lords of All the World: Ideologies of Empire in Spain, Britain and France c. 1500–c. 1800* (New Haven, CT: Yale University Press, 1995); Karuna Mantena, *Alibis of Empire: Henry Maine and the Ends of Liberal Imperialism* (Princeton, NJ: Princeton University Press, 2010); Jennifer Pitts, *A Turn to Empire: The Rise of Imperial Liberalism in Britain and France* (Princeton, NJ: Princeton Unversity Press, 2005).

47. See Diego Panizza, "Political Theory and Jurisprudence in Gentili's *De Iure Belli*. The Great Debate between 'Theological' and 'Humanist' Perspectives from Vitoria to Grotius," (2005), http://www.iilj.org/newsandevents/documents/Panizza.pdf.

48. See Pocock, *The Machiavellian Moment*; Smith, "The Philosophy of Liberty: Locke's Machiavellian Teaching."

49. Alberico Gentili, *The Wars of the Romans: A Critical Edition and Translation of* De Armis Romanis, ed. Benedict Kingsbury, Benjamin Straumann, and David A. Lupher (Oxford; New York: Oxford University Press, 2011), 188–189.

50. In part he draws upon the idea that the Romans were defending the liberty of others, but he also cites the Roman practice of granting citizenship to subjected peoples. See Benedict

Kingsbury and Benjamin Straumann, *The Roman Foundations of the Law of Nations: Alberico Gentili and the Justice of Empire* (Oxford; New York: Oxford University Press, 2010), 73–76. Gentili does retain the Roman distinction between fighting for liberty and fighting for material goods and life, quoting the proverb "Liberty is not properly sold for any amount of gold." Gentili, *The Wars of the Romans: A Critical Edition and Translation of* De Armis Romanis, 198–199.

 51. Machiavelli, *The Discourses of Niccolò Machiavelli*, I:16, p. 156.

 52. While authors always note Hobbes's definition of liberty as the body moving through space unimpeded, the fact that this is an entirely new conception of liberty goes unremarked upon in: Quentin Skinner, "Thomas Hobbes on the Proper Signification of Liberty: The Prothero Lecture," *Transactions of the Royal Historical Society, Fifth Series* 40 (1990); David van Mill, "Hobbes's Theories of Freedom," *The Journal of Politics* 57, no. 2 (1995).

 53. Thomas Hobbes, *Leviathan: With Selected Variants from the Latin Edition of 1668* (Indianapolis: Hackett Pub. Co., 1994), XXI:6.

 54. Ibid., XXI:2.

 55. Skinner, "Thomas Hobbes on the Proper Signification of Liberty," 139.

 56. "[E]very subject has liberty in all those things the right whereof cannot by covenant be transferred. . . . covenants not to defend a man's own body are void." Hobbes, *Leviathan*, XXI:11.

 57. Ibid., XXI:9.

 58. Ibid., XXI:8–9.

 59. Ibid., XXI:8.

 60. Hobbes uses the example of a sinking ship, where passengers throw their goods into the sea to avoid drowning. Ibid., XXI:3.

 61. Both charters begin by affirming respect for the free reign of religious institutions and authority, much as Hobbes makes a nod toward the centrality of the free will. This is parlayed into specific rights to inheritance (including for royal women), protection from unjust taxes, war levies, and confiscations. In Magna Carta, personal protections from arbitrary imprisonment and the right to due process are introduced. As mentioned above, the demand to be consulted in decision-making is present in article 61 but is later stripped from Magna Carta, placing the focus squarely on protections from the actions of the King as opposed to an emphasis on a share of governance. Some of the differences between ancient and modern liberty that Benjamin Constant (1767–1830) astutely examines more than a century later are present even in the late Middle Ages. Benjamin Constant, "The Liberty of the Ancients Compared with That of the Moderns," in *Political Writings*, ed. Biancamaria Fontana (Cambridge, UK; New York: Cambridge University Press, 1988).

 62. Derek Croxton, "The Peace of Westphalia of 1648 and the Origins of Sovereignty," *The International History Review* 21, no. 3 (1999): 583.

 63. Ibid., 577, 579.

 64. Hobbes, *Leviathan*, XIII:11–12.

 65. Locke writes that the state of nature exists between "all *Princes* and Rulers of *Independent* Governments all through the World" and "between a *Swiss* and an *Indian*, in the Woods of *America*." John Locke, "The Second Treatise of Government," in *Two Treatises of Government*, ed. Peter Laslett (New York: Cambridge University Press, 1988), II para. 14. See also Barbara Arneil, *John Locke and America: The Defence of English Colonialism* (Oxford; New York: Clarendon Press; Oxford University Press, 1996); James Farr, "Locke, Natural Law, and New World Slavery," *Political Theory* 36, no. 4 (2008).

66. Hobbes, *Leviathan*, XXI:8.

67. By highlighting features of our material condition that no reasonable person can deny, Hobbes believes he can show everyone that it is their common interest to cooperate with the sovereign—any sovereign.

68. Hobbes, *Leviathan*, XIV:4.

69. There "is no way for any man to secure himself so reasonable as anticipation, that is, by force or wiles to master the persons of all men he can, so long till he see no other power great enough to endanger him. And this is no more than his own conservation requireth, and is generally allowed." Ibid., XIII:4.

70. Ibid., XIV:7.

71. Ibid., XXI:10.

72. The distinction no doubt predates Locke. Gentili writes of the Romans that "Unrestrained jurisdiction was given to the king, but nevertheless not (this is certain) so that he might make a decision in accord with his whim or desire, but so that he might justly decide and apportion. Liberty is not license; it is constrained by law. [Libertas non est licentia; iure cogitur.] And the Romans had the power to boldly refer the matter to law, conscious as they were of their own justice and the injustice of the tyrants." Gentili, *The Wars of the Romans: A Critical Edition and Translation of* De Armis Romanis, 198–199.

73. Locke, "The Second Treatise of Government," II, para. 8.

74. "The *State of Nature* has a Law of Nature to govern it, which obliges every one: And Reason, which is that Law, teaches all Mankind, who will but consult it, that being all equal and independent, no one ought to harm another in his Life, Health, Liberty, or Possessions." Ibid., II, para. 6.

75. "Every one as he is *bound to preserve himself,* and not to quit his Station willfully; so by the like reason when his own Preservation comes not in competition, ought he, as much as he can, *to preserve the rest of Mankind,* and may not unless it be to do Justice on an Offender, take away, or impair the life, or what tends to the Preservation of the Life, Liberty, Health, Limb or Goods of another." Ibid., II, para. 6.

76. Ibid., III, para. 17. On this, see also Andrew Dilts, "To Kill a Thief: Punishment, Proportionality, and Criminal Subjectivity in Locke's Second Treatise," *Political Theory* 40, no. 1 (2012).

77. Locke clarifies this particular point later in his discussion of slavery: "A Liberty to follow my own Will in all things, where the Rule prescribes not; and not to be subject to the inconstant, uncertain, unknown, Arbitrary Will of another man. As *Freedom of Nature* is to be under no other restraint but the Law of Nature. This *Freedom* from Absolute, Arbitrary Power, is so necessary to, and so closely joyned with Man's Preservation, that he cannot part with it, but by what forfeits his Preservation and Life together." Locke, "The Second Treatise of Government," IV, para. 22–23.

78. Ibid., III, para. 18.

79. While it is not entirely clear, even restraint seems to refer *not* to a preemptive restraining of *potential* threats to life (and therefore liberty) but only to the restraint of those who have already done harm or clearly declared their intention to do so. For instance, even though a thief does not declare a design upon one's life and can still be punished, Locke does not contemplate preemptive actions against those who would threaten one's property. Ibid., III, para. 18–20.

80. Ibid., IX, para. 123.

81. Ibid., XVI, para. 180. The language here is unmistakably connected to Locke's discussion of slavery, where he says it is only just in the case of legitimate wars. See ibid., IV, para. 23. However, Locke claims that while those who prosecute just wars may do what they will with the *lives* of their enemies—including enslaving them—they may not confiscate their property except for purposes or reparation. This is so that the inheritance of wives and children will be secure. Ibid., XVI, para 180–183.

82. Ibid., XIV.

83. For instance, he insists that no government can order a subject to physically harm him or herself, no one can be forced to incriminate themselves, and his expectation that subjects will physically resist even lawful attacks against their bodies by the sovereign. Hobbes, *Leviathan*, XXI:11–13.

84. Locke, "The Second Treatise of Government," XVI, para. 176.

85. Ibid., XIX, para. 220, 227.

86. Ibid., II, para. 11.

87. "English Bill of Rights," in *Avalon Project* (Yale Law School, 1689).

88. Anticipating future Supreme Court decisions, Jefferson thought that freedom of speech should also be limited to the extent it had deleterious *physical* effects. He writes in a letter to Madison on August 28, 1789 that while he likes the proposed Bill of Rights, the fourth article should restrict "false facts affecting injuriously the life, liberty, property, or reputation of others or affecting the peace of the confederacy with foreign nations." Thomas Jefferson, "Letter: To James Madison (Excerpt)," in *The Origin of the Second Amendment: A Documentary History in Commentaries on Liberty, Free Government, and an Armed Populace during the Formation of the Bill of Rights*, ed. David E. Young (Ontonagon, MI: Golden Oak Books, 1991), 709.

89. The exception here is religion, where it is understood that the state will not establish or endorse a competing vision of the proper moral order. This is a vestige of the original charters of liberties that provide protections for the church as discussed above and is still present in the idea of conscientious objection to participation in the militia, which I discuss below.

90. Carl Schmitt, *The Crisis of Parliamentary Democracy*, Studies in Contemporary German Social Thought (Cambridge, MA: MIT Press, 1985), 36.

91. One recent book on the origins of modern freedom argues that we can understand the "past three centuries not as the progressive expansion of liberty but as the renaming of threats to them." Jason Caro, *The Origins of Free Peoples* (New York: Continuum International Pub. Group, 2011), 18.

92. Shalhope writes that there were four beliefs informing the Second Amendment: "the right of the individual to possess arms, the fear of a professional army, the reliance on militias controlled by the individual states, and the subordination of the military to civilian control." Robert E. Shalhope, "The Ideological Origins of the Second Amendment," *The Journal of American History* 69, no. 3 (1982): 608.

93. Quoting John Trenchard and Walter Moyle's 1697 argument. In ibid., 603.

94. Virginia's constitution read: " 'That a well-regulated militia, composed of the body of the people, trained to arms, is the proper, natural, and safe defence of a free State; that standing armies, in time of peace, should be avoided, as dangerous to liberty; and that in all cases the military should be under strict subordination to, and governed by, the civil power.' " Ibid., 608.

95. Gregory T. Knouff, "White Men in Arms," in *Representing Masculinity: Male Citizenship in Modern Western Culture*, ed. Stefan Dudink, Anna Clark, and Karen Hagemann (New York: Palgrave Macmillan, 2007), 25, 30.

96. She writes that like most duties "it was commonly regarded as onerous, if not dangerous. Yet, at a crucial moment in English history, when the governing classes seized a rare opportunity to draw up a bill of rights, this long-standing and unpopular duty was transformed into a right." As late as 1639 "most Englishmen did not consider themselves privileged to serve in a militia. In fact, they resented military demands made upon them by their government." Joyce Lee Malcolm, *To Keep and Bear Arms: The Origins of an Anglo-American Right* (Cambridge, MA: Harvard University Press, 1994), 1, 9.

97. For James Harrington "landownership became the essential basis for the bearing of arms." Shalhope, "The Ideological Origins of the Second Amendment," 603.

98. Quoted in ibid., 605.

99. The bourgeois revolutionaries were in good company. Late medieval and early modern aristocrats picked up where the Romans left off in their assumption that only some people were capable of freedom and deserved liberties. The root term *frei* indicates that a person belongs to a particular group and *libertas* referred to privileges guaranteed to a select class of people. I explore the former term in chapter 6.

100. The religious elements of late-seventeenth-century conflicts do appear in the wording of the English Bill of Rights. Citing the confiscation of weapons by the previous Catholic authorities, it guarantees that "Protestants may have arms for their defence suitable to their conditions and as allowed by law." However, the other major sources of the European crisis of authority would prove to be more critical in the justification and implementation of the right to bear arms.

101. Knouff, "White Men in Arms," 31. Knouff emphasizes that whiteness was a fluid concept in the late eighteenth century, which he argues was in part solidified by determinations about who could bear arms. See also Carole Pateman, *The Sexual Contract* (Stanford, CA: Stanford University Press, 1988); Charles W. Mills, *The Racial Contract* (Ithaca: Cornell University Press, 1997).

102. Shalhope, "The Ideological Origins of the Second Amendment," 605.

103. Second Congress, "Militia Act of 1792," http://www.constitution.org/mil/mil_act_1792.htm.

104. Quoted in Shalhope, "The Ideological Origins of the Second Amendment," 606.

105. James Burgh writes " 'The possession of arms is the distinction between a freeman and a slave. He, who has nothing, and who himself belongs to another, must be defended by him, whose property he is, and needs no arms. But he, who thinks he is his own master, and has what he can call his own, ought to have arms to defend himself, and what he possesses; else he lives precariously, and at discretion.' " Quoted in ibid., 604.

106. Ibid., 609.

107. Ibid., 613.

108. David E. Young, *The Origin of the Second Amendment: A Documentary History in Commentaries on Liberty, Free Government, and an Armed Populace during the Formation of the Bill of Rights* (Ontonagon, MI: Golden Oak Books, 1991), 356–360.

109. Both amendments originated in George Mason's Richmond Antifederal Committee. Ibid., 390, 459.

110. John Locke, *A Letter Concerning Toleration*, ed. James Tully, HPC Classics Series (Indianapolis: Hackett Pub. Co., 1983), 46.

111. Young, *The Origin of the Second Amendment: A Documentary History in Commentaries on Liberty, Free Government, and an Armed Populace during the Formation of the Bill of Rights*, 695.

112. The reporter records that Thomas Scott of Pennsylvania argues that many people speculate religion is on the decline and "when the time comes that religion shall be discarded, the generality of persons will have recourse to these pretexts to get excused from bearing arms." Ibid., 703.

113. Ibid., 390, 474, 505. On the failure of a motion to reintroduce see ibid., 697.

114. Ibid., 696–697.

115. Knouff, "White Men in Arms," 37.

116. Young, *The Origin of the Second Amendment: A Documentary History in Commentaries on Liberty, Free Government, and an Armed Populace during the Formation of the Bill of Rights*, 703.

117. Ibid., 697.

118. Ibid., 716.

119. B. Franklin and W. T. Franklin, *Memoirs of the Life and Writings of Benjamin Franklin*, vol. 1 (H. Colburn, 1818), 270.

CHAPTER 5

1. *Iliad* 6:455, 16:833, 20:193.

2. Kurt A. Raaflaub, *The Discovery of Freedom in Ancient Greece*, 1st English ed. (Chicago: University of Chicago Press, 2004), 188.

3. Ibid., 257.

4. Ibid., 193.

5. Ibid., 181, 190–191.

6. Thucydides, *History of the Peloponnesian War*, trans. Rex Warner, Rev. ed. (Harmondsworth, UK; Baltimore: Penguin Books, 1972), 2:36, p. 145.

7. Ibid., 2:41, p. 147.

8. Ibid., 2:39, p.146.

9. Ibid., 2:40, p. 147.

10. Ibid., 2:40, p. 147.

11. Ibid., 2:39, p. 146.

12. Ibid., 2:43, p. 148.

13. Ibid., 2:40, p. 147.

14. Ibid., 2:41, p. 148.

15. Raaflaub, *The Discovery of Freedom in Ancient Greece*, 192.

16. Ibid., 193.

17. The significance of the connection between freedom and violence Pericles makes is perhaps best captured in the following line from the oration, as translated by Thomas Hobbes: "In imitation therefore of these [fallen soldiers] and placing happiness in liberty and liberty in valour, be forward to encounter the dangers of war." Hobbes translation, Perseus online, 2:43.

18. Cited in Raaflaub, *The Discovery of Freedom in Ancient Greece*, 189.

19. "We are free and tolerant in our private lives; but in public affairs we keep to the law. This is because it commands our deep respect. We give obedience to those whom we put in positions of authority, and we obey the laws themselves, especially those which are for the protection of the oppressed, and those unwritten laws which it is an acknowledged shame to break." Thucydides, *History of the Peloponnesian War* 2:37, p. 145.

20. On the evidence regarding and disputes concerning the extent of Athenian slavery, see N. R. E. Fisher, *Slavery in Classical Greece*, Classical World Series (London: Bristol Classical Press, 1993), 40–42, 58.

21. Thucydides, *History of the Peloponnesian War* 2:45–46, p. 151.

22. Aristophanes, *Lysistrata*, ed. Jack Lindsay, Illustrated library (Garden City, NY: Halcyon House, 1950), http://data.perseus.org/catalog/urn:cts:greekLit:tlg0019.tlg007.perseus-eng1.

23. Ibid., ln. 266–272.

24. Ibid., ln. 499.

25. Ibid., ln. 499–513, 1017–10.18.

26. Ibid., ln. 672–695.

27. Ibid., ln. 449, 720.

28. Herodotus, "The Histories," (Cambridge, MA: Harvard University Press, 1920), 5.72. *Lysistrata* also serves as a critical primary source for historians interested in the first democratic revolution. See Josiah Ober, "Democracy's Revolutionary Start," in *Origins of Democracy in Ancient Greece*, ed. Kurt A. Raaflaub, Josiah Ober, and Robert W. Wallace (Berkeley: University of California Press, 2007), 90.

29. Aristophanes, *Lysistrata*, ln. 379.

30. Ibid., ln. 182–183, 1112–1156.

31. Ibid., ln. 617.

32. Ibid., ln. 658.

33. Recent examples of actual sex strikes include one in 2003 in Liberia and 2014 in the Ukraine. News Corp Australia, "'Sex Strike' Urged as Ukrainian Women Take Crimea Fight up to the Russians," http://www.news.com.au/world/sex-strike-urged-as-ukrainian-women-take-crimea-fight-up-to-the-russians/story-fndir2ev-1226866318521; Wikipedia, "Women of Liberia Mass Action for Peace."

34. Aristophanes, *Lysistrata*, ln. 1093–1094.

35. Eva C. Keuls, *The Reign of the Phallus: Sexual Politics in Ancient Athens*, 1st ed. (New York: Harper & Row, 1985), 391–395.

36. Aristophanes, *Lysistrata*, ln. 1153.

37. Ibid., ln. 1135–1137.

38. Leon Harold Craig, *The War Lover: A Study of Plato's Republic* (Toronto; Buffalo: University of Toronto Press, 1996), 3.

39. Jill Frank, "Wages of War: On Judgment in Plato's *Republic*," *Political Theory* 35, no. 4 (2007); Dana Richard Villa, *Socratic Citizenship* (Princeton, NJ: Princeton University Press, 2001).

40. For a more detailed discussion of the critique of violence and warfare in Plato, see Amy L. Shuster and Dustin Ells Howes, "The Pacifism in Plato's *Republic*," *History of Political Thought*, forthcoming.

41. Keuls, *The Reign of the Phallus: Sexual Politics in Ancient Athens*, 402.

42. Plato, "Menexenus," in *The Dialogues of Plato*, ed. Reginald E. Allen (New Haven: Yale University Press, 1984b), 239a–b.

43. Ibid., 239d.

44. Ibid., 240d.

45. Ibid., 240e.

46. Ibid., 242b–c.

47. Ibid., 243b.

48. Ibid., 243e.

49. For another exploration of the contrasts between the oration and Pericles' speech, see Stephen G. Salkever, "Socrates' Aspasian Oration: The Play of Philosophy and Politics in Plato's *Menexenus*," *American Political Science Review* 87, no. 1 (1993).

50. Plato, "Menexenus," 244c–d.

51. Ibid., 245c–d.

52. Fisher, *Slavery in Classical Greece*, 67.

53. Plato, "Menexenus," 249d.

54. Plato, "Apology," in *The Dialogues of Plato*, edited by Reginald E. Allen (New Haven: Yale University Press, 1984a), 38e–39a.

55. Ibid., 40b.

56. Ibid., 32c.

57. Fisher, *Slavery in Classical Greece*, 4.

58. Hannah Arendt, *The Human Condition*, 2nd ed. (Chicago: University of Chicago Press, 1998), 119–120. Marx says that surplus labor was being extracted from slaves, although "overwork [driven by forms of exchange–value] . . . were still the exceptions in antiquity." Karl Marx, *Capital: A Critique of Political Economy*, Vol. I. Translated by Samuel Moore and Edward Aveling, edited by Frederick Engels (Moscow, USSR: Progress Publishers, 1887), 164, https:// www.marxists.org/archive/marx/works/download/pdf/Capital-Volume-I.pdf.

59. Aristotle, *Politics*, trans. Ernest Barker (New York: Oxford University Press, 1998), I:5, 1254b1.

60. Ibid., 1.5, 1254b16–19.

61. "Greeks regard themselves as well born not only in their own country, but absolutely and in all places; but they regard barbarians as well born only in their own country—thus assuming that there is one sort of good birth and freedom which is absolute, and another which is only relative." Ibid., I:6, 1255a32–35.

62. Ibid., III:4, 1277a32–34 and 1277b7–9.

63. "[T]he excellence of a citizen may be defined as consisting in 'a knowledge of rule over free men from both points of view." Ibid., III:4, 1277b15–16.

64. Ibid., VI:2, 1317b1–2.

65. Ibid., I:7, 1255b33–35.

66. Ibid., VII:3, 1325a23–27.

67. Ibid., II:9, 1271b4–5.

68. Ibid., VII.2, 1325a6–8.

69. Ibid., I:13, 1260a3–7.

70. Ibid., VII:17, 1336b3–10.

71. Ibid., I:6, 1255b14–15.

72. Ibid., I:5, 1254b27–34.

73. Ibid., I:5, 1254b38–1255a1.

74. Ibid., I.5, 1254b21–22.

75. Ibid., I:8, 1265b17–26.

76. Ibid., I:5, 1254b9–12.

77. Ibid., VII:2, 1324b40–41.

78. Ibid., I:13, 1260a18.

79. Ibid., I:12, 1259a40–1259b9.

80. Ibid., I:13, 1260a19–30.

81. In the critical discussion of the nature of political rule, Aristotle affirms that the "temperance and courage of a man differ from those of a woman . . . A man would be thought cowardly if his courage were only the same as that of a courageous woman; and conversely a woman would be thought a gossip if she showed no more decorum than that which befits a good man." Ibid., III:4, 1277b21–24.

82. For a discussion of this point see Nicholas D. Smith, "Plato and Aristotle on the Nature of Women," *Journal of the History of Ideas* 21, no. 4 (1983).

83. Aristotle, *Politics*, I:12, 1259b9.

84. Ibid., I:12, 1259b7–8.

85. Thucydides, *History of the Peloponnesian War*, II:37.

86. Aristotle, *Politics*, VI:4, 1319b25–32.

87. Ibid., II:9, 1269b35–37.

CHAPTER 6

1. As has been well documented, many of the prisoners in Guantánamo posed no threat to American citizens. New York Times and National Public Radio, "The Guantanamo Docket" (2015).

2. The massive industrial complex built in conjunction with and by prisoners in the death camp, produced a significant amount of methanol but never the "buna," or synthetic rubber from which the complex took its name. Wollheim Memorial, "Buna for the Wartime Economy," http://www.wollheim-memorial.de/en/buna_in_der_kriegswirtschaft_en and "What Was I.G. Auschwitz Meant to Produce?" http://www.wollheim-memorial.de/en/was_sollte_fabrik_produzieren.

3. *Oxford English Dictionary* (Oxford: Oxford University Press, 2012).

4. For a thoughtful review of some of these issues, see Taras Kuzio, "The Myth of the Civic State: A Critical Survey of Hans Kohn's Framework for Understanding Nationalism," *Ethnic and Racial Studies* 25, no. 1 (2002).

5. Joan Cocks, *On Sovereignty and Other Political Delusions* (New York: Bloomsbury Publishing, 2014), 31–35.

6. Ibid., 41.

7. For a useful application of this critique grounded in feminist theory and attentive to the post-9/11 use of the word "freedom" in connection with sovereignty, see Elisabeth Anker, "Feminist Theory and the Failures of Post-9/11 Freedom," *Politics & Gender* 8, no. 2 (2012).

8. Kurt A. Raaflaub, *The Discovery of Freedom in Ancient Greece*, 1st English ed. (Chicago: University of Chicago Press, 2004), 193.

9. Orlando Patterson, *Freedom: Vol. 1: Freedom in the Making of Western Culture* (New York: Basic Books, 1991), 32.

10. Jean-Jacques Rousseau, "The Social Contract," in *Basic Political Writings* (Indianapolis: Hackett Pub. Co., 1987), 150, 172.

11. Ibid., 205–206.

12. However, Cocks argues that it is possible for the general will to be expressed in a non-sovereign fashion, offering the examples of the environmental movement and the Arab Spring. Joan Cocks, *On Sovereignty and Other Political Delusions*, 37.

13. Rousseau, "The Social Contract," 170–173.

14. However, for an attempt to recover overlooked critiques of sovereignty, see Jeanne Morefield, "Urgent History: The Sovereignty Debates and Political Theory's Lost Voices," *Political Theory*, forthcoming.

15. Liah Greenfeld, *Nationalism: Five Roads to Modernity* (Cambridge, MA: Harvard University Press, 1992), 30–35.

16. Brendan O'Leary, "On the Nature of Nationalism: An Appraisal of Ernest Gellner's Writings on Nationalism," *British Journal of Political Science* 27, no. 2 (1997): 218.

17. Michael Billig, *Banal Nationalism* (London; Thousand Oaks, CA: Sage, 1995).

18. Ernest Gellner, *Nations and Nationalism*, 2nd ed., New Perspectives on the Past (Malden, MA: Blackwell Pub., 2006), 4.

19. Ibid., 33.

20. Benedict R. Anderson, *Imagined Communities: Reflections on the Origin and Spread of Nationalism*, Rev. and extended ed. (London; New York: Verso, 1991), 7.

21. Rudolf Rocker, Michael E. Coughlin, and Paul Avrich Collection (Library of Congress), *Nationalism and Culture* (St. Paul: M. E. Coughlin, 1978).

22. Speaking of his decision to overthrow the Spanish Bourbons, one historian writes: "Napoleon had been motivated neither by an altruistic desire to spread the benefits of freedom and enlightenment, nor by a gigantic strategic combination, nor by an overwhelming clan loyalty that made the creation of family courts centerpiece of French foreign policy." Instead, it was some combination of all of these factors, political opportunity, and personal ambition. Charles J. Esdaile, *Napoleon's Wars an International History, 1803–1815* (London; New York: Allen Lane, 2007), 343–344.

23. On feminism and nationalism, see *Globalizing Feminisms, 1789–1945: Rewriting Histories*, ed. Karen M. Offen (London; New York: Routledge, 2010), Part III and *Between Woman and Nation: Nationalisms, Transnational Feminisms, and the State*, ed. Caren Kaplan, Norma Alarcón, and Minoo Moallem (Durham, NC: Duke University Press, 1999).

24. David Avrom Bell, *The First Total War: Napoleon's Europe and the Birth of Warfare as We Know It* (Boston: Houghton Mifflin Co., 2007), 113.

25. Edmund Burke, *Reflections on the Revolution in France*, ed. J. C. D. Clark (Stanford, CA: Stanford University Press, 2001); Karl Marx, "Manifesto of the Communist Party," in *The Marx-Engels Reader*, ed. Robert C. Tucker (New York: Norton, 1978a), 469–500.

26. Joan Cocks, *On Sovereignty and Other Political Delusions*, 23.

27. Jeanne Morefield, *Covenants Without Swords: Idealist Liberalism and the Spirit of Empire* (Princeton, NJ: Princeton University Press, 2005); Karuna Mantena, *Alibis of Empire: Henry Maine and the Ends of Liberal Imperialism* (Princeton, NJ: Princeton University Press, 2010); Jennifer Pitts, *A Turn to Empire: The Rise of Imperial Liberalism in Britain and France* (Princeton, NJ: Princeton Unversity Press, 2005).

28. John Stuart Mill and Geraint Williams. "Considerations on Representative Government," in *Utilitarianism; on Liberty; Considerations on Representative Government; Remarks on Bentham's Philosophy.* New ed. (London; Rutland, VT: Dent; Tuttle, 1993), 213–214.

29. On the particularly fraught use of the term "self-determination" in the postwar era for African and Asian countries, see Rupert Emerson, *From Empire to Nation: The Rise to Self-Assertion of Asian and African Peoples* (Cambridge, MA: Harvard University Press, 1960), chapter 16.

30. With respect to the expanded surveillance powers of the United States government, some have remarked: "Free choice and diversity—these are the contemporary shibboleths of the liberal discursive construction of 'freedom,' the lodestar of American nationalism, even as it facilitates the consolidation of the power of the state." Minoo Moallem and Iain A. Boal, "Multicultural Nationalism and the Poetics of Inauguration," in *Between Woman and Nation: Nationalisms, Transnational Feminisms, and the State*, ed. Caren Kaplan, Norma Alarcón, and Minoo Moallem (Durham, NC: Duke University Press, 1999), 254.

31. Quoted in Léon Poliakov, *The History of Anti-Semitism*, 4 vols., vol. 3 (Philadelphia: University of Pennsylvania Press, 2003), 300.

32. Meanwhile, the very notion of being German is in the process of being constructed and will not yet fully come to fruition for many decades. Moreover, when German anti-Semitism is finally expressed in the horrors of the Final Solution, the understandable response of many Jews is to seek sovereign freedom of their own. As Cocks points out, this has led to the colonization of Palestinians, thereby perpetuating a cycle whereby the freedom of one group means dominating another. Joan Cocks, *On Sovereignty and Other Political Delusions*, chapter 3.

33. Elisa von Joeden-Forgey, "Race Power, Freedom, and the Democracy of Terror in German Racialist Thought," in *Hannah Arendt and the Uses of History: Imperialism, Nation, Race, and Genocide*, ed. Richard H. King and Dan Stone (New York: Berghahn Books, 2007), 28.

34. John Breuilly, *Nationalism and the State*, 2nd ed. (Chicago: University of Chicago Press, 1994), 371.

35. Adolf Hitler et al., *Mein Kampf, Complete and Unabridged, Fully Annotated* (New York: Reynal & Hitchcock, 1941), 889, italics his.

36. "It often happens that democrats are in the minority. It also happens that they decide on the basis of a supposedly democratic principle in favor of women's suffrage and then have the experience that the majority of women do not vote democratically. Then the familiar program of 'people's education' unfolds: The people can be brought to recognize and express their own will correctly through the right education. This means nothing else but that the educator identifies his will at least provisionally with that of the people, not to mention that the content of the education that the pupil will receive is also decided by the educator. The consequence of this educational theory is a dictatorship that suspends democracy in the name of a true democracy that is still to be created. Theoretically, this does not destroy democracy, but it is important to pay attention to it because it shows that dictatorship is not antithetical to democracy. Even during a transitional period dominated by the dictator, a democratic identity can still exist and the will of the people can still be the exclusive criterion." Carl Schmitt, *The Crisis of Parliamentary Democracy*, Studies in Contemporary German Social Thought (Cambridge, MA: MIT Press, 1985), 28.

37. Carl Schmitt, *The Concept of the Political*, Expanded ed. (Chicago: University of Chicago Press, 2007).

38. Giuseppe Mazzini, Stefano Recchia, and Nadia Urbinati, *A Cosmopolitanism of Nations: Giuseppe Mazzini's Writings on Democracy, Nation Building, and International Relations* (Princeton, NJ: Princeton University Press, 2009).

39. Ernst Renan, "What Is a Nation?" http://ucparis.fr/files/9313/6549/9943/What_is_a_Nation.pdf.

40. Joan Cocks, *On Sovereignty and Other Political Delusions*, 16.

41. Timothy Lang, "Lord Acton and 'the Insanity of Nationality'," *Journal of the History of Ideas* 63, no. 1 (2002): 132.

42. In chapter 1, I discussed the split between communists/socialists who endorsed the use of the state and bureaucratic mechanisms to forward the cause of freedom from those who identified the state—and nationalism in combination with the state in particular—as inseparable from capitalism and the domination of the bourgeoisie. Indeed, both the proper role of violence and the nature of freedom are prominent points of discussion and division among socialists and communists of the last three centuries. It would take another volume to fully explore the wide range of views on these topics. Instead, I will give a very brief and basic lineage that focuses on the issue of violence as relates to freedom with the aim of drawing out themes that will have relevance for Part IV of the book. For more extensive explorations of the history of socialism, see Albert S. Lindemann, *A History of European Socialism* (New Haven: Yale University Press, 1983); Warren Lerner, *A History of Socialism and Communism in Modern Times: Theorists, Activists, and Humanists*, 2nd ed. (Englewood Cliffs, NJ: Prentice Hall, 1993); Albert Fried and Ronald Sanders, *Socialist Thought: A Documentary History*, Rev. ed. (New York: Columbia University Press, 1992). One such work with particular relevance for this study is an attempt to recover a particular understanding of freedom for Marxism: Raya Dunayevskaya, *Marxism & Freedom: From 1776 until Today* (Amherst, NY: Humanity Books, 2000).

43. Ernest Belfort Bax, "The Last Episode of the French Revolution Being a History of Gracchus Babeuf and the Conspiracy of the Equals," http://www.marxists.org/archive/bax/1911/babeuf/index.htm.

44. Philippe Buonarroti, "Manifesto of the Equals," http://www.marxists.org/history/france/revolution/conspiracy-equals/1796/manifesto.htm.

45. Robert Owen and Gregory Claeys, *A New View of Society and Other Writings*, Penguin Classics (London; New York: Penguin Books, 1991), 91.

46. Ibid., 244.

47. Edward Royle, *Robert Owen and the Commencement of the Millennium: A Study of the Harmony Community* (Manchester: Manchester University Press, 1998), 32–33.

48. Charles Fourier, *The Theory of the Four Movements*, ed. Ian Patterson and Gareth Stedman Jones. Cambridge Texts in the History of Political Thought (Cambridge, UK; New York: Cambridge University Press, 1996), 92.

49. Pierre-Joseph Proudhon, "General Idea of the Revolution in the 19th Century," http://fair-use.org/p-j-proudhon/general-idea-of-the-revolution/absorption-of-government-by-the-economic-organism#s6p1.

50. Christopher Caudwell, "Liberty: A Study in Bourgeois Illusion," http://www.marxists.org/archive/caudwell/1938/studies/ch08.htm.

51. Ibid.

52. Ibid.

53. Edward Hallett Carr, *Nationalism and After* (New York: The Macmillan Company, 1945), 24.

54. Among the detractors, see Friedrich A. von Hayek, *The Constitution of Liberty* (Chicago: University of Chicago Press, 1960), 269, 271.

55. See for instance Peter Winn, *Weavers of Revolution: The Yarur Workers and Chile's Road to Socialism* (New York: Oxford University Press, 1986); Deborah Levenson-Estrada, *Trade Unionists against Terror: Guatemala City, 1954–1985* (Chapel Hill: University of North Carolina Press, 1994).

56. See for instance Melvyn Dubofsky and Joseph Anthony McCartin, *We Shall Be All: A History of the Industrial Workers of the World*, Abridged ed., The Working Class in American History (Urbana: University of Illinois Press, 2000), 92–93; Philip Dray, *There Is Power in a Union: The Epic Story of Labor in America*, 1st ed. (New York: Doubleday, 2010), 117–118.

57. Walter Benjamin, "Critique of Violence," in *Reflections: Essays, Aphorisms, Autobiographical Writings* (New York: Harcourt Brace Jovanovich, 1978), 299–300.

58. Georges Sorel and Jeremy Jennings, *Reflections on Violence*, Cambridge Texts in the History of Political Thought (Cambridge, UK; New York: Cambridge University Press, 1999), 43.

59. Ibid., 62.

60. Ibid., 62.

61. Ibid., 182.

62. Ibid., 231.

63. Ibid., 74.

64. Ibid., 165–166.

65. "In the wars of Liberty each soldier considered himself as an *individual* having something of importance to do in the battle, instead of looking upon himself as simply one part of the military mechanism entrusted to the supreme direction of a leader. In the literature of those times one is struck by the frequency with which the *free men* of the republican armies are contrasted with the *automatons* of the royal armies; this was no mere figure of rhetoric employed by the French writers; I have convinced myself, as a result of a thorough personal study of one of the wars of this period, that these terms corresponded perfectly to the actual sentiments of the soldier." Ibid., 240.

66. Ibid., 162–165.

67. Ibid., 286.

68. Rosa Luxemburg, *The Rosa Luxemburg Reader*, ed. Peter Hudis and Kevin Anderson (New York: Monthly Review Press, 2004), 305.

69. Ibid., 351.

70. Luxemburg, "The Nation-State and the Proletariat," in *The National Question*, ed. Horace B. Davies (New York: Monthly Review Press, 1909).

71. Ibid.

72. Luxemburg, *The Rosa Luxemburg Reader*, 180.

73. Ibid., 183.

74. Ibid., 186.

75. Ibid., 191.

76. Rosa Luxemburg references the parallel with the advocates of the First World War in earnest, writing that "In place of the employers and their wage slaves, free working comrades!

Labor as nobody's torture, because everybody's duty! A human and honorable life for all who do their social duty. Hunger no longer the curse of labor, but the scourge of idleness! Only in such a society are national hatred and servitude uprooted. Only when such a society has become reality will the earth no more be stained by murder. Only then can it be said: This war was the last." Ibid., 350.

77. Benjamin, "Critique of Violence," 288–289.

78. Ibid., 277.

79. Ibid., 285.

80. Ibid., 292.

81. "It is not a means but a manifestation. Moreover, this violence has thoroughly objective manifestations in which it can be subjected to criticism. These are to be found, most significantly, above all in myth." Ibid., 294.

82. Ibid., 300.

83. Ibid., 298.

84. Ibid., 299.

85. Ibid., 284–285.

86. Hannah Arendt, *The Human Condition*, 2nd ed. (Chicago: University of Chicago Press, 1998), 216.

87. Ibid., 216.

88. Ibid., 217.

89. Ibid., 218–219.

90. Ibid., 219.

91. Hannah Arendt, "What Is Freedom?" in *Between Past and Future: Eight Exercises in Political Thought* (New York: Penguin Books, 1977).

CHAPTER 7

1. Emmanuel Levinas, *Totality and Infinity: An Essay on Exteriority* (Pittsburgh, PA: Duquesne University Press, 2001), 84.

2. For overview of these issues and a particularly astute attempt to sort through them, see Carisa Renae Showden, *Choices Women Make: Agency in Domestic Violence, Assisted Reproduction, and Sex Work* (Minneapolis: University of Minnesota Press, 2011).

3. Václav Havel, "The Power of the Powerless: Citizens against the State in Central-Eastern Europe," ed. John Keane (Armonk, NY: M. E. Sharpe, 1985); Delia Popescu, *Political Action in Václav Havel's Thought: The Responsibility of Resistance* (Lanham, MD: Lexington Books, 2012).

4. Immanuel Kant and Mary J. Gregor, *The Metaphysics of Morals*, Cambridge Texts in the History of Philosophy (Cambridge, UK; New York: Cambridge University Press, 1996), 106–107.

5. Friedrich Wilhelm Nietzsche and Horace Barnett Samuel, *The Genealogy of Morals*, The Modern Library of the World's Best Books (New York: Boni and Liveright, 1918), 66–69.

6. Friedrich Wilhelm Nietzsche, *Beyond Good and Evil* (Chicago: H. Regnery Co., 1949), 132.

7. Augustine also, however, had an appreciation for the public freedom of the Romans and developed another strain of thought that Arendt picks up in her discussion of the "I-can."

8. Moreover, Arendt laments that when freedom reappears in the modern world it means little more than personal, physical security. She is unclear in her narrative as to how freedom

came to mean this, but I have tried to tell that story in chapter 4. She is probably blind to its origins, in part, because just war theory (as articulated by Augustine in particular) comprises the buried seed that grows into that branch of the Western conception of freedom. In effect, there are no less than three discernible concepts related to freedom coming out of Augustine's thought, albeit by way of many stages of development in other thinkers (the domineering free will, the I-can of public action, and the political justification of violence from necessity).

9. For one of the more important attempts to show why the breach between the social and the political, for instance, needs to be at least partially repaired see Seyla Benhabib, "Hannah Arendt and the Redemptive Power of Narrative," *Social Research* 57, no. 1 (1990): 193–195.

10. For the relevant passages in Augustine, see Augustine, *Concerning the City of God against the Pagans*, trans. Henry Scowcroft Bettenson (Harmondsworth: Penguin Books, 1972), 5:10, 194–195; see also 13:24, 587–589.

11. Hannah Arendt, *The Life of the Mind*, one-volume ed. (San Diego: Harcourt Brace Jovanovich, 1981), II: 141.

12. Arendt, "What Is Freedom?" in *Between Past and Future: Eight Exercises in Political Thought* (New York: Penguin Books, 1977), 163.

13. Ibid., 162.

14. Ibid., 164.

15. Arendt, *The Life of the Mind*, II: 6, 101, 140, 155.

16. Perhaps she intended to bring forth more boldly the connections between our inner and outer experiences at the end of the three volumes of *The Life of the Mind*. Otherwise, the end of the volume on willing would seem to be the natural place to do it, since judgment is primarily oriented toward the past and its role in taking political action is therefore somewhat limited. On the other hand, even at the end of the volume on willing, she seems to emphasize that "preparing the ground for action" and founding a *novus ordo seclorum* involves looking to the accomplishments of the past. So a final volume may have attempted to integrate the various activities of life of the mind and the *vita activa*.

17. Kalyvas tries to solve the problem by suggesting Arendt discovered the "dual quality" of the will; that it is at once the capacity to make a choice but also a capacity to begin something new. Kalyvas suggests that there might be a number of benefits to connecting her description of the free will to political freedom but does not tell us how to do so. See Andreas Kalyvas, "From the Act to the Decision: Hannah Arendt and the Question of Decisionism," *Political Theory* 32, no. 3 (2004): 333–341. See also B. Honig, "Arendt, Identity and Difference," *Political Theory* 16, no. 1 (1988): 91n19; Jean Yarbrough and Peter Stern, "Vita Activa and Vita Contemplativa: Political Thought in *The Life of the Mind*," *Review of Politics* (1981): 323–354.

18. Arendt, *The Life of the Mind*, II:141.

19. "The reason for this is simple: the will, as Nietzsche was later to discover, is incapable of 'willing backwards' . . . The intellect will fabricate a story to make the data fall into place. Without an assumption of necessity, the story would lack all coherence." Ibid., II:140.

20. Ibid., II:142.

21. Arendt, "What Is Freedom?" 167–168. Citing Augustine, *Concerning the City of God against the Pagans*, XII:20.

22. Arendt, "What Is Freedom?" 169. The extent to which Augustine's theory of the free will can be made consistent with a publicly minded moral virtue is controversial. Some would point

to the fact that Augustine endorses the view that slaves can be free, while others argue that the expression of freedom in public life can come through the grace of God and be made manifest in acts of love. Margaret Mary, "Slavery in the Writings of St. Augustine," *The Classical Journal* 49, no. 8 (1954): 363–369; James Wetzel, *Augustine and the Limits of Virtue* (New York: Cambridge University Press, 1992), 221.

23. Kant describes it as the "'power of spontaneously beginning a series of successive things or states.'" Arendt, *The Life of the Mind*, II:6, 20, 29, 30, 110.

24. Ibid., II:110.

25. Arendt, *The Human Condition*, 2nd ed. (Chicago: University of Chicago Press, 1998), 178. "Just as thinking prepares the self for the role of the spectator, willing fashions it into an 'enduring I' that directs all particular acts of volition. It creates the self's *character* and therefore was sometimes understood as the *principium individuationis,* the source of the person's specific identity." Arendt, *The Life of the Mind*, II:195.

26. Arendt, *The Life of the Mind*, II:132.

27. Arendt, *The Human Condition*, 196.

28. The Will is the "unifying force binding man's sensory apparatus to the outside world and then joining together man's different mental faculties . . . directing the senses' attention, presiding over the images impressed on memory, and providing the intellect with material for understanding, the Will prepares the ground on which action can take place." Arendt, *The Life of the Mind*, II:101. This does not make the will omnipotent, but it does give it "primacy." This means that the will has the freedom to reject not only desires but the objects presented to it by the intellect and reason as well. The will inheres in the internal experience of accepting or rejecting what is—it is the "freedom of the will mentally to *take a position.*" See ibid., II:136.

29. "I-will and I-can are not the same—*non hoc est velle, quod posse.*" Arendt, "What Is Freedom?" 159.

30. Harry Frankfurt, "Freedom of the Will and the Concept of the Person," *Journal of Philosophy* 58, no. 1 (1971): 14.

31. Arendt, *The Life of the Mind*, II:142.

32. Ibid., II: 210.

33. Arendt, *The Human Condition*, 233.

34. Primo Levi, *Survival in Auschwitz: The Nazi Assault on Humanity*, trans. Stuart Woolf, 1st Touchstone ed. (New York: Simon & Schuster, 1996), 149.

35. Arendt, *The Life of the Mind*, II:95.

36. According to Arendt, Scotus thought that the debate between freedom and necessity amounted to "an intramural conflict between the willing and thinking ego, a conflict in which the will directs the intellect and makes man ask the question: Why? The reason for this is simple: the will, as Nietzsche was later to discover, is incapable of 'willing backwards'; hence, let the intellect try to find out what went wrong. The question Why?—what is the *cause?*—is suggested by the will because the will experiences itself as a causative agent." Ibid., II:140.

37. On homelessness of thought see ibid., I:199. Arendt discusses how the nowhere non-reality of thought gets confused with reality, so much so that we are often led to wonder if perhaps there is some connection between the two. See ibid., I:45–53.

38. Elizabeth Markovits, *The Politics of Sincerity: Plato, Frank Speech, and Democratic Judgment* (State College, PA: Penn State University Press, 2009); Susan Sara Monoson,

Plato's Democratic Entanglements: Athenian Politics and the Practice of Philosophy (Princeton, NJ: Princeton University Press, 2000).

39. Arendt, *The Life of the Mind*, I:188–189.

40. Some have gone so far as to argue that thinking in extreme circumstances becomes a form of action, because those who are thinking suddenly stand out from the crowd. See Amy L. Shuster, "Hannah Arendt Without Politics," *Spectra: The Aspect Journal* 3, no. 2 (2014), https://spectrajournal.org/index.php/SPECTRA/article/view/139/150.

41. Elizabeth K. Minnich, "To Judge in Freedom: Hannah Arendt on the Relation of Thinking and Morality," in *Hannah Arendt: Thinking, Judging, Freedom*, ed. Gisela T. Kaplan and Clive S. Kessler (Sydney; Boston: Allen & Unwin, 1989), 141.

42. Arendt, *The Life of the Mind*, I:189.

43. Arendt, *The Human Condition*, 324.

44. Arendt, *The Life of the Mind*, I:197.

45. Peirce argues that we move from psychologically uncomfortable states of doubt toward a "fixation" of belief. The upshot of belief is that we have a guide for action, which will be more or less apt depending on which of various more or less desirable means were used to arrive at those beliefs. Charles S. Peirce, "The Fixation of Belief," in *Selected Writings (Values in a Universe of Chance)*, ed. Phillip P. Wiener (New York: Dover Publications, 1966). Arendt says that Scotus believed the will "knows very well how to heal itself of the consequences of the priceless yet highly questionable gift of human freedom . . . Man's normal way of escaping from his freedom is simply to *act* on the propositions of the will." Arendt, *The Life of the Mind*, II:141. It seems clear enough to me that acting on a "proposition" might have something to do with thinking through what the will proposes.

46. Arendt's strong emphasis on the paralyzing and destructive aspects of Socratic thinking seems unjustified even if we bracket all of his questioning of Athenians and consider only the limited role he played in politics (for instance his refusal to fetch Leon of Salamis for the death penalty). For Arendt on Socrates as midwife, see Arendt, *The Life of the Mind*, I:173.

47. Arendt writes "what cannot fail to look like paralysis from the outside—from the standpoint of ordinary human affairs—is *felt* as the highest state of being active and alive. There exist, despite the scarcity of documentary evidence about the thinking experience a number of utterances of thinkers throughout the centuries to bear this out." Ibid., I:173.

48. "You are mistaken, my friend, if you think that a man who is worth anything ought to spend his time weighing up the prospects of life and death. He has only one thing to consider in performing any action; that is, whether he is acting justly or unjustly, like a good man or a bad one." Plato, "Apology," in *The Last Days of Socrates* (New York: Penguin Books, 1993), 28b.

49. There are important and obvious differences between philosophic and political practice. Following Socrates himself, Arendt insists that his activities are not properly understood as political. However, even while Arendt somehow manages to both acknowledge and somehow de-emphasize the fact, we should remember that Socrates' thinking led him—compelled him even—into real conversations with others.

50. Frederick Douglass, *My Bondage and My Freedom* (New York: Dover Publications, 1969); see chapters 1, 8, and especially 11.

51. Douglass, "The Meaning of July Fourth for the Negro," in *The Life and Writings of Frederick Douglass*, ed. Philip Sheldon Foner (New York: International Publishers, 1950), 184.

52. Arendt, *The Life of the Mind*, I:197.

53. Ibid., I:175.

54. Ibid., II:136.

55. Ibid., II:130.

56. Linda M. G. Zerilli, "'We Feel Our Freedom': Imagination and Judgment in the Thought of Hannah Arendt," *Political Theory* 33, no. 2 (2005): 158–188.

57. Kurt A. Raaflaub, *The Discovery of Freedom in Ancient Greece*, 1st English ed. (Chicago: University of Chicago Press, 2004), 256.

58. Josiah Ober, "'I Besieged That Man": Democracy's Revolutionary Start," in *Origins of Democracy in Ancient Greece*, ed. Kurt A. Raaflaub, Josiah Ober, and Robert W. Wallace (Berkeley: University of California Press, 2007), 89.

59. Ibid., 84.

60. Ibid., 89.

61. Ober, *Mass and Elite in Democratic Athens: Rhetoric, Ideology, and the Power of the People* (Princeton, NJ: Princeton University Press, 1989), 68.

62. Ian Mabbett, "Buddhism and Freedom," in *Asian Freedoms: The Idea of Freedom in East and Southeast Asia*, ed. David Kelly and Anthony Reid (New York: Cambridge University Press, 1998), 23. This view, however, must be tempered by the Buddhist doctrine of no self.

63. Buddhists, in a way remarkably similar to Epictetus, have often understood the achievement of freedom as requiring a retreat into an internal world of self-control and discipline. But just as the notion of an internal free will came to have important political consequences in the West, the Buddha's teachings have become part and parcel of conceptions of political freedom in places such as Tibet and Burma.

64. Josef Silverstein, "The Idea of Freedom in Burma and the Political Thought of Aung San Suu Kyi," in *Asian Freedoms: The Idea of Freedom in East and Southeast Asia*, ed. David Kelly and Anthony Reid (New York: Cambridge University Press, 1998), 189.

65. Arendt, *The Human Condition*, 205.

66. Mahatma Gandhi, in *Hind Swaraj and Other Writings*, ed. Anthony Parel (New York: Cambridge University Press, 1997), 73.

67. Gandhi, in *Mahatma Gandhi: Selected Political Writings*, ed. Dennis Dalton (Indianapolis: Hackett Pub. Co., 1996), 146.

68. Gandhi, *For Pacifists* (Ahmedabad: Navajivan Pub. House, 2000 [1949]), 24.

69. She seems to suggest that in certain instances physical violence can be more like speech. For an extensive discussion of this issue, see Dustin Ells Howes, *Toward a Credible Pacifism: Violence and the Possibilities of Politics* (Albany: State University of New York Press, 2009), 113–114.

70. Albert Camus, *The Rebel: An Essay on Man in Revolt*, 1st Vintage International ed. (New York: Vintage Books, 1991), 7–8.

71. Hannah Arendt, *Responsibility and Judgment* (New York: Schocken Books, 2003), 44–45.

72. Mahatma Gandhi, *The Collected Works of Mahatma Gandhi* (New Delhi: Publications Division Government of India, 1999), Vol. 10, 380.

73. Charles de Secondat Montesquieu, *The Spirit of Laws*, Great Books in Philosophy Series (Amherst, NY: Prometheus Books, 2002), I:150.

74. They also require further explanation, given Arendt's skepticism (following Locke) about the role of conscience in politics.

CHAPTER 8

1. Étienne De La Boétie, *The Politics of Obedience: Discourse on Voluntary Servitude* (Whitefish, MT: Kessinger Legacy Reprints, 2010), 13.

2. Herodotus, "The Histories" (Cambridge, MA: Harvard University Press, 1920), 7.139.5.

3. Ibid., 8.143.

4. Ibid., 7.2.3.

5. Indeed, La Boétie went on to serve the French government as an admired judge but died at the age of 33, leaving his library and the fate of his essay in the hands of his friend Montaigne. On the contradictions between the public lives and private thoughts of the two men, see Nannerl O. Keohane, "The Radical Humanism of Étienne De La Boétie," *Journal of the History of Ideas* 1, no. 1 (1977): 119–120.

6. La Boétie, *The Politics of Obedience: Discourse on Voluntary Servitude*, 3.

7. Ibid., 5.

8. Ibid., 6–7.

9. "Tyrants would distribute largess, a bushel of wheat, a gallon of wine, and a sesterce: and then everybody would shamelessly cry, 'Long live the King!' The fools did not realize that they were merely recovering a portion of their own property, and that their ruler could not have given them what they were receiving without having first taken it from them. A man might one day be presented with a sesterce and gorge himself at the public feast, lauding Tiberius and Nero for handsome liberality, who on the morrow, would be forced to abandon his property to their avarice, his children to their lust, his very blood to the cruelty of these magnificent emperors, without offering any more resistance than a stone or a tree stump." Ibid., 18.

10. Ibid., 5.

11. Ibid., 7.

12. "[Nature] has bestowed upon us all the great gift of voice and speech for fraternal relationship, thus achieving by the common and mutual statement of our thoughts a communion of our wills; and since she has tried in every way to narrow and tighten the bond of our union and kinship; since she has revealed in every possible manner her intention, not so much to associate us as to make us one organic whole, there can be no further doubt that we are all naturally free, inasmuch as we are all comrades. Accordingly it should not enter the mind of anyone that nature has placed some of us in slavery, since she has actually created us all in one likeness." Ibid., 8–9.

13. Ibid., 22. For an updated and historically grounded version of this argument as to the role of punishment in symbolically establishing sovereignty and political order, see Keally D. McBride, *Punishment and Political Order*, Law, Meaning, and Violence (Ann Arbor: University of Michigan Press, 2007).

14. La Boétie, *The Politics of Obedience: Discourse on Voluntary Servitude*, 22.

15. On the history of the essay, see La Boétie, "Discourse on Voluntary Servitude, or the Anti-Dictator," ed Harry Kurz (New York: Columbia University Press, 1942), http://www.constitution.org/la_boetie/serv_vol.htm#26.

16. In 2013, his Albert Einstein Institution provided resources for over 1,700 individuals and groups. Albert Einstein Institution, "Annual Report," http://www.aeinstein.org/wp-content/uploads/2014/04/AR-for-print_Part1.pdf. In addition, some of his former students founded the

International Center on Nonviolent Conflict, which serves as an educational resource and clear-inghouse for information on nonviolence.

17. Gene Sharp, *The Politics of Nonviolent Action* (Boston: P. Sargent Publisher, 1973), 37.

18. Gene Sharp and Bruce Jenkins, *Civilian-Based Defense: A Post-military Weapons System* (Princeton, NJ: Princeton University Press, 1990), 10–11.

19. Ibid., 13–14.

20. Ibid., 15.

21. Ibid., 17.

22. Ibid., 17.

23. Ibid., 18.

24. Mary Cawte, "Research Proposals for Nonviolent Defense: Strategy and Tactics. A Review Article of Research on Civilian-Based Defense by Giliam De Valk." *Pacifica Review: Peace, Security & Global Change* 6, no. 1 (1994): 97.

25. Some of those sources and additional research can be found in Peter Ackerman and Jack DuVall, *A Force More Powerful: A Century of Nonviolent Conflict*, 1st ed. (New York: St. Martin's Press, 2000), chapter 5.

26. David Rodin, *War and Self-Defense* (Oxford; New York: Clarendon Press; Oxford University Press, 2002).

27. Jonathan Schell, "The Unconquerable World," in *The Jonathan Schell Reader: On the United States at War, the Long Crisis of the American Republic, and the Fate of the Earth* (New York: Nation Books, 2004), 387–432.

28. Sharp and Jenkins, *Civilian-Based Defense: A Post-military Weapons System*, 33.

29. Gene Sharp, *Social Power and Political Freedom*, Extending Horizons Books (Boston, MA: P. Sargent Publishers, 1980), 42–57.

30. Ibid., 57–60.

31. Ibid., 60–63.

32. Ibid., 45.

33. Ibid., 58.

34. Darius M. Rejali, *Torture and Democracy* (Princeton, NJ: Princeton University Press, 2007); Norval Morris and David J. Rothman, *The Oxford History of the Prison: The Practice of Punishment in Western Society* (New York: Oxford University Press, 1995); Michel Foucault, *Discipline and Punish: The Birth of the Prison* (Pittsburgh, PA: Vintage Books, 1995).

35. Nils Christie, *A Suitable Amount of Crime* (London; New York: Routledge, 2004); Hanns von Hofer, "Punishment and Crime in Scandinavia, 1750–2008," *Crime & Justice* 40 (2011).

36. John R. Sutton, "Imprisonment and Opportunity Structures: A Bayesian Hierarchical Analysis," *European Sociological Review* 28, no. 1 (2012); Matthew DeMichele and Thomas Janoski, "A Regime Theory Approach to Cross-National Incarceration Rate Variation: Three Worlds of Western Punishment, 1960–2002," *Conference Papers—American Sociological Association* (2010).

37. Warren Young and Mark Brown, "Cross-National Comparisons of Imprisonment." *Crime and Justice* 17 (1993): 1–49.

38. The United States imprisons its citizens at a rate four times greater than the world average. Christopher Hartney, "US Rates of Incarceration: A Global Perspective," ed. National Council on Crime and Delinquency (Washington, DC, 2006).

39. Michelle Alexander, *The New Jim Crow: Mass Incarceration in the Age of Colorblindness* (New York; Jackson, TN: New Press; Distributed by Perseus Distribution, 2010); Alec C. Ewald and Brandon Rottinghaus, *Criminal Disenfranchisement in an International Perspective* (Cambridge, UK; New York: Cambridge University Press, 2009); Maya Schenwar, *Locked Down, Locked Out: Why Prison Doesn't Work and How We Can Do Better* (San Francisco: Berrett-Koehler Publishers, 2014); David Cloud, "On Life Support: Public Health in the Age of Mass Incarceration," (Vera Institute of Justice, 2014).

40. On the relationship between crime rates and incarceration rates, see Marc Mauer, "Comparative International Rates of Incarceration: An Examination of Causes and Trends Presented to the U.S. Commission on Civil Rights," *The Sentencing Project* (2003): 12–13; Alfred Blumstein and Allen J. Beck, "Population Growth in U.S. Prisons, 1980–1996," *Crime and Justice* 26 (1999).

41. Yvon Dandurand and Curt T. Griffiths, "Handbook on Restorative Justice Programmes," in *Criminal Justice Handbook Series* (Vienna; New York: United Nations Office on Drugs and Crime, 2006), 23–24. See also National Institute of Justice, "Fundamental Concepts of Restorative Justice," http://www.nij.gov/topics/courts/restorative-justice/pages/fundamental-concepts.aspx.

42. Gandhi, *Hind Swaraj and Other Writings*, ed. Anthony Parel, Centenary ed., Cambridge Texts in Modern Politics (Cambridge, UK; New York: Cambridge University Press, 2009), 61.

43. Ibid., 61.

44. Dandurand and Griffiths, "Handbook on Restorative Justice Programmes," 23–24.

45. Ibid., 22.

46. Isaiah Berlin, Henry Hardy, and Ian Harris, *Liberty: Incorporating Four Essays on Liberty* (Oxford: Oxford University Press, 2002), 190.

47. "It is important to distinguish between liberty and the conditions of its exercise. If a man is too poor or too ignorant or too feeble to make use of his legal rights, the liberty that these rights confer upon him is nothing to him, but it is not thereby annihilated. The obligation to promote education, health, justice, to raise standards of living to provide opportunity for the growth of the arts and sciences, to prevent reactionary political or social or legal policies or arbitrary inequalities is not made less stringent because it is not necessarily directed to the promotion of liberty itself, but to conditions in which alone its possession is of value, or to values which may be independent of it." Ibid., 45.

48. Ibid., 207.

49. This idea dates back to the very earliest explorations of the idea of the free will in the Western tradition. Writing of the relationship between the will and an all-powerful God, Augustine claims that because God is all-powerful "there are some things he cannot do"—such as die or be mistaken. He then writes: "The same applies when we say that it is 'necessary' that when we will, we will by free choice. That statement is indisputable; and it does not mean that we are subjecting our free will to a necessity which abolishes freedom." Augustine, *Concerning the City of God against the Pagans*, trans. Henry Scowcroft Bettenson (Harmondsworth: Penguin Books, 1972), 5:10, 194–195; see also 13:24, 587–589.

50. Hannah Arendt, "What Is Freedom?" in *Between Past and Future: Eight Exercises in Political Thought* (New York: Penguin Books, 1977), 162.

51. Ibid., 164–165.

52. Arendt is particularly concerned about this, noting that Rousseau held that in the ideal state "'citizens had no communications'" and arguing that a state "in which there is no communication between the citizens and where each man thinks only his own thoughts is by definition a tyranny." Ibid., 163, 164.

53. Ibid., 162.

54. For a more extensive discussion of the latter distinction see Dustin Ells Howes, *Toward a Credible Pacifism: Violence and the Possibilities of Politics* (Albany: State University of New York Press, 2009), chapter 5.

55. Berlin's vigorous critique of Rousseau's sovereignty also has much in common with Arendt's. Berlin, Hardy, and Harris, *Liberty: Incorporating Four Essays on Liberty*, 208–212.

56. Arendt, "What Is Freedom?" 166.

57. Kurt A. Raaflaub, *The Discovery of Freedom in Ancient Greece*, 1st English ed. (Chicago: University of Chicago Press, 2004), 184.

58. Ibid., 187.

59. Ibid., 189.

60. Ibid., 189. Raaflaub cites Jacqueline de Romilly in connection with the concept of *eleutherôtatê*.

61. Put another way, just as Aristotle writes that slaves prove they are not fit to be free by the simple fact they are slaves, Athenians proved to themselves and the world that they were free by getting together to dominate others.

62. Immanuel Kant and Mary J. Gregor, *The Metaphysics of Morals*, Cambridge Texts in the History of Philosophy (Cambridge, UK; New York: Cambridge University Press, 1996), IV: 227.

63. Ibid., IV: 225–226.

64. Immanuel Kant, *Religion within the Limits of Reason Alone* (New York: Harper, 1960), 32–34.

65. For an interesting attempt to describe a Kantian politics, see Andrews Reath, *Agency and Autonomy in Kant's Moral Theory* (Oxford; New York: Clarendon Press; Oxford University Press, 2006), chapter 6. For an attempt to argue that Kant's moral theory can be made more consistent with political violence then it might at first appear, see Thomas E. Hill, "A Kantian Perspective on Political Violence," *The Journal of Ethics* 1, no. 2 (1997).

66. Kant, *Religion within the Limits of Reason Alone*, 30. For a helpful reconstruction of his argument and an empirical test bearing out his conclusions, see Vesna Danilovic and Joe Clare, "The Kantian Liberal Peace (Revisited)," 2007.

67. Kant, *Religion within the Limits of Reason Alone*, 29.

68. For a summary of the conventional wisdom in an article that argues against it, see Brian Orend, "Kant's Just War Theory," *Journal of the History of Philosophy* 37, no. 2 (1999): 324–326. See also Orend, *War and International Justice: A Kantian Perspective*, UPCC Book Collections on Project MUSE (Baltimore, MD: Project MUSE, 2014).

69. For a Kantian argument against Kant's view, see Nelson T. Potter, "Kant and Capital Punishment Today," *Journal of Value Inquiry* 36, no. 2–3 (2002).

70. Ronald Terchek, *Gandhi: Struggling for Autonomy*, Twentieth-Century Political Thinkers (Lanham, MD: Rowman & Littlefield Publishers, 1998), 27.

71. On Gandhi's thought as particularly interested in integrating various aspects of life that are often divided conceptually and in practice, see Anthony Parel, *Gandhi's Philosophy and the Quest for Harmony* (Cambridge, UK: Cambridge University Press, 2006). On Gandhi's vision of freedom in relation to his Indian contemporaries, see Dennis Dalton,

Indian Idea of Freedom: Political Thought of Swami Vivekananda, Aurobindo Ghose, Mahatma Gandhi, and Rabindranath Tagore (Gurgaon, Haryana: Academic Press, 1982). On freedom as a particularly complex and multifaceted concept in Gandhi's thought, see Anthony Parel, ed. *Gandhi, Freedom, and Self-Rule*, Global Encounters (Lanham, MD: Lexington Books, 2000).

72. For a particularly good discussion of Gandhi's distinctive approach to means and ends, see Karuna Mantena, "Another Realism: The Politics of Gandhian Nonviolence," *American Political Science Review* 106, no. 2 (2012).

73. On Gandhi's connection to Kant, see Farah Godrej, "Nonviolence and Gandhi's Truth: A Method for Moral and Political Arbitration," *The Review of Politics* 68, no. 2 (2006): 298. On Kant's conception of conscience, see Roger J. Sullivan, *Immanuel Kant's Moral Theory* (Cambridge, UK; New York: Cambridge University Press, 1989), 60–61.

74. Godrej, "Nonviolence and Gandhi's Truth: A Method for Moral and Political Arbitration," 304.

75. Arendt, "What Is Freedom?" 159.

76. Thomas Weber, *On the Salt March: The Historiography of Gandhi's March to Dandi* (New Delhi: HarperCollins Publishers India, 1997). While in this case Gandhi's opponent was the British government his experience recommended the same approach in dealing with overreaching capitalists, describing an entirely nonviolent labor movement. "No matter how oppressive the capitalists may be, I am convinced that those who are connected with labour and guide the labour movement have themselves no idea of the resources that labour can command and which capital can never command. If labour would only understand and recognize that capital is perfectly helpless without labour, labour will immediately come to its own." Mahatma Gandhi, *Trusteeship*, ed. Ravindra Kelkar (Ahmedabad: Navajivan Mudranalaya, 1960), 16.

77. Arendt, "What Is Freedom?" 160. George Kateb writes that Arendt endorses a "discipline that the political actor, possessed of the requisite virtues and attitudes, must impose on himself." This involves becoming fit for public appearance by cultivating "the right spirit" or an approach to politics that values it for its own sake. This, however, is distinguished from Platonic rule, because for Arendt "proper self-rule is no model for interaction with others." Though there are aspects of Gandhi's dualism that suggest his brand of self-rule is Platonic, it is also consistent with the idea that we are in dialogue with ourselves. George Kateb, "Political Action: Its Nature and Advantages," in *The Cambridge Companion to Hannah Arendt*, ed. Dana Richard Villa (New York: Cambridge University Press, 2000), 137, 141, 146.

78. Gandhi, *Village Swaraj*, 1st ed. (Ahmedabad: Navajivan Pub. House, 1962), 11.

79. Some read a proto-environmentalism in this system: Farah Godrej, "Ascetics, Warriors, and a Gandhian Ecological Citizenship," *Political Theory* 40, no. 4 (2012).

80. Mahatma Gandhi, *Constructive Programme, Its Meaning and Place*, 2nd ed. (Ahmedabad: Navajivan Press, 1948), chapters 1, 2, 8.

81. Gandhi, *Village Swaraj*, 80.

82. For instance, he writes: "It has been said that Indian Swaraj will be the rule of the majority community, i.e. the Hindus. There could not be a greater mistake than that. If it were to be true, I for one would refuse to call it Swaraj and would fight it with all the strength at my command, for to me Hind Swaraj is the rule of all people, is the rule of justice." Ibid., 18. On Gandhi

and democratic thought more generally, see Thomas Pantham, "Thinking with Mahatma Gandhi: Beyond Liberal Democracy," *Political Theory* 11, no. 2 (1983).

83. Gandhi, *Village Swaraj*, 17.

84. Ibid., 16.

85. Bilgrami goes so far as to say that "a real distinction here is undeniable as is its theoretical power to claim an alternative way of thinking about morals. It is a commonplace in our understanding of the Western moral tradition to think of Kant's moral philosophy as the full and *philosophical* flowering of a core of Christian thought. But Gandhi fractures that historical understanding. By stressing the deep incompatibility between categorical imperatives and universalizable maxims on the one hand, and Christian humility on the other, he makes two moral doctrines and methods out of what the tradition represents as a single historically consolidated one. And discarding one of them as lending itself ultimately to violence, he fashions a remarkable political philosophy and national movement out of the other." Akeel Bilgrami, "Gandhi's Integrity," *Raritan: A Quarterly Review* 21, no. 2 (2001): 59.

86. Gandhi, *Village Swaraj*, 20.

87. Ibid., 73.

88. For instance: "Strength does not come from physical capacity. It comes from an indomitable will." Mahatma Gandhi, *The Essential Gandhi: An Anthology of His Writings on His Life, Work, and Ideas*, 2nd ed., Vintage Spiritual Classics (New York: Vintage Books, 2002), 157.

89. Gandhi, *For Pacifists* (Ahmedabad: Navajivan Pub. House, 2000 [1949]), 33.

90. Ibid., 33.

91. Hannah Arendt, *The Life of the Mind*, One-volume ed. (San Diego: Harcourt Brace Jovanovich, 1981), 142.

92. She writes: "[T]his I-can sets limitations on the I-will that are not outside the willing activity itself" and "An inherent delight of the will in itself is as natural to the will as understanding and knowing are to the intellect, and can be detected even in hatred; but its innate perfection, the final peace between the two-in-one, can come about only when the will is transformed into *love*." Ibid., 142, 143.

93. Ibid., 136.

94. Though it is not clear whether she would distinguish Pauline love from the love she is describing here, she writes: "[L]ove, in distinction from friendship, is killed, or rather extinguished the moment it is displayed in public." Arendt, *The Human Condition*, 2nd ed. (Chicago: University of Chicago Press, 1998).

95. "At the centre of non-violence is a force which is self-acting. *Ahimsa* means love in a Pauline sense, and yet something more than the 'love' defined by St. Paul, although I know St. Paul's beautiful definition is good enough for all practical purposes." Gandhi, *For Pacifists*, 7.

96. Indeed, while the plurality and spontaneity of others are often experienced as a limit on freedom from the standpoint of the individual, the paradox itself constitutes freedom. As Grafstein writes: "To the holist . . . existing sociopolitical relationships . . . acts more as a filter than a barrier, filtering out not actions but bare motion and behavior. Calling this filter a barrier to action is as misleading as calling the structure of language a barrier to communication. In defining the possible moves one can make, political relationships, like language, constrain and free at the same time." Robert Grafstein, "Political Freedom and Political Action," *Western Political Quarterly* 39, no. 3 (1986): 478.

97. Gandhi unfortunately does. He argues that "man has been steadily progressing toward ahimsa" because, for instance, human history has progressed from cannibalism to meat eating to vegetarianism. Gandhi, *For Pacifists*, 9–10.

98. For examples, see George Lakey and Peace and Conflict Studies Program, "Global Nonviolent Action Database" (Swarthmore College, 2014); Bryan Farrell and Eric Stoner, "Waging Nonviolence," http://wagingnonviolence.org.

CONCLUSION

1. Steven G. Bradbury, "Application of 18usc2340-2340a to the Combined Use [of Certain] Techniques in the [Interrogation] of High Value Al Qaeda Detainees" (Washington, DC: US Department of Justice Office of Legal Council, 2005).

2. Gandhi, *Village Swaraj*, 1st ed. (Ahmedabad: Navajivan Pub. House, 1962), 16.

3. Taiaiake Alfred, "Wasáse: Indigenous Resurgences," in *Colonialism and Its Legacies*, ed. Jacob T. Levy (Lanham, MD: Lexington Books, 2011), 82.

4. Charles de Secondat Montesquieu, *The Spirit of Laws*, Great Books in Philosophy Series (Amherst, NY: Prometheus Books, 2002), I:183.

5 .Ibid., I:185.

6. "Let us first consider what state of things is described by the word 'civilisation'. Its true test lies in the fact that people living in it make bodily welfare the object of life." All of the resources of science and technology have been put into the so-called improvement of warfare and labor, for instance, in order to pursue this end, which has led to unprecedented physical suffering. If the hallmark of Western civilization is to "increase bodily comforts . . . it fails miserably even in doing so." Gandhi, *Hind Swaraj and Other Writings*, ed. Anthony Parel, Centenary ed., Cambridge Texts in Modern Politics (Cambridge, UK; New York: Cambridge University Press, 2009), 35, 37.

7. Mahatma Gandhi, *For Pacifists* (Ahmedabad: Navajivan Pub. House, 2000 [1949]), 10.

8. Dustin Ells Howes, "Terror in and out of Power," *European Journal of Political Theory* 11, no. 1 (2012b).

REFERENCES

Ackerman, Peter, and Jack DuVall. *A Force More Powerful: A Century of Nonviolent Conflict.* 1st ed. New York: St. Martin's Press, 2000.

Adams, Raymond. "Thoreau's Sources for 'Resistance to Civil Government.'" *Studies in Philology* 42, no. 3 (1945): 640–653.

Addams, Jane. "Personal Reactions during War." In *Nonviolence in America: A Documentary History*, edited by Staughton Lynd and Alice Lynd, 91–99. Maryknoll, NY: Orbis Books, 1995.

Albert Einstein Institution. "Annual Report." http://www.aeinstein.org/wp-content/uploads/2014/04/AR-for-print_Part1.pdf.

Alexander, Michelle. *The New Jim Crow: Mass Incarceration in the Age of Colorblindness.* New York, Jackson, TN: New Press; Distributed by Perseus Distribution, 2010.

Alfred, Taiaiake. "Wasáse: Indigenous Resurgences." In *Colonialism and Its Legacies*, edited by Jacob T. Levy, 79–96. Lanham, MD: Lexington Books, 2011.

Anderson, Benedict R. *Imagined Communities: Reflections on the Origin and Spread of Nationalism.* Rev. and extended ed. London; New York: Verso, 1991.

Anghie, Antony. "Francisco De Vitoria and the Colonial Origins of International Law." *Social & Legal Studies* 5, no. 3 (1996): 321–336.

Anghie, Antony. "Rethinking Sovereignty in International Law." *Annual Review of Law and Social Science* 5 (2009): 291–310.

Anker, Elisabeth. "Feminist Theory and the Failures of Post-9/11 Freedom." *Politics & Gender* 8, no. 2 (2012): 207.

Arendt, Hannah. "What Is Freedom?" In *Between Past and Future: Eight Exercises in Political Thought*, 142–169. New York: Penguin Books, 1977.

Arendt, Hannah. *The Life of the Mind.* One-volume ed. San Diego: Harcourt Brace Jovanovich, 1981.

Arendt, Hannah. *The Human Condition.* 2nd ed. Chicago: University of Chicago Press, 1998.

Aristophanes. *Lysistrata*, edited by Jack Lindsay. Illustrated Library. Garden City, NY: Halcyon House, 1950.

Aristotle. *Politics*. Translated by Ernest Barker. New York: Oxford University Press, 1998.

Arneil, Barbara. *John Locke and America: The Defence of English Colonialism*. Oxford; New York: Clarendon Press; Oxford University Press, 1996.

Astin, A. E. *Scipio Aemilianus*. Oxford: Clarendon Press, 1967.

Augustine. *Concerning the City of God against the Pagans*. Translated by Henry Scowcroft Bettenson. Harmondsworth: Penguin Books, 1972.

Bakunin, Mikhail Aleksandrovich. *Marxism, Freedom and the State*. London: Freedom Press, 1950.

Bakunin, Mikhail Aleksandrovich, Grigori Maksimov, Allen McConnell, and Charles Poggi. *The Political Philosophy of Bakunin: Scientific Anarchism*. Glencoe, IL: The Free Press, 1953.

Bales, Kevin. *Disposable People: New Slavery in the Global Economy*. Rev. ed. Berkeley: University of California Press, 2004.

Ballou, Adin. *Autobiography of Adin Ballou, 1803–1890. Containing an Elaborate Record and Narrative of His Life from Infancy to Old Age*, edited by William Sweetzer Heywood. Lowell, MA: The Vox Populi Press, 1896.

Ballou, Adin. *Christian Non-Resistance*, edited by Lynn Gordon Hughes. Providence, RI: Blackstone Editions, 2003.

Bax, Ernest Belfort. "The Last Episode of the French Revolution Being a History of Gracchus Babeuf and the Conspiracy of the Equals." http://www.marxists.org/archive/bax/1911/babeuf/index.htm.

Beard, Mary Ritter. *Woman as Force in History: A Study in Traditions and Realities*. New York: Persea Books, 1987.

Bell, David Avrom. *The First Total War: Napoleon's Europe and the Birth of Warfare as We Know It*. Boston: Houghton Mifflin Co., 2007.

Benhabib, Seyla. "Hannah Arendt and the Redemptive Power of Narrative." *Social Research* 57, no. 1 (1990): 167–196.

Benjamin, Walter. "Critique of Violence." In *Reflections: Essays, Aphorisms, Autobiographical Writings*, 277–300. New York: Harcourt Brace Jovanovich, 1978.

Berlin, Isaiah, Henry Hardy, and Ian Harris. *Liberty: Incorporating Four Essays on Liberty*. Oxford: Oxford University Press, 2002.

Bilgrami, Akeel. "Gandhi's Integrity." *Raritan: A Quarterly Review* 21, no. 2 (2001): 48–67.

Billig, Michael. *Banal Nationalism*. London; Thousand Oaks, CA: Sage, 1995.

Blackmon, Douglas A. *Slavery by Another Name: The Re-enslavement of Black Americans from the Civil War to World War II*. 1st Anchor Books ed. New York: Anchor Books, 2009.

Blumstein, Alfred, and Allen J. Beck. "Population Growth in U. S. Prisons, 1980–1996." *Crime and Justice* 26 (1999): 17–61.

Bock, Gisela, Quentin Skinner, and Maurizio Viroli, eds. *Machiavelli and Republicanism*, Ideas in Context. New York: Cambridge University Press, 1990.

Bradbury, Steven G. "Application of 18usc2340-2340a to the Combined Use [of Certain] Techniques in the [Interrogation] of High Value Al Qaeda Detainees." 20. Washington, DC: US Department of Justice Office of Legal Council, 2005.

Bradley, K. R. *Slavery and Rebellion in the Roman World, 140 b.c.–70 b.c.* Bloomington; London: Indiana University Press; B. T. Batsford, 1989.

Breuilly, John. *Nationalism and the State*. 2nd ed. Chicago: University of Chicago Press, 1994.

Buonarroti, Philippe. "Manifesto of the Equals." http://www.marxists.org/history/france/revolution/conspiracy-equals/1796/manifesto.htm.

Burke, Edmund. *Reflections on the Revolution in France*, edited by J. C. D. Clark. Stanford, CA: Stanford University Press, 2001.

Camus, Albert. *The Rebel: An Essay on Man in Revolt*. 1st Vintage International ed. New York: Vintage Books, 1991.

Cannon, Henry L. "The Character and Antecedents of the Charter of Liberties of Henry I." *The American Historical Review* 15, no. 1 (1909): 37–46.

Caro, Jason. *The Origins of Free Peoples*. New York: Continuum International Pub. Group, 2011.

Carr, Edward Hallett. *Nationalism and After*. New York: The Macmillan Company, 1945.

Caudwell, Christopher. "Liberty: A Study in Bourgeois Illusion." http://www.marxists.org/archive/caudwell/1938/studies/ch08.htm.

Cawte, Mary. "Research Proposals for Nonviolent Defense: Strategy and Tactics. A Review Article of Research on Civilian-Based Defense by Giliam De Valk." *Pacifica Review: Peace, Security & Global Change* 6, no. 1 (1994): 95–106.

Chadha, Yogesh. *Gandhi: A Life*. New York: John Wiley, 1997.

Chafetz, Janet Saltzman, Anthony Gary Dworkin, and Stephanie Swanson. *Female Revolt: Women's Movements in World and Historical Perspective*. Totowa, NJ: Rowman & Allanheld, 1986.

Chenoweth, Erica, and Maria J. Stephan. *Why Civil Resistance Works: The Strategic Logic of Nonviolent Conflict*, Columbia Studies in Terrorism and Irregular Warfare. New York: Columbia University Press, 2011.

Christie, Nils. *A Suitable Amount of Crime*. London; New York: Routledge, 2004.

Cicero, Marcus Tullius. *For Aulus Caecina*. Translated by C. D. Yonge, *The Orations of Marcus Tullius Cicero*. London: Henry G. Bohn, Perseus Digital Library, 1856.

Cicero, Marcus Tullius. *Phillipics*. Translated by C. D. Yonge, *The Orations of Marcus Tullius Cicero*. London: George Bell & Sons, Perseus Digital Library, 1903.

Cicero, Marcus Tullius. *On the Commonwealth*. Translated by George Holland Sabine and Stanley Barney Smith. New York: Macmillan Publishing Company, 1976.

Clavin, Matthew J. *Toussaint Louverture and the American Civil War: The Promise and Peril of a Second Haitian Revolution*. Philadelphia: University of Pennsylvania Press, 2010.

Cloud, David. "On Life Support: Public Health in the Age of Mass Incarceration." 36: Vera Institute of Justice, 2014.

Cocks, Joan. *On Sovereignty and Other Political Delusions*, New York: Bloomsbury Publishing, 2014.

Confortini, Catia Cecilia. *Intelligent Compassion: Feminist Clinical Methodology in the Women's International League for Peace and Freedom*, Oxford Studies in Gender and International Relations. New York: Oxford University Press, 2012.

Congress, Second. "Militia Act of 1792." http://www.constitution.org/mil/mil_act_1792.htm.

Constant, Benjamin. "The Liberty of the Ancients Compared with That of the Moderns." In *Political Writings*, edited by Biancamaria Fontana, 307–328. Cambridge, UK; New York: Cambridge University Press, 1988.

Cornell, Tim. *The Beginnings of Rome: Italy and Rome from the Bronze Age to the Punic Wars (C. 1000–264 BC)*, Routledge History of the Ancient World. London; New York: Routledge, 1995.

Craig, Leon Harold. *The War Lover: A Study of Plato's Republic*. Toronto; Buffalo: University of Toronto Press, 1996.

Croxton, Derek. "The Peace of Westphalia of 1648 and the Origins of Sovereignty." *The International History Review* 21, no. 3 (1999): 569–852.

Dalton, Dennis. *Indian Idea of Freedom: Political Thought of Swami Vivekananda, Aurobindo Ghose, Mahatma Gandhi, and Rabindranath Tagore*. Gurgaon, Haryana: Academic Press, 1982.

Dandurand, Yvon, and Curt T. Griffiths. "Handbook on Restorative Justice Programmes." In *Criminal Justice Handbook Series*. Vienna; New York: United Nations Office on Drugs and Crime, 2006.

Danilovic, Vesna, and Joe Clare. "The Kantian Liberal Peace (Revisited)." 2007, 397–414.

Danziger, Danny, and John Gillingham. *1215: The Year of Magna Carta*. 1st Touchstone ed. New York: Simon & Schuster, 2004.

DeMichele, Matthew, and Thomas Janoski. "A Regime Theory Approach to Cross-National Incarceration Rate Variation: Three Worlds of Western Punishment, 1960–2002." *Conference Papers—American Sociological Association* (2010): 1175–1175.

Demosthenes. *Phillipics*. Translated by J. H. Vince. London: Harvard University Press, Perseus Digital Library, 1930.

Dilts, Andrew. "To Kill a Thief: Punishment, Proportionality, and Criminal Subjectivity in Locke's Second Treatise." *Political Theory* 40, no. 1 (2012): 58–83.

Dmitriev, Sviatoslav. *The Greek Slogan of Freedom and Early Roman Politics in Greece*. Oxford; New York: Oxford University Press, 2011.

Douglass, Frederick. "The Meaning of July Fourth for the Negro." In *The Life and Writings of Frederick Douglass*, edited by Philip Sheldon Foner, v, 181–204. New York: International Publishers, 1950.

Douglass, Frederick. *My Bondage and My Freedom*. New York: Dover Publications, 1969.

Dray, Philip. *There Is Power in a Union: The Epic Story of Labor in America*. 1st ed. New York: Doubleday, 2010.

Drescher, Seymour. *Abolition: A History of Slavery and Antislavery*. Cambridge, UK; New York: Cambridge University Press, 2009.

Dubofsky, Melvyn, and Joseph Anthony McCartin. *We Shall Be All: A History of the Industrial Workers of the World*. Abridged ed., The Working Class in American History. Urbana: University of Illinois Press, 2000.

Dubois, Laurent. *Avengers of the New World: The Story of the Haitian Revolution*. Cambridge, MA: Belknap Press of Harvard University Press, 2004.

Dunayevskaya, Raya. *Marxism & Freedom: From 1776 until Today*. Amherst, NY: Humanity Books, 2000.

Eknath, Easwaran. *Nonviolent Soldier of Islam: Badshah Khan, a Man to Match His Mountains*. 2nd ed. Tomales, CA: Nilgiri Press, 1999.

Emerson, Rupert. *From Empire to Nation: The Rise to Self-Assertion of Asian and African Peoples*. Cambridge, MA: Harvard University Press, 1960.

Engels, Friedrich. *Herr Eugen Dühring's Revolution in Science (Anti-Dühring)*, edited by C. P. Dutt. New York: International Publishers, 1966.

"English Bill of Rights." In *Avalon Project*: Yale Law School, 1689.

Esdaile, Charles J. *Napoleon's Wars an International History, 1803–1815*. London; New York: Allen Lane, 2007.

Ewald, Alec C., and Brandon Rottinghaus. *Criminal Disenfranchisement in an International Perspective*. Cambridge, UK; New York: Cambridge University Press, 2009.

Fanon, Frantz. *The Wretched of the Earth*. New York: Grove Press, 1963.

Farr, James. "Locke, Natural Law, and New World Slavery." *Political Theory* 36, no. 4 (2008): 495–522.

Farrell, Bryan, and Eric Stoner. "Waging Nonviolence." http://wagingnonviolence.org.

Fenton, William N. *The Great Law and the Longhouse: A Political History of the Iroquois Confederacy*, The Civilization of the American Indian Series. Norman: University of Oklahoma Press, 1998.

Fisher, N. R. E. *Slavery in Classical Greece*, Classical World Series. London: Bristol Classical Press, 1993.

Foner, Eric. *Nothing but Freedom: Emancipation and Its Legacy*, The Walter Lynwood Fleming Lectures in Southern History. Baton Rouge: Louisiana State University Press, 1983.

Forsythe, Gary. *A Critical History of Early Rome: From Prehistory to the First Punic War*. Berkeley: University of California Press, 2005.

Foucault, Michel. *Discipline and Punish: The Birth of the Prison*. Pittsburgh, PA: Vintage Books, 1995.

Frank, Jill. "Wages of War: On Judgment in Plato's *Republic*." *Political Theory* 35, no. 4 (2007): 443–467.

Frankfurt, Harry. "Freedom of the Will and the Concept of the Person." *Journal of Philosophy* 58, no. 1 (1971): 5–20.

Franklin, B., and W. T. Franklin. *Memoirs of the Life and Writings of Benjamin Franklin*. Vol. 1: H. Colburn, 1818.

Frey, Sylvia R. "Resistance and Rebellion in American Slave Societies." In *Slavery, Abolition and Social Justice*. Adam Matthew Digital.

Fried, Albert, and Ronald Sanders. *Socialist Thought: A Documentary History*. Rev. ed. New York: Columbia University Press, 1992.

Gandhi, Mahatma. *Constructive Programme, Its Meaning and Place*. 2nd ed. Ahmedabad: Navajivan Press, 1948.

Gandhi, Mahatma. *Trusteeship*, edited by Ravindra Kelkar. Ahmedabad: Navajivan Mudranalaya, 1960.

Gandhi, Mahatma. *Village Swaraj*. 1st ed. Ahmedabad: Navajivan Pub. House, 1962.

Gandhi, Mahatma. *Mahatma Gandhi: Selected Political Writings*, edited by Dennis Dalton. Indianapolis: Hackett Pub. Co., 1996.

Gandhi, Mahatma. *Hind Swaraj and Other Writings*, edited by Anthony Parel. New York: Cambridge University Press, 1997.

Gandhi, Mahatma. *The Collected Works of Mahatma Gandhi*. New Delhi: Publications Division Government of India, 1999.

Gandhi, Mahatma. *For Pacifists*. Ahmedabad: Navajivan Pub. House, 2000 [1949].

Gandhi, Mahatma. *The Essential Gandhi: An Anthology of His Writings on His Life, Work, and Ideas*. 2nd ed., Vintage Spiritual Classics. New York: Vintage Books, 2002.

Gandhi, Mahatma. *Hind Swaraj and Other Writings*, edited by Anthony Parel. Centenary ed., Cambridge Texts in Modern Politics. Cambridge, UK; New York: Cambridge University Press, 2009.

Garrison, William Lloyd. "Declaration of Sentiments Adopted by the Peace Convention." (1838), http://teachingamericanhistory.org/library/index.asp?document=564.

Garrison, William Lloyd. "Declaration of Sentiments of the American Anti-Slavery Convention." *Selections from the Writings of W. L. Garrison* (1852), http://utc.iath.virginia.edu/abolitn/abeswlgct.html.

Gellner, Ernest. *Nations and Nationalism*. 2nd ed., New Perspectives on the Past. Malden, MA: Blackwell Pub., 2006.

Genovese, Eugene D. *From Rebellion to Revolution: Afro-American Slave Revolts in the Making of the Modern World*, The Walter Lynwood Fleming Lectures in Southern History, Louisiana State University. Baton Rouge: Louisiana State University Press, 1979.

Gentili, Alberico. *The Wars of the Romans: A Critical Edition and Translation of* De Armis Romanis, edited by Benedict Kingsbury, Benjamin Straumann and David A. Lupher. Oxford; New York: Oxford University Press, 2011.

Girard, Philippe R. *The Slaves Who Defeated Napoleon: Toussaint Louverture and the Haitian War of Independence, 1801–1804*, Atlantic Crossings. Tuscaloosa: University of Alabama Press, 2011.

Godrej, Farah. "Nonviolence and Gandhi's Truth: A Method for Moral and Political Arbitration." *The Review of Politics* 68, no. 2 (2006): 287–317.

Godrej, Farah. *Cosmopolitan Political Thought: Method, Practice, Discipline*. Oxford; New York: Oxford University Press, 2011.

Godrej, Farah. "Ascetics, Warriors, and a Gandhian Ecological Citizenship." *Political Theory* 40, no. 4 (2012): 437–465.

Gore, Dayo F., Jeanne Theoharis, and Komozi Woodard, eds. *Want to Start a Revolution?: Radical Women in the Black Freedom Struggle*. New York: New York University Press, 2009.

Grafstein, Robert. "Political Freedom and Political Action." *Western Political Quarterly* 39, no. 3 (1986): 464–479.

Green, Judith A. *Henry I: King of England and Duke of Normandy*. Cambridge, UK; New York: Cambridge University Press, 2006.

Greenberg, Karen J., and Joshua L. Dratel. *The Torture Papers: The Road to Abu Ghraib*. New York: Cambridge University Press, 2005.

Greenfeld, Liah. *Nationalism: Five Roads to Modernity*. Cambridge, MA: Harvard University Press, 1992.

Grinde, Donald A., and Bruce E. Johansen. *Exemplar of Liberty: Native America and the Evolution of Democracy*, Native American Politics Series. Los Angeles, CA: American Indian Studies Center, University of California, Los Angeles, 1991.

Grotius, Hugo. *The Law of War and Peace De Jure Belli Ac Pacis Libri Tres*. Translated by Francis W. Kelsey, Essay and Monograph Series of the Liberal Arts Press. Indianapolis: Bobbs-Merrill, 1962.

Grotius, Hugo, Richard Hakluyt, William Welwood, and David Armitage. *The Free Sea*, Natural Law and Enlightenment Classics. Indianapolis: Liberty Fund, 2004.

Gruen, Erich S. *The Hellenistic World and the Coming of Rome*. 2 vols. Berkeley: University of California Press, 1984.

Hallett, Brien. *Declaring War: Congress, the President, and What the Constitution Does Not Say*. Cambridge, UK: Cambridge University Press, 2012.

Harris, William V. *War and Imperialism in Republican Rome, 327–70 bc*. Oxford New York: Clarendon Press; Oxford University Press, 1979.

Hartigan, Richard Shelly. "Saint Augustine on War and Killing: The Problem of the Innocent." *Journal of the History of Ideas* 27, no. 2 (1966): 195–204.

Hartney, Christopher. "US Rates of Incarceration: A Global Perspective," edited by National Council on Crime and Delinquency. Washington, DC, 2006.

Havel, Václav. "The Power of the Powerless: Citizens against the State in Central-Eastern Europe," edited by John Keane, 228 pp. Armonk, NY: M. E. Sharpe, 1985.

Hayek, Friedrich A. von. *The Constitution of Liberty*. Chicago: University of Chicago Press, 1960.

Hegel, Georg Wilhelm Friedrich. *Phenomenology of Spirit*. Translated by Arnold V. Miller. Oxford: Oxford University Press, 1977.

Henry I. "Charter of Liberties." *Medieval Sourcebook* (1100), http://www.fordham.edu/halsall/source/hcoronation.asp.

Herodotus. *The Histories*. Cambridge, MA: Harvard University Press, 1920.

Hill, Thomas E. "A Kantian Perspective on Political Violence." *The Journal of Ethics* 1, no. 2 (1997): 105–140.

Hitler, Adolf, Alvin Saunders Johnson, John Chamberlain, and Rouben Mamoulian Collection (Library of Congress). *Mein Kampf, Complete and Unabridged, Fully Annotated*. New York: Reynal & Hitchcock, 1941.

Hobbes, Thomas. *Leviathan: With Selected Variants from the Latin Edition of 1668*. Indianapolis: Hackett Pub. Co., 1994.

Hochschild, Adam. *To End All Wars: A Story of Loyalty and Rebellion, 1914–1918*. Boston: Houghton Mifflin Harcourt, 2011.

Holt, James Clarke. *Magna Carta*. 2nd ed. Cambridge, UK; New York: Cambridge University Press, 1992.

Holton, Woody. *Forced Founders: Indians, Debtors, Slaves, and the Making of the American Revolution in Virginia*. Chapel Hill: Published for the Omohundro Institute of Early American History and Culture, Williamsburg, Virginia, by the University of North Carolina Press, 1999.

Honig, B. "Arendt, Identity and Difference." *Political Theory* 16, no. 1 (1988): 77–98.

Hornus, Jean Michel. *It Is Not Lawful for Me to Fight: Early Christian Attitudes toward War, Violence, and the State*. Rev. ed., A Christian Peace Shelf Selection. Scottdale, PA: Herald Press, 1980.

Howes, Dustin Ells. *Toward a Credible Pacifism: Violence and the Possibilities of Politics*. Albany: State University of New York Press, 2009.

Howes, Dustin Ells. "Creating Necessity: Well-Used Violence in the Thought of Machiavelli." *symplokē* 20, no. 1–2 (2012a): 145–169.

Howes, Dustin Ells. "Terror in and out of Power." *European Journal of Political Theory* 11, no. 1 (2012b): 25–58.

Hsueh, Vicki. *Hybrid Constitutions: Challenging Legacies of Law, Privilege, and Culture in Colonial America*. Durham, NC: Duke University Press, 2010.

James, Cyril Lionel Robert. *The Black Jacobins*. New York: The Dial Press, 1938.

Jasinski, James. "Constituting Antebellum African American Identity: Resistance, Violence, and Masculinity in Henry Highland Garnet's (1843) 'Address to the Slaves'." *Quarterly Journal of Speech* 93, no. 1 (2007): 27–57.

Jefferson, Thomas. "French Revolution." In *Thomas Jefferson Encyclopedia*. Monticello, 1773.

Jefferson, Thomas. "The New Constitution: To William S. Smith." In *Jefferson Collection*. University of Virginia, 1787.

Jefferson, Thomas. "Letter: To James Madison (Excerpt)." In *The Origin of the Second Amendment: A Documentary History in Commentaries on Liberty, Free Government, and an Armed Populace during the Formation of the Bill of Rights*, edited by David E. Young, 709. Ontonagon, MI: Golden Oak Books, 1991.

Joeden-Forgey, Elisa von. "Race Power, Freedom, and the Democracy of Terror in German Racialist Thought." In *Hannah Arendt and the Uses of History: Imperialism, Nation, Race, and Genocide*, edited by Richard H. King and Dan Stone, 21–37. New York: Berghahn Books, 2007.

Kalyvas, Andreas. "From the Act to the Decision: Hannah Arendt and the Question of Decisionism." *Political Theory* 32, no. 3 (2004): 320–346.

Kant, Immanuel. *Religion within the Limits of Reason Alone*. New York: Harper, 1960.

Kant, Immanuel, and Mary J. Gregor. *The Metaphysics of Morals*, Cambridge Texts in the History of Philosophy. Cambridge, UK; New York: Cambridge University Press, 1996.

Kateb, George. "Political Action: Its Nature and Advantages." In *The Cambridge Companion to Hannah Arendt*, edited by Dana Richard Villa, 130–148. New York: Cambridge University Press, 2000.

Kautsky, Karl. *The Dictatorship of the Proletariat*. Westport, CT: Greenwood Press, 1981.

Kennedy, Hubert. "Johann Baptist Von Schweitzer: The Queer Marx Loved to Hate." *Journal of Homosexuality* 29, no. 4 (1995): 69–93.

Keohane, Nannerl O. "The Radical Humanism of Étienne De La Boétie." *Journal of the History of Ideas* 1, no. 1 (1977): 119–130.

Keuls, Eva C. *The Reign of the Phallus: Sexual Politics in Ancient Athens*. 1st ed. New York: Harper & Row, 1985.

Kingsbury, Benedict, and Benjamin Straumann. *The Roman Foundations of the Law of Nations: Alberico Gentili and the Justice of Empire*. Oxford; New York: Oxford University Press, 2010.

Kishwar, Madhu. "Gandhi on Women." *Economic and Political Weekly* 20, no. 41 (1985): 1753–1758.

Knouff, Gregory T. "White Men in Arms." In *Representing Masculinity: Male Citizenship in Modern Western Culture*, edited by Stefan Dudink, Anna Clark, and Karen Hagemann. New York, NY: Palgrave Macmillan, 2007.

Kropotkin, Petr Alekseevich. *The Conquest of Bread and Other Writings*, edited by Marshall Shatz, Cambridge Texts in the History of Political Thought. Cambridge, UK; New York: Cambridge University Press, 1995.

Kuzio, Taras. "The Myth of the Civic State: A Critical Survey of Hans Kohn's Framework for Understanding Nationalism." *Ethnic and Racial Studies* 25, no. 1 (2002): 20–39.

La Boétie, Étienne De. "Discourse on Voluntary Servitude, or the Anti-Dictator." edited by Harry Kurz. New York: Columbia University Press, 1942.

La Boétie, Étienne De. *The Politics of Obedience: Discourse on Voluntary Servitude*. Whitefish, MT: Kessinger Legacy Reprints, 2010.

Lafayette, Marie Joseph Paul Yves Roch Gilbert du Motier, and Thomas Jefferson. *The Letters of Lafayette and Jefferson*, edited by Gilbert Chinard, The Johns Hopkins Studies in International Thought. Baltimore, MD; Paris: The Johns Hopkins Press, 1929.

Lakey, George, and Peace and Conflict Studies Program. "Global Nonviolent Action Database." Swarthmore College, 2014.

Lamothe, Dan. "US Judge Permits Pentagon to Force-Feed Guantánamo Prisoner but Issues Rebuke." *The Washington Post*, May 23, 2014.

Landers, Jane. *Black Society in Spanish Florida*, Blacks in the New World. Urbana: University of Illinois Press, 1999.

Lang, Timothy. " Lord Acton and 'the Insanity of Nationality.'" *Journal of the History of Ideas* 63, no. 1 (2002): 129–149.

Langan, John. "The Elements of St. Augustine's Just War Theory." *The Journal of Religious Ethics* 12, no. 1 (1984): 19–38.

Lenin, Vladimir Il'ich. "On Revolutionary Violence and Terror." In *The Lenin Anthology*, edited by Robert C. Tucker, 423–432. New York: Norton, 1975.

Lenin, Vladimir Il'ich. *State and Revolution: Marxist Teaching About the Theory of the State and the Tasks of the Proletariat in the Revolution*. Westport, CT: Greenwood Press, 1978.

Lerner, Warren. *A History of Socialism and Communism in Modern Times: Theorists, Activists, and Humanists*. 2nd ed. Englewood Cliffs, NJ: Prentice Hall, 1993.

Levenson-Estrada, Deborah. *Trade Unionists against Terror: Guatemala City, 1954–1985*. Chapel Hill: University of North Carolina Press, 1994.

Levi, Primo. *Survival in Auschwitz: The Nazi Assault on Humanity*. Translated by Stuart Woolf. 1st Touchstone ed. New York: Simon & Schuster, 1996.

Levinas, Emmanuel. *Totality and Infinity: An Essay on Exteriority*. Pittsburgh, PA: Duquesne University Press, 2001.

Lewy, Guenter. *America in Vietnam*. New York: Oxford University Press, 1978.

Lindemann, Albert S. *A History of European Socialism*. New Haven: Yale University Press, 1983.

Livy. *The Rise of Rome: Books One to Five*. Translated by T. James Luce. New ed., Oxford World's Classics. Oxford; New York: Oxford University Press, 2008.

Locke, John. *A Letter Concerning Toleration*, edited by James Tully, HPC Classics Series. Indianapolis: Hackett Pub. Co., 1983.

Locke, John. "The Second Treatise of Government." In *Two Treatises of Government*, edited by Peter Laslett, 265–428. New York: Cambridge University Press, 1988.

Lovejoy, Paul E., and Jan S. Hogendorn. *Slow Death for Slavery: The Course of Abolition in Northern Nigeria, 1897–1936*, African Studies Series. Cambridge, UK; New York: Cambridge University Press, 1993.

Luxemburg, Rosa. "The Nation-State and the Proletariat." In *The National Question*, edited by Horace B. Davies. New York: Monthly Review Press, 1909.

Luxemburg, Rosa. *The Rosa Luxemburg Reader*, edited by Peter Hudis and Kevin Anderson. New York: Monthly Review Press, 2004.

Lynch, John, and R. A. Humphreys. *Latin American Revolutions, 1808–1826: Old and New World Origins*. Norman: University of Oklahoma Press, 1994.

Mabbett, Ian. "Buddhism and Freedom." In *Asian Freedoms: The Idea of Freedom in East and Southeast Asia*, edited by David Kelly and Anthony Reid, 19–36. New York: Cambridge University Press, 1998.

MacGilvray, Eric. *The Invention of Market Freedom*. Cambridge, UK; New York: Cambridge University Press, 2011.

Machiavelli, Niccolò. *The Discourses of Niccolò Machiavelli*. Translated by Leslie J. Walker. London: Penguin Classics, 1970.

Madelin, Louis. *The French Revolution*, The National History of France. London: W. Heinemann, ltd., 1928.

Malcolm, Joyce Lee. *To Keep and Bear Arms: The Origins of an Anglo-American Right*. Cambridge, MA: Harvard University Press, 1994.

Mansfield, Harvey Claflin. *Taming the Prince: The Ambivalence of Modern Executive Power*. Johns Hopkins pbk. ed. Baltimore: Johns Hopkins University Press, 1993.

Mantena, Karuna. *Alibis of Empire: Henry Maine and the Ends of Liberal Imperialism*. Princeton, NJ: Princeton University Press, 2010.

Mantena, Karuna. "Another Realism: The Politics of Gandhian Nonviolence." *American Political Science Review* 106, no. 2 (2012): 455–470.

Mao, Tsetung. *The Selected Works of Mao Tsetung*. 5 vols. Vol. 1. Oxford: Pergamon Press, 1965.

Marsilius of Padua, *Defensor pacis*. Translated by Alan Gewirth. Toronto: University of Toronto Press, Medieval Academy of America, 1986.

Marx, Karl. "Manifesto of the Communist Party." In *The Marx-Engels Reader*, edited by Robert C. Tucker, 469–500. New York: Norton, 1978a.

Marx, Karl. "The Possibility of a Non-violent Revolution." In *The Marx-Engels Reader*, edited by Robert C. Tucker, 522–524. New York: Norton, 1978b.

Marx, Karl, and Friedrich Engels. "After the Revolution: Marx Debates Bakunin." In *The Marx-Engels Reader*, edited by Robert C. Tucker, 542–548. New York: Norton, 1978.

Mary, Margaret. "Slavery in the Writings of St. Augustine." *The Classical Journal* 49, no. 8 (1954): 363–369.

Matthews, Gelien. *Caribbean Slave Revolts and the British Abolitionist Movement*. Baton Rouge: Louisiana State University Press, 2006.

Mauer, Marc. "Comparative International Rates of Incarceration: An Examination of Causes and Trends Presented to the U.S. Commission on Civil Rights." *The Sentencing Project* (2003).

Mayer, Jane. *Dark Side: The Inside Story of How the War on Terror Turned into a War on American Ideals*. 1st ed. New York: Doubleday, 2008.

Mazzini, Giuseppe, Stefano Recchia, and Nadia Urbinati. *A Cosmopolitanism of Nations: Giuseppe Mazzini's Writings on Democracy, Nation Building, and International Relations*. Princeton, NJ: Princeton University Press, 2009.

McBride, Keally D. *Punishment and Political Order*, Law, Meaning, and Violence. Ann Arbor: University of Michigan Press, 2007.

McCormick, John P. "Machiavelli against Republicanism: On the Cambridge School's 'Guicciardinian Moments'." *Political Theory* 31, no. 5 (2003): 615–643.

Mekeel, Arthur J. *The Relation of the Quakers to the American Revolution*. Washington, DC: University Press of America, 1979.

Melzer, Sara E., and Leslie W. Rabine. *Rebel Daughters: Women and the French Revolution*, Publications of the University of California Humanities Research Institute. New York: Oxford University Press, 1992.

Mills, Charles W. *The Racial Contract*. Ithaca: Cornell University Press, 1997.

Minnich, Elizabeth K. "To Judge in Freedom: Hannah Arendt on the Relation of Thinking and Morality." In *Hannah Arendt: Thinking, Judging, Freedom*, edited by Gisela T. Kaplan and Clive S. Kessler, 133–143. Sydney; Boston: Allen & Unwin, 1989.

Moallem, Minoo, and Iain A. Boal. "Multicultural Nationalism and the Poetics of Inauguration." In *Between Woman and Nation: Nationalisms, Transnational Feminisms, and the State*, edited by Caren Kaplan, Norma Alarcón, and Minoo Moallem, 243–263. Durham, NC: Duke University Press, 1999.

Moitt, Bernard. *Women and Slavery in the French Antilles, 1635–1848*, Blacks in the Diaspora. Bloomington: Indiana University Press, 2001.

Monoson, Susan Sara. *Plato's Democratic Entanglements: Athenian Politics and the Practice of Philosophy*. Princeton, NJ: Princeton University Press, 2000.

Montesquieu, Charles de Secondat. *The Spirit of Laws*, Great Books in Philosophy Series. Amherst, NY: Prometheus Books, 2002.

Morefield, Jeanne. *Covenants Without Swords: Idealist Liberalism and the Spirit of Empire*. Princeton, NJ: Princeton University Press, 2005.

Morris, Norval, and David J. Rothman. *The Oxford History of the Prison: The Practice of Punishment in Western Society*. New York: Oxford University Press, 1995.

National Institute of Justice. "Fundamental Concepts of Restorative Justice." http://www.nij.gov/topics/courts/restorative-justice/pages/fundamental-concepts.aspx.

Nemeth, Charles P. *Aquinas and King: A Discourse on Civil Disobedience*. Durham, NC: Carolina Academic Press, 2009.

Nepstad, Sharon Erickson. *Nonviolent Revolutions: Civil Resistance in the Late 20th Century*. New York: Oxford University Press, 2011.

News Corp. Australia, "'Sex Strike' Urged as Ukrainian Women Take Crimea Fight up to the Russians." http://www.news.com.au/world/sex-strike-urged-as-ukrainian-women-take-crimea-fight-up-to-the-russians/story-fndir2ev-1226866318521.

New York Times and National Public Radio. "The Guantanamo Docket." 2015.

Nietzsche, Friedrich Wilhelm. *Beyond Good and Evil*. Chicago: H. Regnery Co., 1949.

Nietzsche, Friedrich Wilhelm, and Horace Barnett Samuel. *The Genealogy of Morals*, The Modern Library of the World's Best Books. New York: Boni and Liveright, 1918.

Oakley, S. P. *A Commentary on Livy, Books VI-X*. 4 vols. Oxford New York: Clarendon Press; Oxford University Press, 1997.

Ober, Josiah. *Mass and Elite in Democratic Athens: Rhetoric, Ideology, and the Power of the People*. Princeton, NJ: Princeton University Press, 1989.

Ober, Josiah. "'I Besieged That Man': Democracy's Revolutionary Start." In *Origins of Democracy in Ancient Greece*, edited by Kurt A. Raaflaub, Josiah Ober, and Robert W. Wallace, 83–104. Berkeley: University of California Press, 2007.

Ogilvie, Robert Maxwell. *A Commentary on Livy, Books 1–5*. Oxford: Clarendon Press, 1965.

O'Leary, Brendan. "On the Nature of Nationalism: An Appraisal of Ernest Gellner's Writings on Nationalism." *British Journal of Political Science* 27, no. 2 (1997): 191–222.

Orend, Brian. "Kant's Just War Theory." *Journal of the History of Philosophy* 37, no. 2 (1999): 323–353.

Orend, Brian. *War and International Justice: A Kantian Perspective*, UPCC Book Collections on Project MUSE (Baltimore, MD: Project MUSE, 2014).

Owen, Robert, and Gregory Claeys. *A New View of Society and Other Writings*, Penguin Classics. London; New York: Penguin Books, 1991.

Oxford English Dictionary. Oxford: Oxford University Press, 2012.

Pagden, Anthony. *Lords of All the World: Ideologies of Empire in Spain, Britain and France C. 1500–C. 1800*. New Haven, CT: Yale University Press, 1995.

Paine, Thomas. "The Constitution of 1795." In *The Complete Writings of Thomas Paine with a Bibliographical Essay, and Notes and Introductions Presenting the Historical Background of Paine's Writings*, edited by Philip Sheldon Foner, 588–593. New York: Citadel Press, 1945.

Paine, Thomas. *Common Sense*, edited by Isaac Kramnick. 2nd ed., Pelican Classics. Harmondsworth: Penguin, 1976.

Pal, Amitabh. "Gandhi Was in Abbottabad, Too." http://www.progressive.org/news/2011/05/161838/gandhi-was-abbottabad-too.

Panizza, Diego. "Political Theory and Jurisprudence in Gentili's *De Iure Belli*. The Great Debate Between 'Theological' and 'Humanist' Perspectives from Vitoria to Grotius." (2005), http://www.iilj.org/newsandevents/documents/Panizza.pdf.

Pantham, Thomas. "Thinking with Mahatma Gandhi: Beyond Liberal Democracy." *Political Theory* 11, no. 2 (1983):165–188.

Parel, Anthony, ed. *Gandhi, Freedom, and Self-Rule*, Global Encounters. Lanham, MD: Lexington Books, 2000.

Parel, Anthony. *Gandhi's Philosophy and the Quest for Harmony*. Cambridge, UK: Cambridge University Press, 2006.

Pateman, Carole. *The Sexual Contract*. Stanford, CA: Stanford University Press, 1988.

Patterson, Orlando. *Slavery and Social Death: A Comparative Study*. Cambridge, MA: Harvard University Press, 1982.

Patterson, Orlando. *Freedom: Vol. 1: Freedom in the Making of Western Culture*. New York: Basic Books, 1991.

Peirce, Charles S. "The Fixation of Belief." In *Selected Writings (Values in a Universe of Chance)*, edited by Phillip P. Wiener, 91–112. New York: Dover Publications, 1966.

Peterson, Merrill D. "Thomas Jefferson and the French Revolution." *The Tocqueville Review* 9 (1988): 15–25.

Pitts, Jennifer. *A Turn to Empire: The Rise of Imperial Liberalism in Britain and France*. Princeton, NJ: Princeton Unversity Press, 2005.

Plato. "Apology." In *The Dialogues of Plato*, edited by Reginald E. Allen, 79–104. New Haven: Yale University Press, 1984a.

Plato. "Menexenus." In *The Dialogues of Plato*, edited by Reginald E. Allen, 329–342. New Haven: Yale University Press, 1984b.

Plato. "Apology." In *The Last Days of Socrates*, 31–70. New York: Penguin Books, 1993.

Pocock, J. G. A. *The Machiavellian Moment: Florentine Political Thought and the Atlantic Republican Tradition*. 2nd pbk. ed. Princeton, NJ: Princeton University Press, 1975.

Poliakov, Léon. *The History of Anti-Semitism*. 4 vols. Philadelphia: University of Pennsylvania Press, 2003.

Popescu, Delia. *Political Action in Václav Havel's Thought: The Responsibility of Resistance*. Lanham, MD: Lexington Books, 2012.

Potter, Nelson T. "Kant and Capital Punishment Today." *Journal of Value Inquiry* 36, no. 2–3 (2002): 267–282.

Proudhon, Pierre-Joseph. "General Idea of the Revolution in the 19th Century." http://fair-use.org/p-j-proudhon/general-idea-of-the-revolution/absorption-of-government-by-the-economic-organism-s6p1.

Raaflaub, Kurt A. *The Discovery of Freedom in Ancient Greece*. 1st English ed. Chicago: University of Chicago Press, 2004.

Reath, Andrews. *Agency and Autonomy in Kant's Moral Theory*. Oxford; New York: Clarendon Press; Oxford University Press, 2006.

Reichberg, Gregory M. "Thomas Aquinas Between Just War and Pacifism." *Journal of Religious Ethics* 38, no. 2 (2010): 219–241.

Rejali, Darius M. *Torture and Democracy*. Princeton, NJ: Princeton University Press, 2007.

Renan, Ernst. "What Is a Nation?" http://ucparis.fr/files/9313/6549/9943/What_is_a_Nation.pdf.

Richards, Leonard L. *Shays's Rebellion: The American Revolution's Final Battle*. Philadelphia: University of Pennsylvania Press, 2002.

Richter, Daniel K., and Institute of Early American History and Culture (Williamsburg, VA). *The Ordeal of the Longhouse: The Peoples of the Iroquois League in the Era of European Colonization*. Chapel Hill: Published for the Institute of Early American History and Culture, Williamsburg, VA, by the University of North Carolina Press, 1992.

Rigstad, Mark. "The Grotian Moment." In *Penal Practice and Culture, 1500–1900: Punishing the English*, edited by Simon Devereaux and Paul Griffiths, 183–209. New York: Palgrave Macmillan, 2004.

Roberts, Adam, and Timothy Garton Ash. *Civil Resistance and Power Politics: The Experience of Non-violent Action from Gandhi to the Present*. Oxford; New York: Oxford University Press, 2011.

Roberts, Michael. *The Age of Liberty: Sweden, 1719–1772*. Cambridge, UK; New York: Cambridge University Press, 1986.

Robespierre, Maximilien. *Virtue and Terror*, edited by Slavoj Zizek, Revolutions. London; New York: Verso, 2007.

Rocker, Rudolf, Michael E. Coughlin, and Paul Avrich Collection (Library of Congress). *Nationalism and Culture*. St. Paul: M. E. Coughlin, 1978.

Rodin, David. *War and Self-Defense*. Oxford; New York: Clarendon Press; Oxford University Press, 2002.

Rousseau, Jean-Jacques. "The Social Contract." In *Basic Political Writings*, 141–227. Indianapolis: Hackett Pub. Co., 1987.

Rowbotham, Sheila. *Women, Resistance and Revolution: A History of Women and Revolution in the Modern World*. New York: Vintage Books, 1974.

Royle, Edward. *Robert Owen and the Commencement of the Millennium: A Study of the Harmony Community*. Manchester: Manchester University Press, 1998.

Salkever, Stephen G. "Socrates' Aspasian Oration: The Play of Philosophy and Politics in Plato's Menexenus." *American Political Science Review* 87, no. 1 (1993): 133–143.

Schell, Jonathan. "The Unconquerable World." In *The Jonathan Schell Reader: On the United States at War, the Long Crisis of the American Republic, and the Fate of the Earth*, 387–432. New York: Nation Books, 2004.

Schenwar, Maya. *Locked Down, Locked Out: Why Prison Doesn't Work and How We Can Do Better*. San Francisco: Berrett-Koehler Publishers, 2014.

Schmitt, Carl. *The Crisis of Parliamentary Democracy*, Studies in Contemporary German Social Thought. Cambridge, MA: MIT Press, 1985.

Schmitt, Carl. *The Concept of the Political*. Expanded ed. Chicago: University of Chicago Press, 2007.

Schock, Kurt. *Unarmed Insurrections: People Power Movements in Nondemocracies,* Social Movements, Protest, and Contention. Minneapolis: University of Minnesota Press, 2005.

Scholz, S. J. "Civil Disobedience in the Social Theory of Thomas Aquinas." *The Thomist* 60, no. 3 (1996): 449–462.

Shalhope, Robert E. "The Ideological Origins of the Second Amendment." *The Journal of American History* 69, no. 3 (1982): 599–614.

Sharp, Gene. *The Politics of Nonviolent Action.* Boston: P. Sargent Publisher, 1973.

Sharp, Gene. *Social Power and Political Freedom,* Extending Horizons Books. Boston, MA: P. Sargent Publishers, 1980.

Sharp, Gene, and Bruce Jenkins. *Civilian-Based Defense: A Post-military Weapons System.* Princeton, NJ: Princeton University Press, 1990.

Showden, Carisa Renae. *Choices Women Make: Agency in Domestic Violence, Assisted Reproduction, and Sex Work.* Minneapolis: University of Minnesota Press, 2011.

Shuster, Amy L. "Hannah Arendt Without Politics." *Spectra: The Aspect Journal* no. 2 (2014), https://spectrajournal.org/index.php/SPECTRA/article/view/139/150.

Silverstein, Josef. "The Idea of Freedom in Burma and the Political Thought of Aung San Suu Kyi." In *Asian Freedoms: The Idea of Freedom in East and Southeast Asia*, edited by David Kelly and Anthony Reid, 187–224. New York: Cambridge University Press, 1998.

Skinner, Quentin. "Thomas Hobbes on the Proper Signification of Liberty: The Prothero Lecture." *Transactions of the Royal Historical Society, Fifth Series* 40 (1990): 121–151.

Smith, Margaret Michelle Barnes. "The Philosophy of Liberty: Locke's Machiavellian Teaching." In *Machiavelli's Liberal Republican Legacy*, edited by Paul Anthony Rahe, lxii, 326. New York: Cambridge University Press, 2006.

Smith, Nicholas D. "Plato and Aristotle on the Nature of Women." *Journal of the History of Ideas* 21, no. 4 (1983): 467–478.

Soboul, Albert. *The French Revolution, 1787–1799: From the Storming of the Bastille to Napoleon.* London: NLB, 1974.

Solanas, Valerie. *SCUM Manifesto.* London; New York: Verso, 2004.

Sorel, Georges, and Jeremy Jennings. *Reflections on Violence,* Cambridge Texts in the History of Political Thought. United Kingdom; New York: Cambridge University Press, 1999.

Spaeth, Barbette Stanley. *The Roman Goddess Ceres.* 1st ed. Austin: University of Texas Press, 1996.

Starkey, Armstrong. *European and Native American Warfare, 1675–1815.* London: UCL Press, 1998.

Strauss, Leo. *Thoughts on Machiavelli.* Chicago: University of Chicago Press, 1978.

Sullivan, Roger J. *Immanuel Kant's Moral Theory.* Cambridge, UK; New York: Cambridge University Press, 1989.

Sutton, John R. "Imprisonment and Opportunity Structures: A Bayesian Hierarchical Analysis." *European Sociological Review* 28, no. 1 (2012): 12–27.

Taylor, Eric Robert. *If We Must Die: Shipboard Insurrections in the Era of the Atlantic Slave Trade,* Antislavery, Abolition, and the Atlantic World. Baton Rouge: Louisiana State University Press, 2006.

Terchek, Ronald. *Gandhi: Struggling for Autonomy,* Twentieth-Century Political Thinkers. Lanham, MD: Rowman & Littlefield Publishers, 1998.

Tertullian. "Apology." In *Apology, De Spectaculis*, edited by T. R. Glover, Gerald Henry Rendall, Walter Charles Alan Kerr, and Marcus Minucius Felix, 1–227. London; New York: W. Heinemann, G. P. Putnam's Sons, 1931.

Thomas, Aquinas. "Summa Theologica." In *On Law, Morality, and Politics*, edited by William P. Baumgarth and Richard J. Regan. Indianapolis: Hackett, 1988.

Thucydides. *History of the Peloponnesian War*. Translated by Rex Warner. Rev. ed. Harmondsworth; Baltimore: Penguin Books, 1972.

Tolstoy, Leo. *The Kingdom of God Is within You*. Translated by Constance Garnett. Rockville, MD: Wildside Press, 2006.

Tooker, Elisabeth. "United States Constitution and the Iroquois League." *Ethnohistory* 35, no. 4 (1988): 305–336.

Trotsky, Leon. *The Defence of Terrorism*. new ed. London: G. Allen & Unwin ltd., 1935.

Tucker, Robert C. *The Marxian Revolutionary Idea*. 1st ed. New York: Norton, 1969.

Tully, James. *Public Philosophy in a New Key*, Ideas in Context. Cambridge, UK; New York: Cambridge University Press, 2008.

Urbainczyk, Theresa. *Slave Revolts in Antiquity*. Berkeley: University of California Press, 2008.

US Select Committee on Intelligence, *Findings and Conclusions,* Committee Study of the Central Intelligence Agency's Detention and Interrogation Program. Washington, DC: US Senate, 2014.

van Mill, David. "Hobbes's Theories of Freedom." *The Journal of Politics* 57, no. 2 (1995): 443–459.

Villa, Dana Richard. *Socratic Citizenship*. Princeton, NJ: Princeton University Press, 2001.

Vitoria, Francisco de. *Political Writings*, edited by Anthony Pagden and Jeremy Lawrance, Cambridge Texts in the History of Political Thought. Cambridge, UK; New York: Cambridge University Press, 1991.

von Hofer, Hanns. "Punishment and Crime in Scandinavia, 1750–2008." *Crime & Justice* 40 (2011): 33–107.

Weber, Thomas. *On the Salt March: The Historiography of Gandhi's March to Dandi*. New Delhi: HarperCollins Publishers India, 1997.

Weightman, M. A. "Self-Defense in International Law." *Virginia Law Review* 37, no. 8 (1951): 1095–1115.

Wetzel, James. *Augustine and the Limits of Virtue*. New York: Cambridge University Press, 1992.

Whipple, Charles K. *Evils of the Revolutionary War*. Boston: New England Non-Resistance Society, 1839.

Wikipedia. "Women of Liberia Mass Action for Peace." http://en.wikipedia.org/wiki/Women_of_Liberia_Mass_Action_for_Peace.

Winn, Peter. *Weavers of Revolution: The Yarur Workers and Chile's Road to Socialism*. New York: Oxford University Press, 1986.

Wright, Henry Clarke. "The Natick Resolution, or, Resistance to Slaveholders the Right and Duty of Southern Slaves and Northern Freemen." Antislavery Literature Project; Arizona State University; EServer, Iowa State University, 1859. http://antislavery.eserver.org/tracts/the_natick_resolution/TheNatickResolutionfinal.pdf.

Yarbrough, Jean, and Peter Stern. "Vita Activa and Vita Contemplativa: Political Thought in *The Life of the Mind*." *Review of Politics* (1981): 323–354.

Young, David E. *The Origin of the Second Amendment: A Documentary History in Commentaries on Liberty, Free Government, and an Armed Populace during the Formation of the Bill of Rights*. Ontonagon, MI: Golden Oak Books, 1991.

Young, Warren, and Mark Brown. "Cross-National Comparisons of Imprisonment." *Crime and Justice* 17 (1993): 1–49.

Zerilli, Linda M. G. ""We Feel Our Freedom": Imagination and Judgment in the Thought of Hannah Arendt." *Political Theory* 33, no. 2 (2005): 158–188.

Ziegler, Valarie H. *The Advocates of Peace in Antebellum America*. 1st pbk. ed. Macon, GA: Mercer University Press, 2001.

INDEX